Here is a weighty tract for the times, in which a dozen Reformed scholars survey the "open theism" of Pinnock, Sanders, Boyd, and colleagues, and find it a confused, confusing, and unedifying hypothesis that ought to be declared off limits. Some pages are heavy sledding, but the arguing is clear and strong, and the book is essential reading for all who are caught up in this discussion.

—J. I. PACKER
Professor of Theology
Regent College

The downsized deity of open theism is a poor substitute for the real God of historic Christianity—as taught by Protestant, Catholic, and Orthodox theologians through the centuries. This book offers an important analysis and critique of this sub-Christian view of God. Well researched and fairly presented.

—TIMOTHY GEORGE
Dean of Beeson Divinity School
Samford University

Open Theism and
the Undermining of
Biblical Christianity

BEYOND
THE
BOUNDS

EDITED BY

JOHN PIPER
JUSTIN TAYLOR
PAUL KJOSS HELSETH

CROSSWAY BOOKS
WHEATON, ILLINOIS

Library of Congress Cataloging-in-Publication Data
Beyond the bounds : open theism and the undermining of biblical
Christianity / edited by John Piper, Justin Taylor, and Paul Kjoss Helseth.
    p. cm.
    Includes bibliographical references and index.
    ISBN 13: 978-1-58134-462-2 (TPB : alk. paper)
    ISBN 10: 1-58134-462-7
    1. God—Omniscience.   2. Free will and determinism—Religious
aspects—Christianity. I. Piper, John, 1946- . II.Taylor, Justin, 1976- .
III. Helseth, Paul Kjoss, 1962- .
BT131 .B49   2003
231—dc21   2002155192

VP		16	15	14	13	12	11	10	09	08	07
17	16	15	14	13	12	11	10	9	8	7	6	5	4	3

CONTENTS

CONTRIBUTORS

Chad Owen Brand. Ph.D., Southwestern Baptist Theological Seminary. Assistant Professor of Christian Theology, The Southern Baptist Theological Seminary; Associate Professor of Christian Theology, and Chairman, Department of Bible and Theology, Boyce College.

A. B. Caneday. Ph.D., Trinity Evangelical Divinity School. Professor of Biblical Studies, Northwestern College.

William C. Davis. Ph.D., University of Notre Dame. Associate Professor of Philosophy, Covenant College.

Russell Fuller. Ph.D., Hebrew Union College. Assistant Professor of Old Testament Interpretation, The Southern Baptist Theological Seminary.

Wayne Grudem. Ph.D., University of Cambridge. Research Professor of Theology and Bible, Phoenix Seminary.

Paul Kjoss Helseth. Ph.D., Marquette University. Assistant Professor of Bible and Philosophy, Northwestern College.

Michael S. Horton. Ph.D., Wycliffe Hall, Oxford. Associate Professor of Apologetics and Historical Theology, Westminster Theological Seminary in California.

John Piper. D.Theol., University of Munich. Preaching Pastor, Bethlehem Baptist Church, Minneapolis.

Mark R. Talbot. Ph.D., University of Pennsylvania. Associate Professor of Philosophy, Wheaton College.

Justin Taylor. Director of Theological Resources and Education, Desiring God Ministries.

Bruce A. Ware. Ph.D., Fuller Theological Seminary. Professor of Christian Theology; Senior Associate Dean of the School of Theology, The Southern Baptist Theological Seminary.

Stephen J. Wellum. Ph.D., Trinity Evangelical Divinity School. Associate Professor of Christian Theology, The Southern Baptist Theological Seminary.

Foreword

John Piper

The stunning thing about open theism in American Christianity is how many leaders do not act as though it is a departure from historic Christianity and therefore a dishonor to Christ and pastorally damaging. Some have seen the departure clearly and said so. For example, Thomas Oden, a Methodist minister and the Henry Anson Buttz Professor of Theology and Ethics at Drew University, writes in *Christianity Today,* "The fantasy that God is ignorant of the future is a heresy that must be rejected on scriptural grounds." His warning to the church is sobering: "Keeping the boundaries of faith undefined is a demonic temptation that evangelicals within the mainline have learned all too well and have been burned by all too painfully."[1] Oden's indictment points toward the baleful heart of open theism and the broken heart of those who love the historic biblical vision of God.

The Baleful Heart of Open Theism

The heart of open theism is the conviction that humans and angels can be morally responsible only if they have ultimate self-determination— and have it to the degree that their self-determination rules out God's ability to render or see any of their future free acts as certain.[2] Therefore, open theism's most obvious departure from historic Christianity is its denial of the exhaustive, definite foreknowledge of God. This departure

---

[1] Thomas C. Oden, "The Real Reformers Are Traditionalists," *Christianity Today* 42, no. 2 (9 February 1998): 45.

[2] Gregory Boyd, and all open theists, distance themselves from the view that says there is compatibility between human responsibility, on the one hand, and God's ability to render future free acts certain, on the other hand. Thus Boyd says that his view of "self-determining freedom" "contrasts with 'compatibilist' freedom, which sees human (and angelic) freedom as compatible with determinism. This view is thus sometimes called 'incompatibilistic freedom'" (Gregory A. Boyd, *Satan and the Problem of Evil: Constructing a Trinitarian Warfare Theodicy* [Downers Grove, Ill.: InterVarsity Press, 2001], 428).

is obscured by the protest of open theists that they *do* affirm the omniscience of God. They argue that self-determining free will creates choices that have no reality before they are created and therefore are not possible objects of knowledge—even to God. They would say that not to know a no-thing does not undermine omniscience. And, they add, truly free choices are no-thing before they are made. The clearest statement of this protest is from Gregory Boyd's book, *Letters from a Skeptic*:

> In the Christian view God knows all of reality—everything there is to know. But to assume He knows ahead of time how every person is going to freely act assumes that each person's free activity is already there to know—even before he freely does it! But it's not. If we have been given freedom, we create the reality of our decisions by making them. And until we make them, they don't exist. Thus, in my view at least, there simply isn't anything to know until we make it there to know. *So God can't foreknow the good or bad decisions of the people He creates until He creates these people and they, in turn, create their decisions.*[3]

Boyd clarifies this in his more scholarly books by affirming that God can indeed know with certainty some future volitions of man and angels, if God himself overrules the self-determining will and inclines it in a certain direction.[4] In other words, God can know ahead of time what *he* intends to do in his freedom, but not what *we* intend to do in our freedom. He can know with certainty what we will choose if he intrudes on our self-determination and renders our choice certain. But at that point, to the degree that God renders our choice certain, our accountability dis-

---

[3] Gregory Boyd, in Gregory A. Boyd and Edward K. Boyd, *Letters from a Skeptic: A Son Wrestles with His Father's Questions About Christianity* (Wheaton, Ill.: Victor, 1994), 30, emphasis added. Cf. his statement in *God of the Possible: A Biblical Introduction to the Open View of God* (Grand Rapids, Mich.: Baker, 2000): ". . . future free decisions do not exist (except as possibilities) for God to know until free agents make them" (120). Similarly, Clark Pinnock wrote in 1990, "Decisions not yet made do not exist anywhere to be known even by God. They are potential—yet to be realized but not yet actual. God can predict a great deal of what we will choose to do, but not all of it, because some of it remains hidden in the mystery of human freedom. . . . God too faces possibilities in the future, and not only certainties. God too moves into a future not wholly known . . ." ("From Augustine to Arminius: A Pilgrimage in Theology," in *The Grace of God, the Will of Man: A Case for Arminianism*, ed. Clark H. Pinnock [Grand Rapids, Mich.: Zondervan, 1989; Minneapolis: Bethany, 1995], 25-26).

[4] Boyd would say that there is a category of actions that God can foreknow with certainty, but which he does not determine, namely, acts done by people whose self-wrought characters are so solidified in good or evil that they cannot do otherwise. For those agents who have "eternalized" themselves in this way, God can even determine, if he chooses, some of their future volitions. For further explanation and interaction, see the chapters in this volume by Wellum, Ware, and Helseth.

appears.[5] Therefore, in the view of open theism most good and evil choices that humans make are unknown by God before they happen.[6]

THE BROKEN HEART OF THOSE WHO LOVE THE HISTORIC BIBLICAL VISION OF GOD

Oden's words above also point to the broken heart of those who love the historic biblical vision of God. Oden said, "Keeping the boundaries of faith undefined is a demonic temptation that evangelicals within the mainline have learned all too well and have been burned by all too painfully." The failure of many Christian leaders to see the magnitude of error in open theism has left churches and denominations and schools with no clear boundary between what is tolerably Christian and what is not. This is painful and will become more so.

It remains one of the most stunning things in evangelicalism today that so many leaders can treat as optional what C. S. Lewis and two thousand years of Christian witness called "mere Christianity." In his usual blunt and clear way, Lewis said, "Everyone who believes in God at all believes that He knows what you and I are going to do tomorrow."[7] The fact that leaders today so readily nullify the intended impact of that sentence, by protecting the Christian legitimacy of open theism, is not a statement about Christian orthodoxy but about leaders who have lost their hold on it. We have prepared this book to address the issue of boundaries and, we pray, bring some remedy to the present and impending pain of embracing open theism as a legitimate Christian vision of God.[8]

---

[5] Boyd's version of open theism "does not entail that God can never exercise coercive power in his interactions with free creatures" (*Satan and the Problem of Evil*, 185). God can indeed act so as to render human choices certain. But such choices lose their moral goodness or evil to the degree that God renders them certain: "*To the extent* that humans or angels are self-determining, to *that* extent their moral responsibility must be irrevocable" (ibid.).

[6] I say "most" rather than "all" because Boyd grants that the good and evil choices that persons make who are already fixed or "eternalized" in their character can be foreknown by God. See note 4.

[7] C. S. Lewis, *Mere Christianity* (New York: Collier, 1952), 148.

[8] Robert Strimple points out, concerning the denial of God's exhaustive foreknowledge, "Here Christians face the denial not simply of one of the distinctives of Reformation theology but of a fundamental truth held in common by every historic branch of the Christian church" ("What Does God Know?" in *The Coming Evangelical Crisis: Current Challenges to the Authority of Scripture and the Gospel*, ed. John H. Armstrong [Chicago: Moody, 1996], 139). This includes historic Arminianism. Jacobus Arminius affirmed, for example, "The fourth decree, to save certain particular persons and to damn others . . . rests upon the foreknowledge of God, by which he has known from eternity which persons should believe according to such an administration of the means serving to repentance and faith through his preceding grace and which should persevere through subsequent grace, and also who should not believe and persevere" (quoted in Carl Bangs, *Arminius: A Study in the Dutch Reformation* [Nashville: Abingdon, 1971], 352).

INTRODUCTION

Justin Taylor

C. S. Lewis once wrote, "Everyone who believes in God at all believes that He knows what you and I are going to do tomorrow."[1] But this is precisely what open theists deny. That is why many would concur with Timothy George, who says, "Open theism teaches a sub-Christian view of God that is unworthy of a robust biblical faith. I have no sympathy for this view and think it would be a great mistake for evangelicals to welcome it within the bounds of tolerable theological diversity."[2]

It is crucial to understand that open theism is not just another intramural squabble among evangelicals. It is not a debate about second-order doctrines, minutiae, or peripheral matters. Rather, it is a debate about God and the central features of the Christian faith. The contributors to *Beyond the Bounds* stand with a growing chorus of contemporary scholars who have made clear what is at stake in this debate. D. A. Carson argues that open theism "so redefines the God of the Bible and of theology that we wind up with a quite different God." Wayne Grudem contends that open theism "ultimately portrays a different God than the God of the Bible." And R. Albert Mohler, believes that "The very identity and reality of the God of the Bible is at stake."[3] Open theism is, at its roots, a question about the nature of

---

[1] C. S. Lewis, *Mere Christianity* (New York: Collier, 1952), 148.

[2] Timothy George, personal correspondence (4 November 2002); used with permission. George was one of the two external, non-voting participants in Bethel College and Seminary's Committee for Theological Clarification and Assessment, which examined Boyd's teaching. For a brief history of the intersection between the Baptist General Conference and open theism, see John Piper with Justin Taylor (appendix by Millard Erickson), *Resolution on the Foreknowledge of God: Reasons and Rationale* (Minneapolis: Bethlehem Baptist Church, 2000); and Piper, "We Took a Good Stand and Made a Bad Mistake: Reflections on the Baptist General Conference Annual Meeting, St. Paul, June 25-28, 2000" (www.desiringgod.org/library/fresh_words/2000/070500.html).

[3] Carson, Grudem, and Mohler, from their endorsements of Bruce A. Ware, *God's Lesser Glory: The Diminished God of Open Theism* (Wheaton, Ill.: Crossway, 2000), 1-2.

God.[4] The essays in this book contend that open theism presents us with a different God—a God compatible, perhaps, with contemporary sentiments, but one who is not the God of the Bible.

THE PURPOSE AND STRUCTURE OF THIS VOLUME

Some may legitimately ask why another response to open theism is needed, given that a number of fine critiques have already emerged,[5] and more are on the way,[6] documenting its serious flaws in terms of exegesis, hermeneutics, philosophy, and piety. One reason that this present volume is needed is the evolving nature of open theism. Open theists have continued to introduce nuances, qualifications, and new proposals. When this happens, counter-arguments must become more refined so as to take into account the strongest version of openness theology. For example, in his most recent book on open theism, Gregory Boyd argues that his version of "neo-Molinism" accounts for roughly the same degree of divine providential control as that of traditional Molinism.[7]

---

[4] I am aware of Boyd's argument that open theism "is not really about God's nature at all" but rather "about the nature of the future" (*God of the Possible* [Grand Rapids, Mich.: Baker, 2000], 15). Or to put it another way, "The debate over the nature of God's knowledge is not primarily a debate about the scope or perfection of God's knowledge. All Christians agree that God is omniscient and therefore knows all of reality perfectly. The debate over God's knowledge is rather a debate over the *content of reality* that God perfectly knows. It has more to do with the doctrine of creation than it does with the doctrine of God" (Gregory A. Boyd, "The Open-Theism View," in *Divine Foreknowledge: Four Views*, ed. James K. Beilby and Paul R. Eddy [Downers Grove, Ill.: InterVarsity Press, 2001], 13). This distinction depends upon Boyd's insistence that open theists "affirm God's omniscience as emphatically as anybody does" (*God of the Possible*, 16). But Boyd and company have redefined omniscience. The traditional doctrine of omniscience does not merely affirm that *"at any time God knows all propositions such that God's knowing them at that time is logically possible"* (William Hasker, "A Philosophical Perspective," in Clark Pinnock, et al., *The Openness of God: A Biblical Challenge to the Traditional Understanding of God* [Downers Grove, Ill.: InterVarsity Press, 1994], 136). Rather, the doctrine of omniscience "requires that any agent is omniscient if and only if he knows all truths and believes no falsehoods" (William Lane Craig, "The Middle-Knowledge View," in Beilby and Eddy, eds., *Divine Foreknowledge: Four Views*, 137). Craig's conclusion is correct: "The debate over the nature of God's foreknowledge *is* primarily a debate about the scope and perfection of God's knowledge" (Craig, "A Middle-Knowledge Response," in Beilby and Eddy, eds., *Divine Foreknowledge: Four Views*, 55). Secondly, Boyd himself seems unwittingly to agree that this debate concerns the attributes of God. On the very same page as his *denial* that this issue is "about God's nature at all," he claims that "Scripture describes the openness of God to the future as *one of his attributes of greatness"* (*God of the Possible*, 15, emphasis added). How can "the openness of God" *not* be "about God's nature at all" when it is at the same time about an "attribute of greatness"?

[5] See especially, Ware, *God's Lesser Glory;* and John M. Frame, *No Other God: A Response to Open Theism* (Phillipsburg, N.J.: Presbyterian & Reformed, 2001). See also my working bibliography on open theism, included at the end of this book.

[6] Projected works include those by D. A. Carson, Steven C. Roy, Mark R. Talbot, and Stephen J. Wellum.

[7] Gregory A. Boyd, *Satan and the Problem of Evil: Constructing a Trinitarian Warfare Theodicy* (Downers Grove, Ill.: InterVarsity Press, 2001), 130. Molinism, named after Luis de Molina

This necessarily qualifies, to some degree, early criticisms of his project. His philosophical defense of libertarian free will[8] means that critics are no longer able to charge open theists with assuming free will apart from argumentation. The details of these discussions need not detain us here; the point is that new responses are needed to a theology that is in many ways still evolving.

There is a more fundamental reason, however, for why we have felt it necessary to assemble this book. Despite a number of fine critiques, there remain a number of important issues that require a coherent, sustained response. These crucial issues can be summarized as five questions, which have become the five major sections of this book:

1. Have unbiblical philosophical influences decisively distorted traditional Christian theology, as openness proponents maintain? Conversely, has openness theology itself been tainted with unbiblical philosophy?
2. What are the philosophical presuppositions and cultural conditions leading to the development and relative acceptance of open theism?
3. How are we to understand anthropomorphic language and the role it plays in revelation and the interpretive process?
4. What is at stake in the debate about open theism? Does open theism logically undermine the essentials of our faith, including the inerrancy of Scripture, the trustworthiness of God, and the gospel of Christ?
5. Finally, what biblical criteria should biblically faithful churches and parachurch organizations follow in drawing new boundaries to exclude doctrinal aberrations? And why should open theism be considered "beyond the bounds" of biblical Christianity?

(1535–1600), is a philosophical position that understands exhaustive definite foreknowledge to be compatible with libertarian freedom. In Molinism, God has a degree of providential control via his "middle knowledge," such that he knows exhaustively not only all that *will be* but also all that *would be* given different circumstances. On the basis of this knowledge, God chooses to actualize a particular world. For an explanation of Boyd's *neo*-Molinism, see *Satan and the Problem of Evil*, 127-133. For interaction with his proposal, see the chapters in this volume by Wellum, Ware, and Helseth.

[8] See especially chapter 2 of *Satan and the Problem of Evil*.

We are not attempting an exhaustive response to open theism[9]; doing so would require many volumes. Our goal is more modest: to focus on these issues, attempting a clear, fair, and accurate analysis that will assist the church in these days of controversy.

CHARITY IN CONTROVERSY

We know that some will view the very existence of this volume—with its title, its argument, and its conclusions—as incompatible with Christian charity and humility. Some will even brand it as an example of theological bigotry. Those who believe open theism is beyond the bounds of biblical Christianity can expect to be viewed as members of an "evangelical Taliban" that would "highjack the evangelical movement."[10] A full-scale response to this criticism lies outside the scope of this introduction. However, at least five principles justify and necessitate our engagement in this polemical theology.

1. *Controversy is required when essential truths are called into question.* Every significant doctrinal teaching in the church has been refined in the furnace of controversy. This work argues that open theism undermines the heart of biblical Christianity: the inerrancy of Scripture, the trustworthiness of God, and the gospel of Christ. What are we to do when such serious disagreements arise? John Stott provides the answer: "The proper activity of professing Christians who disagree with one another is neither to ignore, nor to conceal, nor even to minimize their differences, but to debate them."[11] Christ himself was a controversialist,[12] and the early church followed his lead. The church today must follow in these steps. Stott writes:

> We seem in our generation to have moved a long way from this vehement zeal for the truth which Christ and his apostles displayed. But if we loved the glory of God more, and if we cared more for the eternal good

---

[9] For example, this work contains neither an exegetical defense of exhaustive definite foreknowledge nor a historical survey of the development and defense of this doctrine. Both have been nicely handled in Steven C. Roy, "How Much Does God Foreknow? An Evangelical Assessment of the Doctrine of the Extent of the Foreknowledge of God in Light of the Teaching of Open Theism" (Ph.D. diss., Trinity International University, 2000). For Roy's historical survey, see chapter 2 of his thesis. For his exegetical work, see chapters 4, 5, and the appendix in his dissertation.

[10] John Sanders, "Is Open Theism Evangelical?" (plenary address at the annual meeting of the Evangelical Theological Society, Colorado Springs, 15 November 2001), 22, 23.

[11] John R. W. Stott, *Christ the Controversialist* (Downers Grove, Ill.: InterVarsity Press, 1970), 22.

[12] Ibid., 18, passim.

of the souls of men, we would not refuse to engage in necessary contro-versy, when the truth of the gospel is at stake. The apostolic command is clear. We are "to maintain the truth in love," being neither truthless in our love, nor loveless in our truth, but holding the two in balance.[13]

2. *Truth and love are necessary companions in doctrinal disputes.* There is no biblical or logical contradiction between controversy and compassion, contention and contrition, criticism and Christlikeness. Paul insisted that edification of the body of Christ required "speaking the truth in love" (Eph. 4:15, ESV) so that the church would not be like "children, tossed to and fro by the waves and carried about by every wind of doctrine" (v. 14).[14] The solution to doctrinal drift is spoken truth with a heart of love to the glory of God and for the good of his church.

3. *We must distinguish between a tolerant spirit toward persons that manifests itself in love, and a tolerant mind toward ideas that is never able to come to a knowledge of the truth.* "Tolerance" today is a dis-position rarely defined but routinely insisted upon without distinctions. The fruit of this fuzzy thinking manifests itself in the church as a refusal to condemn *ideas* for fear that one might offend *individuals*. Stott, how-ever, insists that we return to a biblical distinction:

> We need to distinguish between the tolerant mind and the tolerant spirit. Tolerant in spirit a Christian should always be, loving, under-standing, forgiving and forbearing others, making allowances for them, and giving them the benefit of the doubt, for true love "bears all things, believes all things, hopes all things, endures all things" [1 Cor. 13:7]. But how can we be tolerant in mind of what God has plainly revealed to be either evil or erroneous?[15]

Chesterton would have agreed. He wrote, "The object of opening the mind, as of opening the mouth, is to shut it again on something solid."[16]

---

[13] Ibid., 19.

[14] An application of how this was worked out in Paul's ministry can be seen in his rebuke of Peter in Antioch (Gal. 2:11-14). D. A. Carson's analysis reinforces the principles commended in this introduction: "Thus unless we are prepared to charge him with international-class hypocrisy, the apostle Paul is fully persuaded that his rebuke of the apostle Peter is entirely within the constraints of Christian love. Indeed, at one level, it is motivated by love" (D. A. Carson, *Love in Hard Places* [Wheaton, Ill.: Crossway, 2002], 150).

[15] Stott, *Christ the Controversialist*, 8.

[16] G. K. Chesterton, *The Autobiography*, vol. 16 of *The Collected Works of G. K. Chesterton* (San Francisco: Ignatius, 1988), 212.

4. *We must love and pray for the good of those whom we critique.*
John Newton exhorts us to remember our spiritual duties in the context
of theological contention:

> As to your opponent, I wish, that, before you set pen to paper against
> him, and during the whole time you are preparing your answer, you may
> commend him by earnest prayer to the Lord's teaching and blessing.
> This practice will have a direct tendency to conciliate your heart to love
> and pity him; and such a disposition will have a good influence upon
> every page you write. . . . [If he is a believer,] in a little while you will
> meet in heaven; he will then be dearer to you than the nearest friend you
> have upon earth is to you now. Anticipate that period in your
> thoughts. . . . [If he is an unconverted person,] he is a more proper object
> of your compassion than your anger. Alas! "He knows not what he
> does." But you know who has made you to differ [1 Cor. 4:7].[17]

5. *Finally, we must commune with God in the doctrines for which
we contend.* John Owen argued that true communion with God is not
only the *goal* of doctrinal contention but also the *means* by which it is
to be conducted:

> When the heart is cast indeed into the mould of the doctrine that the
> mind embraceth,—when the evidence and necessity of the truth abides
> in us,—when not the sense of the words only is in our heads, but the
> sense of the thing abides in our hearts—when we have *communion
> with God in the doctrine we contend for*—then shall we be garrisoned
> by the grace of God against all the assaults of men.[18]

As we seek to exemplify the spirit of this counsel, may the Lord be
merciful to us all. We present these essays with the humble hope that
God would use this book for the magnification of his name, the edification of his church, and the advancement of his kingdom.

Soli Deo gloria.

---

[17] John Newton, "On Controversy" [Letter XIX], vol. 1 of *The Works of the Rev. John Newton*
(Edinburgh: Banner of Truth, 1985), 269.

[18] John Owen, *The Glory of Christ*, vol. 1 of *The Works of John Owen*, ed. William H. Gould
(London: Johnstone & Hunter, 1852; reprint, Edinburgh and Carlisle, Pa.: Banner of Truth,
1959), lxiii-lxiv, emphasis added.

ACKNOWLEDGMENTS

First and foremost, we thank our Lord Jesus Christ, the embodiment of grace and truth, for his mercy over our lives. Christ is all, and before him we bow with gratitude and joy.

We are thankful to many who have contributed to this project. Noël Piper and Lea Taylor love and support us in countless ways through all that we do. "An excellent wife who can find? She is far more precious than jewels" (Prov. 31:10). Hovald and Betty Helseth have been a constant source of prayer, encouragement, and love. It is a delight and privilege to honor them (Ex. 20:12). Our colleagues at Desiring God Ministries, Bethlehem Baptist Church, and Northwestern College are joyful and serious comrades in the cause of God and truth.

A special word of thanks goes to Matt Perman for producing the subject index, Carol Steinbach and Sara June Davis for providing the Scripture index, and Michael Thate for proofreading the entire manuscript and assembling the person index. Thank you, friends, for your labors of love!

We also extend our thanks to the entire team at Crossway Books—especially Lane Dennis, Marvin Padgett, Bill Deckard, and Jill Carter—for their assistance with this book, but more importantly, for embracing and supporting the vision of God and truth behind it.

PART ONE

Historical Influences

1

THE RABBIS AND THE CLAIMS OF OPENNESS ADVOCATES

Russell Fuller

I. INTRODUCTION

The Old Testament is the battleground in the theological struggle between the advocates of the openness view of God and the advocates of the traditional view of God. The openness view, a recent and rare position,[1] challenges important, vital, and cherished teachings about the character and nature of God. It represents a seismic shift not only in theology but also in history and in exegesis. Because its teachings and implications are so thoroughgoing and so far-reaching,[2] Christians must weigh its claims carefully and test its doctrines meticulously. Both sides of the dispute, to be sure, lay claim to the Bible—especially the Old Testament—to substantiate their position. To validate the claims of the openness view, then, one may appeal to a disinterested third party, like a referee, an umpire, or a judge to evaluate impartially the evidence. Because the Old Testament is the common possession of Christians and Jews, and because the Old Testament is in the front lines of this conflict, the early Rabbis of the Talmud and the Midrash, like a referee or a judge,

---

[1] Gregory Boyd, for instance, states, "Still, I must concede that the open view has been relatively rare in church history. In my estimation this is because almost from the start the church's theology was significantly influenced by Plato's notion that God's perfection must mean that he is in every respect unchanging—including in his knowledge and experience. This philosophical assumption has been losing its grip on Western minds over the last hundred years, which is, in part, why an increasing number of Christians are coming to see the significance of the biblical motif of divine openness" (*God of the Possible: A Biblical Introduction to the Open View of God* [Grand Rapids, Mich.: Baker, 2000], 115).

[2] See part 4 of this volume, "What Is at Stake in the Openness Debate?"

can test the historical, exegetical, and theological claims and teachings of the openness view. Under Rabbinic scrutiny and examination, however, the openness view fails, its lethal errors exposed, its inaccurate claims concerning history, theology, and exegesis repudiated.

II. HISTORICAL CLAIMS OF THE OPENNESS VIEW

Advocates of the openness view, of course, will immediately object, challenging the impartiality of the Rabbis. Indeed, John Sanders, an advocate for the openness view, claims that Greek philosophy influenced both Christian and Jewish thinking about God. Sanders, who insists that "Hellenistic rational theology . . . had a profound impact on Jewish and Christian thinking about the divine nature," writes:

> Where does this "theologically correct" view of God come from? The answer, in part, is found in the way Christian thinkers have used certain Greek philosophical ideas. Greek thought has played an extensive role in the development of the traditional doctrine of God. But the classical view of God worked out in the Western tradition is at odds at several key points with a reading of the biblical text. . . .[3]

Furthermore, Sanders claims that Philo, the first-century Jewish Hellenist, bridged the gap between Greek philosophy and the Old Testament, profoundly affecting Jewish and Christian theology. "Philo of Alexandria," says Sanders, "was a Jewish thinker who sought to reconcile biblical teaching with Greek philosophy. To him goes the distinction of being the leading figure in forging the biblical-classical synthesis. Both the method and the content of this synthesis were closely followed by later Jewish, Christian and Muslim thinkers."[4] Hence, Sanders's historical claims—of Greek philosophical influence and of Philo's role in transmitting Greek thought to Judaism—allegedly disqualify the Rabbis as impartial judges.

Modern Rabbinic authorities, however, deny that Greek philosophy influenced the Rabbis. They were not philosophers, nor students of phi-

---

[3] John Sanders, "Historical Considerations," in Clark Pinnock, et al., *The Openness of God: A Biblical Challenge to the Traditional Understanding of God* (Downers Grove, Ill.: InterVarsity Press, 1994), 68, 59. Boyd persistently argues that Plato influenced the classical (traditional) view of God. See, for example, Boyd, *God of the Possible*, 115, 130-132.

[4] Sanders, "Historical Considerations," 69; cf. 72.

losophy, having only limited or casual interest in the subject,[5] as the Reformed (liberal) C. G. Montefiore asserts:

> Another point to remember in regard to Rabbinic literature is that it comes from men whose outlook was extraordinarily limited. They had no interests outside Religion and the Law. They had lost all historic sense. They had no interest in art, in drama, in *belles lettres,* in poetry, or in science (except, perhaps, in medicine). They had no training in philosophy. How enormously they might have benefited if, under competent teachers, they had been put through a course of Greek philosophy and literature. . . . The Old Testament was practically the only book they possessed . . . Yet this Bible, with all that it implied, is their world, their one overmastering interest. They picked up, it is true, many current ideas, opinions, superstitions, in a fluid, unsystematic form. But all *that* was by the way and incidental. . . . The Rabbis, for good or for evil, knew no philosophy.[6]

From the other side of the theological aisle, the Orthodox H. Loewe concurs: "The dialectics which Halakah involved made up, to no small extent, for the lack of philosophy. The Rabbis were no philosophers . . . and, as Mr Montefiore says, their outlook was limited. . . . They had but a casual acquaintance with Greek thought."[7]

This casual acquaintance, of course, had no discernable influence on the Rabbis. Abraham Cohen speculates that although some Rabbis may have been aware of Greek philosophy, "the interest in metaphysical speculation which characterized the thinkers of Greece and Rome was not shared by the teachers of Israel to any great extent."[8] G. F. Moore cannot find Greek philosophy in Rabbinic thought: "The idea of God in Judaism is developed from the Scriptures. The influence of contemporary philosophy which is seen in some Hellenistic Jewish writings—the Wisdom of Solomon, 4 Maccabees, and above all in Philo—is not recognizable in normative Judaism, nor is the influence of other religions. . . ."[9] Similarly, Adin

---

[5] Max Kadushin, *The Rabbinic Mind,* 2nd ed. (New York: Blaisdell, 1965), 273; Efraim E. Urbach, *The Sages: Their Concepts and Beliefs,* trans. I. Abrahams (Jerusalem: Magnes, 1975), 29.

[6] C. G. Montefiore, in C. G. Montefiore and H. Loewe, *A Rabbinic Anthology* (New York: Meridian, 1960), xix-xx, xlii. The emphasis is his.

[7] H. Loewe, in ibid., xcv.

[8] Abraham Cohen, *Everyman's Talmud* (New York: Schocken, 1975), 27.

[9] George Foot Moore, *Judaism,* vol. 1 (Cambridge, Mass.: Harvard University Press, 1927), 115.

Steinsaltz declares: "Some of the mishnaic and talmudic sages were acquainted with Greek and classical literature, but this knowledge had almost no impact on their way of thinking where talmudic scholarship was concerned. In this they differed greatly from Egyptian Jewry which tried to combine Greek culture with Judaism."[10] Saul Lieberman, arguably the greatest Rabbinic authority of the last century and a leading expert on Hellenistic influence in Judaism, admits that some purely Greek ideas penetrated into Rabbinic circles, but these were limited to ethical principles and Greek legal thought.[11] Rabbinic literature, for example, abounds with Greek and Roman legal terms, and quotes verbatim from Gentile law books.[12] Nevertheless, Lieberman emphatically rejects the influence of Greek philosophy on Rabbinic thought. The Rabbis never quote a Greek philosopher, never use Greek philosophic terms,[13] and they mention only one prominent Greek philosopher: Epicurus, the embodiment of infidelity and "symbol of heresy," whose views the Rabbis regarded as worse than atheism, and whose advocates the Rabbis excluded from the world to come.[14] Lieberman concludes: "They [the Rabbis] probably did not read Plato and certainly not the pre-Socratic philosophers. Their main interest was centered in Gentile legal studies and their methods of rhetoric."[15]

In fact, the Rabbis distrust, resist, and even despise Greek philosophy. The Talmud, for instance, indicates the proper time to study Greek philosophy:

> Ben Damah the son of Rabbi Ishmael's sister once asked Rabbi Ishmael, May one such as I who have studied the whole of the Torah learn Greek wisdom? He thereupon read to him the following verse, *This book of the law shall not depart out of thy mouth, but thou shalt meditate therein day and night.* (Josh 1:8) Go then and find a time that is neither day nor night and learn then Greek wisdom.[16]

---

[10] Adin Steinsaltz, *The Essential Talmud*, trans. Chaya Galai (New York: Basic, 1976), 99.

[11] Saul Lieberman, *Texts and Studies* (New York: Ktav, 1974), 217, 225-226.

[12] Ibid., 225-226.

[13] Ibid., 223. Lieberman confirms the observation of Harry A. Wolfson, the distinguished Harvard historian: "In the entire Greek vocabulary that is embodied in the Midrash, Mishnah, and the Talmud there is not a single technical [Greek] philosophic term" (Harry A. Wolfson, *Philo*, vol. 1 [Cambridge, Mass.: Harvard University Press, 1948], 91-92).

[14] Lieberman, *Texts and Studies*, 222-223. The Rabbis also mention Oenomaus, an obscure second-century Cynic philosopher, and regard him as the greatest Gentile philosopher (Genesis Rabbah lxviii 20). Clearly, the Rabbis were not keeping close score of their Greek philosophers.

[15] Ibid., 228.

[16] Menachot 99b.

Other Rabbis were more to the point, equating the breeding of swine to the learning of Greek philosophy: "Cursed be the man who would breed swine and cursed be the man who would teach his son Greek wisdom."[17] The Rabbis distrusted Greek philosophy, with its naturalism and rationalism, because it threatened religious faith and eroded traditional Rabbinic training. One Rabbi reported: "There were a thousand pupils in my father's school, of whom five hundred studied Torah and five hundred studied Greek philosophy; and from them none were left but myself and my nephew."[18] The Rabbis even exclude the Epicureans, who deny providence, from the world to come.[19] Cohen well summarizes the Rabbinic attitude toward Greek philosophy: "So far as Greek thought [philosophy] is concerned, there is almost unanimity against it."[20]

This hostility, of course, arises from their differences. Greek philosophers trusted in reason and the senses; the Rabbis trusted in God and the Prophets. Greek philosophers believed in a pagan god subject to law, nature, and fate; the Rabbis, in the God who transcended all these. Greek philosophers connected God to the world pantheistically or semi-pantheistically; the Rabbis separated God from his creation. Greek philosophers rejected supernaturalism, providence, and creation *ex nihilo;* the Rabbis heartily embraced them all. The occasional similarity—the notion of divine perfections or of certain monotheistic ideas—is coincidence or, more likely, the result of general revelation (Rom. 1:18ff). In the end, Greek philosophy and Rabbinic thought are like oil and water, like iron and clay: they cannot mix, they cannot adhere.

Historians are just as emphatic as the Rabbis and modern Rabbinic authorities in rejecting Sanders's claim. Solomon Grayzel, for instance, writes:

> For the Jews of Judea did not come in touch with the highest Greek civilization, not even with as high a Greek culture as surrounded the Jews of Alexandria. Even if they had met the real Greek culture, that

---

[17] Baba Qamma 82b.

[18] Baba Qamma 83a and Cohen, *Everyman's Talmud,* 27. The antecedent of "from them" is somewhat unclear. It may refer to the one thousand pupils, or more likely from the context, it refers to the five hundred pupils who studied Greek philosophy (so Cohen, *Everyman's Talmud,* 178). The Rabbis forbid the teaching of Greek wisdom to children, though exceptions were allowed. See Saul Lieberman, *Hellenism in Jewish Palestine* (New York: The Jewish Theological Seminary in America, 1962), 100-104.

[19] Sanhedrin 10.1.

[20] Cohen, *Everyman's Talmud,* 178.

of the famous Greek philosophers and poets, the Jews would still have rejected it as inferior to the culture of Judaism, though they might have had some respect for it.[21]

Likewise, G. F. Moore, also a historian of religion, states:

> The Jewish conception of God is derived from the Bible, and from the purest and most exalted teachings of the Bible, such as are found in Exod 33ff, Hosea, Deuteronomy, Jeremiah, Isaiah 40-5, and the Psalms. Monotheism was reached, as has been already observed, not from reflections on the unity of nature or of being, but from the side of God's moral rule in history, and it has therefore a more consistently personal character than where the idea of unity has been derived from physical or metaphysical premises.[22]

Allen R. Brockway rejects Greek philosophical influence, in particular Plato's influence, on the Rabbis: "The rabbis who re-invented Judaism during the second century did so, not on the basis of Platonism, but on grounds of a new intellectual contention. They held that the categories of purity established in their oral teachings as well as the Scriptures were the very structures according to which God conducted the world."[23] The Qumran discoveries only solidify these sentiments, as Emil Schürer confirms: "Moreover, recent research has shown that the Rabbis possessed an undeniable but limited knowledge of Greek culture. . . . The evidence emerging from the manuscript discoveries in the Judaean Desert largely confirms the conclusions reached so far."[24]

Since Greek philosophy did not influence the Rabbis, Philo cannot bridge Greek philosophy with Rabbinic theology, thus wrecking Sanders's second historical claim. Philo, in fact, had little or no influence on the Rabbis. "Philo's ultimate influence was considerable," writes historian Jenny Morris, "but not, as far as one can discern, on Jewish thought. . . .

---

[21] Solomon Grayzel, A History of the Jews (New York: Jewish Publication Society of America, 1947), 48.

[22] George Foot Moore, History of Religions, vol. 2 (New York: Charles Scribner's Sons, 1949), 69.

[23] Jacob Neusner, Alan J. Avery-Peck, William S. Green, eds., The Encyclopaedia of Judaism, vol. 1 (Leiden: Brill, 2000), 48. Contrast this statement with Boyd's lament of Plato's influence on classical theism (Boyd, God of the Possible, 115, 130-132).

[24] Emil Schürer, The History of the Jewish People in the Age of Jesus Christ (175 B.C.–A.D. 135), rev. and ed. G. Vermes, F. Millar, and M. Black, vol. 2 (Edinburgh: T & T Clark, 1979), 78.

Jewish literature written in Greek was to be of minimal interest to the rabbinic schools of Palestine after the fall of the Temple."[25] Similarly, G. F. Moore asserts: "Neither his [Philo's] conception of a transcendent God, nor the secondary god, the Logos, by which he bridges the gulf he has created between pure Being and the phenomenal world, and between God so conceived and man, had any effect on the theology of Palestinian Judaism."[26] The Rabbis even disregard Philo's exposition of biblical law.[27] In fact, the Rabbis simply ignore Philo, as Ronald Williamson indicates: "His [Philo's] life and works have a significant place within the history of Judaism (though for a long time not recognized by Judaism). . . ."[28] That is, the Rabbis did not recognize Philo. Harry A. Wolfson asserts that the Rabbis knew Philo (and Greek philosophy) only from hearsay.[29] Rabbinic Judaism refused not only to read Philo but also to preserve his writings, as Seymour Feldman relates: "Nevertheless, it must be admitted that Philo's project had little impact upon Jews and Judaism. . . . So complete was the Rabbinic commitment to systematic purity at the expense of Platonism that Philo's own work was not preserved within Judaism but only became known as a result of the work of Christian copyists."[30] While Sanders celebrates Philo as "the leading figure in forging the biblical-classical synthesis . . . followed by later Jewish, Christian and Muslim thinkers,"[31] the Rabbis, in fact, snubbed him.

To buttress his historical claim that classical theism is the product of a classical-biblical synthesis, Sanders appeals to two authorities who, he argues, defend this synthesis: the late philosopher and theologian H. P. Owen, and the eminent patristics scholar G. L. Prestige.[32] Owen, to be sure, occasionally agrees with the openness view. He seems to deny, based on philosophical reasoning, God's foreknowledge of future free actions, for example.[33] Moreover, he denies, or at least redefines, divine

---

[25] Jenny Morris, in ibid., vol. 3.2, 888-889.

[26] Moore, *Judaism*, 1:212.

[27] Ibid., 214.

[28] Ronald Williamson, *Jews in the Hellenistic World: Philo* (Cambridge: Cambridge University Press, 1989), 306.

[29] Wolfson, *Philo*, 1:91.

[30] Neusner, et al., *The Encyclopaedia of Judaism*, 2:711.

[31] Sanders, "Historical Considerations," 69.

[32] John Sanders, *The God Who Risks: A Theology of Providence* (Downers Grove, Ill.: InterVarsity Press, 1998), 307.

[33] H. P. Owen, *Concepts of Deity* (New York: Herder & Herder, 1971), 30-33, 144.

immutability.[34] Nevertheless, Sanders misleads when he quotes Owen—
"So far as the Western world is concerned, theism has a double origin: the
Bible and Greek philosophy"—and then states: "Classical theism is the
product of the 'biblical-classical synthesis.'"[35] Owen is not saying that
Greek philosophy corrupted scriptural teaching, as Sanders clearly implies
in his citing of Owen, but that the Fathers and Philo used Greek philosophy for expression and for amplification of the divine attributes that the
Scriptures teach. Owen writes, "All the divine properties I named in the
preceding paragraph [infinite, self-existence, incorporeality, eternity,
immutability, impassibility, simplicity, perfection, omniscience, and
omnipotence] are implied in the Bible; but the expression and, still more,
the amplification of them were due to the influence of Greek philosophy."[36] To say that the Fathers (not the Rabbis) used Greek philosophical
vocabulary and concepts to explain scriptural truths accurately reflects
Owen, but to say or to imply that Greek philosophy distorted or corrupted
scriptural truths misrepresents Owen.[37] Owen even equates classical
theism with Christian theism because "it arose within the context of orthodox belief in Biblical revelation."[38] Clearly, Owen believes that classical
theism (or Christian theism) comes from biblical revelation.

Similarly, Sanders misreads and misrepresents G. L. Prestige. Prestige
never claims that the Fathers derived their theism from a classical-
biblical synthesis. In fact, he states that the Fathers inherited Hebrew
theism[39] and that the "main trunk of the Christian idea of God," that is,
the divine perfections, which Prestige and the Fathers called transcen-

---

[34] Ibid., 144.

[35] Sanders, *The God Who Risks*, 141. By "classical," Sanders means Greek theism; Owen usually
means traditional or standard theism, not just Greek theism, but occasionally he interchanges the
terms "classical theism" and "Christian theism" (Owen, *Concepts of Deity*, 2).

[36] Owen, *Concepts of Deity*, 1.

[37] Owen differs with Aquinas on occasion, usually on philosophical grounds, but I cannot find a
statement where Owen states or implies that Greek philosophy has perverted the biblical teachings
of the Fathers.

[38] Owen, *Concepts of Deity*, 2. Owen's three other arguments are: "Secondly, although there are
extensive parallels to many aspects of Christian theism in the writings of non-Jewish and non-
Christian philosophers in the ancient world, there are some aspects that seem to be
unparalleled. . . . Thirdly, even where there are parallels there is nothing in any non-Christian
source that is philosophically comparable to the statements of theism given by Aquinas and those
Christian thinkers who are directly or indirectly indebted to him. Fourthly (and consequently),
throughout the Christian era non-Christian philosophers, as well as Christian ones, have almost
always discussed theism in one or other of its Christian formulations" (ibid.). Owen defines
classical theism "as belief in one God, the Creator, who is infinite, self-existent, incorporeal,
eternal, immutable, impassible, simple, perfect, omniscient and omnipotent" (ibid., 1).

[39] G. L. Prestige, *God in Patristic Thought* (London: SPCK, 1952), xviii.

dence, comes from the Hebrew Prophets[40] not from Plato.[41] Owen does not support Sanders's historical claims; Prestige refutes them—Sanders has fallen on his own sword.

Sanders's historical claims and appeals are hopeless, in whole and in part. They should raise the eyebrows, if not the hackles, of historians. These errors are serious, ominous with implications and grave with consequences for the openness view.

III. THEOLOGICAL CLAIMS OF THE OPENNESS VIEW

One such consequence is that their theological claims are partially joined at the hip to their historical claims. The openness view, in fact, recognizes and concedes that Judaism and Christianity maintain the traditional view of God. This concession, however, is potentially embarrassing—have virtually all Jews and virtually all Christians throughout history misread the Old Testament? To explain their concession and to avoid this embarrassment, openness advocates thus advance a historical argument appealing to the influence of Greek philosophy. Their argument, though implied, is clear: if the Rabbis and church fathers had followed the Bible instead of Greek philosophy, they too would have embraced an open view of God. But this explanation has already failed because their historical argument has completely collapsed.

Still, it is helpful to observe the insuperable chasm between Rabbinic theology and openness theology, because the same chasm separates traditional Christian theology from openness theology. Moreover, it is helpful to understand the actual source of Rabbinic theology, because Rabbinic theology and traditional Christian theology drink from the same well. Modern Rabbinic authorities describe the Rabbinic view of divine providence, foreknowledge, and even foreordination, in words that would bring a smile to the divines of Dordt or Westminster. Kaufmann Kohler, for example, depicts God's sovereign rule over human affairs as follows:

> . . . God is Ruler of a moral government. Thus He directs all the acts of men toward the end which He has set. Judaism is most sharply contrasted with heathenism at this point. Heathenism either deifies nature

---

[40] Ibid., xx, 26.
[41] Ibid.

or merges the deity into nature. Thus there is no place for a God who knows all things and provides for all in advance. . . . On the other hand, Judaism sees in all things, not the fortuitous dealings of a blind and relentless fate, but the dispensations of a wise and benign Providence. It knows of no event which is not foreordained by God. . . . A divine preordination decides a man's choice of his wife and every other important step of his life.[42]

Similarly, G. F. Moore describes the Rabbinic view of God's providence most compellingly and appropriately:

Nothing in the universe could resist God's power or thwart his purpose. His knowledge embraced all that was or is or is to be. . . . The history of the world is his great plan, in which everything moves to the fulfillment of his purpose, the end that is in his mind. Not only the great whole, but every moment, every event, every individual, every creature is embraced in this plan, and is an object of his particular providence. All man's ways are directed by God (Ps 37, 23; Prov 20, 24). A man does not even hurt his finger without its having been proclaimed above that he should do so.[43]

The tension between divine sovereignty and free will in Rabbinic theology does not, however, lessen God's foreordination or foreknowledge:

That man is capable of choosing between right and wrong and of carrying the decision into action was not questioned, nor was any conflict discovered between this freedom of choice with its consequences and the belief that all things are ordained and brought to pass by God in accordance with his wisdom and his righteous and benevolent will.[44]

Likewise, Efraim Urbach declares, "The Gemara deduces . . . that the deeds of man that are performed with understanding and in conformity with the laws of ethics and the precepts of religion can assure the desired results only if they accord with the designs of Providence, 'which knoweth what the future holds.'"[45] And finally, Alan J. Avery-Peck writes:

---

[42] Kaufmann Kohler, *Jewish Theology* (New York: Macmillan, 1918), 167-170.
[43] Moore, *Judaism,* 1:115, 384-385.
[44] Ibid., 1:454.
[45] Urbach, *The Sages,* 266.

While thus avowing the existence of free will, the rabbis generally focus on the idea that, from the beginning, God knew how things would turn out, such that all is predestined. This idea emerges from the comprehension that the world was created as a cogent whole, with its purpose preexisting the actual creation. The rabbis thus understand all that was needed to accomplish God's ultimate purpose has [*sic*] having been provided from the beginning of time. . . . In the Rabbinic view, there are no surprises for God. All is in place and ready for the preordained time to arrive.[46]

Calvin and Knox could hardly ask for more.

But the Rabbis are their own best witnesses. The Rabbis testify that God foreknows all things. "Everything is foreseen, yet freedom of choice is given," says Rabbi Akiba,[47] whom Tanchuma bar Abba echoes: "All is foreseen before the Holy One, blessed be He."[48] Rabbi Hanina states: "Everything is in the hands of heaven except the fear of God."[49] And Rabbi Joshua ben Hananiah responds in a similar way to the Romans:

> The Romans asked R Joshua b. Hananiah: Whence do we know that the Holy One, blessed be He, will resurrect the dead and knows the future? [After quoting Deut 31:16, which foretells many future free actions] He replied: Then at least you have the answer to half, viz., that He knows the future.[50]

According to the Rabbis, God foreknows a man's thoughts before he thinks them or even before he exists. Rabbi Haggai in the name of Rabbi Isaac says, "Before thought is formed in the heart of man, it already is revealed before you."[51] Likewise, Rabbi Yudan says, "Before a creature is actually created, his thought is already revealed before you."[52] Rabbi

---

[46] Neusner, et al., *The Encyclopaedia of Judaism*, 1:317, 319.

[47] Aboth 3.15. J. Israelstam comments aptly: "The verb sfh often means *looking ahead* in time or distance. When this is said of God, '*foreseen*' is, strictly speaking, not applicable or admissible, as God is independent of time and space," i.e., there is with Him neither past nor future nor distance, and He 'sees' everything at once" (J. Israelstam in I. Epstein, *The Babylonian Talmud* tractate *Aboth* [London: Soncino Press, 1935], 38).

[48] Tanchuma, Shelach 9.

[49] Niddah 16b.

[50] Sanhedrin 90b.

[51] Genesis Rabbah ix 3.

[52] Ibid.

Eleazar ben Pedath teaches that, unlike man, God judges perfectly through his foreknowledge:

> Unless a mortal hears the pleas that a man can put forward, he is not able to give judgment. With God, however, it is not so; before a man speaks, He already knows what is in his heart. . . . He understands even before the thoughts have been created in man's mind. You will find that seven generations before Nebuchadnezzar was born, Isaiah already prophesied what would be in his heart. . . . Surely, if God could foresee seven generations before, what he would think, shall He not know what the righteous man thinks on the same day?[53]

Moreover, God foreknows man's deeds. Rabbi Abbahu says, "At the beginning of the act of creating the world, the Holy One, blessed be he, foresaw the deeds of the righteous and of the wicked."[54] God foreknows, based on his foreordination, even mundane events, such as marrying a woman or purchasing a field. Rab Judah says:

> Forty days before the embryo is formed an echo issues forth on high announcing, "The daughter of So-and-so is to be a wife to So-and-so. Such and such a field is to belong to So-and-so" . . . as is illustrated by what occurred to Raba, who overheard a certain fellow praying for grace saying: "May that girl be destined to be mine!" Said Raba to the man: "Pray not grace thus; if she be meet for you, you will not lose her, and if not, you have challenged Providence." . . . Thus said Rab . . . from the Torah, from the Prophets and from the Hagiographa it may be shown that a woman is [destined to] a man by God.[55]

In fact, God foreknows and foreordains even the most insignificant events: "No man bruises his finger here on earth unless it was so decreed against him in heaven."[56]

Yet, the question remains: Where did the Rabbis get these views? Greek philosophy was a false guide, unable to show us the way. Perhaps another religion—Zoroastrianism, or the constantly mutating pagan

---

[53] Exodus Rabbah xxi 3.
[54] Genesis Rabbah ii 5.
[55] Moed Qatan 18b.
[56] Rabbi Hanina in Chullin 7b. For additional Rabbinic quotes on God's omniscience, see A. Marmorstein, *The Old Rabbinic Doctrine of God* (New York: Ktav, 1968), 153-160.

religions—influenced the Rabbis? This is another false notion, without advocate or evidence. But surely we are kidding ourselves. One needs only to grasp keenly the obvious to answer the question. Indeed, the modern Rabbinic authorities have already instructed us in the way, having pointed us to the answer, both natural and simple—the Old Testament. This, in turn, answers a related question. Where did the Fathers and the church get their views of God? The same Old Testament, of course. The apostles simply maintained the traditional view of God, revealed to them in the Old Testament, taught to them by their rabbis, and affirmed to them by their Lord. The Fathers and Christians have believed this ever since.[57] Have the Rabbis misread their Old Testament for centuries? Have Christians misread the same Old Testament—and the New Testament—for centuries? Openness advocates must answer yes, but common sense, supported by the evidence, must answer no.

Openness advocates cannot sustain their claim that the Fathers incorporated Greek philosophy into the church's theology. Sanders cites no evidence; Boyd furnishes only his estimation. Granted, Sanders and Boyd appeal to a few similarities between Greek philosophy and Christian theism, but these similarities do not prove that the Fathers synthesized biblical and Greek philosophical ideas into the church. They have not proved and cannot prove their assertions. They simply beg the question. To prop up their faltering claim and to sidestep their obligation to prove their claim, Sanders and Boyd must put the infection of Greek philosophy into the church before the earliest of the Fathers. This neatly and artfully explains everything: why all the Fathers were duped, and why no evidence exists to prove when the infection occurred—everything just happened so early. The claims of Sanders and Boyd are more like a modern conspiracy theory—the lack of evidence only confirms the conspiracy—than actual history.

---

[57] This is clearly the view of G. L. Prestige: "I have not given any assessment of the Hebrew theism which Christianity inherited. It lies outside my scope, and must for present purposes be taken for granted. My readers will, however, detect repeated signs that it formed the basis of patristic theism. In fact, these chapters really show how Hebrew theism looked to sympathetic Hellenistic minds" (Prestige, *God in Patristic Thought*, xviii). This Hebrew theism, moreover, came from the Prophets: ". . . how early Christendom sought both to establish and safeguard the supremacy of God in ways appropriate to a people trained to think in the schools of Greek philosophy, from which modern European thought is derived, and also to present the truth of His spiritual nature and moral holiness, which had been taught by the Hebrew prophets as corollary to His divine power. God was firmly held to be supernatural in the deepest and truest sense. Philosophically, this idea was expressed by the word huproche, which may fairly be translated transcendence" (ibid., 25). Prestige equates transcendence with infinite perfection (ibid., xx).

IV. EXEGETICAL CLAIMS OF THE OPENNESS VIEW

Of course, openness theology hinges on their distinctive interpretation of anthropomorphisms.[58] Boyd defines the openness hermeneutic as follows:

> First, there are certainly passages in the Bible that are figurative and portray God in human terms. You can recognize them, because what is said about God is either ridiculous if taken literally, or because the genre of the passage is poetic. However, there is nothing ridiculous or poetic about the way the Bible repeatedly speaks about God changing his mind, regretting decisions, or thinking and speaking about the future in terms of possibilities.[59]

At first glance, the Rabbis seem to agree with Boyd. Rabbi Aibu, for instance, said: "God said, I made a mistake that I created the evil principle in man, for had I not done so, he would not have rebelled against me."[60] Another Rabbi describes God as "regretting the evil inclination, and saying, 'What damage have I wrought! I regret that I have created it in my world.'"[61] Here at last, the openness advocates perhaps might claim Rabbinic support.

But not quite. First, openness advocates, unlike the Rabbis, artificially distinguish between physical anthropomorphisms and nonphysical anthropomorphisms (anthropopathisms). The openness advocates reject physical depictions of God, understanding them anthropomorphically, but they accept mental and emotional depictions of God (anthropopathisms), understanding them literally. The Rabbis, however, recognize no such subtlety. In fact, Rabbinic literature, especially Midrash, relishes anthropomorphisms, physical and nonphysical, even to excess: God is the best man in Adam's wedding; he mourns the destruction of the flood, like a father over a son; he negotiates with Abraham over the destruction of Sodom and Gomorrah, telling Abraham to correct him and to teach him, and he will do as Abraham

---

[58] Of course, this is not the only exegetical error of the openness view. Bruce Ware cogently demonstrates that openness exegesis, if consistently applied, compromises God's knowledge not only of the future but also of the present and of the past (Bruce A. Ware, *God's Lesser Glory: The Diminished God of Open Theism* [Wheaton, Ill.: Crossway, 2000], 67, 74-86).

[59] Boyd, *God of the Possible,* 118.

[60] Genesis Rabbah xxvii 4.

[61] Tanna de Be Eliyyahu, 62. These Rabbis, to be sure, have God confessing a mistake, something Boyd tries to dodge and duck; but unmistakably, Boyd all but asserts that God is mistaken about future free actions (Boyd, *God of the Possible,* 56, 59-62).

says. The Rabbis can even occasionally outwit God. Rabbi Eliezer, for instance, once tried every possible method of convincing his fellow Rabbis of a Halakic rule: he performed miracles, and God even spoke from heaven to confirm Rabbi Eliezer's opinion. But Rabbi Nathan responded: "We pay no attention to a heavenly voice. For already from Sinai the Law said, 'By a majority you are to decide.' (Exod 23:2) Rabbi Nathan [later] met Elijah and asked him what God did in that hour. Elijah replied, 'He [God] laughed and said, "My children have conquered me.""[62] Certainly, the Rabbis did not take such Midrashic statements or anthropomorphisms literally[63]; the Rabbis clearly teach otherwise—God is incorporeal, immutable, and perfect in all his ways.[64]

But how, then, should these anthropomorphisms be understood? Modern Rabbinic authorities generally furnish two answers. First, anthropomorphisms are necessary because of the limitations of human language and of human understanding, as Loewe and Montefiore write:

> We must remember that many Rabbis, in spite of their learning, were simple folk; it was with simple folk that they had to deal. Anthropomorphisms were unavoidable. But they were often mitigated by such caveats as *Kebayakol* ('If it be proper to say so'). . . . In all such cases, the Rabbis, like most teachers of religion, ascribe human methods of action to the Deity, but, concurrently with such ascription, they always maintain God's unlikeness to man—His omniscience, for example, and His foreknowledge.[65]

Perhaps Kohler expresses the Rabbinic view best:

> We cannot help attributing human qualities and emotions to Him the moment we invest Him with a moral and spiritual nature. When we speak of His punitive justice, His unfailing mercy, or His all-wise providence, we transfer to Him, imperceptibly, our own righteous indignation at the sight of a wicked deed, or our own compassion with the sufferer, or even our own mode of deliberation and decision. Moreover, the prophets and the Torah, in order to make God plain to

---

[62] Baba Mesia 59b.

[63] For a fuller discussion of the nature of anthropomorphic language in Scripture, see the essays by A. B. Caneday and Michael Horton in this volume.

[64] For God's infinite perfections, see Marmorstein, *The Old Rabbinic Doctrine of God*, 148-217; and Cohen, *Everyman's Talmud*, 1-26.

[65] Loewe (xcvi) and Montefiore (36) in *A Rabbinic Anthology*.

the people, described Him in vivid images of human life, with anger and jealousy as well as compassion and repentance, and also with the organs and functions of the senses—seeing, hearing, smelling, speaking, and walking. The Rabbis are all the more emphatic in their assertions that the Torah merely intends to assist the simple-minded, and that unseemly expressions concerning Deity are due to the inadequacy of language, and must not be taken literally. "It is an act of boldness allowed only to the prophets to measure the Creator by the standard of the creature," says the Haggadist. . . .[66]

Second, these anthropomorphisms reflect the Rabbinic doctrine of the "imitation of God," which portrays God as obeying his own commandments, studying Torah, praying to himself, and wearing phylacteries and prayer-shawls, so that his people can imitate his ways.[67] Thus, anthropomorphisms help us to recognize and to follow God, bringing God near to man, and assisting man to become like God.

The Rabbis, in fact, explain their anthropomorphisms. Ishmael ben Elisha states, "We borrow terms from His creatures to apply to Him in order to assist the understanding."[68] Moreover, as noted above by Montefiore, the Rabbis frequently temper or soften the bolder anthropomorphisms with the disclaimer, "If it is proper to say so." Rabbi Judah, for example, in commenting on Zechariah 2:8, says: "It does not say 'the apple of the eye,' but 'the apple of His eye,' that is, of God's eye, for, if it is proper to say so, the Scripture refers to Him who is above, only that it paraphrases [to avoid too great an anthropomorphism]."[69] The Rabbis also refer to a biblical anthropomorphism, but stress God's unlikeness to man:

A human king goes forth to war, and the provinces by which he passed draw near to him, and tell him their needs, but they are told, "He is

---

[66] Kohler, *Jewish Theology*, 76.

[67] Cohen, *Everyman's Talmud*, 7-8. As for these seemingly irreverent anthropomorphisms of the Midrash, Montefiore explains: "The naïve, but daring, anthropomorphism(s) . . . may seem almost flippant to modern readers. The apparent flippancy is not due to any Rabbinic lack of deep reverence for God or of fervent love; it may rather be said that this very reverence and love produced a certain intimate familiarity, which may be compared to the familiarity of a loving son who is on very intimate terms with his father, and can even make jokes about him to his face" (Montefiore, *A Rabbinic Anthology*, 341).

[68] Mekhilta xix 19.

[69] Sifre Numbers, Beha'aloteka, 84. Montefiore (*A Rabbinic Anthology*, 64) supplies the bracketed phrase.

excited, he is going forth to war; when he returns victorious, come then, and ask of him your needs." But God is not like that. The Lord is a man of war, He fights against the Egyptians; but the Lord is his name. . . .[70]

Furthermore, the Tiqqune Sopherim and the Targums, with their tendency to remove or to mollify anthropomorphisms, indicate that the Rabbis understood them figuratively.

Accordingly, the Rabbis understand anthropomorphisms, such as God's regretting, figuratively. Commenting on Genesis 6:6, Ramban (Nachmanides), a Rabbinic commentator of the Scriptures, writes: "The Torah speaks in the language of men. The purport is that they rebelled, and grieved his Holy Spirit with their sins." Similarly, Ibn Ezra and Rambam (Maimonides), also Rabbinic commentators, interpret the passage anthropomorphically. The Mishnah relates that God created the rainbow on the eve of the first Sabbath because God foreknew the flood, as Alan J. Avery-Peck states:

> For instance, rather than God's surprise at human sinfulness, described at Gen. 6:5-6, which leads God to bring a flood (Gen 6:6), the rabbis understand the rainbow to have been created before the first Sabbath. This means that God already knew that people would sin, that there would be a flood, and that, afterwards, God would promise never again to destroy the earth and would offer the rainbow as a sign of that commitment. In the Rabbinic view, there are no surprises for God.[71]

Boyd's comment on Genesis 6:6—"Doesn't the fact that God regretted the way things turned out (to the point of starting over) suggest that it *wasn't* a foregone conclusion at the time God created human beings that they would fall into this state of wickedness?"[72]—mirrors the argument of a Gentile who denied God's foreknowledge to Rabbi Joshua ben Qorha:

> Gentile: Do you not maintain that the Holy One, blessed be he, sees what is going to happen?
>
> Rabbi: Indeed so.

---

[70] Mekhilta (Lauterbach, vol. 2), 32-34.
[71] Alan J. Avery-Peck, in Neusner, et al., *Encyclopaedia of Judaism*, 1:318-319.
[72] Boyd, *God of the Possible*, 55.

Gentile: But lo it is written, And it grieved him in his heart (Gen 6:6).

Rabbi: Did you ever have a son?

Gentile: Yes.

Rabbi: And what did you do?

Gentile: I was happy, and I made everybody happy.

Rabbi: But did you not know that in the end he would die?

Gentile: Rejoice in the time of joy, mourn in the time of mourning.

Rabbi: And that is the way things are done before the Holy One, blessed be he. For R Joshua b Levi said, "For seven days the Holy One, blessed be he, went into mourning for his world before he brought the flood, as it is said, And it grieved him in his heart (Gen 6:6), and further it says, For the king grieved for his son (2 Sam 19:3)."[73]

In short, the Rabbis interpret Genesis 6:6 anthropomorphically, without rejecting God's foreknowledge.[74]

Certainly, the Rabbis and modern Rabbinic authorities understand human descriptions of God anthropomorphically. They do not distinguish between physical and nonphysical anthropomorphisms. They do not contradict their theology by their exegesis. They simply communicate about God as anyone must, by using human language analogously to communicate divine and spiritual realities.

V. Conclusion

Clearly, Christians must reject the claims of the openness view: its historical claims are misinformed—the Rabbis follow Moses and Isaiah, not Plato and Aristotle; its theology is misguided—the Rabbis maintain that God foresees and foreordains even future free actions; and its exegesis is

---

[73] Genesis Rabbah xxvii 6.

[74] The Rabbis interpret other passages, for example, Genesis 22:12—"Because now I know that you fear God"—as God's foreknowledge actualized. Rambam states: "At the beginning Abraham's fear of God was latent; it had not become actualized through such a great deed, but now it was known in actuality, and his merit was perfect, and his reward would be complete from the Eternal, the God of Israel." Rashi and Nachmanides interpret Genesis 22:12 likewise.

mistaken—the Rabbis interpret anthropomorphisms figuratively. In the end, the openness view requires too much. It requires us to believe that Christians and Jews have misunderstood history, theology, and exegesis for thousands of years. It requires a new history and a new exegesis to support its new theology. It then requires a new hymnbook, a new prayer book, and a new liturgy. Next it requires a new Bible, and finally, a new God. It requires too much; it supplies too little. Instead of requiring a new religion, let us reject the claims and the teachings of the openness view, and let us maintain those cherished and precious scriptural truths of God's infinite knowledge and perfections that have always comforted and consoled his saints. Here, we will find rest for our souls.[75]

---

[75] I would like to thank Bruce Ware and Stephen Wellum, my colleagues, for their helpful suggestions.

2

GENETIC DEFECTS OR ACCIDENTAL SIMILARITIES? ORTHODOXY AND OPEN THEISM AND THEIR CONNECTIONS TO WESTERN PHILOSOPHICAL TRADITIONS

Chad Owen Brand

Open theism has become front-page news in evangelical theological circles. Professors cannot teach any subject in the intellectual theological disciplines these days without paying some attention to what open theists are saying. And the discussion does not go very far before someone starts wondering where all of this came from. Did Clark Pinnock, Gregory Boyd, John Sanders, and others get their ideas from the Bible? Or were they driven to their model by some set of philosophical presuppositions? Casual observers have noted similarities between open theism and process theology. Is this new view simply process thought dressed up in a more evangelical garb? And while we are at it, we might also field questions from those on the other side of the fence who wonder whether and to what degree traditionalism has been influenced by philosophical concerns. Were the Nicene Fathers simply recapitulating Platonism? Are their contemporary children propagating biblical theology or Hellenistic philosophy?

Questions about how theological systems are related to philosophical systems have been around for some time. They have surfaced again, though, in the controversy over open theism. It seems imperative, therefore, for us to take a long look at open theism and its philosophical connections, and to open again the same questions with regard to orthodoxy. And it will be necessary not only to ask whether there are similarities between these theological systems and various philosophical projects, but whether those similarities entail borrowing, dependence, and synthesis. The fact that there are occasional similarities between two schools of thought is neither here nor there. But if, for instance, a system of thought employs the same set of arguments to prove the same basic ideas for the same purposes as does another system, and if one can establish a historical connection between the two, then that might entail more than an accidental similarity. This essay will probe whether traditionalism or open theism are doing just that.

I. The Accusation Against Traditional Christian Orthodoxy

Open theists have consistently made the claim that historic, traditional Christian orthodoxy, which they equate with classical theism, holds to views that arise more from philosophical commitments than from Scripture.[1] Specifically, they accuse the traditional position of leaning on classical Greek philosophy and of filtering Scripture through a Hellenistic grid.[2] Against this purported heritage, authors such as Pinnock, Sanders, and Boyd defend their own approach, which they see as constituting an alternative position both to traditionalism and to process theology, and as being thoroughly evangelical. They further claim

---

[1] This essay defines *classical theism* as that system of thought which, under the influence of or parallel to Aristotelian or Stoic thought, crystallizes such divine attributes as immutability and impassibility, and defines God in terms that do not allow for the possibility of his having a genuine relationship with the world (Bruce Demarest, "Process Trinitarianism," in *Perspectives on Evangelical Theology*, ed. Kenneth S. Kantzer and Stanley N. Gundry [Grand Rapids, Mich.: Baker, 1979], 29). On the other hand, in this essay I will argue that "traditional Christian orthodoxy" (or *traditionalism*), which I am distinguishing from classical theism, has preferred to allow the Bible to speak to these issues and so to produce a theology which sees God as relational though still in some sense immutable (Ronald H. Nash, *The Concept of God: An Exploration of Contemporary Difficulties with the Attributes of God* [Grand Rapids, Mich.: Zondervan, 1983], 30). There is no terminological consensus in the contemporary discussion; therefore, some scholars have used the term "classical theism" to designate what I am calling "traditionalism," and vice-versa.

[2] While open theists sometimes recognize that traditionalists have not all adopted the full classical theistic system, they still maintain that the modifications are not nearly thorough enough (Clark H. Pinnock, *Most Moved Mover: A Theology of God's Openness* [Grand Rapids, Mich.: Baker, 2001], 75).

that their position is driven not by prior philosophical commitments but by biblical exegesis.

Not a New Allegation

The claim against traditionalism is, of course, nothing new. In the nineteenth century various theologians in the liberal/revisionist tradition complained that orthodoxy constituted the victory of Athens over Jerusalem. Adolf von Harnack alleged that everything from Nicaea to Thomas Aquinas (and beyond in scholasticism) resulted from the Hellenization of theology.[3] He saw what he perceived to be the "gradual disappearance" of the "Enthusiastic and Apocalyptic," which were prominent in the New Testament, and their replacement by a synthesis of the "Greek spirit" with a newly revised "Jewish religion" that came to its final apex in Catholicism.[4] Harnack claimed that the first real "fusing" of Platonism and Christianity was found in Origen, though there were "elements" of such in people such as Justin and Clement.[5] Harnack was not alone in making such allegations,[6] and representatives from schools of thought such as neo-orthodoxy and the biblical theology movement in the twentieth century have beaten the same drum.[7]

The Open Theist Critique

Open theists have added their "amen" to the analysis of Harnack and allege that most orthodox theologians Hellenized the great tradition for several reasons. One, traditionalists were driven to articulate orthodox theology in the face of various challenges from heretics in the early church, a challenge which caused them to seek ammunition outside the Hebrew heritage of the faith. Two, they faced the difficulty of defend-

---

[3] Adolf von Harnack, *History of Dogma*, trans. Neil Buchanan (Gloucester, Mass.: Peter Smith, 1976), 1:43-59.

[4] Ibid., 51, 54. Though it took till the fourth century for this new tradition to become dominant, Harnack argues that it began as early as A.D. 95 with the work of Clement of Rome. He identifies the moralizing tendency of the apostolic fathers and the synergism of thinkers from Tertullian to Pelagius with this Jewish element. See on the apostolic fathers T. F. Torrance, *The Doctrine of Grace in the Apostolic Fathers* (Grand Rapids, Mich.: Eerdmans, 1959), 133-141.

[5] Adolf von Harnack, *Outlines of the History of Dogma*, trans. Edwin Knox Mitchell (New York: Star King, 1957), 152-154.

[6] See, for instance, Ludwig Feuerbach, *The Essence of Christianity*, trans. George Eliot (New York: Harper & Row, 1957), 285-287.

[7] Michael S. Horton, "Hellenistic or Hebrew? Open Theism and Reformed Theological Method" (chapter 6 in this volume and *Journal of the Evangelical Theological Society* 45 [2002]: 318).

ing respective traditions over against each other in the various scholastic movements in history, a difficulty which sent many theologians scurrying to Aristotelian, Ramist, and other alien forms of discourse. Three, they felt compelled to respond to the threat of unbelief, deism, and atheism in the face of the Enlightenment, and the resulting *apologia* became tinged with modern thought-forms.

Clark Pinnock and Robert Brow offer this general assessment of the problem with the traditional model of understanding God: "The difficulty with classical theism, so influenced by Hellenism, is that it makes God impassive and unable to relate."[8] Sanders contends that the bridge from Greek philosophy to Christian theology was Philo, since he attempted to harmonize the Old Testament with Greek thought.[9] Both the patristic tradition and the scholastic tradition of Anselm and Thomas simply followed suit.[10] Augustine's interpretation of God so controlling the world that there are "no surprises" arises from his Hellenistic tendency to render God as an absolute principle rather than a person—contrary to the biblical portrait.[11] In the Bible the emphasis is on God's "vulnerability and openness" not on his immutability and omnipotence.[12] The Greek tradition, then, has done the Christian heritage a great disservice.[13]

It is not only the Greek tradition that manipulated Christian thought, though. In a similar manner, theology in the medieval and Reformation West was bent by the impact of Latin legal traditions, "causing the image of God as judge to predominate in an unbiblical manner."[14] Though God is at the same time "parent" and judge, the first of those terms is the more appropriate when dealing with redemption, say the openness advocates, but Calvin and Anselm "have led us astray when they have interpreted

---

[8] Clark H. Pinnock and Robert C. Brow, *Unbounded Love: A Good News Theology for the Twenty-first Century* (Downers Grove, Ill.: InterVarsity Press, 1994), 50. They continue, "It removes God from the process of real involvement with the world and makes it hard to envisage real conversation with the three persons of the Trinity" (ibid.).

[9] John Sanders, "Historical Considerations," in Clark Pinnock, et al., *The Openness of God: A Biblical Challenge to the Traditional Understanding of God* (Downers Grove, Ill.: InterVarsity Press, 1994), 69-71.

[10] For an even more determined statement of this position, see Pinnock, *Most Moved Mover*, 69-70.

[11] Sanders, "Historical Considerations," 81.

[12] Pinnock and Brow, *Unbounded Love*, 9-10.

[13] It needs to be noted at the outset that neither open theists nor revisionists are usually very specific when they talk about the Greek influence. This point will be taken up later in this essay.

[14] Pinnock and Brow, *Unbounded Love*, 9; Pinnock, *Most Moved Mover*, 72.

salvation in heavily forensic and legal terms."[15] Likewise, Thomas, since he derived his conception of the divine attributes from reason rather than revelation, is guilty of the "Christianization of Greek" and the "Hellenization of Christian" thought.[16]

Open theists tend to see traditionalism as operating within an essentially monochromatic dimension in its theological formulation. For instance, in critiquing the traditional view of sin and forensic justification, Pinnock and Brow argue that for the traditionalists, "sin is defined primarily as disobedience to the rules."[17] In another place they contend that "Calvinism has tended to regard [God's] wrath as a function of divine holiness and to sever its relation to love."[18] Again, they maintain that traditionalists believe that God has to be "coaxed" by Jesus into loving sinners, since he is merely angry with them.[19] Pinnock offers a similar critique of Donald Bloesch's views on salvation, alleging that for Bloesch, whom open theists consider an ally on some issues, "conversion is not a personal event."[20] Anyone who has read Bloesch's works on the theology of conversion or historic Christian piety will raise an eyebrow or two at such an assessment. It seems critical to open theists, though, that they characterize their opponents as simplistic, as committed to alien philosophical systems of thought, and as being willing to adopt any schema that presents itself in order to win their apologetic and polemical battles.

II. Traditional Orthodoxy: Jerusalem, or Athens?

Is it the case that the critics of traditional theism are correct? We will first take a look at what traditionalists have said in response to the challenge

---

[15] Pinnock and Brow, *Unbounded Love*, 9, 26-30, 38-39. These thinkers have joined a veritable plethora of contemporary left-wing evangelicals who wish to jettison the concepts of satisfaction and substitutionary atonement in favor of less "violent" and less punitive conceptions of the work of Christ on the cross. See, for instance, J. Denny Weaver, *The Nonviolent Atonement* (Grand Rapids, Mich.: Eerdmans, 2001); and Joel B. Green and Mark D. Baker, *Recovering the Scandal of the Cross: Atonement in New Testament and Contemporary Contexts* (Downers Grove, Ill.: InterVarsity Press, 2000). Pinnock also objects to Anselm's "perfect being" theology (Pinnock, *Most Moved Mover*, 70).

[16] Pinnock, *Most Moved Mover*, 71.

[17] Pinnock and Brow, *Unbounded Love*, 63.

[18] Ibid., 67. Their option is to argue that God's wrath arises from "injured love," and is an indicator of "God's response to humanity's treatment of him" (ibid., 68).

[19] Ibid., 101.

[20] Clark H. Pinnock, "The Holy Spirit in the Theology of Donald G. Bloesch," in *Evangelical Theology in Transition: Theologians in Dialogue with Donald Bloesch*, ed. Elmer C. Colyer (Downers Grove, Ill.: InterVarsity Press, 1999), 132.

from liberals and open theists. Second, we will examine the writings of two thinkers in the orthodox tradition who have aroused the ire of the critics. Third, we will seek to determine whether and to what degree open theism is itself a system which is grounded on philosophical assumptions.

Connected To, Influenced By, and Borrowing From

At the outset, it is important to be specific about what we mean when we say that a position is "influenced by" a philosophical or cultural tradition. When we argue that a belief is grounded in or influenced by some other tradition, we have to make clear the degree to which such alleged "borrowing" has actually taken place. We also need to demonstrate that the alleged connection between the two systems actually is the case. It is not enough simply to demonstrate that some parallels exist. In making historical comparisons, it is often considered a damning indictment if one can assert that some group is "like the Nazis," or "just like the Ku Klux Klan," for instance. But most such comparisons are facile and, therefore, inconsequential.

In a similar manner, we need to be precise about the degree to which a theological argument is related to a philosophical movement or tradition. There is no doubt that theologians do their work in cultural and historical contexts and that they are influenced by their intellectual environments. But how are they influenced? Is their relationship with the prevailing ideologies tangential, or intimate? To what degree are there parallels between the two systems of thought? Are they mostly influenced to ask certain questions due to the thought of their times, or are their answers tinged, consciously or otherwise, with the dogma of the hour? In terms of the question raised by this essay, to what degree is there a "synthesis"[21] between these systems, i.e., between the philosophy of the Greeks and the theological formulations of Christian traditionalists? If there is no clear evidence of synthesis, then the burden of proof is on the critic to establish a relationship of borrowing, infection, or syncretism. Even if some taint can be found, it will be important to discern the degree to which that has determined the direction of the theological project in

---

[21] This is the term used by C. Andresen, "The Integration of Platonism into Early Christian Theology," in *Studia Patristica*, vol. 85, pt. 1, ed. Elizabeth A. Livingstone (Berlin: Akademie, 1984), 399-413.

question. That is, the most likely scenario is one in which biblical ideas will have been mixed with certain influences from the local culture. But which is dominant and determinative of the overall direction of the theological program in question? It seems that the questions are not as simplistic as some would maintain.

What "Traditional Orthodox" Theologians Say

If one were to read only the works of revisionists and open theists, one would get the impression that all conservatives and other representatives of the more traditional position were followers of the Platonists and had never given thought to that fact. Nothing could be further from the truth. Traditionalists have criticized classical theism for centuries, and the recent surge of conservative evangelical scholars, including those who have taken up arms against open theism, is no exception.

What revisionists and open theists have often left unsaid in their condemnation of the traditionalist's "Hellenization" of theology is that in most of the debates which culminated in confessional statements or which produced supposedly rationalistic theologies, the opponents of the traditionalists were themselves attempting to philosophize the faith. Arianism, for instance, denied the deity of Christ based on the premise of the absolute transcendence of God as "the unoriginate source . . . of all reality," and the presupposition that the world was unable to bear his direct impact.[22] Sanders, in his discussion of Arianism, ignores this fact, and notes only that Arius rejected the static view of God which was developing in his time and argued rather for a model which would posit change and suffering within God.[23] But this is surely not an adequate analysis. Arius was an Aristotelian and so was convinced that if one used a different name to describe an entity, such a designation suggested a difference in *ousia*. This was the basis of the Arians' rejection of the orthodox affirmation that Christ was *homoousios* with the Father.[24] So, while it is true that the Arian party at Nicaea wanted to use only biblical language in the wording of the Creed, that was primarily because such a move would felicitously support the specific philosophical ontology which stood behind

---

[22] J. N. D. Kelly, *Early Christian Doctrines* (New York: Harper & Row, 1960), 227.

[23] Sanders, "Historical Considerations," 77.

[24] Gerald Bray, *The Doctrine of God,* Contours of Christian Theology (Downers Grove, Ill.: InterVarsity Press, 1993), 127.

Arian Christology. It was necessary, though, to take a step beyond a mere repetition of biblical verses to clarify all of the issues involved:

> A doctrinal hermeneutic was required, in which scripture and tradition were encountered creatively and profoundly, in order to recast their ideas and interpret their narratives in new images and terms. A theology of repetition—whether of biblical texts or liturgical formulae—left too many theological loose ends. The ideas behind the familiar formulae of the New Testament and the liturgy of the church had to be re-imagined and recreated through conceptual innovation, unless they were to become dead metaphors, petrified verbal moments from the past. The Nicene crisis instantiates a general phenomenon to which we shall return later in the present study: the perceived need to transfer theological reflection from commitment to the limits and defining conditions and vocabulary of the New Testament itself, in order to preserve its commitment to the New Testament proclamation.[25]

While one might quibble over one or two of the phrases in McGrath's statement, the fundamental idea is certainly correct—that Christians must state their faith in terms that are completely faithful to the Bible but which also speak to their own day.[26] Parroting biblical words and phrases is no guarantee that one's position truly represents Scripture.

Early Christians did employ the categories found in their contemporary traditions. In the Greek world the Christian faith appropriated the language of classical thought in an attempt to counter pagan philosophy.[27] That was not necessarily unfitting. Revelation itself employs the language of Hellenism as well as the language of Hebraism "in order to reach the intelligentsia of every age."[28] The apologists and church fathers drew upon concepts provided by the creative thinkers of their time and earlier times in order to render the message of faith intellectually respectable and credible. Much of what they affirmed is still needful, especially the work of those persons, such as Athanasius, who did not base the

---

[25] Alister McGrath, *The Genesis of Doctrine: A Study in the Foundations of Doctrinal Criticism* (Oxford: Basil Blackwell, 1990), 7.

[26] John Jefferson Davis, *Foundations of Evangelical Theology* (Grand Rapids, Mich.: Baker, 1984), 11-42.

[27] Donald G. Bloesch, *Holy Scripture: Revelation, Inspiration and Interpretation*, Christian Foundations, vol. 2 (Downers Grove, Ill.: InterVarsity Press, 1994), 285.

[28] Donald G. Bloesch, *God the Almighty: Power, Wisdom, Holiness, Love*, Christian Foundations, vol. 3 (Downers Grove, Ill.: InterVarsity Press, 1995), 29.

heart of their thinking primarily on secular models.[29] He derived his *homoousios* doctrine, not from Hellenic roots, but from the "I am" sayings of Jesus in John.[30] This same spirit can be found in Tertullian, who, though he claimed to believe in the incarnation "because it was absurd," still relied on reason to be the criterion for determining exactly what was absurd.[31] All of this led Harry Wolfson to observe that the Fathers "did not battle as partisans of certain opposing schools of Greek philosophy; they battled only as advocates of opposing interpretations of Scripture."[32]

The truth of the gospel, though, always transcends such Hellenistic linguistic forms and cognitive development, even as it transcends the popular Jewish expectation of a militaristic Messiah.[33] It is important to note that danger always lurked beneath the surface of such undertakings. The tendency of theology to succumb to the rationalistic spirit is ancient. In the early church Justin Martyr, Clement of Alexandria, and Tatian made major concessions to rationalism in an attempt to demonstrate that Christianity was the most perfect of philosophies. Justin, for instance, made use of the Stoic concept of the Logos and sought to convince his hearers that the divine Logos had become incarnate in Jesus Christ. The court is still out on the degree to which he subverted the incarnation to Stoicism. Some of the early apologists erected the superstructure of their theological systems on foundations laid by their opponents. Reflection has shown that these foundations were not always compatible with the structure which was erected upon them. Rationalism is also apparent in many medieval churchmen. John Scotus Erigena argued that reason was prior to theological authority and that true authority is simply truth found by the power of reason and handed down in writing by the Fathers

---

[29] Donald G. Bloesch, *The Ground of Certainty* (Grand Rapids, Mich.: Eerdmans, 1971), 29-30. Athanasius declared that he did not prove his case against Arius by the wisdom of the Greeks but rather by the "faith that clearly precedes . . . argumentation" (Athanasius, *The Life of Antony and the Letter to Marcellinus*, ed. and trans. Robert C. Gregg [New York: Paulist, 1980], 88).

[30] He noted that *ousia* is simply a form of *einai* (T. F. Torrance, *Christian Doctrine of God* [Edinburgh: T. & T. Clark, 2002], 118-119).

[31] Tertullian, *On Prescription Against Heretics* 7, in *The Ante-Nicene Fathers*, vol. 3, trans. Peter Holmes, ed. Alexander Roberts and James Donaldson (Grand Rapids, Mich.: Eerdmans, n.d.).

[32] Harry A. Wolfson, "Philosophical Implications of Arianism and Apollinarianism," *Dumbarton Oaks Papers* 12 (1958): 13.

[33] Bloesch, *God the Almighty*, 207. "We should resist both the Hellenizing and the Judaizing of the faith without abandoning its Hellenistic matrix and Jewish roots" (ibid., 211). "Theology and philosophy tend to reflect the spirit of the age (*Zeitgeist*), though an authentic biblical theology will invariably go counter to the mood of the times" (Donald G. Bloesch, "The Missing Dimension," *Reformed Review* 26 [1973]: 167).

for later use. Even so conservative a thinker as John Feinberg recognizes that classical theism sometimes supervened on the earlier theologians, especially Thomas, and altered their perspectives.[34]

Augustine: Christianized Neoplatonist, or Biblical Theologian?

Early theologians employed the language of their intellectual world in explicating their views. So, Justin Martyr identified Christ with the Logos of Stoicism, while Augustine spoke of God as Absolute Form and the Supreme Substance.[35] Such considerations did not blind them to the contours of the biblical revelation and its emphasis on God as the Father of Jesus and as the redeemer of mankind, but did allow them to engage the intellectuals of their day on their own ground.[36] The question is: Did they explicitly or implicitly import Hellenism into Christian theology, and if so, to what degree?

Open theist writers contend that Augustine did Hellenize the faith, and did so in a damaging manner.[37] The African Father certainly sought, especially in his early career, to synthesize the teachings of "certain Platonists"[38] with those of the Apostles and Prophets. Augustine's pilgrimage, through Manicheanism, then on to the Academicians (such as Cicero), and finally to Neoplatonism just before the gospel found him, is well known.[39] Anyone reading his early writings will detect a strong Neoplatonic strain, so that even as late as The Enchiridion (ca. 422, eight years before Augustine died) one finds him using the definition of evil as privation.[40] No doubt some

---

[34] John S. Feinberg, No One Like Him: The Doctrine of God, Foundations of Evangelical Theology (Wheaton, Ill.: Crossway, 2001), 62-67. See also Nash, The Concept of God, 40-52, for a critique of the Thomistic synthesis of theology and philosophy.

[35] Kelly, Early Christian Doctrines, 96-98, 271-279; Bloesch, God the Almighty, 208-209. Certainly the philosophical overtones of this language were balanced over against biblical, evangelical emphases. Justin broke with Platonism by affirming that God is Creator, and Augustine made it clear that the God of the Bible is a living God and that the distinctions within the Trinity are relational rather than substantive (ibid., 208; Geoffrey Bromiley, Historical Theology: An Introduction [Grand Rapids, Mich.: Eerdmans, 1979], 95).

[36] See Curtis Chang, Engaging Unbelief: A Captivating Strategy from Augustine and Aquinas (Downers Grove, Ill.: InterVarsity Press, 2000), 66-93; and Jaroslav Pelikan, The Emergence of the Catholic Tradition (100–600), The Christian Tradition, vol. 1 (Chicago: University of Chicago Press, 1971), 295-297.

[37] Sanders, "Historical Considerations," 80-85; Pinnock, Most Moved Mover, 69.

[38] Augustine, Confessions, trans. Henry Chadwick (Oxford: Oxford University Press, 1991), 7.9.

[39] Peter Brown, Augustine of Hippo: A Biography, new edition (Berkeley: University of California Press, 2000), 23-107; Augustine, Confessions, 1-10.

[40] Augustine, Enchiridion, trans. S. D. Salmond (Edinburgh: T. & T. Clark, 1877), 11-14. Of course, on this subject, there is no final canonical answer as to the definition of evil which satisfies

Platonic elements stayed with Augustine right down to the end,[41] though one might question the degree to which his anthropological and ontological dualisms arise from his reading of Plotinus or of Paul.[42]

Was Augustine's mature theology then an amalgam of Paul and Plotinus? Pinnock says yes, and argues that Plotinus actually wins out, as Pinnock labels Augustine's theology as "pagan."[43] Sanders likewise claims that even in his mature years, Augustine used Neoplatonism "to interpret the Bible."[44] He further criticizes Augustine's doctrine of predestination as being linked to a Hellenistic notion of impassibility. The earlier Fathers had argued that God foresees who would have faith, and then "elects those who will,"[45] while Augustine contended for a rejection of libertarian free will and a strong doctrine of predestination as unilateral. Sanders has either misread or misrepresented this tradition in his critique of Augustine's contribution to predestinarian theology,[46] but that is merely

---

all evangelical theologians, so it may be inappropriate to criticize Augustine too harshly for his borrowing from the Neoplatonists here. Chang notes that his definition of evil as privation shows that "he refused to accept that violence and death are intrinsic to human life and desires" (Chang, *Engaging Unbelief*, 87). See also the discussion in G. R. Evans, "Evil," in *Augustine Through the Ages: An Encyclopedia*, ed. Allan D. Fitzgerald (Grand Rapids, Mich.: Eerdmans, 1999), 340-344.

[41] This is best seen in his discussion of the Platonists in *City of God*. Here he commends such Platonic insights as that God is the Supreme Good, that humans need the light of God to see clearly, and that philosophers ought to love God. He also poses the possibility that Plato had read the Hebrew prophets, though he does not argue strongly for this (Augustine, *The City of God Against the Pagans*, trans. R. W. Dyson [Cambridge: Cambridge University Press, 1998], 8.4-8.14).

[42] Even evangelical scholars are not in agreement on these issues, but it would seem that, among evangelicals, more would hold to an anthropological (holistic) dualism than to monism. Compare, for instance, Wayne Grudem, *Systematic Theology: An Introduction to Biblical Doctrine* (Grand Rapids, Mich.: Zondervan, 1994), 472-489; with E. Earle Ellis, *Christ and the Future in New Testament History* (Leiden: E. J. Brill, 2000), 147-178; and Nancey Murphy, *Reconciling Theology and Science: A Radical Reformation Perspective* (Kitchener, Ont.: Pandora, 1997), 47-62.

[43] The title of the chapter in which he details orthodoxy's flight from the Bible is, "Overcoming a Pagan Inheritance" (Pinnock, *Most Moved Mover*, 65-112). He states that Augustine preferred being to becoming and that the African theologian put God in a box (ibid., 69).

[44] Sanders, "Historical Considerations," 81; cf. Pinnock, *Most Moved Mover*, 69.

[45] Sanders, "Historical Considerations," 81.

[46] I contend that Sanders has misread the evidence here. With the exception of Origen and Athanasius, there is little discussion of predestination in the Ante-Nicene Fathers. Further, as far as I have been able to tell, there is no discussion of election based on foreseen faith in these thinkers. On Athanasius, see F. Stuart Clarke, "Lost and Found: Athanasius's Doctrine of Predestination," *Scottish Journal of Theology* 29 (1976): 442. For Origen's view, in which he argues for election based on foreseen merit, not, as Sanders argues, foreseen faith, see Origen, *De Principiis* 2.9.7 in *The Ante-Nicene Fathers*, vol. 4, ed. A. Cleveland Coxe, trans. Frederick Crombie (Grand Rapids, Mich.: Eerdmans, n.d.); and Origen, *In Epistolam ad Romanos Commentariorum*, in *Origenis Opera Omnia*, ed. Carol Henric Eduard Lommatzsch (Berlin: Haude & Spener, 1837), 7.17. For a fuller treatment of Augustine and his influence on Calvin and Luther, see Paul Jacobs, *Prädestination und Verantwortlichkeit bei Calvin* (Neukirchen: Erziehungsvereins, 1937). Pelikan also makes the case that Augustine had a remarkable awareness of the doctrine of predestination, "more thoroughgoing than that of any major thinker since Paul" (Pelikan, *Emergence of the Catholic Tradition*, 297).

an aside to the question of whether Augustine's position was in fact an out-
growth of his doctrine of impassibility. Sanders also rejects Augustine's
doctrine of immutability and Augustine's belief that ultimately God does
not "change his mind."[47] Further, Sanders argues that since Augustine was
"sensitive to the suffering involved in friendship and love," he developed
a dislike for any interpersonal models of the Godhead.[48]

Is all of this so? Let me first state that I do not think it imperative
to defend everything that Augustine believed. His ecclesiology was
clearly more Catholic than Protestant, and even in his soteriology there
were elements that the Reformed tradition does not accept.[49] Further, his
treatment of the Donatists laid the groundwork for the later Inquisition,
in that he supported the imperial proscription of that sect, though he
himself would not have condoned the use of force in dealing with sec-
tarians or heretics. So, in my response to the interpretation of the Bishop
of Hippo offered by the open theists, I want to make it clear that I am
not an apologist for his whole theological project.

I would argue that some of the concerns expressed by Sanders and
Pinnock are legitimate, while others stem from the fact that their model
of theology simply is at odds with that of the African Father. Augustine
was not simply a Neoplatonist in bishops' garb. In 386, Augustine
accepted Christianity "without reservation and in opposition to the
Neo-Platonist, Porphyry, who had most helped him, perhaps, at this
stage."[50] Though Neoplatonism had an impact on Augustine, as culture
always has some impact on the thinkers of each era, it is clear that where
the Bible contradicted Plotinus, Augustine went with the Bible.[51] In
terms of defining his doctrine of God, "Neoplatonic elements were
unmistakably present in this definition, but in setting it forth Augustine
believed himself to be—and he was—expressing the catholic creed."[52]

Augustine is a classic example of a thinker who combined philosophical considerations with biblical narrative. At times, the philosoph-

---

[47] Sanders, "Historical Considerations," 82.

[48] Ibid., 84.

[49] Augustine did not hold to a consistent *sola fide*, he held that infant baptism was regenerative, and he did not believe that all of those who once were regenerate would persevere to the end.

[50] John J. O'Meara, ed., "Introduction," St. Augustine, *Against the Academics*, Ancient Christian Writers, vol. 12 (Baltimore: Westminster, 1950), 197.

[51] John Burnaby, *Amor Dei: A Study of the Religion of St. Augustine* (London: Clarke, 1938), 163.

[52] Pelikan, *Emergence of the Catholic Tradition*, 297.

ical concerns outweighed the biblical. His commitment to divine simplicity and his affirmation of impassibility show that the Neoplatonic elements never completely left his consideration.[53] But these were always counterbalanced with his belief in redemption, in God's involvement in the world, and in the supremacy of Scripture over all of the intellectual machinations of man. As for his doctrine of predestination, Augustine took his cue primarily from an exegesis of Paul and John.[54] This is in contrast to the earlier Fathers, who, with the exception of Athanasius, generally developed their views on libertarian free will as a response to the deterministic position of the Gnostics.[55] In other words, Sanders has it backwards when he contends that Tertullian and Origen were biblicists in their understanding of human freedom while Augustine was following the Hellenistic footpath.[56] Quite the opposite is actually the case.

There are, then, Hellenizing tendencies in Augustine. But there are also anti-Hellenizing tendencies. It may be that he is guilty of too strong a doctrine of impassibility. But this did not prevent him from affirming the genuine possibility of knowing God personally. In fact, Augustine has gone down in history as an evangelical mystic, in a vein similar to Jonathan Edwards. What is clear is that his theology was not merely baptized paganism, as Pinnock maintains.

Carl F. H. Henry: Modern Rationalistic Thinker, or Biblically Motivated Apologist?

In the contemporary evangelical context few thinkers have been painted with the brush of "rationalism" more thoroughly than Carl Henry. He has been at the forefront of evangelicalism's attempts to carve out a scholarly theological alternative to the reductionist traditions which were current in Continental theology. This alone has made him a marked man. But more than this, Henry's tendency to write in a polemical fashion on the topics of revelation, anthropology, and the doctrine

---

[53] Feinberg, *No One Like Him*, 432.

[54] Predestination is God's "foreknowledge and preparation of those acts of kindness by which those who are saved are saved" (Augustine, *The Gift of Perseverance*, in *The Nicene and Post-Nicene Fathers*, vol. 5, trans. Philip Schaff [Grand Rapids, Mich.: Eerdmans, n.d.], 14.35).

[55] J. B. Mozley, *A Treatise on the Augustinian Doctrine of Predestination* (London: John Murray, 1883), 126-147; John M. Rist, *Augustine* (Cambridge: Cambridge University Press, 1994), 268-283.

[56] Sanders, "Historical Considerations," 81-82.

of God has resulted in more attention being paid to him than to those who have been less committed to apologetics in these sensitive areas. One of the first thinkers to accuse Henry of being a modernist was Hans Frei.[57] He noted that theological typology and theological method cut across the ordinary lines of distinction between liberal and conservative paradigms. "For example, a contemporary liberal theologian like David Tracy of the University of Chicago will look more like a conservative and evangelical theologian such as Carl Henry than he will like many a fellow liberal in regard to the basic affirmation that theology must have a foundation that is articulated in terms of basic philosophical principles."[58] Since Henry's theological method incorporates many features of rational discourse, the Yale theologian categorizes him with others who deploy similar methodology, regardless of the actual content of their theological system. Frei observes that Henry criticized Karl Barth for his failure to submit his theological reflections to "the law of contradiction, the so-called congruity postulate, and the criterion that all propositions must be arrangeable in the form of axioms and theorems."[59] This sort of intellectual move constitutes sufficient grounds for Frei to lump the evangelical theologian together with the revisionist Tracy.

Several evangelical scholars have also posited that Henry has made concessions to the modernist worldview. Stephen Spencer wrote, "Carl F. H. Henry's writings display this recourse to modernist epistemology as the sole alternative to subjectivism and relativism (whether modernist or postmodernist), despite Henry's frequent criticisms of modernism and his call for us to reject both modernism and postmodernism."[60] Spencer then claims that evangelicals who hold such views believe that

---

[57] Hans W. Frei, *Types of Christian Theology*, ed. George Hunsinger and William C. Placher (New Haven, Conn.: Yale University Press, 1992), 24-25. This volume was assembled from lectures given by Frei in 1983 and 1987. See also Hans W. Frei, "Response to 'Narrative Theology: An Evangelical Appraisal,'" *Trinity Journal* 8 (Spring 1987): 23-30. This is Frei's reply to Henry's criticisms of narrative theology.

[58] Frei, *Types of Christian Theology*, 24. Frei's estimate that classical liberal theology is non-foundationalist is subject to serious question. Murphy demonstrates convincingly that the liberal theological tradition associated with Friedrich Schleiermacher, Shailer Mathews, Harry Emerson Fosdick, and Gordon Kaufman is explicitly foundationalist (Nancey Murphy, *Beyond Liberalism and Fundamentalism: How Modern and Postmodern Philosophy Set the Theological Agenda* [Valley Forge, Pa.: Trinity, 1996], 22-28).

[59] Frei, *Types of Christian Theology*, 24.

[60] Stephen R. Spencer, "'Evangelical Modernists'? Evangelical Responses to Postmodernism and Postliberalism" (paper presented at the southwestern regional meeting of the Evangelical Theological Society, Dallas, 21 March 1997), 7.

"Christian [*sic*] have no right to proclaim Christianity universally true without first establishing its truthfulness—which seems to mean proving it them [*sic*]."[61] In other words, such Enlightenment-influenced evangelicals equate the apologetic task of the church with its dogmatic task. In contrast to what he believes he sees in the methodology of Henry, Spencer proposes that "truth is not objective, if that means that it is self-existing or impersonal, abstract. Rather, truth is rooted in the triune God. Truth is what this tri-personal God knows and says. . . . Truth is personal because God is truth."[62] Spencer seems to be saying that evangelicals who adopt this kind of "modernist epistemology," such as Henry, have forgotten this fact.[63]

Donald Bloesch insists that there is a rationalistic trajectory in much of evangelical theology. Modern theologians, under the influence of Enlightenment rationalism, have incorporated methodologies which are explicitly founded upon either "the logic of deduced conclusions . . . or the logic of evidential confirmations."[64] In this they often allow philosophical concerns to determine the form of their theological methodology.[65] Bloesch argues that Carl Henry has provided real assistance to evangelicals in identifying the ontological immanentalism of modern theology and in warning the church about capitulating to the dangers of modernity. He insists, however, that Henry has not been circumspect enough to avoid *epistemological immanentalism* and that he has in effect called the church to "a return to the rationalistic idealism

---

[61] Ibid. He makes this claim after critiquing R. Albert Mohler's criticism of Stanley Grenz on the grounds that Grenz refused "to begin theology by establishing the role of Scripture in Christian theology" (ibid., 6). It ought to be noted, for the sake of accuracy, that Mohler does not use the word "begin" in his critique. He says, rather, quoting from Grenz, that "Grenz . . . suggest[s] that efforts to establish the role of Scripture in Christian theology are 'ultimately unnecessary'" (R. Albert Mohler, "The Integrity of the Evangelical Tradition and the Challenge of the Postmodern Paradigm," in *The Challenge of Postmodernism: An Evangelical Assessment,* ed. David S. Dockery [Wheaton, Ill.: Victor, 1995], 80). It is one thing to believe in the need to "begin" (one assumes, both chronologically and apologetically) the theological project by establishing the foundational role of Scripture; it is quite another to contend that such a project is ultimately a necessary component of the theologian's task.

[62] Spencer, "Evangelical Modernists," 9.

[63] Charles Scalise offers a similar criticism when he contends that Henry begins with an architectonic prolegomena and an elaborate doctrine of revelation, an approach which results in an "Enlightenment-fueled transformation of the doctrine of revelation from a secondary doctrine waiting in the wings to the primary doctrine on center stage" (Charles J. Scalise, *From Scripture to Theology: A Canonical Journey into Hermeneutics* [Downers Grove, Ill.: InterVarsity Press, 1996], 37).

[64] Donald G. Bloesch, *The Holy Spirit: Works and Gifts,* Christian Foundations, vol. 5 (Downers Grove, Ill.: InterVarsity Press, 2000), 35.

[65] Donald G. Bloesch, *The Battle for the Trinity* (Ann Arbor, Mich.: Servant, 1985), 70.

of the early Enlightenment."[66] Further, Henry's strong focus on propositional revelation drives him to find the unity in Scripture in a logical system of shared beliefs.[67] Other evangelicals could be added to this group of rationalists,[68] as could the work of certain thinkers out of a more liberal tradition, such as Pannenberg,[69] whose theology allows the world "to become another criterion for faith beside the God of the Bible."[70]

The most wide-ranging indictment of Henry as a modern thinker has been offered by James William McClendon, Jr. This theologian argues that Henry's theological method fits neatly into the modern paradigm, as his "philosophical work" is characterized by the "four recurrent marks" of that epistemological paradigm: it is "human-centered, universalizable, reductionist, and foundationalist."[71] Modern thought is *anthropocentric* in that it makes human nature the measure of all things.[72] It tends to *universalization* by assuming that "what matters for anybody must matter for every-

---

[66] Donald G. Bloesch, *A Theology of Word and Spirit*, Christian Foundations, vol. 1 (Downers Grove, Ill.: InterVarsity Press, 1992), 253; cf. idem, *Holy Scripture*, 81.

[67] Carl F. H. Henry, *God, Revelation and Authority*, vol. 4 (Waco, Tex.: Word, 1979; reprint, Wheaton, Ill.: Crossway, 1999), passim.

[68] Other contemporary (or recent) evangelicals whom Bloesch would designate as rationalistic are R. C. Sproul, E. J. Carnell, the early Clark Pinnock, John Gerstner, J. Oliver Buswell, Millard Erickson, and John Warwick Montgomery. His criticisms of Carl Henry seem to relate primarily to Henry's later works (specifically his six-volume magnum opus). Bloesch's earlier writings tend to praise Henry's contribution. See, for instance, Bloesch, *Ground of Certainty*, 22 n. 21; idem, *Evangelical Renaissance* (Grand Rapids, Mich.: Eerdmans, 1973), 26-28, in which he actually perceives Henry to be among those who resist "elevat[ing] the Bible unduly" in the move toward a strong doctrine of inerrancy. The list of rationalistic theologians from the past includes Clement of Alexandria, Abelard, John Locke, Francis Turretin, Charles Hodge, and Benjamin Warfield (Bloesch, *Holy Scripture*, 40, 65, 81; idem, *A Theology of Word and Spirit*, 252-253; idem, *Evangelical Renaissance*, 42).

[69] Avery Dulles, "Pannenberg on Revelation and Faith," in *The Theology of Wolfhart Pannenberg*, ed. Carl E. Braaten and Philip Clayton (Minneapolis: Augsburg, 1988), 187.

[70] Bloesch, *Holy Spirit*, 44.

[71] James William McClendon, Jr., "Christian Knowledge in the Sunset of Modernity" (paper presented at the New Orleans Baptist Theological Seminary, February, 1998), 8. It ought to be noted that this is an unpublished paper. It must be read, therefore, in the context of McClendon's published opinions on these matters.

[72] McClendon contends that "post-medieval (i.e., modern) theology," both orthodox and liberal, moved in a conscientiously anthropocentric direction: "Instead, modern theologians located morality and reality alike in *human beings*—in a word, modernity was deliberately anthropocentric" (James William McClendon, Jr., *Systematic Theology: Doctrine* [Nashville: Abingdon, 1994], 49, italics in the original). There is some ambiguity in McClendon's use of terms. In personal correspondence with this author he indicated his preference for the term "modern" over the term "modernist" in referring to Henry. Yet, in his systematic theology book he also lumps conservatives with other advocates of "modernity" whom he refers to as "modernists" (ibid., 49-50). In his writings, then, he has not made clear the distinction he wishes to draw between these terms.

body."[73] This tendency assumes that one set of experiences will provide the norm for the rest of culture and is, thus, "imperialistic" in
its approach to knowledge.[74] Further, modern thought is *reductionist* in its trend toward reducing everything to its components in
a manner analogous to the scientific tendency to reduce analysis to
molecules, atoms, and subatomic particles, an approach to be found
in positivism,[75] rather than to widen the angle to a more expansive
investigation.[76]

McClendon also accuses Henry of being a narrow foundationalist.[77]
Foundationalism refers to the tendency of Cartesian and, to some extent,
Lockean epistemologies to construct all of knowledge upon self-evident
and indubitable foundations.[78] It is the attempt to find an Archimedean
Point from which one's entire system can be recursively built. Descartes
wistfully proffered, "I shall have the right to entertain high hopes, if I am
fortunate enough to find only one thing which is certain and indubitable."[79] Descartes sought to ground his system in a set of rational first
principles, principles which were, then, metaphysical in orientation. The

---

[73] Idem, "Sunset of Modernity," 2. "It is not assumed (though it may be true) that the standards
of adequacy appropriate in one community are appropriate in others. . . ." (James William
McClendon, Jr. and James M. Smith, *Convictions: Defusing Religious Relativism*, 2nd ed. [Valley
Forge, Pa.: Trinity, 1994], 43).

[74] McClendon and Smith, *Convictions*, 8.

[75] Ibid., 20.

[76] For a thorough treatment of this idea, see Nancey Murphy, *Anglo-American Postmodernity:
Philosophical Perspectives on Science, Religion and Ethics* (Boulder, Colo.: Westview, 1997),
12-34; idem, *Theology in the Age of Scientific Reasoning* (Ithaca, N.Y.: Cornell University Press,
1990), 58-78.

[77] By "narrow foundationalist," McClendon seems to be accusing Henry of holding what others
call "hard" or "rigid" foundationalism, that is, the kind of logically constructed, self-contained
system that is characteristic of Cartesianism and logical positivism. Such a system begins with
absolute certitude and then constructs its "house of knowledge" from this indubitable starting
point. I would argue that Henry does not employ such a model, since, though he believes the Bible
to be without error, his appeal to "rationality" is more modest. The only Archimedean Point in
his argument is God—not an epistemological system. What Henry does employ is what some have
called a sort of "soft" or "modest" foundationalism with regard to rationality. Modest
foundationalism recognizes both that the rational basis for an argument is always subject to
critique and that a sound argument might be constructed inductively, and not merely deductively
from the first principles of the system. I contend that this is precisely what Henry does, as he
develops his case for truth not from reason, but from the exegesis of Scripture. See Robert Audi,
The Structure of Justification (Cambridge: Cambridge University Press, 1993), 117-165. For an
evangelical treatment, see Millard J. Erickson, "Foundationalism: Dead or Alive?" *The Southern
Baptist Journal of Theology* 5, no. 2 (Summer 2001): 20-32.

[78] McClendon, "Sunset of Modernity," 2.

[79] René Descartes, *Discourse on Method and the Meditations*, trans. F. F. Sutcliffe
(Harmondsworth: Penguin, 1968), 95. Hegel hailed Descartes for erecting a "metaphysics of
understanding." Hegel believed he was destined to bring this project to completion (G. W. F.
Hegel, *Hegel's Lectures on the History of Philosophy*, trans. E. S. Haldane and F. H. Simson,
vol. 3 [New York: Humanities, 1968], 220-230).

empirical form of foundationalism came to its most consistent expression in the logical positivism of such figures as Carnap, Ayer, and the early Wittgenstein. Wittgenstein began the *Tractatus* with the observation, "The world is all that is the case."[80] After spending seventy tortuous pages delineating what can and cannot be included in his theory of the declarative sentence, he concluded it with, "What we cannot speak about we must consign to silence."[81] Common to both the Cartesian and the positivist systems is the belief that philosophy is "largely an exercise in epistemology."[82]

Henry uses the word *reason* to refer simply to "man's intellect, mind or cognitive powers."[83] Henry views reason in theology as an instrument for recognizing truth, though not as a *source* of truth or as a tool for *constructing* models of cognition based on the autonomous reflection on empirical data or on universal principles not derived from Scripture. The very notion of revelation "gives no quarter to the idealistic illusion that human reason is intrinsically capable of fashioning eternal truth."[84] Reason is "man's logical capacity."[85] Again, "Christian doctrines are not derived from experimental observation or from rationalism, but from God in his revelation."[86] As a means of recognizing truth, reason can serve a verification role, a way of testing the truth claims of Christianity,[87] since it has the ability to "recognize and elucidate" truth. But even the divine image in humans does not enable them either to intuit or to generate truth claims.[88]

---

[80] Ludwig Wittgenstein, *Tractatus Logico-Philosophicus*, trans. D. F. Peers and B. F. McGuiness (London: Routledge & Kegan Paul, 1961), 1.0.

[81] Ibid., 7.0.

[82] John E. Thiel, *Nonfoundationalism* (Minneapolis: Fortress, 1994), 6.

[83] Walter E. Johnson, "A Critical Analysis of the Nature and Function of Reason in the Theology of Carl F. H. Henry" (Ph.D. diss., New Orleans Baptist Theological Seminary, 1989), 41.

[84] Carl F. H. Henry, *God, Revelation and Authority*, vol. 1 (Waco, Tex.: Word, 1976; reprint, Wheaton, Ill.: Crossway, 1999), 225-226.

[85] Ibid., 1:377; idem, *Remaking the Modern Mind* (Grand Rapids, Mich.: Eerdmans, 1946), 220.

[86] Henry, *God, Revelation and Authority*, 1:223. "We cannot commit others to the truth of revelation simply by theoretical argument" (idem, *Remaking the Modern Mind*, 215).

[87] Christianity is distinguished by its "objective truth, and must adduce the method of knowing and the manner of verification by which every man can become personally persuaded" (ibid., 213; idem, *Toward a Recovery of Christian Belief: The Drift Toward Neo-Paganism* [Wheaton, Ill.: Crossway, 1990], 37). For a brief discussion of how the Bible employs such an approach to verifying truth claims, see David L. Wolfe, *Epistemology: The Justification of Belief*, Contours of Christian Philosophy (Downers Grove, Ill.: InterVarsity Press, 1982), 78-82.

[88] Henry, *God, Revelation and Authority*, 1:226. Henry's views on the role of reason place him within the Anglo-American tradition, which sees reason as instrumental, rather than the Continental tradition, which views reason as teleological and normative. Reason in the Anglo-American tradition refers to the ability of persons to understand given data and might include the

Henry has repeatedly observed that the language of the Bible is clear and understandable and is in the form of "objectively intelligible statements."[89] He is not sympathetic with Barth's concern that human language is an inadequate vehicle for the communication of divine truth. "If language is the product of sin, conditioned by man's perverted nature and unsuitable even when revelation grasps it, there arises the question whether God would or could use it."[90] That does not mean that the "words we use are identical with the objects they designate," but rather that we can have some confidence that God would not deceive us by using language that has no real correspondence to reality.[91] Furthermore, Henry observes that the Bible does not present us an "extended treatise" on religious epistemology, and does not endorse a "single correct system of epistemology," and so it would be "unjustifiable to identify any one scheme as biblical."[92]

Is then his doctrine of God dependent on Scripture, or on Hellenistic or modernist philosophical conventions? Henry is convinced that theology can be constructed without appeal to a dialectical method and without conceding that doctrines contradict one another. He affirms that it may be difficult at times for theologians to understand the relationship between such doctrines as divine election and human responsibility, but he will not concede that they flatly contradict one another. He appeals to the law of noncontradiction, not to determine the truth of revelation but only as a negative test for truth.[93] "Logical consistency is not a positive test of truth, but a negative test; if it were a positive test, logical consistency would accredit all views, however conflicting, that consistently follow from differing starting points."[94]

---

ability to adjudicate between claims to truth by use of canons of rationality, such as consistency, but does not itself determine what that truth is. It is thus an inherently skeptical approach to rationality. Henry differs from the Anglo-American tradition, as seen, for instance, in Hume, in that he *does* believe in the possibility of knowing truth, a possibility dependent ultimately on seeing the world through the lens of Scripture.

[89] Ibid., 1:223.

[90] Idem, *God, Revelation and Authority*, vol. 3 (Waco, Tex.: Word, 1979; reprint, Wheaton, Ill.: Crossway, 1999), 287. Neither does sin affect human logic in any direct fashion. Its effect is on the will, not on the ability of humans to draw correct deductions (Johnson, "Reason in the Theology of Carl Henry," 47).

[91] Henry, *God, Revelation and Authority*, 3:289.

[92] Idem, *God, Revelation and Authority*, 1:224. See also James Emery White, *What Is Truth? A Comparative Study of the Positions of Cornelius Van Til, Francis Schaeffer, Carl F. H. Henry, Donald Bloesch, Millard Erickson* (Nashville: Broadman & Holman, 1994), 94, for further treatment of this question.

[93] Johnson, "Reason in the Theology of Carl Henry," 51.

[94] Henry, *God, Revelation and Authority*, 1:235.

Is Henry, then, a rationalist? That would depend on what one means by the term. Henry did not reject the designation for himself, as long as he had the right to give his own definition of the term.[95] Henry's use of the apparatus of logical, even Aristotelian, discourse, with its appeal to theorems, proofs, and so on, gives his expositions a "rational" feel. Likewise, he was convinced that the biblical revelation was credible and reasonable:

> The main issue for the intellectual world is whether the biblical reve-
> lation is credible; that is, are there good reasons for believing it? I am
> against the paradox mongers and those who emphasize only personal
> volition and decision. They tell us we are to believe even in the absence
> of good reasons for believing. Some even argue that to seek to give
> good reasons for the faith within us is a sign of lack of trust or an exer-
> cise in self justification. This is nonsense. Against any view that faith
> is merely a leap in the dark, I insist on the reasonableness of Christian
> faith and the "rationality" of the living, self-revealed God.[96]

Henry then affirms that revelation is rational, but he denies that one can construct theology on positivist or rationalist grounds. So, his discussions are highly rational, and his methodology employs rigorous appeals to logical analysis. But his God is not the God of Plato or Plotinus, nor is his method merely scholastic. Henry's rationalism is more in line with the Anglo-American tradition, in which reason functions as a means of coming to truth but does not itself provide the content of truth, an approach one finds in the Continental tradition of Descartes and Kant. Reason is functional, not normative or teleological. Further, Henry's presuppositionalism served as a counterpoint to his understanding of reason, a commitment on his part which further insulates him from falling prey to traditional forms of autonomous Rationalism.

Augustine and Henry: Hellenists or Hebrews?

Our two models, Augustine and Carl Henry, are perfectly comfortable in engaging the thought forms of their time. They are fluent in the philo-

---

[95] Johnson, "Reason in the Theology of Carl Henry," 53-54.

[96] Carl F. H. Henry, "The Concerns and Considerations of Carl F. H. Henry" (interview in *Christianity Today* 13 [May 1976]: 21, quoted in Johnson, "Reason in the Theology of Carl Henry," 55).

sophical currents and cultural artifacts that make up the prevailing worldviews from their own respective ages. They are willing to use the tools afforded them by their culture, and, at times, those tools even impinge somewhat on the grammar of their theology. At the same time, though, both of these men are thoroughly committed to Scripture and to drawing their theology from that book rather than the "books of the Platonists." While we may wish to tweak Augustine here or there and to suggest to him that a few of his proposals might be slightly more tainted with Platonic influence than they ought to be, in general, all of his ideas can be traced to the Bible. Of course, one might disagree with his interpretation, but that is a different issue, now, is it not? Similarly, I might not wish to structure some of my arguments in the same fashion as does Henry—with theorems, corollaries, and the other accoutrements of formal debating style. But style is one thing—substance is another.

III. The Other Side of the Question: Is Open Theism Philosophically or Biblically Driven?

Now the time has come to put the shoe on the other foot. There are several questions that one ought to pose here: What is the driving force behind the open theist position? Are its fundamental and unique theological moves compelled by biblical exegesis? Are there clear indicators of philosophical and cultural influence which have come from alien systems of thought? This essay will ask only the third question directly, but will attempt to assess the answers to the other two questions along the way.

Parallels with "Certain Greeks"

The Greek tradition was not merely confined to Platonism and Stoicism. Other ancient philosophers proposed models which were not top-heavy on the issue of Being, but of Becoming. Heraclitus taught that all was in flux, and so established a "processive" school of thought long before Plato was born. Others in the Greek tradition promoted the notion of libertarian freedom. It is curious that open theists often point to parallels between traditionalists and the Greeks, as if that in itself is sufficient condemnation, but they rarely confess to the parallels between their own views and those of the philosophers.

Is open theism merely another version of process theology? Geisler and House answer yes, since openness advocates affirm that "God can change in His nature."[97] This would entail a dipolarity in God, and that qualifies this system to be labeled "process." It is not clear, though, that Pinnock, Boyd, and the other key figures in this tradition are arguing that God can change in his nature in the same sense as Geisler and House allege.[98]

Process theology has been "the most influential movement stressing libertarian freedom and divine vulnerability" in this century.[99] Open theists have often praised some elements of process thought:

> We make the love of God a priority; hold to libertarian human freedom; are both critical of conventional theism; seek a more dynamic model of God; contend that God has real, and not merely rational, relationships with the world; believe that God is affected by what happens in the world; say that God knows what can be known, which does not amount to exhaustive foreknowledge; appreciate the value of philosophy in helping to shape theological convictions; connect positively to Wesleyan/Arminian traditions.[100]

They have also distanced themselves from process theology's more objectionable elements, such as dipolarity, metaphysical dualism, and its view of God's dependence on the world. In assessing the relative merits of traditionalism's Platonist tendencies with open theism's process tendencies, Pinnock writes, "Candidly, I believe that conventional theists are more influenced by Plato, who was a pagan, than I am by Whitehead, who was a Christian."[101]

In a book-length debate between open theists and process theolo-

---

[97] Norman L. Geisler and H. Wayne House, *The Battle for God: Responding to the Challenge of Neotheism* (Grand Rapids, Mich.: Kregel, 2001), 263.

[98] Sanders, for instance, argues that God does change his mind regarding decisions he has made and the course he will follow, which entails that he "has been remarkably flexible, innovative and adaptable in working to achieve his goals," but that at the same time he is faithful to his goals, committed to his covenant relationships, and consistent in his character (John Sanders, *The God Who Risks: A Theology of Providence* [Downers Grove, Ill.: InterVarsity Press, 1998], 143-144, 165, 186 [quote is from 186]).

[99] John M. Frame, *No Other God: A Response to Open Theism* (Phillipsburg, N.J.: Presbyterian & Reformed, 2001), 38.

[100] Pinnock, *Most Moved Mover*, 142-143; see also Clark H. Pinnock and John B. Cobb, Jr., "Introduction," in *Searching for an Adequate God: A Dialogue Between Process and Free Will Theists*, ed. Clark H. Pinnock and John B. Cobb, Jr. (Grand Rapids, Mich.: Eerdmans, 2000), ix-xiv.

[101] Pinnock, *Most Moved Mover*, 143.

gians, it seems as though the openness advocates were more interested in their commonalities with the process thinkers than was the case from the other side.[102] I think we ought to give the open theists the benefit of the doubt to make their claim that they are not really process theologians in evangelical guise. I do, however, believe that many of the things they hold in common with process thought, such as libertarian free will, lack of exhaustive divine foreknowledge, and the search for a more dynamic model of God (whatever that means), are seriously problematic. It is also interesting that Pinnock does admit that openness advocates do "appreciate the value of philosophy in helping to shape theological convictions."[103] However, it must obviously be the right kind of philosophy lifted from the correct Greek (or Continental, or Anglo-American) philosophers. Forgive me if I take this as a slight bit of double-dealing.

Parallels with Socinianism

Several thinkers have recently compared open theism to Socinianism, a model which Sanders curiously leaves out of his survey of historical theology.[104] Robert Strimple notes that Faustus Socinus saw his work as a corrective both to Calvinist views on foreordination and to Arminian views on foreknowledge. If the future was foreknown, then, for Socinus, it was also foreordained, since humans had no power of contrary choice. Against this view, Socinus argued for a kind of free will theism in which future contingencies were not settled.[105] This is just about exactly what open theists are proposing. That is not to say that open theists hold to a Socinian view of Christ or of the Trinity (though some of their objections to substitutionary atonement have a Socinian ring), but it is curious that none of them has adduced the Socinian view of free will as a partner position to their own, though it is clear that it is.[106]

---

[102] Pinnock and Cobb, eds., *Searching for an Adequate God*. See especially the essays by David Ray Griffin and William Hasker.

[103] Pinnock, *Most Moved Mover*, 143.

[104] Sanders, "Historical Considerations," 87-90. Here he deals with the Reformation and its aftermath, but with no discussion of Socinus, whose views on some of these issues parallel those of the open theists.

[105] Robert B. Strimple, "What Does God Know?" in *The Coming Evangelical Crisis: Current Challenges to the Authority of Scripture and the Gospel*, ed. John H. Armstrong (Chicago: Moody, 1996), 140-142.

[106] Frame, *No Other God*, 35.

Parallels with Manichaeism

Historic Manichaeism held that two coeternal principles exist alongside each other in the universe, one good and the other evil.[107] The evil has invaded the good, and redemption takes place when humans work to restore the kingdom of light.[108] In the meantime, the two forces are arrayed against each other in a pitched battle, and for all intents and purposes the kingdom of darkness is currently in command of this world. Manichaean theology presents an intrinsic warfare motif with good and evil in battle array.

Clearly Boyd does not hold to the cosmology or the cosmogony of historic Manichaeism, nor does he hold to its bizarre soteriology. He does construe a dualistic ontology in terms of good versus evil, though, in a manner reminiscent of the ancient cult. In addition, he argues that Satan is in command of this world and is, in effect, the sovereign of this world in this age, another feature parallel to the Manichaean view of the relationship between good and evil spirits in this eon. This idea is consistent with Boyd's belief that God does not generally exercise comprehensive sovereignty in the world at this time. He further argues that it is inappropriate to use the word "monotheism" to describe the biblical view of God, since the Bible affirms the existence of the other "gods."[109] Rather, we should speak of a sort of henotheism, or, as he proposes in one place, "monotheopraxis."[110] Satan and the demonic powers are, then, gods who wreak havoc on this world and with whom the true God is in perpetual conflict during this age.[111]

The conflict rages because "God chose to create a quasi-democratic cosmos in which dualism could result," and some of the angelic beings in that universe are now in a state of rebellion.[112] Since Yahweh, "in almost every respect,"[113] mediates his authority by morally responsible angels,

---

[107] S. N. C. Lieu, *Manichaeism in the Later Roman Empire and Medieval China: A Historical Survey* (Manchester: University of Manchester Press, 1985).

[108] Peter Brown, "The Diffusion of Manichaeism in the Roman Empire," in *Religion and Society in the Age of Augustine* (London: Faber, 1972), 94-118.

[109] Gregory A. Boyd, *God at War: The Bible and Spiritual Conflict* (Downers Grove, Ill.: InterVarsity Press, 1997), 119.

[110] Ibid., 120-142.

[111] Ibid., 143-167.

[112] Ibid., 176.

[113] Ibid., 178. He quotes approvingly the statement of Athenagoras that, though God exercises a general providence, the control of "the particular parts are provided for by the angels over them" (Gregory A. Boyd, *Satan and the Problem of Evil: Constructing a Trinitarian Warfare Theodicy* [Downers Grove, Ill.: InterVarsity Press, 2001], 40).

such a rebellion created a situation in which the evil ones now rule. Boyd interprets Jesus' words in which he refers to Satan as the prince of this world (John 12:31; 14:30) to mean that, "concerning ruling powers over the cosmos, this evil ruler is the highest."[114] Boyd goes on to argue that Satan is the cause of all sickness and infirmity, that ill people are "the casualties of war,"[115] and that this dualistic hermeneutic is the key to understanding the New Testament, especially the ministry of Jesus.

Apart from the proponents of the Word of Faith movement in contemporary charismatic circles, it would be hard to find anyone who makes a stronger case for the sovereignty of Satan in this world and for a warfare dualism than does Boyd in his argument in this soon-to-be trilogy of books.[116] I cannot subject the thesis to any serious analysis due to space limitations, but I will make three observations. First, Boyd's proposal depends on a complete rejection of God's comprehensive sovereignty. If God exercises providential governance over all the details of life and history, then Boyd's proposal breaks down. Though I cannot here make a case for meticulous providence, I will note that Boyd's own approach is intrinsically self-contradictory on this matter, since he believes that God can and does sometimes work in deterministic fashion (the text of Scripture indicates examples in which he does so),[117] but that he does not generally do so. Others have critiqued Boyd on this matter, and I will defer to their observations.[118]

Secondly, Boyd's interpretation of "warfare theodicy" is overdone. He certainly raises important exegetical issues in his interpretation of Jesus' encounters with demonic forces, though he simultaneously makes *more* of the amount of material than is really there[119] and *less* of the

---

[114] Boyd, *God at War*, 181.

[115] Ibid., 184.

[116] The third volume is tentatively titled, *The Myth of the Blueprint* (Downers Grove, Ill.: InterVarsity Press, forthcoming).

[117] Note how Boyd is inconsistent in construing exhaustive, definite foreknowledge in his treatment of Cyrus, Josiah, and Peter's crowing rooster (Gregory A. Boyd, "The Open Theism View," in *Divine Foreknowledge: Four Views*, ed. James K. Beilby and Paul R. Eddy [Downers Grove, Ill.: InterVarsity Press, 2001], 18-23).

[118] See, for instance, David Hunt, "A Simple Foreknowledge Response," in *Divine Foreknowledge: Four Views*, ed. Beilby and Eddy, 48-54. See also the treatment on meticulous providence in John M. Frame, *The Doctrine of God*, A Theology of Lordship (Phillipsburg, N.J.: Presbyterian & Reformed, 2002), 274-288. This is a withering critique of the openness view on this matter from Scripture.

[119] His assertion that Jesus' teachings on the kingdom and his healing ministry are understandable only within a warfare worldview (Boyd, *God at War*, 213) is not entirely wrong. The problem is that Boyd really means that we can understand such teachings of Jesus only within the

material than is really there.[120] Graham Twelftree argues that exorcism was not the key to Jesus' ministry, though "it was at least one of the most important aspects of his ministry."[121] Boyd is careful to argue that sickness and death are "the byproducts of a creation gone berserk through the evil influence of this Satanic army" and that Jesus "many times" (as opposed to "all times") "attributed this to direct demonic involvement."[122] But the overall thrust of his warfare theodicy is that illness is generally demonic in nature and must be confronted accordingly.[123] It is more accurate to say that healing and exorcism are not the same, and that "Jesus did not treat them in the same way."[124]

Thirdly, though openness advocates offer as a major premise their belief in libertarian freedom, the amount of authority and power granted to the "gods" by Boyd virtually eliminates human freedom altogether. What we have here is a substitution of Satanic power for divine power in the drama of history, with humans as not much more than pawns in the game.[125] Perhaps more accurately, human beings do get to make some limited moves in the game, but the "gods" control most of the board, even though we are assured that God is smart enough that he will eventually corner them and checkmate the enemy. My point is that the emphasis on the power of Satan is so pronounced in Boyd's work that libertarian freedom is virtually eviscerated.

Is this a Manichaean or Gnostic presentation? Boyd explicitly claims

---

framework of his (Boyd's) "warfare worldview." I find his warfare worldview, though, to be inconsistent with the full teaching of Scripture.

[120] See *God at War*, 231-234, for his explanation of the man born blind in John 9. He does not discuss Jesus deciding to let Lazarus die because he loved Mary and Martha. Scripture states that the reason behind both situations is the glory of God (John 9:3; 11:4), and there is no mention of warfare.

[121] Graham H. Twelftree, "Demon, Devil, Satan," in *Dictionary of Jesus and the Gospels*, ed. Joel B. Green, Scot McKnight, I. Howard Marshall (Downers Grove, Ill.: InterVarsity Press, 1992), 168.

[122] Boyd, *God at War*, 182-183.

[123] Ibid., 184-185.

[124] John P. Newport, *Life's Ultimate Questions: A Contemporary Philosophy of Religion* (Dallas: Word, 1989), 208.

[125] Boyd's discussion of Chemosh is salient here. In 2 Kings 3:26-27, Israel had been defeating Moab city by city. The king of Moab then sacrificed his own son presumably to Chemosh. The text then notes that Israel left off its attack and returned home. Boyd opines that, "Indeed the text also seems to assume the ability of the Moabite king to influence, and perhaps even to empower, this demonic being through sacrificing his child; the text also seems to assume the ability of Chemosh in this case to rout Israel in battle" (Boyd, *God at War*, 118). The text makes no reference to a "rout," and it is just as likely that Israel left in disgust over the incident of human sacrifice as anything else. The notion that Chemosh had power over Israel, regardless of God's role in the battle, is not a conclusion that comes readily to the reader of this text. Boyd constructs a great edifice of theory upon a very small foundation.

that his position is not.[126] Clearly he is right that his views are quite distinct from historic Manichaeism, but the overt and constant dualism that is present here has Manichaean overtones. If we are to follow the example of open theists in rhetorically labeling other positions when they bear family resemblances at some points, then it would not be unfair to say that there are Manichaean tendencies here.[127]

Parallels with Contemporary Cultural Concerns

Open theists are quite specific about their willingness to allow contemporary culture to stand as a source for theology.[128] Influences from areas of thought such as feminism and postmodernity seem to be rampant in their writings. Several thinkers in this tradition want theologians to revise their language for God to be more inclusive. Pinnock and Brow, for instance, prefer to use the word "parent" rather than "father" when speaking of God.[129] Similarly, though they recognize that Jesus was a male, they contend that "'Son of God' itself is a metaphor, pointing to a social relationship with God; it is not a statement about gender. It would be a radical distortion to depict the incarnation as supporting patriarchalism when its outcome is deliverance from all forms of oppression.[130] Jesus is God's Child who seeks the wholeness and full humanity of everyone."[131] They seem to be arguing that we need to modify "the language of Canaan" in the interests of supporting feminist hermeneutics.[132] Pinnock and Brow's support for feminism is actually quite

---

[126] Boyd, *God at War*, 229, 230.

[127] Pinnock calls traditional orthodoxy "pagan," and regularly speaks of traditionalists "proof-texting," "gate-keeping," using "scare tactics and lying," and other such rhetoric in his denunciation of their views. He does this all the while accusing traditionalists of using shrill rhetoric! (Pinnock, *Most Moved Mover*, 1-24). One would hope that the conversation might be a little more substantial and a little less inflammatory in the future.

[128] See, for instance, Pinnock, *Most Moved Mover*, 153-178.

[129] In their discussion of God as "Father" in *Unbounded Love*, they really say nothing about God as "father," oddly enough, but rather appeal to the readers to recognize the maternal metaphors in Scripture (Pinnock and Brow, *Unbounded Love*, 53).

[130] It may well be that part of Pinnock's dissatisfaction with Augustine stems from the fact that the African Father employed exclusively masculine imagery in conceiving of the Trinity. See the discussion in Millard J. Erickson, *God in Three Persons: A Contemporary Interpretation of the Trinity* (Grand Rapids, Mich.: Baker, 1995), 141-144.

[131] Pinnock and Brow, *Unbounded Love*, 52. From this statement it appears that Pinnock and Brow see any and all forms of "patriarchalism" (including that found in the Bible) as "oppression."

[132] For a withering critique of the attempt to remove "patriarchal" language from theology, see Bloesch, *The Battle for the Trinity*, 43-56.

extreme, leading them even to assert that the Bible "gives us permission to name God in feminine ways."[133]

This tendency is also apparent in open theism's commitment to "relational theology." Sin is sometimes described in terms that are merely relational.[134] Open theists also speak of God's power in relational terms: "Irresistible power can bring forth a world, but only a relational power can make the most delicate of things, a creature independent of it."[135] Also, in their focus on God's love as his basic attribute, open theists emphasize the caring nature of God, but that is not all: "love is more than care and commitment; it involves being sensitive and responsive as well."[136] This appeal to "relationality" is clearly an attempt on the part of Pinnock and others to claim that traditionalists focus on immutability, omnipotence, and transcendence, while the open theist position is committed to God's relationship with humanity. The difficulty is that in attempting to focus on the biblical idea of living in relationship with God, open theists wind up truncating those parts of Scripture, such as the notion that sin is disobedience to the will of God, which are contrary to modern cultural norms. They wind up sounding more like therapists than biblical theologians, and one has to wonder whether this is not a capitulation to culture rather than an appropriation of its insights for hermeneutics.[137] Also, their tendency to sublimate all of God's attributes under the attribute of love is not consistent with Scripture, for the same Bible which states that God is love also features God affirming, "I the LORD your God am holy" (Lev. 19:2, NKJV).[138]

Parallels with Marcionism

Pinnock and Brow contend that God is a father who heals his creatures, not a judge who looms over them in wrath. But they note, "Not all biblical texts make this as clear as others do. The prophet Nahum, for

---

[133] Pinnock and Brow, *Unbounded Love*, 116.

[134] Ibid., 57; Sanders, "Historical Considerations," 89.

[135] Pinnock, *Most Moved Mover*, 96.

[136] Richard Rice, "Biblical Support for a New Perspective," in *The Openness of God*, 15.

[137] David F. Wells, *God in the Wasteland: The Reality of Truth in a World of Fading Dreams* (Grand Rapids, Mich.: Eerdmans, 1994), 60-83. In addition, it simply is not the case that traditionalists are not committed to the need for a genuine relationship between God and human beings. See, for instance, Millard J. Erickson, *God the Father Almighty: A Contemporary Exploration of the Divine Attributes* (Grand Rapids, Mich.: Baker, 1998), 88.

[138] See the excellent analysis and critique of this issue in Frame, *No Other God*, 49-56.

example, does not seem to see it that way from his brief oracle. Perhaps it was not yet revealed to him. Old Testament writers often display a less than Christian point of view when they teach some truth."[139] Two moves are apparent in this statement. First, Nahum had not yet received the fullness of revelation which would later come in Christ—that Yahweh is also Abba. Second, the authors insist that Nahum's comment is sub-Christian, and, therefore, is to be rejected in the light of New Testament revelation.

The first claim is a legitimate hermeneutical move, whether or not one agrees that Pinnock and Brow are correct in their assessment of the text in question. Progressive revelation is a concept that nearly all evangelicals accept, even though the term was first coined by liberals in their polemic against conservative views on Scripture.[140] Defined as "the fact that God progressively revealed himself in event and in Scripture, climaxing the events with the death-resurrection-exaltation of Christ and climaxing the Scriptures with the closing of the canon," progressive revelation is a concept thoroughly consistent with an inductive analysis of Scripture's claims to authority.[141] So, it might be, as Pinnock and Brow claim, that some truth "had not yet been revealed to him." Of course, whether it is appropriate to argue that such a father-judge dichotomy is in fact legitimate exegetically or theologically is quite another question.

The more serious matter here is Pinnock and Brow's claim that "Old Testament writers often display a less than Christian point of view when they teach some truth."[142] This statement is either a sloppy way of repeating the point about progressive revelation, or else it constitutes a more serious charge—that the Old Testament is not merely dispensationally limited, but that it is actually dead wrong.[143] In his more recent work, Pinnock observes that prophets such as Isaiah, Ezekiel, and John

---

[139] Pinnock and Brow, *Unbounded Love*, 71.

[140] J. I. Packer, "An Evangelical View of Progressive Revelation," in *Evangelical Roots: A Tribute to Wilbur Smith*, ed. Kenneth S. Kantzer (Nashville: Thomas Nelson, 1978), 143-158.

[141] D. A. Carson, "Unity and Diversity in the New Testament," in *Scripture and Truth*, ed. D. A. Carson and John D. Woodbridge (Grand Rapids, Mich.: Zondervan, 1983), 83.

[142] Pinnock and Brow, *Unbounded Love*, 71.

[143] The next sentence in the paragraph cited above seems to confirm this estimate that some Old Testament texts are simply miscues: "It is possible to cite texts of judgment, such as the account of the judgment of Sodom and Gomorrah, where there does not seem to be any concern to correct and restore sinners but only to destroy them" (Pinnock and Brow, *Unbounded Love*, 71).

the Baptist uttered prophecies which are contained in Scripture but which never came true.[144]

Pinnock and Brow seem to be committing the same error often attributed to Luther—elevating one truth to such a status that it becomes the touchstone truth, so that even canonical texts are evaluated by the clarity with which they uphold the one criterion. Luther had doubts about the authenticity of the letter of James because it seemed not to affirm justification by faith alone; his doubts were unjustified. Insofar as Pinnock and Brow entertain similar doubts about individual passages of Scripture (mostly Old Testament) which they evaluate as being inferior to the texts which affirm God's nature as Abba, they are guilty of ascribing to a canon within the canon, and they come dangerously close to Marcionism. Their doubts about the truthfulness of some prophecies[145] calls into question the authenticity of their evangelical profession. Perhaps they will be able to make it clear at some point how a theologian can call the truthfulness of Scripture into question and at the same time affirm biblical inerrancy.[146]

IV. CONCLUSION

You may recall that, earlier in this essay, I urged that just showing similarities between two schools of thought does not indicate that one has borrowed from the other or is dependent on the other. Sometimes similarities are just that—similarities. In addition, on some occasions borrowing is not a bad thing—as long as alien ideologies are not imported into the system of thought. The problem comes in when two systems are synthesized in a manner in which a hybrid is produced. Of the four systems which this essay has discussed—classical theism, process theism, open theism, and traditional orthodoxy—the first two are clearly hybrids. What of the last two?

It seems to me that traditional orthodoxy, which, by the way, is not a monolithic tradition (incorporating both classical Arminians and classical Calvinists), contains within itself all the resources it needs to prevent it from becoming a theological hybrid. It appeals to Scripture,

---

[144] Pinnock, *Most Moved Mover*, 50, 51, especially n. 66.
[145] See note 144 above.
[146] For an extended reflection on the incompatibility of open theism and inerrancy, see Stephen J. Wellum's chapter in this book.

seeks to allow Scripture to speak for itself without forcing it into a hermeneutical box, is willing to critique its own deficiencies, and is not overly sensitized to contemporary cultural manipulation. What of open theism? In my opinion, it shares some of the hopefulness of traditionalism in that it examines Scripture, seeking to allow it to speak for itself, being willing to hear new interpretations of texts, and is generally willing to critique its own deficiencies. However, open theism has some characteristics which, in my opinion, make it more susceptible to synthesis and infection from alien thought forms. One problem lies in its tendency to seek the more bizarre interpretations of Scripture and to prefer them above other options. This is repeatedly seen in Boyd's warfare volumes, and is the reason why his theology has a modified Manichaean flavor. Here is another difficulty—the rear-guard action which Boyd (especially) employs to make his hermeneutics work. As I noted earlier, he has to switch gears repeatedly between the times when God does know tomorrow and the times when he does not. These manifold hermeneutical adjustments eventually make his proposal less and less believable, and make it seem more and more as if he is constantly repairing the roof over his theological work shed. But perhaps the most insidious problem with open theism, the one which makes it most susceptible to dogmatic infection by alien theological viruses, is its commitment to contemporary culture as a source for theological knowledge. It is this which infuses feminism, relationalism, processism, and even Marcionism into the mix.

I appreciate open theism in at least one way. Pinnock, Boyd, Sanders, and the others who are pursuing this project will stand there as reminders to the rest of us how important it is not to subjugate our theology to alien thought forms, whether Hellenistic, Teutonic, or Anglo-American. They will shake their fingers at us and tell us, "Don't go that route." At the same time, though, they serve as exemplars of just what happens when we allow our theology to be taken captive by alien thought forms. I'd like to say to them, "You should not go that route, either."

PART TWO

Philosophical Presuppositions and Cultural Context

3

TRUE FREEDOM:
THE LIBERTY THAT SCRIPTURE
PORTRAYS AS WORTH HAVING

Mark R. Talbot

Truly, truly, I say to you, everyone who commits sin
is a slave to sin. . . .
But if the Son sets you free, then you will be free indeed.

—JOHN 8:34, 36

The open theist John Sanders and I have this in common: we have both come to our views on divine sovereignty and human freedom from reflecting on personal tragedies. For Sanders, the key event was the death of his brother. He opens his book *The God Who Risks* like this:

> The police car, lights flashing and siren wailing, sped past me as I was driving home. When I reached the stop sign at the corner, I could see several police cars and an ambulance up ahead at the scene of an accident. Because I was working for the local newspaper as a photographer at the time, I reflexively decided to take some pictures of the accident. When I reached the scene, I could see a semitrailer blocking the road, a motorcycle lying on its side and a white sheet covering something near the truck. Someone approached me and said, "You don't want to take any pictures here. Your brother Dick is lying under the wheels of that truck." The next few minutes are a blur in my memory, but I do recall getting home. I went to my room and prayed,

"God, why did you kill my brother?" As I look back on that prayer, I am fascinated that I asked God such a question. I was a nominal Methodist at the time, and I did not believe that God caused everything that happened. Perhaps I had picked up from the broader culture the belief that God was the cause behind all tragedies ("acts of God," as insurance companies call them). In years to come many a Christian attempted to provide me with "good" reasons why God would have ordained my brother's death.

"Those discussions," Sanders notes, "served to spur my reflection on divine providence for over twenty years."[1]

In my case, the tragedy was my own. When I was seventeen, I fell about fifty feet off a Tarzan-like rope swing, breaking my back and becoming paralyzed from the waist down. I spent six months in hospitals. Initially, I had no feeling or movement in my legs and no bowel or bladder control. I dropped from 200 pounds to 145 pounds because I was so nauseated that I couldn't eat. Once my back had stabilized a little and I had regained some movement in my legs, the doctors tried to help me to regain more by having me crawl to breakfast each morning. At the time, an undetected calcified stone had formed in my bladder. It was causing raging bladder infections that made me completely incontinent. And so as they would put me on the floor each morning, I would wet myself and remain soaked for the rest of the day. When I left the hospital, after the stone was finally discovered and removed, I was able to control my bladder in most situations and walk awkwardly with a cane.

I'm now fifty-two. My accident has had several long-term consequences. Walking is increasingly more difficult, although it is important for me to stay on my feet in order to exercise my legs. I walk by forcing my leg muscles to spasm, which raises my blood pressure and makes it hard to find ways to exercise adequately to stay in cardiovascular shape. Physical discomfort is pretty steady. I have to remain alert to some physiological concerns that most people never have to think about. In the last ten years or so, I have sometimes had sleep-robbing leg spasms. And in this last year, I've learned that my inability to walk has depleted the

---

[1] John Sanders, *The God Who Risks: A Theology of Providence* (Downers Grove, Ill.: InterVarsity Press, 1998), 9.

bone-density in my left hip to the place where, if I take a serious fall, it is likely to break.

I have thought about providence in this context for about thirty-five years. Yet I have reached very different conclusions than Sanders has reached. Sanders concludes that God is not "the ultimate cosmic explanation for each and every thing, including all the bad things we experience."[2] I conclude that nothing happens to us—nothing good *and* nothing bad*—that is not ultimately from God. Sanders thinks that God "takes risks . . . in providentially creating and governing the world," risks that mean that sometimes things turn out "differently from the way God desires."[3] For instance, Adam and Eve's sin "was 'something strange to God' in that it was not planned," and God, therefore, had "to adjust his project in response to this horrible"—and surprising[4]—"turn of events."[5] I think that nothing takes God by surprise because he has ordered—or "ordained"—every event from before creation.[6]

Most fundamentally for this chapter, while Sanders and I both affirm that we should think of God as personal and as someone with whom human beings can have personal fellowship, Sanders claims that this requires us to embrace what he calls "relational theism."[7] Relational theism, he explains, claims that "God has granted us the *libertarian freedom* necessary for a truly personal relationship of love to develop" between him and us.[8] Sanders and other open theists equate libertarian freedom with "significant" or "morally significant" freedom.[9] We can define libertarian freedom in terms of whether someone can make more than one choice at a particular time. Let us say that someone possesses *libertarian freedom* just in case, prior to his making the choice he actu-

---

[2] Ibid., 9-10.

[3] Ibid., 10.

[4] See ibid., 45f.

[5] Ibid., 48.

[6] For excellent, biblically-saturated defenses of the claim that God ordains everything, including sinful human acts, see the fifth chapter of John M. Frame's *No Other God: A Response to Open Theism* (Phillipsburg, N.J.: Presbyterian & Reformed, 2001); the fourth chapter of idem., *The Doctrine of God*, A Theology of Lordship (Phillipsburg, N.J.: Presbyterian & Reformed, 2002); the fourteenth chapter of John S. Feinberg's *No One Like Him: The Doctrine of God*, Foundations of Evangelical Theology (Wheaton, Ill.: Crossway, 2001); and John Piper, "Is God Less Glorious Because He Ordained That Evil Be? Jonathan Edwards on the Divine Decrees," in *Desiring God: Meditations of a Christian Hedonist*, 3rd ed. (Sisters, Ore.: Multnomah, forthcoming).

[7] Sanders, *The God Who Risks*, 12.

[8] Ibid., 282, emphasis added.

[9] Ibid., 214, 251.

ally makes, he could have made a different choice.[10] For instance, libertarians would hold that John's choice to stop and aid a sick homeless woman was free and thus morally significant only if it was possible at that time for John to choose to stop and aid her and it was also possible for John to choose to do something else (such as choose *not* to stop and aid her). In other words, he must have been *at liberty* to make more than one choice.[11]

But if this is what it means to possess significant freedom, then God's granting us such freedom means that it is possible for us "to do things that God does not specifically intend to happen,"[12] things that may put God's plans and purposes at risk. This is because libertarian freedom is *incompatible* with there being any explanation of someone's choosing as he did other than his choosing. In particular, libertarian freedom is incompatible with the claim that God's will is the ultimate explanation for someone's choosing as he did.[13] At least at first glance, Scripture seems to contradict this requirement for libertarian freedom.[14] For instance, Acts 4:27-28 seems to depict Herod and Pontius Pilate, along

---

[10] Philosophical distinctions like this are difficult to grasp; and so it may be helpful to put them in more than one way. Here is the way David Basinger characterizes libertarian freedom: a person is free with respect to performing an action if he has it within his power "to choose to perform action A or choose not to perform action A. Both A and not A could actually occur; which will actually occur *has not yet been determined*" (emphasis added) (see David Basinger, "Middle Knowledge and Classical Christian Thought," *Religious Studies* 22 [1986], 416). See also his *The Case for Freewill Theism: A Philosophical Assessment* (Downers Grove, Ill.: InterVarsity Press, 1996), 26.

[11] For more on this and the compatibilist conception of free will, see William Hasker, "A Philosophical Perspective," in Clark Pinnock, et al., *The Openness of God: A Biblical Challenge to the Traditional Understanding of God* (Downers Grove, Ill.: InterVarsity Press, 1994), 136-138.

[12] Sanders, *The God Who Risks*, 194.

[13] So in developing his position, open theist Gregory Boyd says that "agents are genuinely free only if the agents themselves are the *ultimate explanations* of their own free activity" (Gregory A. Boyd, *Satan and the Problem of Evil: Constructing a Trinitarian Warfare Theodicy* [Downers Grove, Ill.: InterVarsity Press, 2001], 19). He then continues like this:

> If we understand the purpose an agent had in mind in freely carrying out a particular deed, we have understood the *ultimate reason* for the deed. We thus need not assume that there is also a divine reason explaining its occurrence, either as to why it was ordained or specifically allowed [ibid.].

In fact, Boyd is really affirming a bit more than the last sentence suggests. It is not merely that we do not need to assume that there is also a divine reason explaining the occurrence of the deed; it is that we *must not* assert that there is also a divine reason explaining that occurrence. God's will *cannot* be invoked as the ultimate explanation for genuinely free human acts, libertarians insist.

[14] I say "At least at first glance" because Sanders and other open theists acknowledge how verses like these have often been read and then try to explain them in ways consistent with their libertarian commitments. Boyd in fact acknowledges that this is the natural reading of these texts when he says that "In Acts 2:23 and 4:28, . . . God seems to predestine a wicked deed . . . while at the same time holding the perpetrators responsible for it" (*Satan and the Problem of Evil*, 121). He then offers two explanations for how God could predestine Christ's crucifixion while still properly holding the perpetrators responsible for it. Paul Kjoss Helseth surveys and responds to these explanations in the third and fourth parts of his chapter.

with the Gentiles and Israelites, choosing to do exactly what God had predestined them to do (see also Luke 22:22; Acts 2:23; 3:17-19). Moreover, Scriptures such as Proverbs 21:1—"The king's heart is a stream of water in the hand of the LORD; he turns it wherever he will" (cf. Ezra 1:1; 6:22; Dan. 4:34-35)—seem to imply that *all* human choices are ordained by God.[15] Yet if God's will is the final explanation for whatever we choose, then, by libertarian standards, we are not really or significantly free.

Sanders and other libertarians hold that several things would follow if this were the case. First, it would mean that God has not really given us the "room to be genuine"—or "significant"—"others" to him.[16] If he has not granted us libertarian freedom then God, Sanders thinks, would ultimately be manipulating us in a way not unlike how a puppeteer manipulates his puppets. Consequently, our relationship with God would actually be "an I-It relation" rather than a truly personal "I-Thou relationship."[17] And this would mean, Sanders concludes, that the Bible's claim that we can have personal fellowship with God would be a sham. Secondly, it would mean that we could not be held to be "morally responsible for good and evil in a way that really makes a difference."[18] This is because for libertarians like Sanders it is only appropriate to praise or blame someone for choosing to do something if he or she was free to choose otherwise. That person's choice—and that person's choice alone—must be the final explanation of what he or she does.[19] Thirdly, if, contrary to libertarianism, God's will is the ultimate

---

[15] (All Scripture quotations in this chapter are from the English Standard Version of the Bible.) Proverbs 21:1 implies this as soon as we remember that Scripture identifies our *hearts* as the core of our personalities, from which all our good and bad acts come (see Luke 6:45). If, then, God turns the king's heart as easily as we can guide the direction of a small stream of water that is flowing over our hands, then he shapes everything the king does just as he wants. But if God does this with kings, who are of all human beings the most sovereignly powerful, then we ought to expect that he can and does do the same with all of us. In fact, Scripture does not wait for us to universalize this point from this text. In Psalm 33:13-15 we find: "The LORD looks down from heaven; he sees all the children of man; from where he sits enthroned he looks out on all the inhabitants of the earth, *he who fashions the hearts of them all* and observes all their deeds."

[16] Sanders, *The God Who Risks*, 176.

[17] Ibid., 239, 247.

[18] Ibid., 221.

[19] Thus Boyd says:

> As Robert Kane and others have argued, the intelligibility of our convictions about moral responsibility depends on the supposition that the *agent* is the *final* cause and explanation for his or her own behavior. Unless agents have the power *"to be the ultimate creators (or originators) and sustainers of their own ends or purposes,"* he argues, our sense of morally responsible self-determination cannot be rendered intelligible. In other words:

explanation for our choosing as we do, "then why is God not rightfully held responsible for sin"?[20] Why isn't God to be considered the real author of sin?[21] If God's will is in fact the ultimate explanation for *everything* that happens, then what could possibly be wrong with shaking our fists and blaming God for every tragedy?

At one time I found considerations like these to be completely convincing. As time has passed, however, I have found myself led to embrace an alternative conception of human freedom known as *compatibilism.* Compatibilism allows us to take Scriptures like Acts 4:27-28 and Proverbs 21:1 at face value because it allows for more than one explanation of the same event. Compatibilists hold that someone's choice to stop and aid a sick homeless woman is free and morally significant as long as it is voluntary and thus neither physically forced nor psychologically coerced.[22] Yet if we define freedom in this way, then someone's doing something voluntarily is *compatible* with there being another explanation for why the person chose as he did. Perhaps he has so shaped his character that it is completely natural—indeed, inevitable—for him to choose to stop and help sick homeless persons. In such a case, there are then *two* explanations for why this person stopped and aided the sick homeless woman: first, it is because he *chose* to do so; and, secondly, it is because making such a choice was *inevitable* for him, given who he is.[23]

If we embrace a compatibilistic conception of freedom, then we can hold both that those who crucified Jesus did so freely and yet that God somehow predestined those very individuals to make those specific free

---

when we trace the causal or explanatory chains of action back to their sources in the purposes of free agents, these causal chains must come to an end or terminate in the willings (choices, decisions, or efforts) of the agents, which cause or bring about their purpose.

If agents are to be free and morally responsible, Kane is arguing, the buck must stop with them in terms of what ultimately produces and thus explains their behavior [*Satan and the Problem of Evil,* 59-60. Boyd is quoting from Robert Kane, *The Significance of Freedom* (New York: Oxford University Press, 1996).].

[20] Sanders, *The God Who Risks,* 239.

[21] See ibid., 221. In chapter 8 of this volume, Paul Kjoss Helseth argues that Boyd's God is indeed the occasional author of sin.

[22] Psychological coercion would involve something like a person being threatened with some dire consequence—"We will kill your children"—if he doesn't choose a certain way. Concerning compatibilism Sanders says: "According to this view, a person is free to perform an action if she chooses. That is, a person is free [to do some particular thing] as long as she desires to do it. . . . In this schema a person is free as long as she acts on her desires, even if her desires are determined" (ibid., 221).

[23] In specific kinds of instances, Boyd is happy to countenance a form of compatibilistic freedom. See for instance his discussion of Acts 2:23 and 4:28 in *Satan and the Problem of Evil,* 121-123.

choices from before creation. We can hold both that God shapes the hearts of all human beings and yet that he observes—in the sense of judging—all of their deeds (see Ps. 33:15). For we can hold that the same event can have two distinct explanations, one that focuses on God's activity and the other that stresses human choice and responsibility.[24] My goal in this chapter is to show both how and why I have changed my mind in moving from a libertarian to a compatibilistic conception of human freedom and especially to show why Christians should be compatibilists. In the end, I shall argue, open theism rests on reading unbiblical notions of love and fellowship and freedom into the biblical text.

GOD AND THE PROBLEM OF EVIL

In my own case, as I suspect it almost always is, it was at first perfectly natural to think about these issues in libertarian terms. I began to think this way within a couple of years after my accident, when I first began to think seriously about what philosophers call "the problem of evil."[25]

For many people, the "problem of evil" is their biggest hurdle to trusting God. Most simply put, the problem is this: If an almighty and all-good God exists, then why is there any evil? For if God is almighty, then he could prevent evil; and if he is all-good, then he would want to. Evil seems to tell against God's power, or his goodness, or even against his very existence. And it often seems most telling when we—or those we love—are in its grip.

As odd as it may seem, from the moment it happened, my accident's enduring spiritual effect has always been that while I was doubting God's existence before I fell, that fall and the physical difficulties stemming from it have always assured me of God's love. This has been especially true when my paralysis spawns new physiological complications. Consequently, I

---

[24] Because the issues of this chapter are so crucial to our everyday Christian lives, I have been trying to state the differences between libertarianism and compatibilism in the simplest terms. Technically, more needs to be said. For instance, libertarians would be happy to acknowledge that someone's choosing as he did has an explanation ("I chose to go to college because then I could get into Trinity Seminary" or "I chose the chocolate ice cream because I like chocolate ice cream best") as long as that explanation does not imply that the choice was compelled or made inevitable.

[25] A much shorter and less technical version of what I say for much of the remainder of this chapter was first published as an article entitled, "God's Providence Over All," in *Modern Reformation* 11, no. 5 (September/October 2002): 38-43. I am using it with the permission of *Modern Reformation*'s parent organization, the Alliance of Confessing Evangelicals (www.alliancenet.org). A slightly different version of that piece is available in audio form online (www.wheaton.edu/wetn/real/bestof/talbot030402.ram); and in audio and videotape versions from Wheaton College, where I first told my story in a March 2002 chapel address that was part of a series on "Redemptive Curve Balls."

never found myself asking, "Why did this happen to me?" From the beginning it seemed obvious that God was manifesting his love to me through it. Yet after I had been out of the hospital for a while, I did find myself asking, "Why is this *continuing* to happen to me? If the God I love and worship is all-powerful and all-good, then why doesn't he heal me now?"

For a while, I sought a miracle. I went through a stage when I thought that God would heal me, if only I could muster up enough faith. But I eventually came to believe that a miraculous healing wasn't God's will for me—and that this didn't involve any lack of faith on my part. I then tried to give God the opportunity to heal me gradually. During my first two springs at Seattle Pacific University, I spent hours struggling up and down Queen Anne Hill while constantly praying that God would use those labors as the means to restoring my walking.

Finally, it became clear to me that it was not God's will to make me physically whole again. And then I found myself wanting to understand why.

MY FIRST ANSWER: THE "FREE WILL DEFENSE"

My attempt to understand why God did not will to make me physically whole again—and, more generally, to understand God's relation to evil—has gone through three stages. The first stage began as I worked out my first answer to the problem of evil over a year of thinking about that problem for virtually every evening during parts of my sophomore and junior college years. It was my own rude version of what I afterwards learned philosophers and theologians call the free will defense. Free will theists attempt to preserve our belief in God's almightiness and complete goodness by arguing that this world's evils are fully explained in terms of wrong choices made by God's free creatures. *Moral evil* results whenever some morally responsible being decides to do what is wrong. *Natural evil*—any evil in our world that is not moral evil, such as hurricanes, influenza epidemics, and random birth defects—then comes about indirectly as a consequence of moral evil. Open theists are one kind of free will theists, although one of the more radical and unorthodox kinds.[26]

---

[26] For more on free will theism in general, see Basinger's *The Case for Freewill Theism*.

Frame devotes the second chapter of his *No Other God* to tracing open theism's historical precedents. He maintains, as I do, that libertarianism is natural to non-Christian thought. He also points out that Socinianism—which was a sixteenth-century theological movement that was condemned by both Catholics and Protestants as heretical —maintained positions on God's

Sometimes the links between moral and natural evil are obvious. Suppose a drunk driver runs a stoplight and hits another car, crippling its occupant. The long-term pain and disability resulting from that accident is natural evil, but natural evil that clearly has its origin in the moral evil of someone driving drunk. In other cases, such as with influenza epidemics, the links are not so clear. Yet free will theists in general maintain those links are really there.[27] All of creation groans, they remind us, because of Adam's sin (Rom. 8:22-23).

With this distinction between moral and natural evil in hand, free will theists then add this: creatures can be morally responsible only if they are *really free*, which means, according to free will theism, that they must not only be able to choose to do what they actually do but that

---

foreknowledge that are virtually identical with the positions held by today's open theists. The best article on these parallels between Socinianism and open theism is Robert B. Strimple's "What Does God Know?" which is found in John H. Armstrong, ed., *The Coming Evangelical Crisis: Current Challenges to the Authority of Scripture and the Gospel* (Chicago: Moody, 1996). So far as I know, no open theist has commented on the parallels that Strimple demonstrates, although those parallels defeat the claim, sometimes made by open theists, that if the Reformers had been aware of open theism's views they might very well have embraced them. Strimple establishes that Calvin was well aware of such views, because Lelio Socinus pestered him with those views in several letters.

For a graphic "real-life illustration" of how open theism utilizes a free will framework to explain the bad things that can happen to us, see Boyd's story about "Suzanne" in his *God of the Possible: A Biblical Introduction to the Open View of God* (Grand Rapids, Mich.: Baker, 2000), 103-106. The lesson to take from Boyd's illustration is that, according to open theism, God can, with the best intentions, make disastrous mistakes in guiding us, mistakes that he has no chance of avoiding because he cannot unerringly anticipate what significantly free creatures may choose. So God may regret how he has guided us as much as or more than we regret having followed his guidance. (Boyd does argue that, on his view of the matter, God has not, in such an instance, really made a "mistake" [ibid., 61], but Sanders is willing to say that God at times does make mistakes [*The God Who Risks*, 74].)

[27] The situation is now a little more complex than I am representing it. Insofar as the "free will defense" was developed as an answer to the problem of evil, its proponents needed to maintain that the misuse of free will that is labeled "moral evil" accounts for all natural evil, for otherwise there would be some evil that the free will defense did not explain. Yet is all natural evil the result of moral evil or is some natural evil unavoidable given the kind of world that God chose to create? Today, some libertarians believe that some natural evil may be unavoidable. For instance, Sanders sometimes seems to embrace this position, as when he says,

> If it is believed that God created a world in which air currents and water vapor bring needed rain but God cannot prevent these elements from sometimes forming hurricanes, then God takes the risk that people will suffer from them and may turn away from his love [because of that suffering]. Water sustains us but we can also drown in it. Lightning brings essential nitrogen to the soil, but it may also strike us dead. Certain genetic traits make us resistant to malaria, but the same genes make us susceptible to other diseases. The risk of human suffering simply is not avoidable in the world as we know it [Sanders, *The God Who Risks*, 263].

He then, however, raises the possibility that "all natural evils represent either God's punishment on human sin or demonic forces" (ibid., 263). So it is not clear whether Sanders believes that all natural evil is the result of misused free will. And I, in fact, am no longer sure that all natural evil is the result of misused free will. Yet at the time that I came up with my own version of the free will defense, I did think that this was true. (In my own case, the moral evil that had now resulted in the natural evil of my continuing paralysis was that I was much too willing to do dangerous things and take unnecessary risks.)

they must also be free to choose to act differently. Of course, this is the notion of *libertarian freedom* that we have already encountered in Sanders's book. And, as we have already seen, this view of freedom means that even God cannot ordain what his free creatures will choose. For as soon as he would do so, they would no longer be free. So if God is committed to making free creatures, then the "cost" of their being free is the risk that they will make bad or wicked choices. Even an all-powerful God must live with this risk.

As I thought about this in my college years, I reasoned like this: God has created us to love him. But love isn't love if it is coerced. Genuine love, then, requires free will in the free will theist's sense—it requires that we are free to choose to love God or not. God has given us free will hoping that we will freely choose to love him. But in giving us this freedom, he runs the risk of our choosing not to love him. Not loving God is bad; indeed, it is the ultimate source of all of this world's evils. But for God not to have created some free creatures who are capable of love would have been even worse. Consequently, God in his goodness has created free creatures who can love him but who can also do wicked and evil things.

This line of reasoning seemed to explain why God hadn't kept me from having my accident. He could have done so, I thought, only by infringing on my free will. It also seemed to explain why he didn't heal me at some later date. God would not heal me because that would threaten other people's freedom. For if God were to heal me, then it would be obvious that there is a God who will act to remove the sufferings of those who love and worship him. Then God's power and goodness would become so apparent to those who had seen what he had done for me that they would, in effect, be psychologically coerced into worshiping him. Then only fools would freely turn away from him. So just as evil first came into our world because of wrong free choices made by morally responsible human beings, so God really has no choice but to allow it to remain if he is not to make his existence, power, and goodness overwhelmingly clear. For if his existence, power, and goodness were that obvious, then human beings would no longer be free to love him in a way that was truly uncoerced.

My Second Answer: Sometimes God Ordains Real Evils for Our Overall Good

The argument I have just given, except for a couple of my claims, could be given by any open theist.[28] Granted, there may be differences of emphasis. For instance, John Sanders states that his *God Who Risks* "is not about the problem of evil."[29] It is, instead, "about a personal God who enters into genuine give-and-take relations with us."[30] In other words, for Sanders considerations about love take precedence over considerations about free will.[31] It is not that Sanders would categorically deny what I thought about free will at this early stage in my thinking. It is simply that he would qualify those claims by placing them in the larger context of his "relational theism." And so when he does address the problem of evil, he states that his position—rooted as it is in the conviction that God created human beings because he desired to have beings who were "capable of entering into genuine . . . relationships of love with him and one another"[32]—would better be called "the 'logic-of-love defense' instead of the 'freewill defense.' Instead of beginning with human freedom, it starts with the nature of the divine project of producing significant others who are able to enter into reciprocal fellowship with God."[33]

---

[28] We have already noted Sanders's commitment to libertarian freedom. He is careful, however, to put some distance between his own project and the project of free will defenders, as I make clear in footnote 33. Sanders does distinguish between *moral* and *natural* evil, although he refers to moral evil as *sin*. Gregory Boyd ultimately denies that distinction because he denies that there is any "natural" evil. "My argument," he says, "is that there is in fact nothing 'natural' about it. Ultimately, it is as much the result of free agents exercising their will as is 'moral evil'" (*Satan and the Problem of Evil*, 18 n. 14).

Boyd makes almost exactly the same argument as I used to make concerning God's goal in creating us and the conditions under which that goal can be met:

> If love is the goal [of creation], what are its conditions? . . . [T]he first condition of love [is] that it must be freely chosen. It cannot be coerced. Agents must possess the capacity and opportunity to reject love if they are to possess the genuine capacity and ability to engage in love [*Satan and the Problem of Evil*, 52].

[29] Sanders, *The God Who Risks*, 14.

[30] Ibid.

[31] Many of Sanders's claims about God's goal in creating us parallel my early thinking about the same topic: "One of the central, if not *the* central, aims of creation was to produce significant others who could experience the divine love and reciprocate that love both to God and to other creatures" (ibid., 176). But love "does not force its own way" (ibid.). It "allows for creatures to be genuine others" by giving them "[s]pace . . . to freely participate in the fellowship of love" (ibid.). God, in other words, "provides some relational distance" so that he will "not smother [his creatures] with his presence" (ibid., 46).

[32] Ibid., 257.

[33] Ibid., 258. Sanders distances himself a bit from the free will defense because he thinks that free will defenders "tend to affirm the intrinsic (as opposed to instrumental) value of libertarian freedom. At times it is freedom for freedom's sake or, at best, freedom as requisite of morality that is trumpeted" by them (ibid.), he tells us, while he maintains that God has given us free will only because it is necessary for the possibility of a personal relationship of love between him and us.

When I worked out my first answer to the question of why, given the existence of an almighty and all-good God, there is any evil, I did so with very little reference to Scripture and no reference to historical theology. It simply seemed to be the natural answer to my question of why God did not heal me even though he could. But as time passed, I gradually saw that the free will defense was inadequate in various ways. Initially, this involved my realizing that my continuing disability was the chief means by which God kept blessing me and keeping me near to himself. As my accident has had more negative consequences—weakening hands from damaging my ulnar nerves when, losing my balance, I fall on my elbows; coming under permanent risk of stroke from dissecting my left-internal carotid while trying to keep in shape; and so on—I have found that, rather than these things becoming occasions for doubting God's goodness to me, they have become sources of spiritual strength by helping me to see where I *cannot* place my heart.

In other words, I have come to realize that God is protecting me from idolatrous self-sufficiency by taking various goods away from me so that I am not tempted to rest satisfied in them.[34] Each morning as I get up, my disability prompts me to trust God rather than to rely on my own strength. And so, in this second stage of my coming to understand how God works in and through our difficulties, I came to realize that some things that are really evil—Christians are not Christian Scientists who say that evil is illusory—are also really good and that, as such, these evils are actually *ordained* by God.

What does it mean to say that God ordains something? It means that he has eternally willed it to come about.

Free will theists reject the claim that God orders or ordains evil. They want to say that if something is really evil, then God does not will it in any way.[35] Of course, they readily concede that God can and often does bring good out of evil, but that is not the same as saying that God ordains what is really evil for our good.

Yet this is exactly what Scripture claims. Genesis provides us with

---

[34] For a meditation on how this relates to open theism, see John Piper, "How Open Theism Helps Us Conceal Our Hidden Idolatries," available online at www.desiringgod.org/library/fresh_words/2002/041002.html.

[35] This statement will be both corroborated and somewhat qualified in my next two sections. In particular, Boyd's "neo-Molinism," which is discussed in several other chapters in this book, qualifies this statement in significant ways.

one of the clearest examples of this when Joseph summarizes what God was doing through his brothers' wickedness in this way: "As for you," he says to his brothers, referring to their act of selling him into Egypt (see Gen. 37:12-28; 45:4-8), "you meant evil against me, but God meant it for good, to bring it about that many people should be kept alive, as they are today" (Gen. 50:20). The word "evil" here is the Hebrew *ra'* in the feminine singular. And the "it" in Joseph's declaration that "God meant *it* for good" is also feminine singular. So this "it" clearly takes as its antecedent the previous *ra'*. But this means that Joseph's claim is most accurately represented like this: "As for you, in selling me into Egypt you meant evil against me, but God meant that evil event for good."

In other words, Joseph is here referring to just one specific event; namely, his brothers selling him to the Ishmaelites who then took him to Egypt. Yet he explains its occurrence in two different ways: his brothers intended their selling him to do him harm even as God intended that sale for Joseph's and many others'—including his brothers'!—good.[36]

As I began to think more about this, I realized that dual explanations like this one are found throughout the Scriptures.[37] Indeed, they are central to the Bible's interpretation of our Lord's crucifixion. In that case, the most awful act ever done—the crucifixion by "lawless" (that is, wicked) "men" of God's only Son, "the Holy and Righteous One" who is the very "Author of life" (Acts 2:23 and 3:14, 15)—was and is also the most wonderful event that has ever happened because it was the means by which God was reconciling us to himself (see 2 Cor. 5:18-21).

How Do Open Theists Respond to Scriptures Like These?

As Sanders observes, "The story of Joseph's being sold into slavery and his eventual rise to rulership in Egypt commonly serves as *the* paradigm in discussions of providence."[38] So how does he interpret it?

---

[36] Indeed, it was God's intention that through this evil event he would ultimately fulfill his promise to Abraham that in him—in Abraham, that is, through Abraham's offspring—"all the families of the earth shall be blessed" (Gen. 12:3). This is because through his offspring God would bring about the greatest good that sinful humankind can have—that is, reconciliation with God through the life, death, and resurrection of Jesus (see 2 Cor. 5:18-21), Abraham's greatest descendent (see Matt. 1:1).

[37] For more biblical passages that involve these dual explanations, see Wayne Grudem, *Systematic Theology: An Introduction to Biblical Doctrine* (Grand Rapids, Mich.: Zondervan, 1994), 322-327.

[38] Sanders, *The God Who Risks*, 54. For instance, Charles Hodge says, "What is true of the history of Joseph, is true of all history" (*Systematic Theology*, vol. 1 [Grand Rapids, Mich.: Eerdmans, 1986 (orig., 1871)], 544).

Sanders acknowledges that the interpretation I have just given of it "is possible."[39] We can read the story in a way that takes God to be arranging all of the details "in such a way that Joseph inevitably rises to leadership and so saves his family and the Egyptians from famine."[40] Yet he prefers another reading that turns on three observations.

First, "the text explicitly ascribes responsibility for selling Joseph into Egypt to the brothers."[41] Sanders cites Genesis 37:28—

> Then Midianite traders passed by. And they [that is, Joseph's brothers, minus Reuben] drew Joseph up and lifted him out of the pit, and sold him to the Ishmaelites for twenty shekels of silver. They took Joseph to Egypt

—and Genesis 45:4-5—

> So Joseph said to his brothers, "Come near to me, please." And they came near. And he said, "I am your brother, Joseph, whom you sold into Egypt. And now do not be distressed or angry with yourselves because you sold me here, for God sent me before you to preserve life"

—to corroborate this claim.[42] Sanders is obviously assuming that the assignment of responsibility must mean that Joseph's brothers exercised libertarian freedom in choosing to sell him.[43] And if his brothers exercised libertarian freedom in choosing to sell him, then this, of course, would exclude there being two explanations for Joseph's brothers having sold him into Egypt.[44] More specifically and even though this directly contradicts what Genesis 50:20 actually says, it would mean that the event of Joseph's being sold into Egypt should not be explained at all in terms of what God intended, even if God's working to bring good out of the bad intentions of Joseph's brothers was so successful that it

---

[39] Sanders, *The God Who Risks*, 54.

[40] Ibid.

[41] Ibid.

[42] Sanders is considering the whole story of Joseph, as it is found in Genesis from chapter 37 through chapter 50. I shall say more about the crucial verses in chapter 45 in the next paragraph.

[43] See footnote 19 for an argument in support of this assumption.

[44] See the argument for this in the fifth through the seventh paragraphs of the introductory section of this chapter.

seemed appropriate to Joseph to describe the whole event as having been planned by God from the start.[45]

But there are at least two difficulties with this observation. First, in spite of Sanders's claim to the contrary, neither Genesis 37:28 nor Genesis 45:4-5 "explicitly ascribes responsibility for selling Joseph into Egypt to the brothers."[46] Neither the word "responsible" nor any of its synonyms appears in these texts. What the texts do assert is that Joseph's brothers sold him into Egypt. In fact, Genesis 45:4-8 makes a special point of it, since in those verses Joseph twice attributes his presence in Egypt to his brothers' act of selling him ("you sold" [v. 4], "you sold" [v. 5]). Sanders just assumes that if Joseph's brothers sold him into Egypt, then they alone are responsible for his being there. Yet in Genesis 45:4-8 Joseph immediately proceeds twice to attribute his presence in Egypt to God's having sent him there ("God sent" [v. 5], "God sent" [v. 7]). God, it seems, is also responsible for his being there. And then, as Joseph concludes his account of how he came to Egypt, he utterly discounts his brothers' part in his arrival in Egypt and attributes it entirely to God: "So it was not you who sent me here, but God" (v. 8). This seems to be Joseph's way of emphasizing God's primary agency in the chain of events that eventuated in his arrival in Egypt. Thus it becomes very clear that Joseph considered God's will to be the ultimate explanation for his being where he was.

Another difficulty with this observation is that Sanders is obviously assuming that if these texts explicitly ascribe responsibility for selling Joseph into Egypt to his brothers, then this must mean that they exercised libertarian freedom in choosing to sell him. But to assume this just begs the question against the compatibilistic claim that God ordains the acts of human beings while still properly holding them accountable for their deeds. Yet compatibilism seems to be exactly what a text like Luke

---

[45] This is the way another free will theist, Fritz Guy, actually explains Joseph's statement in Genesis 50:20. Guy says:

> divine love is infinitely resourceful. . . . A classic example is the story of Joseph, whose brothers' treachery became the opportunity for such an extraordinary career that he could say to them later, "You meant evil against me; but God meant it for good, to bring it about that many people should be kept alive" (Gen. 50:20). *The divine love was so resourceful in "working for good" that the whole scenario seemed programed in advance* ["The Universality of God's Love," in *The Grace of God and the Will of Man*, ed. Clark H. Pinnock (Minneapolis: Bethany, 1989), 41-42, emphasis added].

[46] Sanders, *The God Who Risks*, 54.

22:22 is assuming ("For the Son of Man goes as it has been determined, but woe to that man by whom he is betrayed!"[47]).

Secondly, Sanders observes that Joseph's description of his brothers' act as evil (see Gen. 50:20), as well as Reuben's description of it as sinful (see Gen. 42:22), militate against ascribing it to God's will, for it "is problematic, to say the least, to ascribe sin and evil to God."[48] But, again, this comment begs the question, for it assumes that an event that is properly described in one way when it is viewed as the product of human choice must be described in the same way when it is viewed as ordained by God. In Genesis 45:4-8, what Joseph attributes to God is *not* the evil inherent in his brothers' act of selling him into Egypt but only the good involved in God's sending him before his brothers into Egypt "to preserve life" (45:5). This gets reiterated in Joseph's descriptions of what God was doing in verses 7 and 8:

> And God sent me before you *to preserve for you a remnant on earth, and to keep alive for you many survivors.* So it was not you who sent me here, but God. *He has made me a father to Pharaoh, and lord of all his house and ruler over all the land of Egypt.*

Indeed, even in its immediate context (see Gen. 50:15-21), Genesis 50:20 does not ascribe any sin or evil to God. As Paul Helm has commented,

> on Joseph's understanding God brought certain events to pass, events which had a beneficial end, and which were in accordance with his covenant promise to Abraham, using the evil intentions and actions of human beings. He does this, according to Joseph, without himself being implicated in the evil, and without diminishing in any way the evil of what was done to Joseph and the responsibility for that evil.[49]

Passages like Luke 22:22, Acts 2:23, and 4:27-28 make it even clearer that Scripture does not assume that an event that is properly described

---

[47] See also Matthew 26:24 and Mark 14:21. So far as I know, no open theist has dealt explicitly with these texts, although Boyd does deal with some other texts concerning Judas's role in Jesus' betrayal. See his *Satan and the Problem of Evil*, 122-123.

[48] Sanders, *The God Who Risks*, 55.

[49] Paul Helm, *The Providence of God*, Contours of Christian Theology (Downers Grove, Ill.: InterVarsity Press, 1994), 104.

in one way when it is viewed as the product of human choice must be described in the same way when it is viewed as ordained by God.

Thirdly, Sanders takes Joseph's claim that what his brothers intended for evil, God intended for good as meaning merely "that God has brought something good out of their evil actions. God was not determining everything in Joseph's life, but God did remain 'with' him,"[50] as Genesis 39:2 states. But Sanders gives us no reason why this interpretation should be preferred over any other.

Sanders concludes that nothing in this story "demands the interpretation that God actually desired [the brothers'] sinful acts. The text does not say," Sanders declares,

> that God caused or necessitated the events. In fact, the text is remarkably silent regarding any divine activity until Joseph's speeches. Until [those speeches], the events could have been narrated without reference to divine activity at all. In fact, unlike the other patriarchal stories, here God is strangely absent. Joseph never invokes God! It is in retrospect that Joseph identifies God's activity in his life working for the preservation of human life.[51]

Of course, Moses may have had a very good reason for not stressing God's part in Joseph's life until late in the story. Such a storytelling device can drive home the point that, even when God seems absent, he actually is present and working all along. The mere fact, then, that we have not yet understood why God has ordained some dreadful event—such as the early death of John Sanders's brother—does not mean that we shall not someday come to realize that God did indeed have a good reason for ordaining it.

What Genesis 45:4-8 does do is to assert God's activity of sending Joseph to Egypt in order to accomplish his own good purposes as often and as strongly—indeed, *more* often and *more* strongly—as it asserts Joseph's brothers' activity of selling Joseph into Egypt in order to harm him. Scripture places Joseph's brothers' agency ("you sold") and God's agency ("God sent") and Joseph's brothers' intention ("you meant") and God's intention ("God meant") in precise parallel when explain-

---

[50] Sanders, *The God Who Risks*, 55.
[51] Ibid.

ing how Joseph's being sold into Egypt came about. No doubt, what God wills is the ultimate explanation for whatever happens—"Our God is in the heavens; he does all that he pleases" (Ps. 115:3)—but this does not mean that human choice cannot be the appropriate proxi-mate—that is, "close" or "near"—explanation for some event's coming about. And the fact that God's will is the ultimate explanation for whatever happens is never taken in Scripture as a reason to deny that human beings are responsible for their choices and what those choices bring about.[52]

MY THIRD AND FINAL ANSWER: *NOTHING* BEFALLS US— NOTHING GOOD *AND* NOTHING EVIL—THAT IS NOT ULTIMATELY FROM GOD

My realization that dual explanations like the one found in Joseph's story are found throughout the Scriptures gave me a new way of understanding God's relationship to evil. In free will theism, God must work to bring good from evils he does not ordain. God works to make good of bad situations. Because he is wise and almighty, he can do a lot to salvage what we have messed up. And because he is good, he does what he can. Yet he is still merely working to repair what he did not ordain. Indeed, if open theism is right, then God is sometimes working to repair what he does not expect. Open theism is free will theism taken to its logical extreme in that it argues that, insofar as God has given us libertarian free will, even he cannot truly know what choices we will make; and so the portion of the future that will be determined by still-unmade free human choices is "open" and unknown to him as well as to us.

This is why Sanders writes that God had "no reason to suspect"

---

[52] Ibid., 45. In an appendix in his book, *Satan and the Problem of Evil,* Boyd states that
> Compatibilists often argue that [Genesis 45:5 and 50:20] . . . illustrate that God ordains evil actions for greater good. While different interpretations are possible, I am largely in agreement with compatibilists on this point. The passage [*sic*] seems to indi-cate that God intentionally orchestrated the evil intentions of the brothers in order to get Joseph into Egypt [ibid., 396].

He then makes three thoughtful comments on these texts, one of which involves his declaration that "if we interpret this episode as evidence of how God always operates, we must accept the consequence that this passage always minimizes the responsibility of human agents" (ibid., 396). But this consequence, as I am about to argue, is exactly what Scripture denies, and so Boyd's compatibilism and my compatibilism (as I develop it in my next section) are not the same. My answers to Boyd's other two points are found further along in this chapter.

that Adam and Eve would sin.[53] He also claims that God and Jesus only realized in the garden of Gethsemane that Jesus would have to be crucified. "The path of the cross," he states, "comes about only through God's interaction with humans in history. Until [Gethsemane] other routes were, perhaps, open."[54] Yet in Gethsemane "Father and Son . . . both come to understand that there is no other way."[55] At that point in Jesus' life, Sanders states, "the canyon narrows even for God."[56] So Father and Son resolve to make the best of it as Jesus proceeds to his death even though, Sanders tells us, they do not know whether this "gambit" will work—whether, in other words, Jesus' death will lead to anyone's salvation.[57]

In the third stage of my attempting to understand God's relation to this world's evils, I realized that I, as a Christian, was obliged to try to understand what *all* of God's Word had to say about this topic. For the Scriptures, like other writings, can be twisted to support almost any position if they are quoted selectively (see 2 Pet. 3:16). For instance, it is only by very selective quotation that Sanders's version of open theism can seem to be a Christian option because several of his claims contradict central biblical themes. What does he do with verses like Luke 24:25-26—"And [Jesus] said to them, 'O foolish ones, and slow of heart to believe all that the prophets have spoken! Was it not necessary that the Christ should suffer these things and enter into his glory?'"? Sanders cites these verses only to dismiss them, although they contradict his claim that until Gethsemane Christ's crucifixion was not God's settled

---

[53] Sanders stresses repeatedly that God's decision to grant us libertarian freedom means that God's existence "is conditioned by the creatures he created" in various ways (*The God Who Risks*, 10). This means that "God takes risks in bringing about this particular type of world" (ibid.). Shockingly enough, Sanders seems to think that these risks include even whether God should ultimately be called either "wise" or "foolish." And thus after "the totally unexpected happens" (ibid., 46) in Genesis 3 when Adam and Eve ate from the tree of the knowledge of good and evil, Sanders states that "God [was] still working for the best interests of the humans, and [his] divine actions [in sending them out of the garden of Eden so that they would not eat from the tree of life and live forever in sin] may be understood as attempts to restore their trust in the divine wisdom and provision" (ibid., 49). He then asks, regarding these attempts, "Is God a fool? Will his attempts at restoration succeed? Only the history of God's activity and the human response to it will tell" (ibid.). And, presumably, if human beings use their libertarian freedom to respond wrongly to God's attempts to restore fellowship with them, then it will become clear that God *is* a fool.

[54] Ibid., 100.

[55] Ibid., 101.

[56] Ibid.

[57] Ibid.

plan for redeeming sinful human beings (see also Matt. 26:24; Luke 22:22; Acts 2:23; Rev. 13:8; etc.).[58]

As I have attempted to understand what the whole Bible says about the problem of evil, I have discovered that Scripture supports what I have sensed since the time of my accident. This is that *nothing* happens to us—nothing good *and nothing bad*—that does not ultimately come from God's hand.

You will recall that I said it is often right after some complication of my accident—a messy fall or something worse—that I feel God's love and care for me most intensely. My sense is not that God will "patch things up" and "make them better" in spite of what has just happened; it is that God's love and care for me somehow *explains* what has just happened to me, no matter how bad in one sense it really is. This is what Scripture both asserts and assumes to be true for those who love God and who have been called according to his purpose (see Rom. 8:28-39; Ps. 30:4-5).

Yet here, if we are not to misunderstand Scripture, we must be very careful. Genesis 50:20 gives us the primary picture: "As for you, you meant evil against me, but God meant [that evil] for good, to bring it about that many people should be kept alive, as they are today." Here Joseph's brothers' evil intention and God's good intention are paralleled, with both referring to and both taken as explaining the same event, but referring to it under different descriptions and explaining it in different ways. By their act, Joseph's brothers meant to do him harm; by means of their act, God meant to do Joseph (and many others) good.

As I shall reiterate, such a passage does not deny or diminish human agency and responsibility, but it suggests, as even open theist Gregory Boyd concedes, that sometimes even wicked human acts happen because God ordains them.[59] Nevertheless, Boyd is correct in claiming that

---

[58] Again, as footnotes 26 and 53 make clear, open theists claim that God's plans and purposes can be thwarted to some degree by the exercise of libertarian free will. But this seems to be directly contradicted by many Scriptures, including Job 42:2, Psalm 115:3, Daniel 4:35, and Philippians 1:6.

[59] See footnote 52 for Boyd's concession. He does, however, think that this passage (along with 45:5), interpreted in a compatibilistic way, diminishes human responsibility. And so he says:

> if we interpret this episode as evidence of how God always operates, we must accept the consequence that this passage [Gen. 45:5] always minimizes the responsibility of human agents. This is the conclusion Joseph himself draws from his observation that God used his brothers to send him to Egypt. "Do not be distressed, or angry with yourselves," he tells them, "for God sent me." If this text is taken as evidence of how God *always* controls human action—if God is involved in each kidnapping and murder the way he was involved in the activity of Joseph's brothers—we must be willing to console every murderer and kidnapper with Joseph's words: "Do not be distressed, or

Genesis 50:20 should not itself "be taken as a proof text of how God usually, let alone always, operates."[60] Boyd is right that even if Joseph's story is paradigmatic of the way God works in and through what is evil, nothing in the story itself warrants our taking what God has done there as representing what he does in every case. In fact, there are many Scriptures that oblige us to think very carefully about the relationship between divine and human agency (see, e.g., Mark 6:1-6; Matt. 23:37; Ezek. 18:30-32). Yet taken as a whole the Scriptures do either assert or assume or imply that God ordains everything, including natural and moral evil. I cannot make the full biblical case for this claim and still make some other crucial points.[61] Here, however, it is perhaps worth noting that open theists still have not acknowledged or grappled adequately with some of the passages in Scripture that witness most decisively to God's foreordination of everything, including free human choices—passages such as Acts 13:48, Ephesians 1:11, and 1 Thessalonians 1:4-6.[62]

---

angry with yourself, for God kidnapped and murdered your victims." We cannot universalize the mode of God's operation in this passage without also universalizing its implication for human responsibility [*Satan and the Problem of Evil*, 396-397].

In response, I would make a couple of observations. First, when we consider Joseph's whole story rather than limiting ourselves to this one verse, it seems likely that Joseph's purpose here in saying what he did was simply to keep his brothers from focusing on their guilt for the moment. For elsewhere, as Sanders points out, Joseph describes his brothers' act as evil (see Gen. 50:20) and Reuben describes it as sinful (see Gen. 42:22). Indeed, Joseph's brothers themselves later describe their act of selling him into Egypt as a "transgression," a "sin," and a case of doing a lot of "evil" to him (see Gen. 50:15-17). The whole story, then, does not diminish human responsibility for the bad things that human beings do nor does it suggest that the brothers took Joseph's remark at this point as lessening their blameworthiness. Secondly, other passages in Scripture that seem to involve exactly the same kind of dual explanation stress human responsibility and wickedness, even as they affirm God's foreordination. Think here particularly of those passages that refer to our Lord's crucifixion, such as Matthew 26:24—"The Son of Man goes as it is written of him, but woe to that man by whom the Son of Man is betrayed! It would have been better for that man if he had not been born" (cf. Luke 22:22)—and Acts 2:23—"this Jesus, delivered up according to the definite plan and foreknowledge of God, you crucified and killed by the hands of lawless [that is, wicked] men." Passages emphasizing God's foreordination as well as human responsibility and culpability are often paired up in Scripture; see, for instance, Proverbs 16:4-5 as well as the previously cited Psalm 33:13-15.

[60] Boyd, *Satan and the Problem of Evil*, 396.

[61] For the full case, see Frame's *No Other God*, chapter 5; Grudem's *Systematic Theology*, chapter 16; Helm's *Providence of God*; R. K. McGregor Wright's *No Place for Sovereignty: What's Wrong with Freewill Theism* (Downers Grove, Ill.: InterVarsity Press, 1996); and John S. Feinberg's *No One Like Him*, especially chapter 14. So far as I know, the best sources for open theists' rebuttals to the biblical case for compatibilistic freedom are found in Sanders's *The God Who Risks* and Boyd's *Satan and the Problem of Evil*. But consult Frame in chapter 6 of his *No Other God*, and Feinberg later on in chapter 14 of his *No One Like Him*. For some Scriptures that imply that God ordains everything, including human choices, see footnote 15, above.

[62] As Frame notes, "Incredibly, neither Sanders's *The God Who Risks* nor Boyd's *God of the Possible* lists Ephesians 1:11 in the Scripture index. Boyd doesn't list Romans 11:36 or Lamentations 3:37-38, either." "In the open theist literature," Frame goes on to observe, "there is a general failure to interact with significant Scripture passages used by the other side." This leads

Let us assume then, for now, that a good case can be made for the claim that, taken as a whole, the Scriptures do either assert or assume or imply that, no matter whether we are dealing with the moral or the natural realms, no matter whether we are focusing on moral good and evil or natural good and evil, absolutely *nothing* comes about that God has not ordained.

"All right," you say, "but *in what sense?* Does God merely *permit* evil things to happen? Or does his ordaining them amount to something more?"

Space does not permit me to make the full case for what I think Scripture shows us here, but I shall state what I believe it shows while citing a couple of Scriptures in support of my view. The biblical view is that God has ordained or willed or planned everything that happens in our world from before creation.[63] God is the primary agent—the primary cause, the final and ultimate explanation—of everything that happens, yet the causal relationship between God and his creatures is such that his having foreordained everything is compatible with—and indeed takes nothing away from—their creaturely power and efficacy.[64] Their

---

him to conclude, "At the very least, it seems that the open theists are not dealing seriously with the strongest biblical evidence against their position" (*No Other God*, 87, including n. 34). I have more to say about the attitudes of several open theists to Scripture in "Does God Reveal Who He Actually Is?" in Douglas S. Huffman and Eric L. Johnson, eds., *God Under Fire: Modern Scholarship Reinvents God* (Grand Rapids, Mich.: Zondervan, 2002), 62-66. Open theism's endorsement of libertarian free will does not bode well for a strong doctrine of biblical authority, in spite of its claims to be a more biblical alternative to classical Christian theism.

In fairness to open theism, Boyd has tried to deal with more of the problematic biblical passages in his *Satan and the Problem of Evil*, especially appendix 5 ("Exegetical Notes on Texts"). My commentary on his treatment of Genesis 45:5 and 50:20 in footnote 59 indicates why I think his comments are often unconvincing.

[63] Regarding Genesis 45:5 and 50:20, Boyd says that

nothing in these texts indicates that God orchestrated the brothers' activity before creation or even before the brothers developed their characters on their own. The text only suggests that *at some point* in the course of God's interaction with humans, God decided that it fit his sovereign purpose to steer the brothers' intentions in the manner we read in Genesis. It wasn't God's original plan that the brothers would acquire the character they did, but in the flow of history it fit his plan to use these brothers in the way he did [*Satan and the Problem of Evil*, 397].

As with Boyd's claim that Genesis 50:20 "should not be taken as a proof text of how God usually, let alone always, operates" (ibid., 396), I willingly concede that we should not attempt to derive the doctrine of God's eternal foreordination of all events from Joseph's story. That doctrine is grounded in other Scriptures, such as Romans 8:29-30; Ephesians 1:4; 1 Peter 1:20; and Revelation 13:8 and 17:8. Open theists, especially in line with their doctrine of *corporate election* (see, e.g., Sanders's *God Who Risks*, 102), attempt to interpret these verses in a way that does not imply that God has eternally foreordained all events.

[64] D. A. Carson puts it well:

(1) God is absolutely sovereign, but his sovereignty never functions in such a way that human responsibility is curtailed, minimized, or mitigated.

activity—as "secondary" or "proximate" causes considered simply on the created level—fully explains what happens in this world, unless we are dealing with a situation in which God has miraculously intervened and thus overridden mere creaturely causality. And this is as true of the relationship between divine and free human agency as it is between divine and natural agency.

So we should hold that human beings are free and fully responsible for their actions, even while holding that what they freely do was ordained by God before creation. It was Joseph's brothers' free and unfettered and wicked intention to do him harm; it was God's free and unfettered and good intention that Joseph's brothers would freely intend to do him harm, but that their free act would actually bring good to him and many others.

But how can this possibly be? How can Joseph's brothers have acted freely and responsibly if what they did was what God had previously ordained? How can God govern the choices of human beings without that entailing that those choices are no longer free? The correct answer to these questions is that we *cannot* understand how these things can possibly be. We cannot understand how some human act can be fully explained in terms of God's having freely intended it without that explanation taking away from the freedom and responsibility of its human intenders. We cannot understand how divine and human agency are compatible in a way that allows the exercise of each kind of agency to be fully explanatory of some event's coming about. Yet—and this is the absolutely crucial point—we *can* understand why we cannot understand it. It is because attempts on our part to understand it involve our trying to understand the unique relationship between the Creator and his creatures in terms of our understanding of some creature-to-creature relationship. But this attempt, it should be clear, involves us in a kind of "category mistake" that dooms our attempt from the start. A *category mistake* involves attempting to think about something under the wrong category. How the Creator's agency relates to his creatures' agency is to be categorized quite differently from how any creature's agency relates

---

(2) Human beings are morally responsible creatures—they significantly choose, rebel, obey, believe, defy, make decisions, and so forth, and they are rightly held accountable for such actions; but this characteristic never functions so as to make God absolutely contingent. D. A. Carson, *How Long, O Lord? Reflections on Suffering and Evil* (Grand Rapids, Mich.: Baker, 1990), 201.

to any other creature's agency. This should be obvious merely by our remembering that God has created everything *ex nihilo*—out of nothing—while all creaturely creation involves some sort of limited action on some pre-existing "stuff."

When Scripture pulls back the veil enough to tell us anything about the relationship between divine and human agency, it merely reveals what Joseph affirms in Genesis 50:20: it affirms both divine and human agency, with both kinds of agency referring to and both explaining the same event, but with each kind of agency explaining that event in its own way. Thus Scripture reveals that both human agency and divine agency are to be fully affirmed without attempting to tell us how this can be.

This holds for passages like Acts 2:23 and 4:27-28 that refer to our Lord's crucifixion, where various phrases in each passage clearly affirm both divine and human agency. Similar statements assuming the ultimate consistency and indeed complementary nature of divine and human agency are found in the accounts of Jonah being cast into the sea (see especially Jonah 1:14-15 and 2:3) and in Luke's account of Paul's shipwreck (Acts 27:13-44).

In summary, as my knowledge of Scripture grew, I found myself prompted to affirm the age-old Christian doctrine of God's complete providence over all, by which he has sovereignly ordained, before the world began, everything that happens, but in a way that does no violence to creation's secondary causes.[65]

BUT DOESN'T THIS RAISE THE PROBLEM OF EVIL AND THE ISSUE OF MORAL RESPONSIBILITY ALL OVER AGAIN?

But doesn't taking God as ordaining everything, including evil human acts, raise many issues, including those raised by libertarians in the second-to-the-last paragraph of my introductory section? I shall close by addressing those issues.

To begin with the final issue raised in that paragraph: If, contrary to libertarianism, God's will is the ultimate explanation for our doing

---

[65] I say "age-old" because it has been held by many of the church's greatest theologians, including Augustine and Aquinas. The final clause of my sentence echoes chapter 3, section 1, of the *Westminster Confession of Faith:* "God from all eternity did by the most wise and holy counsel of his own will, freely and unchangeably ordain whatsoever comes to pass; yet so as thereby neither is God the author of sin; nor is violence offered to the will of the creatures, nor is the liberty or contingency of second causes taken away, but rather established."

whatever we do, "then why," as Sanders asks, "is God not rightfully held responsible for sin?"[66] Mustn't God be taken as an evildoer because he has, in at least one sense, willed what is evil?

In response to these questions, we must first note that Scripture *never* attributes moral evildoing to God, even while it emphasizes that he has ordained and brings about what is evil. To attribute moral evildoing to God merely because he ordains and brings into being what is evil is to make that "category mistake" again; it is to try to think of the relation between God and his world in a way that inevitably smuggles in some illicit creature-to-creature analogy. Scripture stresses how different God is from everything he has made at least partly in order to keep us from drawing such analogies (see Ex. 9:14; Job 42:1-6; Isa. 46:8-11; Jer. 10:6-7; Rom. 9:19-20 and 11:33). God's will is the ultimate explanation for all of the evil we find in this world, but to the degree that some evil event has come about because of some sort of moral wrongdoing, blame for that wrongdoing should be assigned to some creature and not to God.

I do not deny for a moment how hard it can be to avoid holding God responsible for the world's evils simply because he ordains everything. How could a good God ordain the Holocaust? How can he ordain the sexual abuse of even one child? How can he ordain the slow, lingering death of someone I love? Yet, as with all other Christian doctrines, the test of the truth of this doctrine is not that we find it plausible or attractive but that we find it in Scripture. Moreover, wouldn't it prove particularly ironic for us to realize some day that we had been blaming God for some evil that he had ordained for our ultimate good? Romans 8:28 assures us that God works *all things* together for good for those who love God and who are called according to his purpose. How some very evil event could possibly be ordained by God for some Christian's ultimate good may not be apparent as the evil occurs nor even, perhaps, at any time in that Christian's earthly life. Yet stories like Joseph's remind us that appearance and reality are different things. To blame God and hold him responsible for what now seem to us to be unmitigated evils is perilous, given how little we know.

Moving on, then, to the second issue raised in my second-to-the-last

---

[66] Sanders, *The God Who Risks*, 232.

introductory paragraph: If we do not possess libertarian free will, then how, as open theists ask, can we be held morally responsible in any meaningful way? How could it be appropriate to praise or blame someone for voluntarily doing something if God's foreordination of his choice really means, as it does with compatibilism, that he could not have chosen otherwise?

I don't know how to answer these questions completely. But I do know two things. First, Scripture clearly affirms both God's foreordination and human responsibility and culpability. So I should affirm them, too, even if I cannot completely understand how God's foreordination does not negate human moral responsibility.[67] I am even less capable of understanding the orthodox doctrines of how, say, God can be both one and three in one or how God's Son can be fully human and fully divine, yet I must also affirm those doctrines because Scripture affirms them. Secondly, compatibilism's very point is to protect the ascription of moral responsibility in cases where someone acts voluntarily and yet we cannot imagine how he was free to act otherwise. As long as his choice was not psychologically coerced, compatibilists maintain, it is appropriate to take him to be responsible for his choice to some degree. I am espousing a kind of compatibilism where God's exercise of his Creator's agency is compatible with my exercise of my creaturely agency fully explaining (on the creaturely level) why some event has come about. Embracing this kind of compatibilism actually should strengthen our conviction that we must choose and act responsibly. For instance, whenever I am in some dire medical situation, I remind myself of the practical implications of compatibilistic freedom. I know that it is my duty, in that situation, to do everything I can to bring about a good result, for I am obliged to exercise my agency responsibly. Consequently, I must select careful, exceedingly competent doctors who take their tasks with the utmost seriousness; I need to listen to the counsel of several of them; and so on. Yet I also comfort myself in knowing that, at the end of the day, God's hand is in it all—that I would not be in this dire situation if God had not ordained it and that whatever happens is what he has ordained for my good because I am one of his precious children. It is my responsibility to do everything I can to bring the situation to a

---

[67] I reflect a bit more about when we are responsible and blameworthy in my final section.

good conclusion, but it is also my responsibility to take the situation, as dire as it is, as coming from God's hand. In the last analysis, then, my ultimate responsibility is to trust God and let my trust of him show in my interactions with everyone else in the midst of the crisis. And it is only by looking at whatever is happening to me in this way that I can do what Paul urges me to do: "Rejoice always, pray without ceasing, *give thanks in all circumstances;* for this is the will of God in Christ Jesus for you" (1 Thess. 5:16-18).

WHAT KIND OF FREEDOM DOES SCRIPTURE PORTRAY AS WORTH HAVING?

This leads us to the final—and most crucial—issue. Sanders and other libertarians hold that if God has not granted us libertarian free will, then he has not really given us the "room to be genuine"—or "significant"— "others" to him.[68] If he has not granted us libertarian freedom, then God, they charge, is ultimately just manipulating us. Then God would be treating us as objects rather than as persons. And then the Bible's claim that we can have personal fellowship with God would be a sham.

This is the crucial issue because it requires us to think through God's goals in creation and redemption. We must ask not only why God created human beings but also what their final state will be. Sanders identifies "God's project"[69] as his "seeking to create a people of whom he is proud to be their God."[70] These people will "love and trust him in response to his love and manifest their love of God in effective action to others."[71] In other words, God "sovereignly wills to have human persons become collaborators with him in achieving the divine project of mutual relations of love."[72] But these love-relations must involve "genuine give-and-take,"[73] which requires God to grant us libertarian freedom. Indeed, only persons possessing libertarian freedom are capable of entering into fellowship with other persons, because "fellowship

---

[68] Sanders, *The God Who Risks*, 176.
[69] Ibid., 124.
[70] Ibid., 125.
[71] Ibid., 124.
[72] Ibid., 12.
[73] Ibid., 14.

requires reciprocity."[74] And reciprocity necessarily involves "a kind of risk."[75] For in reciprocal relations, Sanders maintains,

> the two parties are dependent on each other to uphold the value of the relationship. If one party backs out and rejects the other, the one rejected bears the pain involved in the loss of love. . . . Personal relations entail the risk of failure in that the relationship may be broken and love may not materialize.[76]

Consequently, Sanders designates his kind of risky, relational theism as "the fellowship model"[77] of Christian theism.

It is true that Scripture identifies fellowship with God the Father (see 1 John 1:3-6) and with his Son (see 1 Cor. 1:9; Phil. 3:10; 1 John 1:3) and with the Holy Spirit (see 2 Cor. 13:14; Phil. 2:1) as at least one of the benefits or blessings of Christ's work. Indeed, our current fellowship with God in Christ through the Holy Spirit is a foretaste and pledge of a greater and more perfect fellowship that is yet to come (see Rev. 21:3; 2 Cor. 4:14; Rom. 8:9-11)—the fellowship we shall enjoy in the eschaton, when the imperfect will have been made perfect (see 1 Cor. 13:10) and our redemption will be complete.

Asking "What will this perfected fellowship be like?" throws some of the more profound differences between compatibilists and libertarians into sharp relief. More specifically, our profound disagreements concerning the nature of sin and salvation start to stand out. Sanders highlights some of these differences when he argues for what he calls "the fellowship model of salvation"[78] over and against its compatibilist counterpart. As he says, compatibilists understand "sin as a condition that must be changed."[79] It is "a state of corruption in which humans find themselves, and this condition manifests itself in sinful behavior. Typically," he continues, this sinful condition

> is explained as a result of inheriting a sinful nature. In compatibilistic terms this sinful (Adamic) nature is the remote cause that produces sin-

---

[74] Ibid., 211.
[75] Ibid.
[76] Ibid.
[77] Ibid., 195.
[78] Ibid., 247.
[79] Ibid., 238.

ful desires. [Yet for compatibilists, as long as] we do what we desire, we are free. Due to our sinful nature we are [however] only free to sin. We can never desire God because our sinful nature excludes such "good" desires. In order to confess Jesus as Lord, [then,] we need to have the remote cause of our desires replaced by a new entity or condition that produces a desire to confess Jesus. Obviously, we are in no position to bring this about. God is the sole and complete cause that replaces our sinful nature with a regenerate nature. There is nothing we can do to initiate this change or aid in bringing it about for, so to speak, there is no one home for God to address.[80]

Salvation, then, for compatibilists, consists in God's changing our nature so that we are no longer slaves to sin (see John 8:34; Rom. 6:6). It consists in Christ setting us free (see John 8:36; Rom. 6:7) so that we can choose to present ourselves to God as slaves of righteousness (see Rom. 6:12-19). When we were slaves to sin, we were "free from"—that is, unimpeded by—righteousness. But in Christ we are released from the absolute domination of sin and thus enabled to choose that which leads to holiness and eternal life (see Rom. 6:20-22).

In contrast, Sanders tells us, libertarians characterize sin as "a broken relationship with God."[81] We have broken this relationship by misusing our libertarian free wills—by "refusing to respond in love to the divine love."[82] As libertarians see it, we can restore this relationship by just choosing to will rightly, by simply choosing to love and trust God once again. Our making this choice, Sanders stresses, requires God's "enabling grace."[83] But enabling grace, for libertarians, consists merely in God's revelation of his mercy and love, in his appealing to us without himself changing us. For if enabling grace were anything more—if, in particular, God's enabling grace worked upon our wills in an irresistible way—then God would be transgressing the interpersonal boundaries that are necessary if he is to have "a reciprocal relationship of love with us."[84] He would then be treating us impersonally—as objects—by forcing his will on ours.

---

[80] Ibid.
[81] Ibid., 243.
[82] Ibid.
[83] Ibid., 245.
[84] Ibid., 246.

This possibility Sanders condemns in the strongest terms. Compatibilists believe that when God elects to change a human heart, he acts irresistibly—"For we know, brothers loved by God, that *[God] has chosen you,* because our gospel came to you not only in word, but also in power and in the Holy Spirit and with full conviction" (1 Thess. 1:4-5). Such irresistible grace is anathema to Sanders. Irresistible grace, he concedes, "may be thought of positively as divine liberation from an invincible prison."[85] Yet it "may also be seen negatively as *divine rape* because it involves nonconsensual control. . . . Of course, the desire God forces on the elect is a beneficent one—for their own good—but *it is rape nonetheless.*"[86] Libertarians, in contrast, hold that "God does not rape us, even for our own good."[87]

But let us now think about these issues in terms of the perfect fellowship with God and other human beings that we will someday possess. What does Scripture tell us about redemption's final state?[88] It tells us that in "the new heavens and the new earth" (Isa. 66:22; cf. 2 Pet. 3:13; Rev. 21:1) that God is going to make for his redeemed people, creation will be restored and there will be no moral or natural evil. There "the spirits of the righteous" will be perfect (Heb. 12:23) and we shall be like Jesus— the sinless one (see Heb. 4:15)—because there "we shall see him as he is" (1 John 3:2; cf. Rev. 22:4). In that place there will be no more sin and none of its effects—no mourning, no crying, no pain, and no death (see Rev. 21:27, 4; 22:3). Indeed, because creation will no longer be under sin's curse, it will itself "be set free from its bondage to decay and obtain the freedom of the glory of the children of God" (Rom. 8:21).

This "freedom of the glory of the children of God" is not libertarian freedom—it is not the freedom to sin and the freedom not to sin. Even Boyd admits this when he says that "Scripture describes both heaven and hell as eternal, irreversible states."[89] The freedom that God's children will

---

[85] Ibid., 239-240.

[86] Ibid., 240; my emphasis.

[87] Ibid., 246.

[88] On this topic, Sanders professes uncertainty. He says that "The nature of 'heaven' and the question of whether both moral and natural evil will, by divine fiat, immediately cease to exist in such a state raises a number of significant problems" (ibid., 336 n. 99). As he develops these problems in this endnote—and contrary to what the verses I quote in this paragraph state or imply—he is not sure that heaven will be free of sin and pain.

[89] *Satan and the Problem of Evil,* 189. Boyd holds that we start with libertarian freedom, but that such freedom "is always finite and probational" (ibid.). "Those who by God's grace [use] their irrevocable probational freedom as God [intends] ultimately become irrevocably aligned with him,

possess is the freedom of having become completely "dead to sin and alive to God in Christ Jesus."[90] When our redemption is complete, God will, therefore, have granted us the greatest of freedoms—compatibilist freedom—that is, the liberty of having been set completely "free from sin" so that we may become glad and total "slaves to righteousness" (Rom. 6:18).

Initially, libertarianism can seem to be painting an attractive picture with its God who does not compel but only waits and woos. Yet is this what we really want? Is a waiting and wooing God what we hope for when we long for complete redemption?

When I was young, I thought that lots of paths were open to me just for the choosing. As time has gone by, however, I have realized that many of these paths were not really open to me because I *would* not choose them. I have realized that, regarding my responsibility, it does not ultimately matter whether I *could* have chosen them. The fact is, even if I could have chosen them, I was such that I *would not have chosen* them. For instance, I have only my own self to blame for the fact that I would not heed my father's counsel to stay away from dangerous rope swings. Likewise, early in my Christian life, it often seemed to me that I did what was right simply because I chose to do so. I was too quick to believe that I was never really spiritually dead in my transgressions and sins (see Eph. 2:1). It was easy to think that I was never really a slave to sin. Yet as my Christian life progressed, I began to be confronted with the depths of my sin. I began to hunger and thirst for righteousness—indeed, to long for redemption's final state, when by God's grace I will be forevermore freed from sin. This longing is a longing for a kind of compatibilist freedom, when I can be free from even the desire to do what is wrong, when I will always gladly and surely choose to glory in the goodness and righteousness of God in Christ. I long for this kind of perfected freedom, convinced that I shall have it only if God brings it about (see Phil. 1:6).[91]

---

while those who use their irrevocable probational freedom against God become irrevocably set against him in self-absorbed rebellion" (ibid., 191).

[90] When Paul uses this phrase in Romans 6:11, he is telling us Christians how we should think about ourselves now, during our earthly lives, in the light of what we shall yet become.

[91] For Boyd, the transition from the libertarian freedom God grants us at the outset to the compatibilist state that follows is part of what we may call a "natural" process. Our past choices

not only condition our future choices about what we will *do* in life; they also condition the kind of person we will *be* and even the amount of self-determination we have left to decide this matter. Decisions, however small, are not morally neutral activities. Certain decisions tend to create future possibilities, while other decisions squelch them [*Satan and the Problem of Evil*, 199].

When, by God's grace, I realized these things,[92] then libertarian claims about love and fellowship and freedom began to sound a bit thin. I realized that sometimes real love must act without the beloved's consent. Sometimes nonconsensual, unilateral action is necessary if there is to be any possibility of interpersonal love and personal freedom. Suppose I find my wife unconscious and in cardiac arrest. In that condition, she will never love or exercise any kind of personal freedom if I do not work to revive her without her consent. Indeed, my love drives me to act without obtaining her consent. Whether love must act without the beloved's consent depends on the condition that the beloved is in. Compatibilists believe that Scripture asserts—and deeper Christian experience corroborates—that, until God regenerates us, all human beings are not merely spiritually sick but actually spiritually dead in our sin (Eph. 2:1).

Again, as I have begun to recognize just a little portion of my sinfulness, it has become clearer to me how much better my fellowship with my wife would be if I were free from all fickleness as well as from all temptation and sin. The reciprocity our fellowship requires is *not* the kind that only libertarian free will can give; in fact, our relationship flourishes the more we sense that our love for each other is strong and steady. Perfect fellowship rests in the knowledge that its parties will unfailingly affirm the value of their relationship; that neither party is going to back out and reject the other; that the love of each for the other is irrevocably fixed. This is the kind of love and fellowship that the Father and the Son and the Holy Spirit have shared with each other from eternity past. Therefore, it *cannot* be that only those who possess libertarian freedom are capable of entering into fellowship with each other and that all true love must involve some risk. And this kind of invari-

---

In Scripture, however, the transition from the imperfect to the perfect is brought about by God in an instant (see 1 Cor. 15:50-53). It is something that we thank God for, rather than something that we see ourselves as having produced (see 1 Cor. 15:57). It is the same with the beginning of our Christian lives (see Acts 13:48; Eph. 2:1-10; 1 Thess. 1:4-6).

[92] It is important to realize that the controversy between compatibilists and libertarians is not likely to be resolved merely by exegesis. As many libertarians and compatibilists admit, a seemingly convincing biblical case can (at least at first glance) be made for either position. This should not be surprising or disheartening because similar religious stalemates were common in our Lord's day (see John 8:12-58; Acts 5:17-42; Gal. 1:6–5:15). In the face of our profound disagreements, we must persist in examining (see Acts 17:10-12) and reasoning from the Scriptures (cf. Acts 17:1-4, 17; 18:19), testifying to what we take to be the truth (see Acts 10:42; 18:4, 5; Heb. 3:5; 1 John 1:2), while recognizing that Christian truth must ultimately be spiritually discerned (see Deut. 29:2-4; Ps. 119:18; Luke 8:9-10; 1 Cor. 2:1-16).

able love that knows no "shadow due to change" (James 1:17) will someday be the glorious possession of God's saints.

In the thirty-five years since my accident, I have found that my thinking about divine sovereignty and human freedom has shifted profoundly. I no longer ask, "What kind of human freedom is necessary to absolve God from having any part in the evils I see?" for I have become convinced that Scripture represents those evils as ordained by him, in part for the greater good of his saints. Now I ask, "What kind of human freedom is necessary for my heart to be fully fixed in God's righteousness? What will true freedom for God's saints be?" And when I turn to the Scriptures, I find that they answer: "Compatibilist freedom, the freedom to choose to be righteous without the possibility of choosing otherwise." This is the liberty that Scripture portrays as worth having. I know I remain responsible for my past, present, and future sins. Yet I know that, while I must still in this life work out my own salvation with fear and trembling, God is working within me both to will and to work for his good pleasure (see Phil. 2:12-13). I know that he who has chosen to appoint me to eternal life (see 1 Thess. 1:4-5 with Acts 13:48) will complete the work he has begun in me (see Phil. 1:6) when, one day, "in a moment, in the twinkling of an eye, at the last trumpet" (1 Cor. 15:52), he transforms me into the likeness of his sinless Son and thus ushers me into "the freedom of the glory of the children of God" (Rom. 8:21). True freedom is the freedom that God in Christ, in their own unchangeable mercy and faithfulness, work within us. By the gift of that freedom we are indeed set free. It is compatibilist and not libertarian freedom—that is, it is the freedom *not* to sin.

4

WHY OPEN THEISM
IS FLOURISHING NOW

William C. Davis

History is littered with unsuccessful attempts to turn Christians away from the God of the Bible. Many of these failures were too short-lived to merit even a footnote. Too complicated, isolated, or poorly developed, these temporary threats often collapse on their own. But other proposals for changing our understanding of God grow strong enough to deserve a vigorous response by the entire church. The strongest of these challenges in the past drove the church to speak with a single voice, both for the protection of the church and for the sake of God's honor.

Open theism is unquestionably an attempt to change the way Christians think about God. And even though it is relatively new as a self-conscious theological movement, its influence is evident in a surprising number of places. *Christianity Today* treats it as an evangelical option, offering both editorials that praise its proponents and links to the official open theism website. Thomas Nelson publishes and promotes *The Sacred Romance* and *Wild at Heart*. Although John Eldredge, author of one of the books and coauthor of the other, denies being an open theist,[1] these very popular books develop the open theist claim that God's desire for genuine love with free creatures leads him to take risks regarding the future. InterVarsity Press publishes and promotes Clark Pinnock's *The Openness*

---

[1] John Eldredge, *Wild at Heart: Discovering the Secret of a Man's Soul* (Nashville: Thomas Nelson, 2001), 32. He writes, "Trying to reconcile God's sovereignty and man's free will has stumped the church for ages. We must humbly acknowledge that there's a great deal of mystery involved, but for those aware of the discussion, I am not advocating open theism. Nevertheless, there is definitely something wild in the heart of God."

of God and John Sanders's *The God Who Risks*. Baker Books provides publisher's notes for booksellers that identify Gregory Boyd (*The God of the Possible*) and Clark Pinnock (*The Most Moved Mover*) as "evangelicals." Societies and gatherings of Christian scholars such as the Evangelical Theological Society[2] and the Wheaton Philosophy Conference[3] have welcomed and even showcased advocates of open theism.

Any effort to affect evangelical thought would be pleased by half this much success. Academic theologians and philosophers are taking the openness position seriously. Christian bookstores are giving it shelf space alongside the works of traditional theists. And maybe most importantly, the sources Christians are most likely to consult are either giving the movement a "pass" or actively promoting the position. InterVarsity Press, Baker Books, Thomas Nelson, and *Christianity Today* are all "authorities" that evangelicals are likely to trust. Even if evangelical scholars oppose open theism, acceptance by publishers and editors of Christian periodicals may enable the movement to succeed with the broader evangelical audience.

For these reasons and others, more and more evangelicals are finding open theism attractive. We must conclude that the movement has found conditions favorable to its flourishing. The purpose of this chapter is to explain the features of evangelicalism today that encourage the spread of open theism, as well as those features that make it so difficult to inhibit its growth. After sketching the major tenets of open theism, I will attempt to explain why our times are so disposed to finding the openness account of God attractive and to allow it a place in the evan-

---

[2] The relationship between the Evangelical Theological Society (ETS) and open theism has become quite complicated. At its 2001 meeting the ETS passed a resolution affirming the historic view of God's exhaustive foreknowledge. See David Neff's "Scholars Vote: God Knows the Future" in *Christianity Today* 46, no. 1 (7 January 2002): 21. Questions about the impact of the vote are also reported in David Neff's November 19, 2001 internet posting, "Foreknowledge Debate Clouded by 'Political Agenda,'" available at www.christianitytoday.com/ct/2001/147/13.0.html. At the 2002 ETS meeting in Toronto, the members voted by a slim majority to recommend that the executive committee examine charges regarding the compatibility of open theism and inerrancy. See Doug Koop's November 22, 2002 internet posting, "Evangelical Theological Society Moves Against Open Theists: Membership of Pinnock and Sanders Challenged by Due Process," available at www.christianitytoday.com/ct/2002/145/54.0.html. On the prospects for the ETS to set meaningful and effective boundaries, see chapter 10 in this volume.

[3] The October 2000 Wheaton Philosophy Conference theme was "The Providence of God," and a number of open theists (John Sanders, David Basinger, and William Hasker) were invited to present papers. Theologian R. K. McGregor Wright was asked to respond to Sanders, and concluded that open theists were "worshiping a different god." Most in the audience thought Wright had overstepped his place. They assumed that Wheaton would give only solid evangelicals such a prominent place at their conference.

gelical mainstream. The chapter will close with a discussion of what needs to happen for the church to reverse the trend.

I. THE QUESTION: WHY IS OPEN THEISM ON THE RISE NOW?

In order to explain why open theism is flourishing today, I need to answer two prior questions. First, what is "open theism"? And second, why think this rise is a problem? These questions receive attention in other chapters of this book, so my answers will be brief.

"Open theism" aims to rescue our understanding of God's relationship with his creatures from traditional theism.[4] According to advocates of open theism, traditional ("classical") theism overemphasizes God's immutability (unchangingness) and transcendence. Open theism instead stresses God's desire for a love relationship with us, and holds that in pursuit of this relationship God freely set aside his dominance over his creatures.[5] God could have remained transcendently lofty, but out of a desire for truly loving intimacy with us he set his transcendence aside and entered time with us. As a participant in time, God has made himself "open" to a future that is yet to be determined by both his and our choices. The "open" future is largely indeterminate until God and his free creatures collaborate in forming it. If God were to bring about his specific designs without genuinely collaborating with our choices, our free will would be violated and our dignity destroyed.

Proponents of open theism (or an "openness" view of God) believe their understanding of God makes it possible to solve a number of puz-

---

[4] The definitive statements of open theism are found in the works of Clark Pinnock, Gregory Boyd, John Sanders, Richard Rice, David Basinger, and William Hasker. *The Openness of God: A Biblical Challenge to the Traditional Understanding of God*, by Pinnock, Rice, Sanders, Hasker, and Basinger (Downers Grove, Ill.: InterVarsity Press, 1994) is a multi-disciplinary introduction. Gregory A. Boyd's *God of the Possible: A Biblical Introduction to the Open View of God* (Grand Rapids, Mich.: Baker, 2000) is more extensively exegetical; Pinnock's *Most Moved Mover: A Theology of God's Openness* (Grand Rapids, Mich.: Baker, 2001) is more philosophically ambitious.

[5] John Sanders summarizes the position at www.opentheism.org: "Open Theism (also called Free Will Theism) connects with the spirituality of many Christians throughout the history of the church especially when it comes to prayer. Many Christians feel that our prayers or lack of them can make a difference as to what God does in history. The Openness of God is an attempt to think out more consistently what it means that God enters into personal relationships with humanity. We want to develop an understanding of the triune God and God's relationship to the world that is Biblically faithful, finds consonance with the tradition, is theologically coherent and which enhances the way we live our Christian lives. On the core tenets of the Christian faith, we agree, but we believe that some aspects of the tradition need reforming, particularly when it comes to what is called 'Classical Theism.' We believe that some aspects of this model of God have led Christians to misread certain Scriptures and develop some serious problems in our understanding of God which affect the way we live, pray and answer the problem of evil."

zles that have vexed traditional accounts of God. These puzzles include explaining the presence of evil, the efficacy of prayer, human freedom and divine foreknowledge, and the possibility of meaningful worship. But puzzle solving is not their main objective. Their principal aim is to allow Christians to recover the joy of intimacy with their God.[6]

The explicit goal of deepening divine-human intimacy is commendable, and it has led many well-meaning evangelicals to read books by open theists.[7] As a result, Bible study groups, prayer partners, and private devotional lives are all coming under the influence of open theism. Often participants in these devotional activities report a renewed vitality to their spiritual life. God has never felt closer; their prayer life has never been so urgent and meaningful; their worship is alive in a new way.

If these were accounts of deepened relationships with the God of the Bible, they would be grounds for rejoicing. But because this exciting intimacy is with a convenient God ultimately at odds with God's self-revelation in Scripture, sorrow and alarm are more appropriate responses. Feelings of intimacy with a God-substitute should not be satisfying. Urgent prayers to any other God are pointless. And vibrant worship of a human invention is empty. Evangelicals are finding open theism exciting. But the excitement arises from an understanding of God that is not taught by the Bible and has never before been embraced by Christians. Because open theism is tempting evangelicals away from a relationship with the God of the Bible, it must be considered a dangerous development.

II. The First Part of the Answer: The Times Are Favorable

A. The Doctrinal Environment

One of the more striking features of open theism is its theoretical richness. Its foundation is a plausible account of the future as indeterminate,

---

[6] The pastoral focus is especially evident in the work of David Basinger (in the last chapter of *The Openness of God*) and Brent Curtis and John Eldredge, *The Sacred Romance* (Nashville: Thomas Nelson, 1997).

[7] Examples include: Curtis and Eldredge, *The Sacred Romance*; and John Eldredge, *Wild at Heart*. Eldredge denies being an open theist, but it is hard to accept his denial. He emphasizes God's risk-taking in the pursuit of a relationship with humans. The result is unpredictability, apparently even to God. God *"loves to come through*. He loves to show us that he has what it takes. It's not the nature of God to limit his risks and cover his bases. Far from it. Most of the time, he actually lets the odds stack up against him. . . . God's relationship with us and with our world is just that: a *relationship*. As with every relationship, there's a certain amount of unpredictability . . ." (*Wild at Heart*, 31ff.).

humans as radically free, and God as hungry for real love from his crea-tures. From this foundation arises a whirlwind of implications about God's plans, God's relationship to evil, and our role in bringing about the future. And even if its proponents wouldn't all like the label, open theism unquestionably constitutes a systematic theology. As a systematic theology, it arrives at an auspicious time. For at least a century, system-atic work in theology has been drifting farther and farther away from the practical needs and concerns of evangelical believers.[8] The work of main-line liberal theologians pays less and less attention to the actual words of Scripture. Reformed theologians stress God's transcendence so much that it is hard to imagine having a close relationship with him. Theologians working with Arminian assumptions push to one side the puzzles that come with saying that God knows the future with certainty without mak-ing human actions unfree.[9] Evangelicals don't have much affection for doctrine. Given their options, this isn't hard to understand. And it has provided an opportunity for open theism to advance its own system.

The task of alerting the church to the dangers of open theism would be much easier if the movement had nothing righteous to recommend it. But even though its ultimate understanding of God is unbiblical, significant features of the theological methodology of open theists are commendable. It is important for critics of open theism to admit this. If we do not, we are liable to deceive ourselves about the grip that open theism is capable of sustaining among believers. We will be too likely to think that right-thinking evangelicals will come to see through it, believ-ing that all its charms are illusory. Moreover, we will be tempted to think it sufficient to warn our sisters and brothers only in the most general terms, linking openness tendencies to other known demons such as "postmodernism" or "relativism." If openness were attractive only for deceptive or superficial reasons, that might be sufficient. But even though it arises from unjustifiable and unbiblical presuppositions, open theism's methodology has a number of features that give it both imme-diate credibility and even a measure of legitimate appeal.

The most obvious of its laudable features is its careful attention to

---

[8] On this point see Ellen Charry, *By the Renewing of Your Minds: The Pastoral Function of Christian Doctrine* (Oxford: Oxford University Press, 1999).

[9] Sanders's treatment of the standard Arminian understanding of God's knowledge of the future exposes some difficult problems. See his "Why Simple Foreknowledge Offers No More Providential Control Than the Openness of God," *Faith and Philosophy* 14 (1997): 26-40.

the details of the biblical text.[10] Unlike too many theological movements in the last century, open theism offers serious exegetical studies that labor to take the words of Scripture seriously. Its use of Scripture proceeds from presuppositions willing to sacrifice God's honor on the altar of human significance, but it still involves attempts at genuine exegesis. And sincere Christians appreciate honest efforts to take God's words seriously. Christians who have been living off a meager diet of sermons only tangentially related to the text of Scripture will find in the writings of Greg Boyd or John Sanders an attitude about Scripture that is refreshing. Malnourished believers are extremely unlikely to see the role that openness presuppositions about love and freedom are playing. What they'll see and feel is an invitation to take the Bible seriously. Since careful attention to Scripture is crucial to leading people away from openness thinking, any rejection of the movement must not squelch this legitimate desire.

The desire for close attention to the Bible's claims should not be surprising. It has been encouraged by years of evangelical emphasis on daily devotions and corporate Bible study. Emphasis on Bible study also helps to explain the pull exerted by open theism's focus on God's immanence. After a century of theology too often fascinated with God's transcendence and otherness, we shouldn't fault evangelicals for sensing the need to embrace God's immanence and pursue an intimate, growing relationship with him. Realizing the need to affirm both immanence and transcendence can only deepen our understanding of God. Openness pushes the pendulum recklessly far toward the immanence end of our account of God's majesty, but in itself the effort to unsettle rigid and unimaginative theology is welcome.

It is similarly difficult to fault those who are attracted to the willingness of open theists to reconsider the role that ancient Greek thought has played in the development of Christian theology.[11] Traditional theists should always be happy to look again at the history of doctrinal development. Augustine is not inerrant. Thomas Aquinas wasn't inspired the way Paul was when he wrote Galatians. Reason is fallen;

---

[10] Boyd's *God of the Possible* has this feature. Chapter 1 of Pinnock's *Most Moved Mover*, "The Scriptural Foundations," is less exegetically careful.

[11] See especially chapter 2 of Pinnock's *Most Moved Mover*, "Overcoming a Pagan Inheritance," as well as Sanders's historical discussion in *The Openness of God* and *The God Who Risks: A Theology of Divine Providence* (Downers Grove, Ill.: InterVarsity Press, 1998).

and Greek thought is full of unbiblical oddities. Even though open theists are wrong in concluding that Greek thought distorted Christian doctrine, we can commend efforts to revisit our past. And thus we shouldn't be surprised that this feature of openness writing appeals to Christians of good will.[12]

The interest open theists take in the past isn't the problem. Rather, it is their inconsistent approach to it. They insist that the ancient church was easily carried off by Greek thought. Yet they confidently assume that they are *not* being unduly influenced by twentieth-century thinking about freedom, love, and power. This confidence leads them to cast aside two millennia of Christian consensus too easily. Like jurors who overturn the presumption of innocence on the basis of a strong hunch, they overturn the presumption of the Holy Spirit's past guidance on the basis of their strong intuitions about love and freedom. Discerning the appropriate force to give to tradition is certainly a difficult matter. And many academic defenders of open theism are self-conscious about how little weight they are giving to traditional formulas and symbols. But most people attracted to openness thinking have never considered what role tradition ought to play. If in part they are attracted by the attention that open theists pay to the influence of Greek thinking, their interest is appropriate. Critics of open theism need to be careful not to undermine a legitimate interest in our history and a willingness to hold it up to the light of Scripture.[13]

A fourth legitimate strength of the work of many proponents of openness is its emphasis upon pastoral concerns. John Sanders's short answer to the question, "What is open theism?" (at www.openthe-ism.org) professes that the entire system arises from a concern for our relationship with God, and in particular our prayer life. David Basinger's contribution to *The Openness of God* similarly focuses on the ways in which proponents of open theism hope to enable a deeper intimacy between God and his people. Some defenses of openness focus on abstract philosophical matters (the indeterminacy of the future, libertarian vs. compatibilist theories of human freedom, or anti-Molinist

---

[12] For a critique of the open theists' thesis about the role of Greek thought, see chapters 1 and 2 in this volume.

[13] David Lyle Jeffrey addresses this issue in, "Houses of the Interpreter: Spiritual Exegesis and the Revival of Authority," *Books and Culture* 8, no. 3 (May/June 2002): 30-32.

arguments[14]), but the works that appeal to a broad evangelical audience stress the power of open theism to bring believers palpably nearer to God. Tackling very difficult pastoral needs head on, open theism purports to offer answers to an array of perennial problems. It has developed its answers in ways accessible to a nonacademic audience, with little jargon and in user-friendly formats such as devotional guides and websites. And its answers almost never offer "mystery" as the best we can do in answering some of Christianity's thorniest questions. Why does God allow horrendous evil in the world? Why should I pray if God already knows what is going to happen? Does God share in my grief over a particular disappointment or loss? Does God really delight in my worship or work?

Evangelicals worry about these things, and open theism provides answers that appear both rationally plausible and psychologically satisfying. God prevents all the evil he can without violating our freedom. God needs our prayers in order to finalize his plans about what to do next. God's grief is more profoundly empathetic than we can comprehend. Our worship adds to God's growing pleasure in his creation in a way that nothing else can. For Christians who have been languishing under thin, vague, or needlessly abstract teaching, the answers from open theists offer more comfort and satisfaction than they've thought possible. And coming in the midst of a proudly individualistic and self-absorbed age, they are answers that vindicate both God and those hearing the message. God's ways *can* make sense to us; and our actions *are* as independent of God as they feel to us.

Lamentably, these answers come only at the cost of God's majesty. While the proponents of openness are aware that their solutions involve whittling away at God's traditional attributes, to most people such costs are too subtle and abstract to matter. Open theists believe that the gains, however, are gripping and concrete. Critics of the openness view may believe that this is a higher price than God's Word allows us to pay for intellectual satisfaction and psychological solace, but we must not overlook the reality of the intellectual and psychological needs that make open

---

[14] William Hasker has been especially active. See his chapter-length treatments, "The Absence of a Timeless God," in *God and Time: Essays on the Divine Nature*, ed. Gregory Ganssle (Oxford: Oxford University Press, 2002), 182-206; "The Foreknowledge Conundrum," *International Journal for the Philosophy of Religion* 50 (2001): 97-114; and "Anti-Molinism Is Undefeated!" *Faith and Philosophy* 17 (2000): 126-131.

theism attractive. Even though the openness solutions are false and ultimately injurious, these questions are real and deserve attention that is accessible and sensitive. Even when their work injures the church, open theists should not be faulted for addressing these troubling questions.

One final feature of openness offerings deserves to be mentioned: they claim to be pursuing the absolute truth about God and his relationship to us. As buffeted as Christians have been by cultural forces urging tolerant and comfortable pluralism, conscientious children of God know that there is a truth of the matter about God. In part, this can be attributed to an excessive confidence about the power of human reason that has been with us since the Enlightenment; but it is more than that. The Holy Spirit works in each of us to open the eyes of our heart to the truths of the gospel (Eph. 1:18). We are made to see that Christ's work is the only way to be right with God. Other ways are false ways, not equally valid alternatives. Our spiritual ears are opened to hear our master's voice (John 10:27-30). The other competing voices are false masters, not our true master with a muffled voice.

Open theism is consistent with this exclusivist understanding of the gospel. Some of its defenders are unclear on Christ being the only way, but the core doctrine is not a pluralist project. They claim to be pursuing *the* truth about God, not one of many truths about God. The non-Christian world is increasingly hostile to Christian claims to know the truth, especially when the truth conflicts with the beliefs of other groups or religions. An important part of the appeal of openness thinking stems from a righteous desire by evangelicals to assert what the Holy Spirit has enabled them to see and hear. God has revealed himself in Scripture. We can know him. Even more importantly, he wants us to know him as a person, not just as an *idea*. Traditional theists too often have urged the faithful to cling to their idea of God because it is part of a beautiful system or because it is traditional. That is like urging the faithful to partake of the Lord's Supper because the wine is good or because we've been doing it for a long time. Conscientious believers know better, and shouldn't be faulted for seeking out intimacy with God himself. Open theism is a flawed systematic theology, but it is successful in part because it connects theology to the believer's desire to know God more intimately.

B. The Cultural Environment

Although open theists are typically pursuing the objective truth about God and a deeper relationship with him, their conclusions find a receptive audience today because they fit comfortably within recent currents in American thought. Here I will consider four influential trends. The first might be called the "Nietzschean expectation," a generalized suspicion that all authority rests only on power and serves only to maintain power structures. Exacerbating this Nietzschean expectation is an even older fascination with human autonomy. Jealous guarding of human independence is as old as the garden of Eden, but at least since Mill's *On Liberty* what had been a guilty jealousy has swelled and gained extraordinary legitimacy. The third trend is a peculiarly American brand of pragmatism, an antipathy to theory and an impatience with mystery. The recent expansion of American pragmatism is the fourth trend. It might be called "capitulation to Rorty's challenge." This capitulation is resignation to the belief that zeal for the truth is always damaging to community. According to this understanding of community, we must always choose between doctrinal precision and a flourishing life together. In order to see how these cultural currents contribute to the rise of open theism it is necessary to explain each in more detail.

SUSPICION OF AUTHORITY

Resistance to authority is a hardy perennial of human existence, but disdain for the possibility of benevolent authority is relatively new. Reformation, Renaissance, and Enlightenment thinkers had serious misgivings about the way churches and monarchs exercised their power,[15] but in all three of those cases the culture at large believed that rulers could be found who would rise above their own interests. Many looked to their own churches for examples of authorities who exercised power for the good of the governed. Church rulers were expected to be servant-leaders. Most people believed that benevolent authority was possible because they saw it in their priests, elders, and deacons. Similar judg-

---

[15] For influential examples from each era, see Martin Luther, "Address to the German Nobility," in *Martin Luther: Selections from His Writings* (New York: Doubleday, 1972); Montaigne, "On Presumption," in *The Complete Essays of Montaigne,* trans. Donald M. Frame (Palo Alto, Calif.: Stanford University Press, 1989); and Voltaire, "A Treatise on Toleration," in *Reading About the World,* ed. Paul Brians et al., vol. 2 (Orlando: Harcourt, 1999).

ments were formed about successful civic leaders such as George Washington or John Witherspoon.

In the last century, however, confidence about the possibility of self-sacrificial power has been largely undermined. In part this has been the result of a series of wicked rulers, but cynical expectations have been reinforced by efforts to show that all power is oppressive. I will refer to these efforts collectively as the "Nietzschean expectation."[16] According to this line of thinking, humans are like all other animals: they are driven to dominate as much of their environment as they can. Whether we admit it or not, everything we do or say aims to extend our power. No action is ever truly self-sacrificing. No words are ever intended only to heal. And every exercise of power is aimed at keeping the powerless on the outside, marginalized and ineffective. This view paints a dismal picture of humans and human authority. But because we are fallen, it is a plausible picture. We know our own hearts well enough to know that it accurately describes us far too often. And we have seen others use power this way most, if not all, of the time. Apart from the restraining work of the Holy Spirit, it could well be a complete picture of humanity.[17]

The Nietzschean expectation is common in Western culture, but its influence is also evident among evangelical Christians. Along with the rest of our times, we are cynical of authority. We have long given up on disinterested benevolence from our political leaders. Skillful management of the economy, relief from foreign entanglements, and some measure of "homeland security" is all we dare to hope for. Expectations about our neighbors and friends are similarly less trusting than they were even fifty years ago. Most tragically, however, this cynicism about authority has infected our thinking about spiritual authority. We have seen too many corrupt church leaders and are quick to be suspicious of the motives and abilities of human spiritual leaders. Sadly, we are also tempted to believe that God's power is susceptible to the tendency to oppress his subjects.

---

[16] After Friedrich Nietzsche, the late nineteenth-century German philosopher and literary critic. The connection between oppressive power and authority is central to Nietzsche's work. See especially *On the Genealogy of Morals* (Indianapolis, Ind.: Hackett, 1998). His works are still very popular and many influential thinkers of the twentieth century have extended this expectation in their work. Albert Camus, Michel Foucault, and Jacques Derrida all build explicitly on Nietzsche's work.

[17] Richard Mouw's *He Shines in All That's Fair* (Grand Rapids, Mich.: Eerdmans, 2001) argues for this conclusion.

Open theists offer a God who has renounced absolute power, defusing the threat posed by the Nietzschean expectation. Instead of the God of the Bible whose sovereign rule is all-powerful without being oppressive, the God of the open theists willingly sets aside sovereign command out of a jealous regard for the autonomy of his human creatures. Even though open theists would agree that God's rule is not oppressive, their portrayal of God avoids the question. The God of the open theists chooses not to run the risk of being labeled a tyrant.[18]

INFATUATION WITH LIBERTY

One of the defining myths of Enlightenment modernism is the conviction that individual liberty is always a good thing. Freedom to pursue my own understanding of the good life, freedom to do as I please so long as it doesn't hurt anyone else, and freedom to be true to myself are all seen as unmixed goods. Near the heart of this myth is the belief that significance depends on autonomy, the right to be a law unto myself. Submission that compels beyond what I would choose on my own is slavery, no matter how it is dressed up. Even vows that I voluntarily took in the past are ultimately inimical to real liberty.

Personal autonomy, the power of genuine alternate choice, is an obvious possession for most evangelicals. Philosophers refer to this as a "libertarian" understanding of human freedom.[19] On this view, people are free only if they could (really) have done otherwise than they did when they made their choice. It is not enough for them to *think* that they could have done otherwise. They really had to have been able to do other than they did. Consider an example. If my arms are tied securely behind my back, I am *able* to choose to keep my arms still. But because

---

[18] Consider Eldredge in *The Sacred Romance,* 76: "Satan mounted his rebellion through the power of one idea: God doesn't have a good heart. Though it seems almost incomprehensible, he deceived a multitude of the heavenly host by sowing the seed of doubt in their minds that God was somehow holding out on them. After the insurrection is squelched, that question lingers in the universe like smoke from a forest fire. Sure, God won, but it took force to do it. Power isn't the same thing as goodness. As the lead actor in the story, God *seems* generous and self-giving, but perhaps he's just big. Maybe his motive is simply to be in charge. At the end of Act II, our hero's heart has been called into question." Eldredge argues that God vindicates the goodness of his heart by giving humans freedom "in order for a true romance to occur" (77). Whether Eldredge would affirm God's exhaustive knowledge of the future is unclear. His emphasis on the need for risk taking and freedom in order for there to be a "true romance," however, is clearly in line with the emphases of open theism, and especially of the work of John Sanders.

[19] A clear statement of the libertarian view of freedom that finds it obviously true can be found in Scott Davison's chapter, "Divine Providence and Human Freedom," in *Reason for the Hope Within,* ed. Michael J. Murray (Grand Rapids, Mich.: Eerdmans, 1998), 217-237.

I can't really do anything else, calling that a *free* choice is inappropriate. If my arms are untied (and no new restraints are imposed), then if I choose to leave my arms behind my back the choice is free. I could have done otherwise. The libertarian theory of freedom holds that a choice is free only if it is really possible to do otherwise.[20]

The philosophical implications of this view of freedom are far-reaching. Here, however, it is sufficient to note only two things. First, this understanding of what it means to be free is thought to be an undeniable fact about human existence. We are aware of what it feels like to be free (and what it feels like not to be free); and on this subject no authority can be superior to the way things clearly seem. Second, with this understanding of freedom, a person's life is insignificant and morally pointless unless the person is free in the libertarian sense.[21] When it is later discovered that this kind of freedom is very hard to reconcile with God's exhaustive foreknowledge, God's omniscience becomes a threat both to the highest recognized authority (how things seem) and to human moral significance (which depends on libertarian freedom). Open theists offer to preserve us from having to choose between God's claims to know the future in detail and our freedom, and they promise to make God's Lordship over history no threat to our significance.

Along with this confidence about libertarian freedom of choice has come an individualistic understanding of social realities. Most evangelicals willingly accept that humans are each God-like unmoved movers in their morally significant choices. And because this is a fundamental fact, no grouping of individuals can ever really be more than a temporary and voluntary collection of people. We may say that in marriage husband and wife become "one flesh," but this is thought to be either poetry or a veiled allusion to sexual intimacy. We may sing, "We are one in the Spirit / We are one in the Lord," but we can't mean it literally. The "body of Christ" must be a metaphor, not a reality. Otherwise, our liberty would be constrained by our connection to each other.

Even worse, because it is popular to define human freedom first and

---

[20] For a fuller explanation and critique of libertarian freedom, see Mark R. Talbot's chapter in this volume.

[21] An influential source for this position is the work of Kierkegaard. See his *Journals and Papers*, VII:I A 181 (Hong and Hong 1251) in *Søren Kierkegaard's Journals and Papers*, ed. Howard V. Hong and Edna H. Hong (Bloomington, Ind.: Indiana University Press, 1970). This is a prominent theme in most existentialist thought.

everything else in light of it, the most natural description of our relationship with God is one of mutual dependence. The common view is that, like God, we are radically independent in our free choices. It may be gauche to say, "God needs me," or, "God is powerless until I choose to heed his call," but it follows from this exalted view of human freedom. And quite a number of evangelicals are comfortable believing what it is gauche to say: our freedom gives us the power to make God either modify his plans around our choices or wait for circumstances more favorable to his purposes. Open theists insist that God is omni-resourceful, able to get his way in most circumstances without resorting to freedom-violating force.[22] And while omni-resourcefulness falls well short of the sovereign omnipotence of traditional theism, thinking of God in this way makes God's power no threat to our freedom.

Such an exalted understanding of human freedom is typically qualified, however. Even open theists concede that God doesn't depend on us in order to realize his general plans. But if he wants us to be significant, responsible contributors to the realization of his plans, then God must lay aside his ability to get his will by force. In line with our culture's infatuation with liberty, evangelical thinking about freedom loosens the connections between husbands and wives, and between members of churches. And it makes us receptive to the idea that God is dependent upon us in order to fulfill his designs. I am not here suggesting that open theists hope to loosen their ties to their spouses, or even to make God dependent upon them. The point is only that we live in an age when jealous regard for our autonomy makes us increasingly willing to accept these implications. This is fertile soil for the growth of open theism.

IMPATIENCE WITH MYSTERY

A third feature of American culture disposing evangelicals toward open theism is our pragmatic spirit. Noted by visitors since de Tocqueville in the first part of the nineteenth century,[23] Americans share a preference for doing over theorizing. We are a nation that gets things done, willing to

---

[22] According to at least Boyd, Rice, Pinnock, and Hasker, God can usually get his way. Typically God does this by managing the circumstances in ways highly likely to result in our freely choosing what he desires. In some cases, though, God must force events. But open theists expect that these cases are rare, and may never involve overriding human freedom. For interaction with Boyd's proposal in particular, see chapter 8 in this volume.

[23] Alexis de Tocqueville, *Democracy in America* (New York: Bantam, 2000), orig. 1835.

explain why things work only after seeing that the theory has a use. We are offended by loose ends, delayed closure, and complexity not rewarded by increased efficiency. In theological matters this expresses itself as distaste for doctrinal wrangling and impatience with mystery. Both of these sentiments advance the fortunes of open theism. Following the Bible's caution against presuming to comprehend God, traditional theism is willing to admit that some questions can be answered only with submission to the mystery of God's majesty. More satisfying to American sensibilities, though, is open theism's offer of mystery-free explanations. And when traditional theists attempt to expose open theism's dangers, they are accused of committing the social crime of pointless disputation. Deliverance from mystery makes open theism attractive to American evangelicals. Moreover, the prospect of unpleasant theological debates does more than offend. It threatens beliefs currently in vogue about the nature of a healthy community.

PRAGMATISM ABOUT COMMUNITY

In "Solidarity or Objectivity?" Richard Rorty expresses an increasingly common American expectation, arguing that we must choose between two conceptions of our life together.[24] On the one hand, we can choose to pursue genuine, flourishing community (solidarity), but that will be possible only if we abandon the myth that there are community-transcending truths. On the other hand, we can pursue a life based on community-transcending truths (such as universal human rights), but to do so means abandoning any expectations about achieving real community. This second alternative he calls "objectivity." This choice between objective truth and real community, he insists, is both momentous and unavoidable. Rorty's aim is to draw all Americans into the common project of liberal democracy. Evangelical Christians have largely rejected his suggestion that the church is a threat to a thriving American community. But they have internalized two of his conclusions about the nature of true community.

The first of these conclusions about community concerns the relationship between consensus and authority. According to Rorty, the only

---

24 Richard Rorty, "Solidarity or Objectivity?" in *Post-Analytic Philosophy*, ed. John Rajchman and Cornel West (New York: Columbia University Press, 1985), 3-19.

legitimate foundation for authority is the consent of the governed. For Americans this should sound familiar (it is presumed in the Declaration of Independence). In the case of civil government, the consent of the governed is very important. But spiritual authority in the church does not rest ultimately upon consent. God calls his people out of the world into a body; and God sets apart people to shepherd them. When Christians think about church authority the way they think about civil authority, they come to expect that their consent is always necessary to command their obedience. They are also tempted to resent even legitimate exercises of church discipline. And they are even tempted to think it tyrannical of God to rule merely according to the counsel of his own will. Open theists exploit this temptation, offering a God who constrains his rule by the choices of his creatures. While the God of the open theists does at times find it necessary to override human choices, it is only as a last resort. Cooperative creation of the future is what the openness God desires, since any other kind of rule destroys community.

A second conclusion about community advanced by Rorty and influencing evangelicals concerns the pursuit of truth.[25] Rorty argues that fascination with the truth destroys community. It is not possible, according to Rorty, to pursue both real community and community-transcendent truth. Community is maintained by a commitment to each other that bears with differences over theoretical detail. Anyone who insists that some should be excluded for the sake of the truth is a threat to the peace of the community. With this understanding of a flourishing community, tolerance is the preeminent virtue. Church discipline is viewed as a destructive power play, an expression of political ambition rather than love. Because open theism is a direct rejection of central doctrines about God's knowledge and relationship to his creatures, it can only benefit from an environment in which doctrinal disputes are widely viewed as threats to Christian community. Churches will be tempted to find a way to tolerate open theism as only a minor divergence from their doctrinal standards. To view it as more than a minor divergence would demand a doctrinal dispute that would undermine the peace of the body.

---

[25] For a clear instance of Rorty's influence on evangelical thought, see Philip Kenneson, "There Is No Such Thing as Objective Truth, and It's a Good Thing, Too," in *Christian Apologetics in the Postmodern World*, ed. Timothy R. Phillips and Dennis L. Okholm (Downers Grove, Ill.: InterVarsity Press, 1995), 155-170.

As long as truth is thought to be a threat to community solidarity, open theism will be safe.

C. The Spiritual Environment

Current doctrinal and cultural environments are conducive to the rise of open theism. But they aren't sufficient in themselves to account for it. Why, then, is the openness understanding of God so attractive right now? The short answer is that the spiritual climate of American evangelicalism is peculiarly disposed to find it attractive and succumb to its charms. Two features of our current situation combine to nurture the spread of open theism. In the first place, unmet spiritual needs and ecclesiastical individualism make evangelicals receptive to the claims of open theists. This receptivity alone is not a sufficient explanation, however, since the church should possess the means to protect its members from such unbiblical teachings. But impediments to open theism that ought to be protecting the church are absent or malfunctioning. I will discuss the receptive environment first.

With the rest of our culture, American evangelicals possess a number of felt needs that are not being met. Many of these needs are legitimate. Reconciliation with our neighbors, a place in a vital community, intimacy with God, and intellectual stimulation are just a few of the good things that we righteously desire. And despite the universality of these desires, American culture is inimical to realizing them. Divorce rates, frantic work demands, and an entertainment industry geared to passive and individual pleasures all contribute to a brooding sense of alienation and abandonment. Real friendships are old-fashioned; neighbors you trust are distant memories; families that nurture are endangered. The legitimate need for loving relationships and a safe home is often unmet. Very few think of the church as a likely place of remedy. Even evangelicals are hungry for reliable promises of mutual commitment.

Part of our desire for mutual commitment is a desire for stability, but evangelicals have also absorbed our culture's preference for novelty, and this includes theological novelty. With the rest of American culture, evangelicals increasingly prefer the young, the new, and the immediate. Skillfully managed new ideas are likely to get a hearing just because of their "buzz." Distribution options without any editorial control enable a mounting flood of new ideas and "hype" to circulate. This puts pressure on publishers of even Christian books to acknowledge the latest idea, deepening the perception that the idea is "mainstream" and worthy of consideration. Open theists have benefited from this trend, receiving increased attention simply because their ideas are new.

THE EMERGENCE OF EXTRA-ECCLESIAL CHRISTIANITY

The broader culture's suspicion regarding authority finds an evangelical expression in the growth of "para-church" substitutes. Church alternatives or supplements are numerous: InterVarsity Christian Fellowship, Bible Study Fellowship, Campus Crusade for Christ, Promise Keepers, Baptist Student Union, homeschooling networks, and so forth. All of these organizations meet real and important needs, and the problem is not their existence. The problem is rather the extent to which they can allow their participants to treat the organization as their spiritual home. Sometimes even against the intentions of the organizers, these groups can take the place of the local church as the center of their participants' spiritual lives. The success of the para-church organization can become more important than the health of the local church. The participants can come to care more about pleasing others in the para-church organization than about pleasing fellow members of their local church. Some even come to believe that active participation in a para-church group is an adequate substitute for being a church member at all.

However, even the most spiritually vital and biblically faithful para-church organizations cannot offer authoritative spiritual oversight. Because they are not created as substitutes for churches, they do not have leaders set apart by ordination; they do not typically administer the sacraments; and they don't receive members by baptism or the taking of vows. And because they are not churches, they cannot presume that their leaders are set apart by the Spirit for the care of believers. The Spirit may empower their work, but they may not claim to exercise discipline as Christ's representative. The ordained overseers of churches may do so. Whatever title is used (e.g., elder, deacon, brother, priest), the New Testament is clear that leaders set apart by ordination are crucial to the life of the church.[26] Para-church organizations often do good and important work, and they regularly provide faithful church members with edifying opportunities for fellowship, service, and mutual encouragement. But they can also unwittingly suggest that properly ordained spiritual oversight is unnecessary.[27] In an age that already assumes that all associations are voluntary human constructions, these organizations can easily reinforce among their participants the broader culture's confusions about personal autonomy and the expectation that every association—even the church—is a voluntary human construction.

Love of personal liberty manifests itself among evangelicals in two ways that are especially helpful to the rise of open theism. The first is a clear preference for explicitly voluntary Christian associations. Churches rightly require vows from church members. These vows bind the members beyond a passing enchantment with the group. Para-church groups offer the benefits of "membership" without any vows and without any submission to ordained leaders. A second manifestation of the love of autonomy is the conviction that every Christian is equipped to make choices without any authoritative guidance. Clear guidance about devotional materials or theological literature is hard to find anywhere in evangelical Christianity. In part this is because Christians are not asking for it. Para-church individualism may encourage the belief that every believer is competent to be his or her own shepherd.

Confident autonomy and suspicion of binding authority are not the only forces encouraging evangelicals to find their spiritual home outside of specific churches. Culturally popular expectations about the relationship between authority and real community also play a role. Evangelicals have largely accepted the suggestion that any exercise of authority undermines community. As a result, they are less likely to seek spiritual nurture inside a structure that requires submission to ordained shepherds. But they still know that intimate fellowship is vital to spiritual growth. Para-church groups provide a visible home among

---

[26] See 1 Peter 5:1-4; 1 Timothy 3:1-7; and especially Acts 20:17ff: "From Miletus, Paul sent to Ephesus for the elders of the church. When they arrived, he said to them . . . 'Keep watch over yourselves and all the flock of which the Holy Spirit has made you overseers. Be shepherds of the church of God, which he bought with his own blood. I know that after I leave, savage wolves will come in among you and will not spare the flock. Even from your own number men will arise and distort the truth in order to draw away disciples after them. So be on your guard!'" (NIV).

[27] For a similar line of reasoning, see Brian Habig and Les Newsom, *The Enduring Community: Embracing the Priority of the Church* (Jackson, Miss.: Reformed University Press, 2002).

informally committed believers. These are communities built on consensus, not submission. These groups often construct impressive and effective systems of accountability, but it is voluntary accountability to leaders whose authority is ratified by individual members. It is not submission to shepherds set apart by God's ordination. This falls short of the rich life of the church possible in submission to God-ordained shepherds, but it is considerably better than the emptiness of modern life. And with fewer and fewer models of community built on submission, for many evangelicals these consensus-based communities are the only alternatives to the modern emptiness that they know.

Within Christian communities defined by consensus, "doctrine" is the acknowledged enemy of unity. The pursuit of theological discipline is always unpleasant because it attacks group consensus, the real foundation of the voluntary association. Accordingly, almost all the fundamentals are negotiable for the sake of peace within the community. Peace is the precondition for the maintenance of the community, instead of being the consequence of mutual submission to God's Word and to the shepherds he is holding responsible. And because peace must precede community, differences of age, ethnic culture, economic status, or education are inevitably problematic. Even though Christian community is supposed to be a picture of the irrelevance of these divisions for those captured by the Spirit, we are instead drawn to more and more homogeneous spiritual "homes." College ministries offer young adults a community experience without the inconvenience of restless little children, older believers they ought to imitate and respect, and the marginally educated. Segment-specific Bible studies cater to similarly narrow demographic groups.

These developments make it less and less likely that Christians will be willing to support the unpleasant task of excluding or even denouncing errors that hurt the church. Having gained a degree of acceptance, open theism will be very hard to condemn clearly. And para-church Christianity will find it even more difficult than churches with ordained leaders. The movement of evangelicals out from under ordained oversight provides open theists with a safe environment. This is especially evident among Christian theologians and philosophers. A significant amount of theological discussion today takes place out from under the oversight of ordained shepherds. Participants act as Christian intellectuals at-large, submitting to no oversight other than the good will of the conference organizers. Open theism benefits from this arrangement. Once the conference begins, no one has the right to offer an authoritative judgment about the assertions of open theists. And if anyone does call the orthodoxy of open theism into question, then the openness position gains the advantage of being seen as a victim of intolerance.

In parallel with the move of evangelicals to para-church identities, more and more Christian theologians and philosophers are treating professional associations as their own para-church homes. Groups like the American Academy of Religion, the Society of Biblical Languages, and the Society of Christian Philosophers can become for professional Christian scholars a kind of spiritual home. They easily become places where Christian academics have their talents nurtured. They find Christians with similar challenges and burdens who are able to appreciate the peculiar struggles they face as believers with academic gifts and responsibilities. Unlike the local church or a particular denomination, these groups offer spiritual encouragement without the inconvenience of ordained spiritual oversight. Academic freedom is respected to an almost unlimited degree. The oversight that exists is carried out by other academics and is typically limited to procedural rather than substantive matters. The threat of having mere engineers, contractors, or salespeople question their work doesn't arise. For these academics, the core of their Christian life—where their faith intersects with their most cherished activities—can come to be located outside of the local church and its ordained oversight. As with other para-church homes, it is extra-ecclesial Christianity.

The absence of functioning ordained oversight in these academic organizations forces the opponents of open theism into an impossible situation. The move of academics away from ordained oversight has been consistent with the twentieth-century suspicion that any exercise of authority rests either on consensus or on the oppressive use of power. According to the Nietzschean expectation, even apparently principled stands are just disguised impositions by those with the power to get their way. Unless handled very carefully, efforts to exclude open theism from such organizations threaten to confirm these expectations about power, consensus, and spiritual authority.

SHEEP WITHOUT SHEPHERDS

Cultural trends and evolving thinking about church identity have provided fertile soil for the growth of open theism. But the speed of its move into the mainstream has also depended on the failure of efforts to impede it. Critics of openness have been sounding an alarm, but in general the God-ordained means for protecting God's flock are malfunctioning. While many strategies could effectively arrest the spread of openness influence, the only authority that can legitimately command obedience is the collective judgment of overseers set apart by ordination. Conservative scholars may be able most clearly to explain the dangers posed by open theism's understanding of God and his dealings with his people, but only ordained overseers have the biblical authority to condemn the error. Open theists have enjoyed the absence of effective resistance because the link that should exist between academics and ordained overseers is broken.

Complicating matters, the link has been broken for a long time. Both liberal and conservative Christian academics have drifted away from doing their work as church members. For a variety of reasons, evangelical Christian scholars find it natural to see their work as independent of ordained spiritual oversight. One reason is the insistence that academic freedom is inconsistent with ecclesiastical oversight. Another reason for the drift is the tendency for nonacademic overseers to greet scholarly work with either suspicion or a yawn. This response from ordained overseers has encouraged evangelical academics to seek their main spiritual encouragement for their work in extra-ecclesial organizations. These tendencies to resist oversight and to suspect theological expertise are mutually reinforcing. The result is a downward spiral away from a healthy community in which academic talents are encouraged to flourish under the careful oversight of God's appointed shepherds.

Movement away from a productive partnership between academics and ordained overseers has reached a point favorable to the spread of open theism. In the absence of mutual trust between theologians and ordained leaders, peace is maintained by a kind of détente. Theologians remain nominally under ordained oversight in exchange for the "freedom" to explore within very wide boundaries. Overseers exclude only the blatantly rebellious in exchange for the prestige of retaining influential authors and professors. This arrangement might work reasonably well if the church were composed only of academics and ordained leaders. But they aren't the whole church, and neither group has the luxury of pretending that they are. Both the academics and the overseers have their gifts primarily for the building up of the body. And the current peace-preserving relationship is hurting the church, denying it guidance that it needs.[28]

Speculation by open theists about God's relationship to his creatures might seem like the benign work of ivory-tower academics. Far too often philosophers and theologians busy themselves with issues and disputes that are as impractical as they are heated. But the work of open theists is different. They are publishing articles, books, and web discussions that are widely read, especially by other academics and authors. These readers, in turn, exert their own influence as seminary professors, college teachers, and writers of devotional literature. Pastors, youth workers, Bible-study leaders, and Sunday school teachers have their thinking shaped by professors, teachers, and popular authors. This chain of influence from academic open theists to Bible studies can already be seen. In this case at least, ivory-tower speculation is having very practical consequences.

Ordained church overseers do not have the option of treating open theism as a passing fad. And even though the link is broken between academics and overseers, both must take steps to work together to give believers the guidance that they have every right to expect. Does God know the future? Church members can easily find books, Bible study groups, and even sermons that offer conflicting opinions. How they answer that question has profound implications for the progress of their spiritual life, the kinds of prayers they offer, and their approach to worship. Is God frustrated by specific acts of evil? Once again, the range of answers that they can find in print and elsewhere is staggering. And the answers believers settle on will affect their ability to give an answer for their faith, as well as affecting their appreciation for Christ's sacrificial death. The questions are many and far-reaching, and many entrusted by

---

[28] The evolution of church leadership away from spiritual oversight and toward professional management is helpfully discussed by Darryl Hart in, "Whatever Happened to Office? Ordination and the Crisis of Leadership in American Protestantism," *Touchstone* 6, no. 3 (Summer 1993): 12-16.

God with the spiritual nurture of believers are apparently unwilling or unable to give the guidance they need and should expect.

Reluctance to offer specific guidance is understandable given the Nietzschean expectation, but in some cases careful shepherds will need to warn against specific views. Before this suggestion is drowned out by the howls of Christian scholars, I hasten to add that specific exclusion should not happen very often.[29] It is necessary in the case of open theism precisely because it has been developed in detail and published widely apart from effective ordained oversight. When new theological systems are developed and widely distributed apart from ordained supervision, specific exclusion is much more likely both to be necessary and to be injurious to the peace and health of the church. Until the link of trust between academics and overseers is repaired, it is likely that the church will frequently have to choose between disturbing the peace by wholesale public rejections and enduring the confusion that attends disjointed local efforts to counter errors.

However it is delivered, the shepherding guidance that Christians need most is denomination-specific. Pastors and other ordained leaders of their local congregations should be the first place Christians are looking for suggestions about what to read and warnings about errors to avoid. These local leaders, in turn, ought to be able to look to their conferences and broader assemblies for guidance. No denomination can effectively make spiritual demands of authors and teachers outside their membership, so no assembly or conference can decide for everyone what is or is not acceptable. But they can and must give guidance to their members. And members ought to be looking to them for direction and warnings. Evangelical church members have a right to hear from their local and denominational leaders whether open theism is an acceptable understanding of God. As it turns out, clear guidance of this kind is hard to achieve.

TWO EFFORTS AT GUIDANCE BY EXCLUSION

In June of 2000, the Baptist General Conference considered two resolutions relating to open theism. Their deliberations focused on the crucial openness contention that God does not know the future

---

[29] For specific criteria, see Wayne Grudem's chapter in this volume.

exhaustively (because the future won't exist until free creatures make their choices). The first of the two resolutions asked the Conference to say clearly that God does know the future exhaustively. It read:

> Be it resolved that we, the delegates of the Baptist General Conference (who are also the delegates of Bethel College and Seminary) affirm that God's knowledge of all past, present and future events is exhaustive; and, we also believe that the "openness" view of God's foreknowledge is contrary to our fellowship's historic understanding of God's omniscience.[30]

This resolution passed. Had it been the Conference's only word on open theism, the entire denomination would have had the benefit of clear guidance. Pastoral efforts to discourage their congregations from being seduced by openness thinking would have been strengthened. Staffing decisions by the denominational college and seminary would have been simplified. Members of Conference churches would have been spared the distress and confusion of wondering whether questions about God's foreknowledge have answers.

But it was not the only word from the Conference on the matter. On the day of the vote, a second resolution was added to the agenda. It read:

> Be it resolved that the statement on the doctrine of God in the 1951 Affirmation of Faith is sufficiently stated; and, in regard to the subject of Open Theism, as delegates of the Baptist General Conference (who are also the delegates of Bethel College and Seminary) we affirm that [Open Theist] Dr. [Greg] Boyd's views did not warrant his termination as a member of the Bethel College faculty and by inference that his views fall within the accepted bounds of the evangelical spectrum.[31]

This resolution also passed. While it is possible to reconcile these two assertions (by stipulating that open theism is an insignificant deviation from the Bible's teaching[32]), the passage of this second resolution leaves

---

[30] Quoted from John Piper, "We Took a Good Stand and Made a Bad Mistake: Reflections on the Baptist General Conference Annual Meeting, St. Paul, June 25-28, 2000." Available at www.desiringGod.org/library/fresh_words/2000/070500.html.

[31] Quoted from Piper, "We Took a Good Stand." This formulation combines the resolution and the relevant portion of the "Position paper" by the Bethel board of trustees referred to in the resolution.

[32] Ibid.

the membership of the Baptist General Conference with very mixed signals about the Bible's teaching on God's foreknowledge. Open theists would have us believe that before the foundation of the world God didn't *know* whether any would ever respond to the gospel call. (Since those responses were still in the future, they would say that before the foundation of the world there was nothing that God could know about them.) Is this an insignificant deviation from the Bible's teaching? The Conference's decisions make it hard to tell.

Christians looking for guidance on how to think about open theism are likely to find this outcome confusing. The timing of the second resolution suggests that it was introduced to prevent the Conference from speaking clearly. But the Baptist General Conference was not the only denomination that attempted to provide their membership with clear guidance. The following year (2001) the Southern Baptist Convention overwhelmingly passed a resolution affirming God's exhaustive foreknowledge. In a statement that open theists should find hard to accept, the Convention said (in part):

> Be it further RESOLVED, that we confess and proclaim that the omniscience of God extends to all creation and throughout all time, to all things actual and potential, even to the thoughts and actions of His conscious creatures, past, present, and future . . . [33]

In this case, the message was unmixed, giving the membership of the Convention direction on an important matter.

Many other denominations have confessional standards or affirmation statements that implicitly reject the central claims of open theism. But in most cases the denominations have not acted officially to make these implicit judgments explicit. Members of these denominations are left to recognize the connection between the church standards and draw the inferences for themselves. While this does provide some help to the church, it is considerably less than most Christians would find beneficial. Both the Southern Baptist Convention and the Baptist General Conference are to be commended for tackling the matter

---

[33] See www.sbc.net/resolutions/amResolution.asp?ID=574, as well as "Resolution on the Power, Knowledge, and Changelessness of God," SBC, June, 1999.

directly, even if the outcome in one case was more confusing than it needed to be.

Clear guidance is hard to find in the church today, and ordained leaders are certainly fallible. Even so, these leaders are the ordinary means by which God cares for the flock. They make mistakes, but we are encouraged to presume that the Spirit works through their collective judgment. We look to them for wisdom because we expect that they are given an extra measure of discernment along with their peculiar level of accountability before God. In the absence of clear guidance from shepherds set apart for the care of the flock, Christians today are increasingly left to draw their own conclusions about the claims of open theism. As a result, the doctrinal, cultural, and spiritual climate grows in importance. Christians are disposed by this climate to pay special attention to new and plausibly biblical attempts to enrich their relationship with God in ways that they can understand. These environmental forces favor treatments of God that soften his awesome majesty, affirm human importance, and satisfy our hunger for answers. Open theism offers a God that meets American expectations admirably.

III. The Rest of the Answer: A God for Our Times

While defenders of open theism insist that they are only attempting to correct the defects in the traditional understanding of God, the God of open theism is conveniently consistent with the kind of deity that American evangelicals will find comfortable. Some have argued that the open God is a capitulation to process philosophy,[34] but despite the provocative points of contact between process philosophy and open theism, I am more struck by the way the open God fits current American expectations about power, freedom, mystery, and community. Even if proponents of openness were motivated by zeal to rescue the God of the Bible from Greek distortions, what they have produced is a God of American distortions. In the place of a static tyrant, they have erected

---

[34] The work by proponents of open theism on process thought is worthy of attention. Consider Boyd's *Trinity and Process: A Critical Examination and Reconstruction of Hartshorne's Di-Polar Theism Towards a Trinitarian Metaphysics* (New York: Peter Lang, 1992); and David Basinger, *Divine Power in Process Theism: A Philosophical Critique* (New York: SUNY, 1988).

the ultimate American parent. The God of open theism is soothingly free from mystery and gratifyingly zealous to affirm our autonomy.

The combination of expectations about power, autonomy, and community current in contemporary thought is relatively new in American life. But confidence that it ought to be easy to make sense of God is not. Open theism appeals to the American distaste for mystery on a range of issues. How can we be truly free and God majestically sovereign? No problem: God's sovereignty is limited by our freedom. Why is there so much evil in the world? God wasn't able to prevent it without violating human autonomy. Why would God have us pray if he already knows what we'll ask? He only knows generally what we're likely to ask. The future is undetermined until we make our choices. Until we pray, there is nothing for God to know about our specific requests; so God can't decide until *then* how to respond. He can know what we'll ask before we ask it only in a general way. Open theism claims to resolve one classic mystery after another.

A comprehensible God satisfies American sensibilities, but release from mystery is not the most attractive feature of the openness model for American evangelicals. In line with popular misgivings about the possibility of truly benevolent power, the God of open theism is unwilling to exercise sovereign power. Embodying the only kind of power that today's culture finds comfortable, the open God renounces the imposition of his own will, settling instead for persuading or out-maneuvering his creatures. The open theist insists that this is the pursuit of a genuine love relationship, but even concerning genuine love the openness model is strikingly appropriate to our times. The loving relationship the open God seeks is much more like the relationship *Parents* magazine counsels its readers to pursue with their children.[35] Expecting sovereign authority to destroy intimacy, the open God accomplishes just what he can manage by manipulation. This is a long way from the God of Ephesians 1, who accomplishes everything according to the counsel of his own will. The apostle Paul explains God's love for us in Christ in terms of God's sovereign, independent will, not in spite of it. Unlike open theists, Paul makes no mention of risk, or mutual dependence, or open-

---

[35] *Parents* magazine emphasizes the importance of a child's autonomy. For a representative sample of its advice about managing the dangers facing children, see Dianne Hales, "Raising Kids in an R-Rated Culture" (*Parents* [March 1, 2001]), available at www.parents.com/articles/ages_and_stages/3105.jsp.

ness to an indeterminate future. Consistent with the rest of his epistles, Paul in Ephesians describes God in love claiming a people even though they hate God; Paul has no uncertainty about whether God will succeed. For Paul, divine love takes no risks.

Drawing on a different Pauline theme, open theists offer the husband-wife relationship as a clearer model of the love relationship that God is pursuing with his people.[36] Their goal is to emphasize God's care to guard the autonomy of his human creatures. But the husband-wife model doesn't capture the divine-human relationship that open theists ultimately have in mind. Even after God has divested himself of sovereign power for the sake of intimacy, the God of open theism is still dramatically more powerful, knowledgeable, and good than his human creatures. This is not the relationship of mutual dependence found in healthy marriages. Because of this, a better analogy for the relationship between the open God and his creatures would be the relationship between a morally excellent parent and an infant child. This analogy would preserve the power, knowledge, and goodness gap. But even this analogy doesn't secure precisely what open theists intend, since on this model it wouldn't make sense for God to guard our autonomy jealously. Loving parents know better than to submit their wise judgments to the whims of their infant children.

In order to capture the principal features of the openness account of God's relationship to his creatures, it is necessary to find an analogy that preserves both the gap between us and God in power, knowledge, and moral excellence, and God's zeal to protect human autonomy. Jealous regard for our autonomy is crucial because, like many evangelicals today, the open God believes that responsibility and significance are impossible without libertarian freedom. On the open theist account, God can have morally significant creatures only if he is willing to constrain his own freedom by our free choices. Accordingly, the open God makes only general plans, since specific plans would leave no room for truly free input from his creatures. And the open God awaits the choices of his creatures before making final decisions about what he will do. This is not the picture of God in the Scriptures.[37] It is rather the picture of a

---

[36] John Sanders used this analogy extensively in his presentation to the 1999 meeting of the Evangelical Theological Society in Orlando, Florida.

[37] See especially Romans 8:28-30; Ephesians 1; and Isaiah 45. God is consistently praised as the Lord of history who knows the end from the beginning and the specific details in between.

parent today looking to coax his or her teenage child into a meaningful mutual relationship. Evangelicals today have no trouble recognizing the challenges this open God faces. They understandably find it easy to identify with such a God. Open theism provides them with precisely the kind of father they wish they had had as teenagers. It also flatters their expectations about the centrality of their autonomy. Even God must contend with it in order to realize his ends.

The best analogy for the relationship between the open God and his free creatures is not that of a questing lover; it is instead that of a very resourceful parent of wayward teenage children. The creator of the universe pursues communal intimacy with us the same way a parent pursues a mutual relationship with his or her teenage child. Promises of delight and warnings about blessings unrealized are combined with the careful organizing of circumstances. And still the open God can't guarantee that any particular person will seek him out. Once again, evangelicals will recognize this model of fatherly solicitude. As teenagers who were able to frustrate their parents, or as teenagers wishing for parental intimacy, or as parents seeking intimacy with their children, the open God is very likely to make sense to evangelicals today. This is a God we both understand and empathize with. Open theism gives us a God for our times: a God like us.

IV. A WAY FORWARD

It is tempting to lay all the blame for the rise of open theism at the feet of its proponents, but they certainly have had a lot of help. Currents of thought within the culture have contributed to a climate in which the open God is particularly attractive. And with only a few notable exceptions—Crossway Books, Presbyterian and Reformed Publishing, and *World* magazine, to name three—Christian academics, publishers, bookstores, and reviewers have done too little to guard the church against this dangerous new system of doctrine. But just as ordination sets apart Christian leaders for the exercise of spiritual authority without oppression, it also carries with it peculiar responsibility for shepherding God's people. Ultimately, much of the blame for the rise of open theism must fall on ordained overseers who have chosen to allow it. In order to see how important it is for the church to take the threat of open theism seriously, consider the following story:

At the end of a wholesome date, Richard and Janine visit a Christian bookstore looking for something they can read together. In their early twenties and evangelicals serious about their faith, they want a book they can discuss that will draw them closer to God and to each other. Neither has a particular title in mind, but they agree to look first for a book about God. Holding hands, they head for the "Theology/Christian Living" shelves.

What they find is bewildering. The shelf at eye level has numerous promising titles lined up: *Knowing God; The Openness of God; A Hunger for God; Engaging God's World;* and *Pray with Your Eyes Open.*[38] They reject the last of them because the title doesn't mention God. Opening *Knowing God,* they discover that it was written before they were born. Since they want something current, they set it aside. Because something like "engaging" is close to both their hearts, the table of contents of *Engaging God's World* grabs their attention. The first chapter, "Longing and Hope," looks very promising. But the other chapter titles—"Creation" and "The Fall"—don't, so they decide against it.

Pleased that they are agreeing about these choices so easily, Richard and Janine each pull down one of the two remaining books. Richard studies the back cover of *The Openness of God,* while Janine thumbs through *A Hunger for God.* Both are encouraged by what they find. Richard had considered attending Wheaton College, and *The Openness of God* has a recommendation from a Wheaton professor. Janine had been thinking about fasting as a spiritual exercise, and *A Hunger for God* promises to explain the practice. They exchange books. Janine is attracted by the back-jacket promise that *The Openness of God* offers a "more consistently biblical" understanding of God that is "more true to the actual devotional lives of Christians." Uninterested in giving up any meals, Richard agrees that *A Hunger for God* isn't as promising as *The Openness of God.* They are impressed by the ease with which they reached a decision and head to the checkout counter.

---

[38] The books are arranged alphabetically by author: J. I. Packer, *Knowing God* (Downers Grove, Ill.: InterVarsity Press, 1973); Clark Pinnock, et al., *The Openness of God;* John Piper, *A Hunger for God* (Wheaton, Ill.: Crossway, 1997); Cornelius Plantinga, *Engaging God's World* (Grand Rapids, Mich.: Eerdmans, 2001); and Richard Pratt, *Pray with Your Eyes Open* (Phillipsburg, N.J.: Presbyterian & Reformed, 1987).

The clerk at the cash register asks, "Did you find everything you were looking for?" Richard says he thinks so, but goes on to ask what the clerk thinks of their choice. The clerk says he hasn't read the book, but thinks he has a *Christianity Today* article that mentions it. Rummaging around under the counter he pulls out an old issue turned to an editorial entitled, "God vs. God."[39] Richard and Janine both read the first few paragraphs. They learn that while traditional theism is boring, open theism is a dynamic new evangelical alternative. Pleased with the thought of a cutting-edge way of deepening their relationship, Richard and Janine each buy a copy of the book. Even before they leave the store they set a dinner-date to discuss the first chapter.

Richard and Janine were careful about their selection, looking for guidance from more than one source and considering more than one option. But while the purchase of two copies of *The Openness of God* has only miniscule cultural impact, it is nonetheless a significant victory for the cause of open theism. Richard and Janine are fairly typical evangelicals. They love God and want to know him better, and they were easily persuaded that studying *The Openness of God* would be rewarded with spiritual growth.

Nearly everyone involved in this story bears some responsibility for the harm that this choice of a book will inflict. And what is needed in response is a community-wide effort to repair the systems of guidance and encouragement that should have been there for Richard and Janine. Efforts to reestablish a healthy relationship between ordained shepherds and the flock within the body of Christ will be crucial. Humanly speaking, however, it is hard to see how this can happen. One serious impediment to moving forward is a pervasive distrust within the body of Christ. Idea-shaping academics, reporters, and publishers too often don't trust ordained shepherds, finding excuses to avoid real submission to ordained oversight. Ordained leaders too often don't trust idea-shapers, thinking it necessary to protect the faith against reckless academics, reporters, and publishers who crave novelty and flirt with edgy ideas. Neither group is humanly likely to make the first trusting move toward responsible leadership and submissive industry.

Responsible leadership by ordained shepherds will need to take

---

[39] *Christianity Today* 44, no. 2 (7 February 2000): 34-35. The editorial as a whole is slightly more balanced than its opening paragraphs.

much more seriously the needs of those they are called to guard and nurture. More needs to be done to provide church members with pointed guidance about what is worth reading and which new ideas need to be held suspect. The amount of work this will involve is considerable. Pastors and other ordained shepherds don't have the time to review all the books that members of their churches are likely to pick up. And even if they had the time, many of them as individuals would struggle to discern some of the more subtle threats. Happily, these shepherds have a resource available in a growing stable of theologically trained lay people—both men and women—who can be called upon. Just as the leaders of a church would call upon talented carpenters in the church to reinforce a defective ceiling, they should be calling upon talented academics to provide informed guidance about theological developments.

Making use of these theological talents in the service of the church would provide needed guidance. It would also draw the academics into the life of the church, making it a place where their talents are valued and nurtured. Reestablishing the needed trust between academics and shepherds won't be easy, but it can be done. Humanly speaking, the first move will need to come from academics who volunteer to submit drafts of their work to spiritual overseers for comment and counsel. The resulting dialogue and guidance may be strained at first, but the entire church would benefit from the expanded circle of discussion and accountability. I submitted a serious draft of this chapter to my pastor at Lookout Mountain Presbyterian Church and asked for guidance about its assertions. He made copies for all thirty of the church's elders, and they responded with written questions and comments. If they had collectively counseled against any part of my argument, then I would have been obligated to make changes. They didn't ask for changes as a body, but their individual observations and suggestions were exceptionally helpful. What many academics would expect to be a confining experience was for me a blessing.[40]

Boldness in the pulpit is another challenge facing ordained leaders. The popularity of open theism has exposed a handful of issues that traditionalist churches have avoided. While evangelical pastors have been

---

[40] I need to thank in particular Pastor Joseph Novenson for facilitating my search for oversight. Through his efforts I had the benefit of specific help from Assistant Pastor David Arthur and elders Robert Ashlock, Bunky Blalock, Benjamin Dady, Robert Holt, and Ted Hope.

boldly denouncing sins of addiction, impurity, and hatred, they have been needlessly shy about addressing the legitimate needs for intimacy with God, a vital prayer life, peace regarding God's providence, and the bewilderment of grief. The various strains of evangelicalism have different weaknesses on these questions. Reformed pulpits stress God's majestic sovereignty in a way that makes an intimate relationship with God difficult to discuss. Arminian pulpits stress the necessity of our response to God's invitation in a way that makes it hard to resist the openness conclusion that God depends upon our decisions. Evangelical pastors of all kinds need to be boldly moving beyond their safely rutted paths, applying God's Word about himself as the sovereign, loving Lord to the real perplexities, anxieties, and sorrows of their flocks.

By the same token, Christian authors and other idea-shapers need to be addressing these legitimate felt needs in print.[41] Their efforts need to be coordinated with pastors and ordained shepherds, to identify both the most pressing needs and the most accessible means of meeting those needs. Another truckload of dry theological exercises may enhance academic careers and encourage fellow academics, but it won't do much to meet the needs of the rest of the church. Internet discussions, articles in magazines that evangelicals actually read, Sunday school curricula, and devotional guides are all more likely to extend the kind of encouragement and guidance that the church can and will hear. And in order to reduce confusion, the authors of these tools need to make explicit in print who their overseers are. This will provide their readers with a model of submission. It will also dramatically increase the confidence with which their works will be read.

Finally, church members need to seek out and honor guidance from their ordained shepherds. We have too little practice at this. Persuaded by the myth that we are all reliable judges of what is good for us spiritually, we seek out guidance only as a last resort. Sermons that can hold our attention might be challenging for a day or so; but if the speaker is dull, we feel little obligation to work to hear God's Word to us. When buying devotional literature or children's videos, we might consult our

---

[41] Works of this kind are starting to appear. Carolyn Curtis James, *When Life and Beliefs Collide* (Grand Rapids, Mich.: Zondervan, 2001), is a moving account of drawing near to God while affirming God's sovereignty. Douglas Kelly's *If God Already Knows, Why Pray?* (Ross-shire, U.K.: Christian Focus, 1995) answers hard questions about the efficacy of prayer without dragging God into time.

friends' opinions or sales figures. But most of us would benefit from asking our elders or deacons for advice as well. God has provided us with shepherds for precisely these kinds of needs.

I have used "we" and "us" here because the problem of holding spiritual overseers at arm's length is my problem as much as anyone else's. The culture in which we live makes uncommitted, minimally submitting Christianity seem both inevitable and sufficiently healthy. Open theism unopposed will thrive in this freedom-intoxicated, authority-distrusting age. The spiritual health of the body is a sufficient reason to work on restoring the relationship between ordained overseers and their flocks. Undermining the climate that is encouraging the rise of open theism will be a happy by-product of the effort.

In closing, consider what might happen next in the story of Richard and Janine if the church were healthier. Between buying copies of the book and the date for discussing it, they attend a worship service at the church where they are both members. The sermon text (providentially) is 1 John 4:8, "Whoever does not love does not know God, because God is love" (NIV). The pastor specifically deals with the "recent suggestion" that love involves taking risks, and shows why it is unbiblical to say that "God is love" means that God takes real risks. Richard thinks of Janine repeatedly during this close discussion of love. Janine, however, is made uncomfortable by the sermon because she has already read the first chapter of the book they bought and agreed to discuss. The next day Richard shares her anxiety when he reads the chapter. When they finally meet to discuss the book, neither is enthusiastic about using *The Openness of God* as the basis for getting to know each other. Together they ask a church leader to suggest an alternative. Two dog-eared copies of Richard Pratt's *Pray with Your Eyes Open* wind up sharing a prominent place on their family bookshelf for years.[42]

---

[42] I am indebted to my wife Lynda, my father Theron Davis, and my students Asha Garretson, Elizabeth Mehne, Katie Mesh, Cameron Moran, Josiah Roe, and Ryan Wright for research assistance and helpful comments on preliminary drafts of this chapter.

PART THREE

Anthropomorphisms, Revelation, and Interpretation

5

Veiled Glory:
God's Self-Revelation in Human
Likeness—A Biblical Theology
of God's Anthropomorphic
Self-Disclosure

A. B. Caneday

Truly you are a God who hides himself,
O God and Savior of Israel.
—ISAIAH 45:15

I. Introduction: Suppression and Reification of Anthropomorphism

Open theism did not burst upon the contemporary theological scene. The "new" view of God did not make its first appearance with the publication of *The Openness of God* in 1994.[1] Nor did Robert Brow's essay "Evangelical Megashift"[2] first bring open theism to evangelicalism in 1990. Clark Pinnock introduced open theism to evangelicalism in 1986

---

[1] Clark Pinnock, et al., *The Openness of God: A Biblical Challenge to the Traditional Understanding of God* (Downers Grove, Ill.: InterVarsity Press, 1994).

[2] John MacArthur, Jr., points to the essay by Robert Brow as the emergence of open theism into the public square. See MacArthur, "Open Theism's Attack on the Atonement," in *Bound Only Once: The Failure of Open Theism,* ed. Douglas Wilson (Moscow, Ida.: Canon, 2001), 95ff. See Robert Brow, "Evangelical Megashift," *Christianity Today* 34, no. 3 (19 February 1990): 12-14.

in his essay, "God Limits His Knowledge."[3] In his essay, Pinnock claimed, "God anticipates the future in a way *analogous to our own experience.*"[4] Pinnock admitted that he embraced open theism, for he cited philosopher Richard Rice's book, *The Openness of God: The Relationship of Divine Foreknowledge and Human Free Will,* as a longer presentation of the view he advocated in his essay.[5] Open theism quietly crossed evangelicalism's threshold in 1986, took up residence, and now sues for squatter's rights.[6] That open theism could gain entrance and take up residence within evangelicalism hints at defects and lack of vigilance within. How could the open view of God, previously excluded as heterodoxy under other designations, gain residence within evangelicalism?[7]

Crucial to making their case, open theists claim that they correct a flaw in traditional Christian theism. The alleged flaw is preference for "the Greek philosophical way of speaking of God (impassible, immutable, timeless, etc.)" in place of "the anthropomorphic way (father, changeable, suffering, etc.). The church has followed this path for so long that we now take this way of thinking for granted."[8] John Sanders rejects

---

[3] In *Predestination and Free Will: Four Views of Divine Sovereignty and Human Freedom,* ed. David Basinger and Randall Basinger (Downers Grove, Ill.: InterVarsity Press, 1986), 141-162. Pinnock indicates his theological shift in two essays, one published in 1985 and this one in 1986. For detailed assessment of Pinnock's theological shift, see A. B. Caneday, "God in the Image and Likeness of Adam—Clark Pinnock's Use of Scripture in His Argument 'God Limits His Knowledge,'" *Journal of Biblical Apologetics* 1 (2001): 20-27.

[4] Pinnock, "God Limits His Knowledge," in *Predestination and Free Will,* ed. Basinger and Basinger 157, emphasis added. Pinnock claims, "God is omniscient in the sense that he knows everything which can be known, just as God is omnipotent in the sense that he can do everything that can be done. But free actions are not entities which can be known ahead of time. They literally do not yet exist to be known. God can surmise what you will do next Friday, but cannot know it for certain because you have not done it yet."

[5] Ibid., 144 n. 2. Pinnock incorrectly cites Rice's book as *The Openness of God: The Relationship of Divine Foreknowledge and Human Free Will* (Minneapolis: Bethany, 1985). That was the former title of Rice's book first published in 1979 by Review & Herald Publishing, a Seventh Day Adventist publishing house in Nashville. However, Rice's ideas met stiff resistance from fellow Adventists. In 1985, when he reprinted the book as *God's Foreknowledge and Man's Free Will,* Bethany published it. For details, see Robert A. Morey, *Battle of the Gods: The Gathering Storm in Modern Evangelicalism* (Southbridge, Mass.: Crown, 1989), 109.

[6] Several essays that promote open theism are tucked away in a book that bears the innocuous title, *The Grace of God and the Will of Man: A Case for Arminianism* (ed. Clark H. Pinnock [Grand Rapids, Mich.: Zondervan, 1989]). For example, see Richard Rice, "Divine Foreknowledge and Free-Will Theism" (121-139); and John Sanders, "God as Personal" (165-180).

[7] Despite protests from open theists against this theological association, that open theism resurrects a foundational belief of Socinianism should alert all concerning its heterodoxy. See especially Robert B. Strimple, "What Does God Know?" in *The Coming Evangelical Crisis: Current Challenges to the Authority of Scripture and the Gospel,* ed. John H. Armstrong (Chicago: Moody, 1996), 139-153.

[8] Sanders, "God as Personal," 168. Two essays address both aspects of Sanders's complaint. See Douglas M. Jones, "Metaphor in Exile," in *Bound Only Once,* ed. Wilson, 31-51; and Michael S. Horton, "Hellenistic or Hebrew? Open Theism and Reformed Theological Method" (chapter 6 in this volume; and *Journal of the Evangelical Theological Society (JETS)* 45 [2002]: 317-341).

the classic interpretation of passages that depict God as "repenting." Sanders objects, "On what basis do these thinkers claim that these biblical texts do not portray God as he truly is but only God as he appears to us? How do they confidently select one biblical text as an 'exact' description of God and consign others to the dustbin of anthropomorphism?"[9]

From childhood, we learned that the Bible guides us to think of God with proper imagery, for it asks, "To whom then will you liken God, or what likeness compare with him?" (Isa. 40:18, NRSV).[10] We learned that some imagery intrinsically draws analogies that lead us to wrong concepts of God, if not idolatry. For example, the imagery of God as a chess player intuitively seemed a grotesque caricature of how God relates to his creatures. Its repugnance is gone for open theists who claim, God "anticipates and ingeniously outmaneuvers his opponents" as a master chess player.[11] They readily characterize God with categories drawn

---

[9] John Sanders, *The God Who Risks: A Theology of Providence* (Downers Grove, Ill.: InterVarsity Press, 1998), 68. Sanders's accusations against evangelical theology echo those of Sally McFague, *Metaphorical Theology: Models of God in Religious Language* (Philadelphia: Fortress, 1982); idem, *Models of God: Theology for an Ecological Nuclear Age* (Philadelphia: Fortress, 1987). There are differences between McFague and Sanders, but both derive their views of God from human experience. Nevertheless, because Sanders wants to win evangelicals to his view of God, he tries to find support in the Bible by examining Scripture "through the lens of divine risk taking . . . in order to see what should be said concerning a risk-taking god" (*The God Who Risks*, 14). By contrast, McFague is more candid about her "quest of a feminine model for expressing the divine-human relationship" (*Metaphorical Theology*, 61) because she does not speak from within evangelicalism. Thus, she dismisses the Bible as authoritative.

McFague wanders into some proper criticism of evangelicalism in her assault upon evangelical faith: "On the issue of the truth of religious language, there are continuing, powerful, conservative religious movements which insist on the literal reference of language to God. Religious conservatism is a widespread tendency within contemporary culture, not restricted to groups which call themselves 'evangelicals' or 'fundamentalists.' This tendency is linked with fear of relativizing Scripture through historical criticism and a refusal to accept a plurality of interpretive perspectives. The Bible, says this movement, *is* the Word of God; the Bible is inerrant or divinely inspired; the words and images of the Bible are authoritative and appropriate words and images for God. The Bible is a sacred text, different from all other texts, and not relative and pluralistic as are all other human products. The Bible becomes an idol: the fallible, human words of Scripture are understood as referring correctly and literally to God. . . . It derives from the understanding of what counts as 'true' in our culture. . . . Translated into religious terms, 'true' religious language is also a copy of what it represents; in other words, a literal or realistic representation of God's nature. If the Bible says that God is 'father' then God is literally, really, 'father'; the word 'father' and the associations of that word truly refer to God's nature" (*Metaphorical Theology*, 4-5). I will demonstrate, for example, that "father" properly belongs to God and only derivatively belongs to humans because God made us in his image and likeness.

[10] Unless otherwise noted, Scripture translations in this chapter are my own.

[11] Gregory A. Boyd, *God of the Possible: A Biblical Introduction to the Open View of God* (Grand Rapids, Mich.: Baker, 2000), 51. For his explicit appeal to the chess player imagery, see page 128. "One beats a computerized chessboard because he knows how it was programmed and thus knows every move it *will* make. The other beats a person by anticipating every possible move he *might* make. Which is the more praiseworthy champion? Clearly the latter, for the first victory took very little intelligence. Why, then, should we regard a God who knows all that *will* happen to be wiser than a God who can perfectly anticipate and respond to all that *might* happen?" See also, Gregory A. Boyd, *Satan and the Problem of Evil: Constructing a Trinitarian Warfare Theodicy* (Downers Grove, Ill.: InterVarsity Press, 2001), 112-114.

from our modern therapeutic culture that prizes "self-esteem" and regards "vulnerability" as virtuous. Gregory Boyd says, "It takes a truly self-confident, sovereign God to make himself *vulnerable.*"[12] "God as risk taker" is a dominant imagery among open theists.[13] Furthermore, under the influence of modern culture, Sanders claims, "God . . . *has healthy self-esteem,*" and later, on the same page, he says, "God *is worried* . . ."[14] As Sally McFague constructs an image of God for an ecological and nuclear age, so open theists have constructed an image of God for a therapeutic age. Open theists, however, do not employ their descriptive language as anthropopathic (read *analogical*) portrayals of God, but as descriptive of God as he is in himself, for they transmute figurative portraits of God into glossy pictures.[15] They look at God's created analogies and suppose they reveal God just as he is in himself.

Besides importing modern therapeutic terms into Christian talk about God, open theists challenge the foundations of Christian theology on the premise that "God anticipates the future in a way *analogous to our own experience.*" To assert this premise is to commit a *referential fallacy.*[16] All anthropomorphisms and anthropopathisms are inherently referential, for they entail analogy. They sketch an implicit likeness and unlikeness between Creator and creature. Open theism's referential fal-

---

[12] Boyd, *God of the Possible,* 149, emphasis added. Cf. Boyd's section, "God Gets Frustrated" (62-63).

[13] Sanders, *The God Who Risks,* 11. He argues, "When certain metaphors (for example, God as king) reign for so long in theology, we risk being conditioned to overlook aspects of God's relationship with us. When this happens, we need new 'iconoclastic' metaphors that reveal to us something that we overlooked. It is my contention that the metaphor of God as risk taker opens up new ways for us to understand what is at stake for God in divine providence." Throughout his book, Sanders repeatedly refers to God's creation as "God's project," a mechanistic imagery that counters his efforts to portray God as relational. See my comments in, "Putting God at Risk: A Critique of John Sanders's View of Providence," *Trinity Journal* 20 NS (1999): 135.

[14] Sanders, *The God Who Risks,* 64, emphasis added.

[15] Garrett Green insightfully observes, "Talking about a 'picture of God,' for example, strikes us as naïve or blasphemous, while the notion of an 'image of God,' though it may be controversial, is taken seriously. The key lies in the use or function: a picture reproduces; an image exemplifies. An image is a picture in which nonessential features have been suppressed and essential ones highlighted. A picture, we might say, represents features indiscriminately; an image, by contrast, represents selectively. An image is both more and less than a picture: more insofar as it makes a claim about what is definitive or essential to the object; less insofar as it may be less complete or 'literal.' A picture shows us something; an image seeks to show us what that something *really* is" (*Imagining God: Theology and the Religious Imagination* [Grand Rapids, Mich.: Eerdmans, 1998], 93-94).

[16] For this, see A. B. Caneday, "The Implausible God of Open Theism: A Response to Gregory A. Boyd's *God of the Possible: A Biblical Introduction to Open Theism," Journal of Biblical Apologetics* 1 (2000): 66-87; "Putting God at Risk," 131-163; "God in the Image and Likeness of Adam," 20-27; and "Critical Comments on an Open Theism Manifesto," *Trinity Journal* 23 NS (2002): 103-107.

lacy inverts this implicit analogy intrinsic to God's self-disclosure in human likeness. The fallacy is to forget that we are analogues of God and to regard ourselves as the fundamental reference point for ascriptions concerning God. The error is to project back upon God our creaturely restrictions of qualities received from him who made us in his image and likeness.

Open theists criticize those they oppose for allegedly adopting a Greek view of a static God, and simultaneously, they are impatient with the same theologians for understanding God's self-disclosure in humanlike qualities as figurative. Open theists reject explanations of God's anthropomorphic self-portrayals, such as "changing his mind," as figurative. They do so because they believe that if these passages portray God figuratively, they do not give us true access to God and true knowledge of God, for they do not provide a true portrait of God.[17] They insist that passages that portray God as "changing his mind" disclose "to us the very nature of God."[18] They *reify* God's self-disclosures in terms of human-like qualities. They transmute figurative portrayals of God into literal portraits.[19] We need to address this problem. However,

---

[17] Sanders, *The God Who Risks,* 69. Sanders complains, "Claiming that biblical texts asserting that God 'changed his mind' are merely anthropomorphisms does not tell us what they mean. If, in fact, it is impossible for God to change his mind, then the biblical text is quite misleading. Asserting that it is a nonliteral expression does not solve the problem because it has to mean something. Just what is the anthropomorphic expression an expression of? Thus, classical theists are left with the problem of misleading biblical texts, or, at best, meaningless metaphors regarding the nature of God."

[18] Ibid., 38.

[19] Gregory A. Boyd, "Christian Love and Academic Dialogue: A Reply to Bruce Ware," *JETS* 45 (2002): 240, argues, "[E]verybody, including Ware, takes some texts as literal and other texts as figurative. No evangelical thinks that the incarnation is figurative, for example, but all agree that expressions of God's 'right arm' are." Boyd confuses categories. He confounds *texts* and *events*. *Texts,* themselves, are neither "literal" nor "figurative." Rather, texts *describe* or *portray* things, including events, literally or figuratively. Boyd also confuses *literal* and *figurative.* The fact that Scripture portrays God's qualities figuratively hardly renders God's qualities unreal. Boyd unveils the gravity of his error when he says, "No evangelical thinks that the incarnation is figurative, for example, but all agree that expressions of God's 'right arm' are." Here, it becomes obvious that Boyd thinks figurative means *not real. Figurative* is a literary and rhetorical category. It is not an existential category. Though the Bible often portrays the Son's incarnation figuratively, it does not suggest that the incarnation is not literal in the sense of real.

In the same essay, note 5 (p. 240) illustrates the "logic" of Boyd's confusion. He states, "When I speak of texts being 'literal,' I am not thereby denying that there is a metaphorical element in them. I simply mean they have a similar meaning when applied to God as they have when applied to humans. Hence, for example, to say that passages that speak of God 'changing his mind' is [*sic*] 'literal,' I mean only that it has [*sic*] a similar meaning as when humans are said to 'change their mind.' But, obviously, the very concept of 'changing one's mind' is a metaphor depicting a change of intention. No one *literally* 'changes their minds' [*sic*]." Follow Boyd's reasoning. First, he confuses categories at two levels. He wrongly describes *texts* as *literal* rather than the things texts portray or describe, even if represented figuratively. By literal, he means *real* or *actual,* neither of which stands opposite *figurative* in the literary sense. Second, Boyd switches the category of figure of speech under question, specifically *anthropomorphism,* to the broadest use of *metaphorical,*

before we rush to correct open theism's error, open theists may have a legitimate complaint, at least to a degree, concerning some evangelical formulations.

Bruce Ware offers a working definition of anthropomorphism: "A given ascription to God may rightly be understood as anthropomorphic when Scripture clearly presents God as transcending the very human or finite features it elsewhere attributes to him."[20] Open theists take issue with Ware's use of this definition to explain Numbers 23:19 and 1 Samuel 15:29 as proof that "God never changes his mind." For example, Sanders focuses upon Hosea 11:8-9:

> How can I give you up, Ephraim?
>   How can I hand you over, Israel?
> How can I treat you like Admah?
>   How can I make you like Zeboiim?
> My heart is changed within me;
>   all my compassion is aroused.
> I will not carry out my fierce anger,
>   nor will I turn and devastate Ephraim.
> For I am God, and not man—
>   the Holy One among you.
> I will not come in wrath.

About this passage, Sanders argues, "Following Ware we have a real problem on our hands because the Bible teaches both (1) that God cannot change his mind because he is not human and (2) that God literally

which bears the sense *figurative.* Third, he reduces the biblical anthropomorphism found in the expression *nāḥam* (*relent*) to a simplistic translation that favors his theological assumptions, namely "change of mind." Fourth, without recognition, Boyd measures God by humans; God's "change of mind" "has a similar meaning as when humans . . . change their mind." Fifth, apparently unaware of his own definitional legerdemain, Boyd switches "change of mind" from its proper category, *anthropomorphism,* to an improper category, *metaphor,* in the narrow sense. This is evident when he claims, "But, obviously, the very concept of 'changing one's mind' is a metaphor depicting a change of intention. No one *literally* 'changes their minds' [*sic*]." He began the paragraph by broadening anthropomorphism to metaphorical in the sense of figurative. He ends the paragraph by replacing anthropomorphism with metaphor in the narrowest sense, based upon his preferred English translation of *nḥm.* Without saying anything meaningfully correct, Boyd thinks he has given ample support for his "straightforward" reading of the Bible.

Without awareness, Boyd continues to equivocate in his use of "literal" and "metaphorical" despite extended demonstrations of his error. See, e.g., Caneday, "The Implausible God of Open Theism," 67-70.

[20] Bruce A. Ware, "An Evangelical Reformulation of the Doctrine of the Immutability of God," *JETS* 29 (1986): 442. See also idem, *God's Lesser Glory: The Diminished God of Open Theism* (Wheaton, Ill.: Crossway, 2000), 86.

does change his mind because he is not human."[21] Ware may have responded to Sanders's overstatement and thus missed the force of the argument.

Consider the passage. Through the prophet Hosea, the Lord speaks as one who deliberates over what to do with Israel, and as he deliberates, he speaks as one who remembers his covenant promise to Abraham. The Lord depicts himself as one whose compassion is aroused. He undergoes a change of heart, so that he will not destroy Israel because he is God and not a man who easily becomes captive to his passions, especially anger. Sanders reifies Hosea's anthropomorphic imagery. Of this passage, Ware correctly says, "Rather, it affirms that God, unlike humans, is absolutely faithful to his covenant promises."[22] Yet, even this statement entails anthropomorphism, for to say that God is "unlike humans" is to employ analogy and anthropomorphism, albeit by way of negation. God's self-portrayal through Hosea's prophecy is thoroughly anthropomorphic. God's asking deliberative questions is as anthropomorphic as his admission of change of heart. The same is true of God's self-restraint concerning his anger and wrath.

Sanders may legitimately fault evangelicals for inadequate consideration of biblical anthropomorphisms. Yet, Sanders only gives lip service to the idea that "*All* scripture is anthropomorphic," quoting Herman Bavinck, for he selectively eliminates figurative language from passages that speak of God's repentance and reduces the passages to literal portrayals of God.[23] Sanders states, "If God decides to disclose himself to us as a personal being who enters into relationship with us, who has purposes, emotions and desires, and who suffers with us, then we ought to rejoice in this anthropomorphic portrait and accept it as *disclosing to us the very nature of God.*"[24] This, of course, is contradictory, for in the end, Sanders takes as *literal* the very passages most evangelicals believe are figurative portraits of God.[25] Sanders is inconsistent and

---

[21] Sanders, *The God Who Risks*, 68.

[22] Ware, *God's Lesser Glory*, 89. This well-written book, published in response to Boyd's *God of the Possible* within the same year (2000), unfolds an excellent argument against open theism.

[23] Sanders, *The God Who Risks*, 22. Sanders is not wrong about the centrality of anthropomorphism in Scripture. His error is that he misunderstands how anthropomorphism functions and thus reifies it selectively to fit his preconceived notion of what God must be like.

[24] Ibid., 38, emphasis added.

[25] For an incisive critique that exposes Sanders's equivocation concerning God's metaphorical and anthropomorphic self-disclosures, see Jones, "Metaphor in Exile," 31-51.

confused. He tries to praise anthropomorphism: "The personal God . . . is a God who is not afraid of anthropomorphism."[26] Yet he transmutes God's figurative representations into literal portraits of God that "disclose to us the very nature of God."[27]

Open theism is a current theological trend that results from a quest to know God as he truly is in himself. This quest seems right. What could be godlier than to want to know God as he is in himself? Philip petitioned Jesus, "Show us the Father, and that will be enough for us" (John 14:8). Moses entreated the Lord, "Show me your glory, I pray" (Ex. 33:18). The Lord's responses to both are instructive, for both asked for more than God will reveal. Every quest to know God as he is in himself is elusive, for as the invisible God reveals himself to us he hides himself from us, lest he consume us. Hence, every pursuit to know God as he is in himself, unless checked by Scripture, eventually exchanges the glory of God for the image and likeness of the creature. Discontent with true knowledge of God as he has revealed himself, open theism would have us reify biblical anthropomorphisms so that we can know God as he truly is in himself. Despite protests to the contrary, open theism would have us exchange the glory of God for an image of ourselves by transmuting God's anthropomorphic self-disclosures, that give us true knowledge and access to God, into literal portrayals of himself "that disclose to us the very nature of God," but in our likeness.

Classical Christian theology has not escaped influence by Enlightenment and post-Enlightenment philosophers who disparaged anthropomorphism.[28] This "iconoclastic bias," born in philosophy and transferred to theology, "is the assumption that the least metaphoric concept of God is the best."[29] It is tempting to suppose that we can know God as he truly is in himself. We may think we honor God by abstracting him from the very form and manner in which he reveals himself to

---

[26] Sanders, *The God Who Risks*, 38.

[27] Ibid.

[28] Concerning the influence of Thomas Hobbes and John Locke, see Jones, "Metaphor in Exile," 34ff. On the influence of post-Enlightenment philosophers such as Immanuel Kant, G. W. F. Hegel, and Ludwig Feuerbach, see Green, *Imagining God*, 9-27. Green argues that Kant and Hegel have negatively induced some Christian theologians to disparage biblical imagery by using philosophical reasoning to release "the pure religious essence from its entrapment in the imaginative forms" (18). Feuerbach, in his *The Essence of Christianity*, envisaged twentieth-century thinkers coming of age and growing out of dependence upon illusory religion or the "childlike condition of humanity" (23).

[29] Green, *Imagining God*, 95. See Green's instructive endnote 18, p. 164.

us, namely in human form and likeness. To represent God with abstract philosophical concepts may seem more suitable for our transcendent God than to conceive of him as an actor on the earthly stage, engaged in this drama that seems so utterly human. But is it? Do we really sanctify the Lord in our hearts and uphold his majesty by capturing him with philosophical abstractions? If we represent God with philosophical abstractions, we will tend to exaggerate either God's transcendence or his immanence. We will conceive of God either as held captive by his own creation or as depersonalized.[30] It is necessary to steer the theological vessel away from Scylla, the yawning cave of idolatry, toward which open theism will take it. Yet, we must always be alert lest we overcorrect and steer into Charybdis, the vortex of divine aloofness, by focusing upon God's transcendence to the reduction of his immanence.[31]

Will evangelical theology emerge from the open theism controversy strengthened or weakened, chastened or hardened? This largely depends upon whether or not the church and its theologians are willing for God to admonish us with the rod of heterodoxy. Michael Horton rightly alerts us, "This debate, as all challenges to orthodoxy, is a tremendous opportunity for us once more to rediscover for ourselves the richness of scriptural teaching."[32] His words capture the heartbeat of this essay. This essay first seeks to demonstrate that God's design of creation accounts for Scripture's rich imagery with which the Creator reveals himself to his creatures. Then it offers a biblical-theological sketch of God's self-revelation to his creatures in human likeness with imagery of God's self-revelation in the Old Testament as foreshadowing his disclosure in and through the Word incarnate in the New Testament. It shows that Scripture leads us to affirm that God reveals himself to us while he simultaneously hides himself from us. The essay addresses the implica-

---

[30] Even if we prefer philosophical categories, we cannot escape the fact that we still have to speak of God with human categories (anthropomorphism), for we are human. Try to say something about God that does not have some referential connection to creation and especially to humans. Categories that open theists dislike, such as "impassible" or "immutable," are still anthropomorphic in nature, for their references are to contrasting qualities in humans.

[31] For an excellent presentation of this same theme, see Michael S. Horton, "A Vulnerable God Apart from Christ? Open Theism's Challenge to the Classical Doctrine of God," *Modern Reformation* 10, no. 3 (May/June 2001): 33. Horton says, "Only by staying with Scripture has orthodoxy in the modern period been able to resist somewhat the pendulum of modern thought as it swings between hyper-transcendence (God as practically uninvolved in the world) and hyper-immanence (God as practically identical with the world)."

[32] Ibid. The theme of this particular issue of *Modern Reformation* suggests that heterodoxy has a chastening value for the church—"Our Debt to Heresy: Mapping Boundaries."

tions of God's veiled glory, analogically revealed, for both classical Christian theology and open theism. Therefore, this essay first seeks to chasten our own classical Christian flirtation with suppressing anthropomorphism by abstraction and to chide open theism's courtship with idolatry when it reifies anthropomorphism.

II. IMAGE OF GOD—BIBLICAL FOUNDATIONS FOR GOD'S SELF-REVELATION

Image of God and Popular Definitions of "Anthropomorphism"

Open theists trade upon popular but deficient definitions of anthropomorphism to oppose carefully nuanced presentations by notable theologians of the church, such as John Calvin. They seem to have gained a popular hearing and following, but their discussions of anthropomorphism and of God's figurative self-portrayals in Scripture are deficient both as critiques of those they oppose and as presentations of what Scripture truly portrays.

One popular definition of anthropomorphism states that it is, "A figure of speech used by writers of Scripture in which human physical characteristics are attributed to God for the sake of illustrating an important point. . . . Anthropomorphisms essentially help to make an otherwise abstract truth about God more concrete."[33] At least five flaws tend to attach to popular definitions of anthropomorphism. First, they prompt us to suppose that anthropomorphism occurs in only a few biblical passages that seem to detract from God's character, such as ascribing body parts or repentance to God. Yet, if one attentively reads classic writings on biblical interpretation and theology, one finds Christian scholars are careful to clarify that *all of God's self-revelation is anthropomorphic.*[34] Second, definitions of anthropomorphism tend to reflect the Enlightenment's influence with talk of "abstract truth of God"

---

[33] Stanley J. Grenz, David Guretzki, and Cherith Fee Nordling, *Pocket Dictionary of Theological Terms* (Downers Grove, Ill.: InterVarsity Press, 1999), 11.

[34] See, e.g., Milton Terry, *Biblical Hermeneutics: A Treatise on the Interpretation of the Old and New Testaments* (New York: Eaton & Mains, n.d.; Grand Rapids, Mich.: Zondervan, 1974), 103 n. 1. Terry offers a variety of anthropomorphisms in Scripture and quotes Tayler Lewis (*The Divine Human in the Scriptures* [New York: R. Carter, 1860], 43)—"Why talk of anthropopathism as if there were some special absurdity covered by this sounding term, when any revelation conceivable must be anthropopathic? . . . There is no escape from it. Whatever comes in this way to man must take the measure of man. . . . The thoughts and feelings thus aroused would still be human, and partake of the human finity and imperfection. In their highest state they will be but shadows of the infinite, figures of ineffable truths."

made "more concrete," as if the "concrete" were an accommodation to those with weak capacity.[35] The Bible, however, is rich and replete with figurative portrayals of God yet empty of abstract or theoretical representations of deity.[36] Third, popular definitions imply that anthropomorphism is a "human device" for representing God, another influence of the Enlightenment. The Bible safeguards against this erroneous notion by condemning as idolatry all human devices for conceiving of God. God is the source of anthropomorphic portraits of himself. God made us in his image; he forbids us to cast him in our image. It is not the sculptor's chisel but the chisel of the mind that first fashions God in our likeness. A fourth flaw often attaches to popular definitions of anthropomorphism. Too readily, the standard of human expectation concerning what God must be like becomes an independent arbiter of reasoning and logic to strip away from the figurative biblical portrayal of God everything that is incompatible with one's own concept of God.[37] As such, anthropomorphism tends to become a heuristic device of systematic theology, freewheeling and not tethered to evident markers and indicators within the biblical text. Fifth, definitions of anthropomorphism rarely show adequate reflection upon prominent indicators of the Bible's creation accounts. Especially notable for understanding how and why God discloses himself to humans as if he were human is the fact that God made us from the "dust of the earth" as his image and likeness.

---

[35] Paul Helm unwittingly opens himself up to this charge when he says, "The statements about the extent and intensity of God's knowledge, power and goodness must control the anthropomorphic and weaker statements, and not vice versa" (see Paul Helm, *The Providence of God* [Downers Grove, Ill.: InterVarsity Press, 1994], 52). On the next page, Helm makes statements that should have corrected the above statement. While appealing to John Calvin's doctrine of accommodation, he restricts, too much, what is properly anthropomorphic in Scripture. A better guide on Calvin's doctrine of accommodation is Michael Horton's chapter in this volume. Martin Luther wisely observed, "That Scripture thus assigns to God the form, voice, actions, emotions, etc., of a human being not only serves to show consideration for the uneducated and the weak; but we great and learned men, who are versed in the Scriptures, are also obliged to adopt these simple images, because God has presented them to us and has revealed Himself to us through them" (Martin Luther, *Lectures on Genesis: Chapters 6-14,* vol. 2 of *Luther's Works,* trans. George Schick [St. Louis: Concordia, 1960], 46).

[36] Cf. Herman Bavinck, *The Doctrine of God,* trans. William Hendricksen (Grand Rapids, Mich.: Eerdmans, 1951; Edinburgh: Banner of Truth, 1977), 114.

[37] In *The God Who Risks,* Sanders accuses classical Christian theists of this: "God, it is claimed, is a term for which only certain properties are 'fitting' (*dignum Deo*). Any God worth his salt must conform to our intuitive notions of deity or get out of the deity business. Since the biblical depiction of God does not, according to some people, measure up to what is fitting for God to be, the doctrine of divine accommodation is enacted to protect the Bible from charges of falsehood" (33). Sanders does not recognize that he is guilty of this repeatedly.

"Anthropomorphism" bears different senses ranging from broad to narrow. To attribute human characteristics or purposes to any inanimate object—animals, plants, or other natural phenomena—or to God is to use anthropomorphism. For example, to describe a rushing river as "angry" is to represent it anthropomorphically. However, Christians tend to use "personification" to name any figure of speech that represents inanimate objects or abstract ideas with human qualities and reserve "anthropomorphism" strictly for describing God with human features and qualities.

Purists of terminology also tend to distinguish *anthropomorphism* (i.e., God's self-disclosure in human form) from *anthropopathism* (i.e., God's self-disclosure with human qualities—passions, feelings, attitudes, etc.). For others, anthropomorphism bears a broader use to include any ascription of human features or qualities to God.[38] While it is necessary that we distinguish individual anthropomorphisms in the biblical text from metaphors and other figures of speech in their narrower sense, this essay calls upon Christians to recognize that all of God's self-revelation is analogical or anthropomorphic. The term "anthropomorphism" is properly broad because God's Word does not simply contain "anthropomorphism" as one figure of speech alongside metaphor, simile, synecdoche, and others. Rather, God's Word *is* intrinsically anthropomorphic, for the Bible *is* God's speech to humans in human language. God's speaking to humans *is* anthropomorphism. Anthropomorphism is a description of God's revelation; anthropomorphism is not a description of our interpretation of Scripture.[39] The fact that God revealed himself anthropomorphically does not warrant us to subscribe to "anthro-

---

[38] Cf. G. B. Caird, *The Language and Imagery of the Bible* (Philadelphia: Westminster, 1980), 172-182.

[39] Some continue the same confusion that characterized much of the discussions between Dispensationalists and Covenant Theologians during the latter half of the last century. Some open theists take the term "anthropomorphism," which properly describes *how* God reveals himself, and unreflectively turn it into an adjective to describe a human hermeneutic or method of interpretation. Observe Boyd's carelessness in two examples: (1) "Hence it is tempting to *anthropomorphically assume* that God must face similar difficulties" (emphasis added). (2) "Some, like [Bruce] Ware, can't fathom this infinite intelligence and thus *anthropomorphically reduce* God's future to one possible future and insist that even then one must be meticulously controlled" (*Satan and the Problem of Evil*, 129-130, emphasis added). The problem with Boyd's latter statement is not restricted to his expression "anthropomorphically reduce." The expression "God's future" is surely problematic. (Cf. the strange title: *Does God Have a Future? A Debate on Divine Providence*, by Christopher A. Hall and John Sanders [Grand Rapids, Mich.: Baker, 2003].) Also, ponder the incoherence of his faulting Ware for not being able to "fathom this infinite intelligence." Can anyone fathom infinite intelligence? Does Boyd fathom infinite intelligence? If so, then he falls under his own indictment of Calvin (98-99). See also the confusion of terminology in Amos Yong, "Divine Omniscience and Future Contingents: Weighing the Pre-

pomorphic interpretation." We are not to read the Bible anthropomorphically. Rather, we are to recognize that the Bible *is* anthropomorphic in character. Therefore, I propose the following definition of anthropomorphism, a definition that emerges from the soil of Scripture: *Because God formed Adam from the "dust of the earth" and breathed into his nostrils the breath of life, making him in his own image and likeness, God makes himself known to his creatures in their likeness, as if he wears both their form and qualities, when in fact they wear his likeness.*

Image of God—Creature Distinguished from Creator

From where does God's self-revelation derive its anthropomorphic nature? Sanders answers that God's self-disclosure to humans requires us "to presuppose a shared context between God and the creation."[40] He means that God shares "the conditions of our existence, including our language, history and spatio-temporal world. This is our context, and the biblical revelation asserts that God enters into that context with us by being in relation to us."[41] To explain revelation as anthropomorphic, Sanders logically posits a "shared context," and then insists that God exists within "the conditions of our existence," an amazing affirmation. However, anthropomorphism is not a heuristic device that derives from systematic theology's logical postulates. Rather, anthropomorphism is of the essence of God's self-revelation in Scripture.[42] It derives from the fact that God formed Adam from the "dust of the

---

suppositional Issues in the Contemporary Debate," *Evangelical Review of Theology* 26 (2002): 240-264. Yong states, "If God is not fully revealed but remains partially hidden in the language of revelation itself, *allegorical* and especially *spiritualistic interpretations* of the text are required in order to keep one from being deceived that he or she has fully understood what is ultimately incomprehensible" (emphasis added).

[40] Sanders, *The God Who Risks*, 24. "Anthropomorphic language does not preclude literal predication to God. Of course, the question must be asked, What is it to which the anthropomorphisms refer? If God shares the same context with us by entering into relation with us, as the biblical revelation presupposes, then we have a basis for our language about God. What I mean by the word *literal* is that our language about God is reality depicting (truthful) such that there is a referent, an other, with whom we are in relationship and of whom we have genuine knowledge" (25).

[41] Ibid. For a critique of Sanders's reasoning, see Jones, "Metaphor in Exile," 37ff.

[42] Horton's excellent historical-theological study "Hellenistic or Hebrew?" (chapter 6 in this volume) shows that the view argued in this essay is the classic Christian and Reformed view: "Thus, Calvin and the Reformed do not use analogy as a fall-back strategy when they find something that does not fit their system. Rather, it is the warp and woof of their covenantal approach, a necessary implication of the Creator-creature relationship as they understand it. *All* of God's self-revelation is analogical, not just some of it. . . . Transcendence and immanence become inextricably bound up with the divine drama of redemption. Revelation no less than redemption is an act of condescension and grace" (210).

earth" in his image. Through Moses, God is pleased to disclose himself as one who, as a potter, fashions mankind and beasts from the dust of the earth (Gen. 2:7-8, 19).[43] The anthropomorphic imagery appeals to human imagination. The analogy is rich, for God is an unusual potter. As a potter's hands mold a vessel, God, who has no hands, formed Adam.[44] Likewise, God the potter, who has no lungs, "breathed into his nostrils the breath of life, and the man became a living being."[45]

As it was with the birds of the air and the beasts of the field, with which Adam shared the earth, God formed man from the "dust of the ground." From the ground (*'ădāmāh*), God formed man (*'ādām*).[46] This vividly makes the point that God made man from the earth and for the earth; man is an earthly creature (Gen. 2:8, 15; Ps. 115:16). The biblical narrative sharply distinguishes man from God: "In the beginning, God created," but man was formed from the "dust of the ground" by God.[47] God is creator; man is the creature formed by the creator to bear his image.

Against Sanders, Scripture does not warrant positing a "shared context between God and creation." Humans and animals share the same context of existence, for God formed both from the "dust of the ground"; both are earthly. Even so, as Creator, God distinguished man from beasts by making man in his image and likeness. Simultaneously, man is like God and unlike God, which, by definition, is what likeness implies.[48] God bestowed his likeness upon man, but man is of the earth,

---

[43] The Hebrew verb *yāṣar* denotes "to form" or "to fashion." When used as a synonym for *bārā'* (create) and *'āśāh* (make), its emphasis is on shaping or forming of the object (T. E. McComiskey, "*yāṣar*," *Theological Wordbook of the Old Testament* [Chicago: Moody, 1980], 1:396).

[44] The comments of Douglas Wilson on Isaiah 40:13ff are fitting: "Only God holds the oceans in the palm of His hand, and He is able to do this because He doesn't have any hands" (Wilson, "The Loveliness of Orthodoxy," in *Bound Only Once*, ed. Wilson, 25).

[45] Cf. A. Berkeley Mickelsen, *Interpreting the Bible* (Grand Rapids, Mich.: Eerdmans, 1963): "Philosophers who dislike anthropomorphisms may say that some unthinking person might conceive of God as a man on his knees testing his lung capacity. But such dangers are worth the risk because the gain made possible by this use of figurative language far outweighs any such possible loss. God made man alive by imparting life from himself to man" (314-315).

[46] For rationale why I use *man* for *'ādām*, see Vernard Eller, *The Language of Canaan and the Grammar of Feminism* (Grand Rapids, Mich.: Eerdmans, 1982), 13ff. Though Genesis 2:7-8 focuses upon the order of creation, first the man and then the woman, the use of *'ādām* bears significance like its use in Genesis 1:26.

[47] Cf. John H. Sailhamer, *The Pentateuch as Narrative: A Biblical-Theological Commentary* (Grand Rapids, Mich.: Zondervan, 1992), 98. He states, "In the light of the special treatment given to humanity's creation in chapter 1 [Gen 1:26ff], the emphasis on human creatureliness in chapter 2 is not without importance."

[48] Cf. Green, *Imagining God*, 131. "Whether in everyday speech or in philosophical discourse, to say that one thing is *like* another necessarily implies a degree of unlikeness as well; otherwise one would say 'the same as.'"

a creature. God is not like man, for man is only an image or resemblance of him. This accounts for God's analogical self-disclosure to humans. God, who is not human, reveals himself to humans *as though he were human* (i.e., analogically or anthropomorphically).

Apprehension of God and relation to God are ours only in terms of analogies that derive from the fact that God made man in his own image. God's imprinted image is organic. The Creator-creature analogy yields the Bible's five primary analogical relationships within which we relate to God: (1) king and subject; (2) judge and defendant/litigant; (3) husband and wife; (4) father and child; and (5) master and slave. God, who made his creatures in his own image, is pleased to disclose himself to us in keeping with the God-like adornment with which he clothed us. Here is the essence of anthropomorphism. God reveals himself to us in human terms, yet we must not compare God to us as if we were the ultimate reference point. God organically and indelibly impressed his image upon man so that our relationships to one another reflect his relationships with us. We do not come to know God as creator *ex nihilo* because we know ourselves to be creative and imagine him to be greater. Instead, man creates because we are like God. God is the original; we are the organic image, the living copy. We do not rightly speak of God as king by projecting onto him regal imagery because we think it is fitting for God. Rather, bowing before God who has dominion is proper because man, as king over creation, is the image of kingship; God, the true king, is the reality that casts the image of the earthly king.[49] It is not as if God looked around his creation and found marital union between male and female to be a fit pattern for his relationship with humans. "Male and female he created them" that they may "become one flesh" (Gen. 2:24). The union of husband and wife is an earthly image or copy of the heavenly union of God, the true husband, with his people, the true bride. Paul understood marriage in Genesis 2:24 this way, for he cites the passage and explains, "This is a profound mystery—but I am talking about Christ and the church" (Eph. 5:32).[50]

---

[49] Terry states, "The Lord is king, not borrowing this title from the kings of earth, but having lent his own title to them—and not the name only, but so ordering, that all true rule and government upon earth, with its righteous laws, its stable ordinances, its punishment and its grace, its majesty and its terror, should tell of Him and of his kingdom which ruleth over all—so that 'kingdom of God' is not in fact a figurative expression, but most literal: it is rather the earthly kingdoms and earthly kings that are figures and shadows of the true" (*Biblical Hermeneutics*, 245).

[50] Cf. discussions by Eller, *Language of Canaan*, 37-47; and Terry, *Biblical Hermeneutics*, 245. See also John Piper, *Brothers, We Are Not Professionals: A Plea to Pastors for Radical Ministry* (Nashville: Broadman & Holman, 2002), 245-254.

Because God made man analogous to himself, God exploits that analogy when he reveals himself to us. "Man was created as an analogue of God; his thinking, his willing, and his doing is therefore properly conceived as at every point analogical to the thinking, willing, and doing of God."[51] The whole human reflects God's image and likeness. Though what we are bears sin's corruption and is in need of trans-formation by God's grace, even human anger and jealousy, though unredeemed, have some similarities to God's qualities.[52] God is pleased to redeem us, including the qualities he has given us, so that anger, exercised without sinning (Eph. 4:26), is properly described as a quality fitting "the new man who in God's likeness is created in true righteousness and holiness" (v. 24).[53] Anger, jealousy, and speech, redeemed by God, are qualities fitting the new man, for they reflect God. They are God-like, godly.

It is not enough to say that anthropomorphisms are human ascriptions to God. "Rather, our human qualities are themselves but a reflection of God's person and attributes."[54] Biblically speaking, we should understand anthropomorphisms first as God's self-ascriptions, for he is pleased to reveal himself to us in keeping with his own image and likeness into which he molded us from the dust of the ground. Thus, as Silva suggests, given that God does not have a body, the question we should ask is not "How can God speak or hear or see?" but "How can *we* see or hear or speak?"[55] What is the answer? God, who does not have hands, formed man from the dust of the ground as he made man in his image and likeness. Our capacities to speak, to hear, and to see reflect our Creator's qualities.

---

[51] Cornelius Van Til, "Nature of Scripture," in *The Infallible Word*, ed. N. B. Stonehouse and Paul Woolley (Philadelphia: Presbyterian & Reformed, 1947), 273.

[52] Cf. Horton, "Hellenistic or Hebrew?" 331. Horton states, "The anger that God condemns in us (Prov 29:11, 22; 22:24; 1 Cor 13:5) is different from the anger that fills him with holy wrath, whatever similarities there may be."

[53] Take note that the underlined portion of Paul's phrase in Ephesians 4:24— *ton kata theon ktisthenta*—denotes *godliness* in 2 Corinthians 7:10, 11; 11:2.

[54] Moisés Silva, *God, Language, and Scripture: Reading the Bible in the Light of General Linguistics*, Foundations of Contemporary Interpretation, vol. 4 (Grand Rapids, Mich.: Zondervan, 1990), 22.

[55] Ibid., 22-23.

Image of God—Mankind Distinguished from
All Other Created Things

The account of creation emphasizes that God formed both humans and animals from the earth. Furthermore, Genesis makes it clear that both animals and humans derive their lives from God, for "living creature" fittingly describes both (Gen. 2:7, 19; 1:20, 21, 24, 30; 9:12, 15). Like humans, most animals have eyes, ears, and mouths that make sounds. Yet, the creation account distinguishes mankind from animals.

The biblical narrative of Genesis sets apart creation of man from creation of everything else, especially of living beings, with four distinctive statements. First, the personal command, "Let us make" stands in contrast to the impersonal command—"Let there be"—which is the command that introduces creation of everything else. Second, the narrative describes the making of each creature as "according to its own kind," but when God makes man, the narrative alters the pattern and says, "God created man in his own image" (Gen. 1:27). The image of God distinguishes humans from other living creatures. God did not make man "according to his own kind." Man's likeness does not terminate upon himself; his likeness points away from himself to God, for God shares his likeness with man. Distinct from a bull or a mouse, man is the earthly image of his creator. The narrative emphasizes this distinction by stating it twice and in chiasmus: "So God created man in his own image, in the image of God he created him" (Gen. 1:27). The emphasis of the text is upon the unity of man. God's making the woman from a portion derived from the side of man reinforces this unity, for she does not derive directly from the ground as Adam does. God made Adam from the ground (*'ǎdāmāh*), but he made woman from the side of Adam (*'ādām;* Gen. 2:21-22).[56] Third, in contrast to God's creation of other living beings, the narrative identifies God's creation of man as entailing two sexes: "male and female he created them" (Gen. 1:27). Together, male and female constitute man made in God's image and likeness.[57] Fourth, Genesis links God's creation of humans in his own image

---

[56] According to Genesis 2:23, Adam highlights this with a phonetic wordplay: "This is now bone of my bones and flesh of my flesh; she shall be called 'woman' [*'ishāh*], for she was taken out of man [*'ish*]."

[57] See Eller, *Language of Canaan*, 22-32. Eller states, "In summary, here are two levels of discourse: Level 1 with man as an indivisible integer, and Level 4 with mankind constituted of males and females. Both levels are true and both essential to a proper understanding of the passage. Yet even

and likeness with dominion over land and water beasts, plants, and earth. "Let us make man in our image, in our likeness, and let them rule over the fish of the sea and the birds of the air, over the livestock, over all the earth, and over all the creatures that move along the ground" (Gen. 1:26).[58] Though dominion over creatures and plants of the earth distinguishes humans from animals and all other created things, Genesis does not restrict the image of God to man's dominion over fish, birds, ground animals, and seed-bearing plants. Because God made Adam in his likeness, God distinguished him from animals and plants by giving him unique responsibilities and abilities as his image bearer. God placed Adam in the garden to till it and care for it (Gen. 2:15).

Likewise, God sharply distinguishes humans from animals by enabling humans to project thoughts that encompass moral choices and their consequences. "And the LORD God commanded the man, 'You may freely eat of every tree of the garden; but of the tree of the knowledge of good and evil you shall not eat, for in the day that you eat of it you shall die'" (Gen. 2:16-17). God made Adam in his own image, thus integrating within him deductive reasoning capacity and moral accountability. Adam had not yet experienced death. Yet because he bore God's likeness, he knew that by eating of the forbidden tree he would bring calamity upon himself, calamity not worth investigating by eating.

God impresses upon Adam how he differs from other "living beings," with which he shares the earth, by having him name the animals. At the same time, God instructs Adam that despite similarities animals have with him, there are profound differences. God gives Adam dominion over them. Animals do not speak; Adam does, for he names the animals. Adam recognizes a distinctive boundary between himself and other living beings, for there is no fitting companion among the animals that is his equal or essential complement (Gen. 2:18-20). So God makes woman from a portion of Adam's side, that he might have a suit-

---

though both are necessary, the verse creates a clear priority between them. However, that priority is not here expressed in terms of chronology; only one act of creation is being described. Yet priority there most certainly is; the order of the two statements could not be reversed. Not only does the first statement come *first;* it is doubled for emphasis; and the 'image of God' is ascribed to it alone. Man always is to be thought of as an undifferentiated unity before he is analyzed into constituents (of whatever sort). And although it is not explicit in this verse, we have seen that very quickly to be made explicit is the idea that, even on Level 4, the male and female constituents are to represent a molecular bonding rather than separated atoms. However the account is read, the *unity* of the race takes precedence over any of the *constituencies* of which it is composed" (33-34).

[58] Cf. Sailhamer, *Pentateuch as Narrative,* 94-95.

able helper and complement that derived from his own flesh and would bring him wholeness in union with her (vv. 21-22). As Adam breathes only because God breathed life into him, so also the woman's life is not inherent within her, for she also derives her life from God. Together they exist solely at the pleasure of their Creator. If the Lord withdraws his breath from them, they will return to the dust (Ps. 104:29; Job 34:14-15). Also, unlike animals, the man and the woman have God-like qualities of self-awareness, purposeful desires, and knowledge of righteousness as ones who stand before God (Gen. 2:23-25). Thus, humans know themselves to have personality and individuality that fundamentally distinguishes them from animals. With purposeful desires that mark them off from animals, man and woman have deep innate desires to unite again as one flesh in union that is God-like.

Speech characterizes God and man, not animals. Adam recognizes this when on the sixth day he speaks names for the animals while learning God's lesson that he stands far above the animals. It is against this backdrop that Genesis 3 tells of the woman conversing with the serpent that should not be talking. Animals do not speak, but inexplicably the serpent talks. Adam can speak, but he remains silent. Thus, without a word of admonition from Adam, the woman falls prey to the serpent's deception, and Adam falls prey to the woman's seduction to eat the forbidden fruit (Gen. 3:13; 3:12).

Image of God—Source of God's Anthropomorphic Revelation

Even though the man and the woman knew God because God made them in his image and likeness, they suppressed this truth, and the crafty serpent enticed the woman. The serpent's temptation promised knowledge of "good and evil," as God knows "good and evil." The woman expected that the fruit would infuse her with wisdom, so she ate the fruit and gave some to the man. Together, they exchanged the truth of God's warning for the lie of the serpent, "You will not surely die." They believed the forbidden fruit would make them like God, so they ate in order that, on their own, they might "be like God, knowing good and evil." Discontented with bearing God's likeness as his endowed gift, they pursued what they *were* already (God's likeness) by eating the fruit of the tree that God forbade. Because they heeded the serpent and did not

worship and serve their Creator, they exchanged their created glory as
the image of God for their ironic, elusive, and futile quest to "be like
God" on their own terms. They became idolaters. Ironically, their eyes
opened, not to their likeness to God, but to their nakedness, to their
deformed and distorted imaging of God.[59]

The creation narrative tells in story form that the image of God
functions as the link that gives humans inherent knowledge of God.
What is remarkable in the narrative, following the sin in the garden, is
the way the biblical text portrays God. The Lord, who created man
(ʾādām) from the ground (ʾădāmāh), walks in the garden, calling out,
"Where are you?" When Adam answers, the Lord asks two more questions: "Who told you that you were naked? Have you eaten from the
tree that I commanded you not to eat from?" God reveals himself to the
man and the woman in the form and likeness he had given them when
he made them. Does the narrative mean that God has a body, after all,
with feet and a mouth, and that he looks like Adam? Does God have
body sensation for heat and cold? Does God have eyes? Is God's vision
limited? Was God ignorant concerning where Adam and Eve were and
that they were hiding? Was God ignorant of how the man and the
woman discovered that they were naked? Was God lacking knowledge
that they had eaten fruit from the forbidden tree? Will not a so-called
"straightforward reading of the text" yield positive responses to all these
questions? Are there any indicators in the narrative that guard us from
answering these questions incorrectly?

Genesis 3:8-11 sketches a portrait of God who shows himself in
human form and likeness. Moses *truly* portrays God as walking in the
garden and calling out to Adam with audible words. If we take the Bible
literally, are we not obliged to accept this portrayal of God to the man
and the woman? This, however, is not to say that the narrative portrays
God *as he truly is in himself*. Note the placement of the modifier "truly."
That the story *truly* portrays God as walking in the garden is to say no
more than that God took on Adam's form as he revealed himself to the
sinful couple. To conclude that the text portrays God *as he truly is* (i.e.,
as he is in himself), one must say that God has a physical body, that he
has physical feet, that he has a physical mouth. It is unwarranted to con-

---

[59] Cf. Genesis 3:1-7 with Romans 1:18-23. The latter passage seems to be a generalized
commentary on the former.

clude that, since God disclosed himself in human form, God has physical features—body, feet, mouth—as Adam does. While we must avoid *physicalizing* God, on the basis of Genesis 3:8-11, we must also protect against *etherealizing* God, as if Moses' narrative does not portray God as *truly* revealing himself to Adam and Eve in the garden. It seems reasonable to conclude that the Lord *truly* revealed himself to the sinful pair in human form, that he wore Adam's form, just as God likely had done previously with Adam on the Sixth Day during the naming of the animals and the formation of woman.

Likewise, if we claim that the narrative of Genesis 3:8-11 portrays God *as he truly is in himself,* we must also claim that God does not fully know either the present or the past, based upon the questions he asks. The Lord's questions are as much God's self-revelation in human likeness as his walking and speaking are self-disclosures in human form. "Where are you? Who told you that you were naked? Have you eaten from the tree that I commanded you not to eat from?"—such questions are not seeking information, as if God does not know. Rather, precisely because God knows, he uses questions to draw from the man and the woman acknowledgment that they lusted for wisdom and grasped after his likeness on their own terms. The Lord is showing himself *anthropomorphically.* His questions are *anthropomorphic* in character. That is to say, his interrogatives are the kinds of questions we humans ask of one another, not because we do not know the answers to our questions, but precisely because we do know.[60]

Therefore, to the man and woman who attempted to cover their shame with fig leaves and by hiding in the foliage of the garden, the Lord framed his questions *as if he were human,* as if he were a human prosecutor. His line of questioning suggests the proceedings of a court session, much like in Genesis 4:9-10: "Where is your brother Abel? . . . What have you done?"[61] These are the questions a prosecutor, who knows the facts of the case, asks a defendant, to seek not information but conviction. Each question tightens the noose of conviction around Cain. Likewise, each question the Lord asks of Adam skillfully draws

---

[60] Cf. John 6:5-6: "When Jesus looked up and saw a great crowd coming toward him, he said to Philip, 'Where shall we buy bread for these people to eat?' He asked this only to test him, for he already had in mind what he was going to do."

[61] Cf. Sailhamer, *Pentateuch as Narrative,* 106.

him into conviction with his own words of response.[62] The Lord's questions are anthropomorphic in nature (i.e., framed in human terms).

God made mankind in his image and likeness. Therefore, God reveals himself to us with reference to ourselves. The image of God is his revelatory nexus integrated into our very being. He discloses himself to us with reference to his likeness in us. Thus, apart from this first analogical revelation imprinted upon us, we would know nothing about God, for "without knowledge of self there is no knowledge of God," and "without knowledge of God there is no knowledge of self."[63] The same interchange is true concerning knowledge of creation, so to this first analogical self-disclosure of himself, God associates all other revelation. God implanted within us both an intrinsic awareness of deity and an inherent sense of our own dignity over all other created things.[64] Calvin affirms, "Lest anyone, then, be excluded from access to happiness, he . . . revealed himself and daily discloses himself in the whole workmanship of the universe. As a consequence, men cannot open their eyes without being compelled to see him. Indeed, his essence is incomprehensible; hence, his divineness far escapes all human perception."[65] Because God's creation is "the appearance of things invisible" (Heb. 11:3), it is "a sort of mirror in which we can contemplate God, who is otherwise invisible."[66] Therefore, God has imprinted his indelible signature upon his whole creation. All creation points as unmistakably to its creator, God, as finely crafted furniture is its artisan's signature. Because God invested all of creation to reflect his glory (Rom. 1:20), it provides rich metaphorical imagery by which he reveals himself throughout Scripture.[67] The psalmist does not impose anthropomorphism upon the heavens; God

---

[62] Ibid.

[63] John Calvin, *Institutes of the Christian Religion* (Philadelphia: Westminster, 1960), 1.1.1 and 1.1.2.

[64] Ibid., 1.3.1 and 1.5.1-3. Calvin states, "To prevent anyone from taking refuge in the pretense of ignorance, God himself has implanted in all men a certain understanding of his divine majesty" (1.3.1).

[65] Ibid., 1.5.1.

[66] Ibid.

[67] Ibid., 1.5.2. Calvin states, "But upon his individual works he has engraved unmistakable marks of his glory, so clear and so prominent that even unlettered and stupid folk cannot plead the excuse of ignorance. Therefore the prophet very aptly exclaims that he is 'clad with light as with a garment' [Ps. 104:2p.]. It is as if he said: Thereafter the Lord began to show himself in the visible splendor of his apparel, ever since in the creation of the universe he brought forth those insignia whereby he shows his glory to us, whenever and wherever we cast our gaze."

invested the heavens with speech that translates itself into every human tongue:

> The heavens declare the glory of God;
>   the skies proclaim the work of his hands.
> Day after day they pour forth speech;
>   night after night they display knowledge.
> There is no speech or language
>   where their voice is not heard. (Ps. 19:1-3, NIV)

God, who created the heavens and the earth, "rested on the seventh day from all his work" (Gen. 2:2). The creation story continues, "So God blessed the seventh day and hallowed it, because on it God rested from all the work that he had done in creation" (v. 3, NRSV). Did God get tired because of his labors? Did God cease (*shābat*) his creative work because he grew weary? Until recently, who except young children would have raised these questions? Now, thanks to open theists, theologians have to address these questions. The answer is deceptively easy. One might argue that *shābat* means "to cease." Nevertheless, Exodus 31:16-17 complicates the matter: "Therefore the Israelites shall keep the sabbath, observing the sabbath throughout their generations, as a perpetual covenant. It is a sign forever between me and the people of Israel that in six days the LORD made heaven and earth, and on the seventh day he rested, and was refreshed" (NRSV). That the Lord "rested and was refreshed" (*yināpēš*) is more difficult, especially in view of Exodus 23:12: "Six days you shall do your work, but on the seventh day you shall rest, so that your ox and your donkey may have relief, and your homeborn slave and the resident alien may be refreshed." That God reveals himself as taking "rest" from his creative work and being "refreshed" on the seventh day triggers tension in our minds, because they do not seem fitting activities for God. The tension intensifies when we read passages such as Psalm 121. The psalmist says,

> My help comes from the LORD,
>   the Maker of heaven and earth.
>
> He will not let your foot slip—
>   he who watches over you will not slumber;

> indeed, he who watches over Israel
> will neither slumber nor sleep. (Ps. 121:2-4, NIV)

Surely, the human need for refreshment hardly suggests that God grew tired in his work and had to refresh himself. The creature is not the determinative reference point. The biblical text orients the analogy so that the referential point is God. God's pattern of creation and rest established the earthly analogy that Israel was to carry out in its building of the tabernacle.[68] In Exodus 31:12-17, it is clear that the Lord established the sabbath as a *sign* (*'ôt*). As a sign, the sabbath does not terminate upon itself. It points to the original, to God's eternal rest, for Moses ceases his literary description of the succession of days and nights as he tells of the day when God "ceased from all the work of creating" (Gen. 2:3). Of the days of creation, God hallowed only the seventh day, the climax of his work, thus foreshadowing the climax of his redemptive work in the Last Day. Humans, made in his image, enter into the perpetual seventh day with him by imitating him who ceased from his work and was refreshed (Heb. 4:10).[69]

Understanding all figurative language with which God reveals himself begins with the creation account in Genesis 1. Most basic is the fact that God made man in his image and likeness. The Creator made us, his creatures, to be his analogues. There is a right and a wrong way to think about God as he reveals himself in human likeness.[70] Right and biblical thinking is to recognize that in some profound way, we humans reveal something of God's glory. For whatever God's talking, asking questions, relenting, planning, loving, etc., conveys concerning God, these qualities do so not because God borrows them from us. Rather, the Lord bestowed his own qualities upon us and invested those qualities with

---

[68] Sailhamer, *The Pentateuch as Narrative*, 309. He observes, "Just as God made the world, so Israel is to make the tabernacle. Like God's work, it is to be a holy work and is to be carried out by observing the holy times. The Israelites' work on the tabernacle was not holy merely because they were working on a holy structure. The work was holy because it was sanctified by the sign of the Sabbath. As such, the building of the tabernacle in the wilderness is a paradigm of all of Israel's work."

[69] Calvin, *Institutes*, 2.8.29; 2.8.30.

[70] "Scripture . . . has no hesitation in speaking anthropomorphically of God. It ascribes all manner of activity to him. Of this activity we cannot think otherwise than spatially and temporally. So we are face to face with the choice either of thinking of God as altogether like unto ourselves, or of thinking ourselves the finite analogues of the fullness of his being. As we cannot do the first without wiping out the difference between Creator and creature, we are compelled to do the latter" (Cornelius Van Til, *An Introduction to Systematic Theology* [Nutley, N.J.: Presbyterian & Reformed, 1976], 212).

image significance so that our talking, asking questions, relenting, planning, loving, choosing reflect God-likeness.

III. VEILED REVELATION—FROM ANTHROPOMORPHISM TO INCARNATE WORD

As we read the Bible, especially the Old Testament, the action and events may seem to us as separate stories, each with its own moral.[71] Even worse, we may lose sight of the fact that the whole Bible is God's revelatory voice and that each portion contributes to the whole. If we read the Bible correctly, we will enter into the world the Bible portrays and accept its presuppositions and affirmations concerning God. The biblical drama requires the presence of the Lord God as the leading actor in its story line. Yet the Bible also requires that we acknowledge God as the scriptwriter, director, and producer of this grand drama. If we correctly read the Bible, therefore, we recognize that the Bible's story line stretches along the history of God's redemption of his creation, with the First Man and Second Man, each with his significant role at creation and consummation, respectively. Integral to this history of redemption are progressive sequences of God's revelation that reach completion and fulfillment in the disclosure of God's Last Adam, Jesus Christ. The New Testament writers understood the Old Testament this way: "After God spoke long ago to the fathers by the prophets in many portions and many ways, in these last days he spoke to us by his Son, whom he appointed heir of all things, through whom also he made the ages" (Heb. 1:1-2).

Christians readily recognize how the sacrificial lamb of the first Passover foreshadowed the *true* Passover lamb, Jesus Christ (Ex. 4:22-23; 11:1–12:29; 1 Cor. 5:7). Likewise, believers understand that Jesus Christ is the *true* (i.e., real) bread, the bread from heaven, that manna foreshadowed to the Israelites long ago (John 6:32). More difficult to recognize is how God's anthropomorphic self-revelation, throughout the Old Testament, foreshadows God's disclosure in the incarnate Word, Jesus Christ, who is "the image of the invisible God" (Col. 1:15). Though this deserves much more attention, the following discussion concentrates on three crucial links between Old Testament revelation in

---

[71] For an excellent source for correcting "moralistic readings" of the Bible, see Graeme Goldsworthy, *Preaching the Whole Bible as Christian Scripture* (Grand Rapids, Mich.: Eerdmans, 2000).

which God clothes his glory with human similitude (anthropomor-phism) and New Testament revelation in which God clothes his glory with human flesh.

Anthropomorphic Theophany—God's Veiled Glory

"Show me your glory, I pray" (Ex. 33:18) is a bold request for Moses, a mere man, to ask of God. This is especially true because he interceded on behalf of Israel, who had already broken covenant with the Lord. Moses and Joshua had just returned from the mountain with the covenant tablets when the people imitated Adam's sin when they "exchanged their Glory for an image of a bull, which eats grass" (Ps. 106:19-20; Exodus 32).[72] The Lord favored Moses, who interceded for the covenant-breaking nation, and spoke "face to face" with him, "just as a man speaks to his friend" (Ex. 33:11; Num. 12:6ff). The Lord calls Moses to the mountain for renewal of the covenant. Unlike the first giv-ing of the covenant, when the Israelites saw the glory of the Lord settle upon the mountain as a cloud and "like a consuming fire on top of the mountain" (Ex. 24:15-17, NIV), this time, Moses alone is to see the Lord's glory. To Moses' bold request, the Lord responds,

> "I will make all my goodness pass before you, and will proclaim before you the name, 'The LORD'; and I will be gracious to whom I will be gracious, and will show mercy on whom I will show mercy. But," he said, "you cannot see my face; for no one shall see me and live." And the LORD continued, "See, there is a place by me where you shall stand on the rock; and while my glory passes by I will put you in a cleft of the rock, and I will cover you with my hand until I have passed by; then I will take away my hand, and you shall see my back; but my face shall not be seen." (Ex. 33:19-20, NRSV)[73]

---

[72] The Hebrew of Psalm 106:20 reads, "and they exchanged their glory," but the LXX of Codex Alexandrinus reads, "and they exchanged *his* glory" (*tēn doxan autou*). The RSV, NRSV, and ESV preserve this variant by supplying the referent, God, for the pronoun: "They exchanged the glory of God for the image of an ox that eats grass."

[73] Sailhamer observes, "In the first revelation of God's glory at Sinai, Moses explained to the people that its purpose had been 'to test you, so that the fear of God will be with you to keep you from sinning' (20:20). After the incident with the golden calf, however, the revelation of God's glory had a quite different purpose. When Moses asked to see God's glory, the Lord answered, 'I will cause all my goodness to pass in front of you. . . . I will have mercy on whom I will have mercy, and I will have compassion on whom I have compassion' (33:19). Surprisingly, what Moses learned about God's glory after the 'great sin' (32:30) of the golden calf was not further fear of God but rather that he was a gracious God, full of compassion" (*The Pentateuch as Narrative*, 315).

The Lord will show all his goodness to whomever he chooses to be merciful. It is because of God's mercy that he reveals himself to Moses as though he were a man. He seems to have a body. He speaks of his face. He converses with Moses. He appears to have a hand, though large enough to cover Moses. He even seems to have a posterior side. Yet God is unlike any human, for he is awesome, even fearsome. No one can see his face and live. This does not refer merely to sight of a physical form but to full exposure to the Lord's glory or character as summed up in the expression, "all my goodness." His glory is his name or character of goodness, graciousness, and mercy. It is also because of God's mercy that he veiled his brilliant glory from Moses to preserve his life when he descended in a cloud and then "passed before him" (Ex. 34:6). As the Lord passed by, he proclaimed,

> "The LORD, the LORD, a God merciful and gracious, slow to anger, and abounding in steadfast love and faithfulness, keeping steadfast love for the thousandth generation, forgiving iniquity and transgression and sin, yet by no means clearing the guilty, but visiting the iniquity of the parents upon the children and the children's children, to the third and fourth generation." (Ex. 34:7, NRSV)

Moses witnessed a private theophany at the renewal of the covenant. When Moses descended the mountain with the tablets of covenant renewal, the skin of his face shone (Ex. 34:29). Thus, Moses carried both the Law covenant and the glory of God with him back into the camp of the Israelites. On the mountain, Moses interceded for the people, and when he returned from his meeting with God, he was both mediator of God's covenant Law and mediator of God's covenant presence.[74] The Lord, who veiled himself from Moses even in the act of self-disclosure, veiled himself from Israel as he revealed himself through his earthly mediator who veiled his face as his skin reflected the radiance of God's glory.[75]

---

[74] Scott J. Hafemann, *Paul, Moses, and the History of Israel* (Peabody, Mass.: Hendrickson, 1995), 222.

[75] Ibid., 223. Hafemann explains, "The veil of Moses makes it possible for the glory of God to be in the midst of the people, albeit now mediated through Moses, without destroying them. As such, the veil . . . functions in the same way as the fence around the bottom of Mt. Sinai in Exod. 19:12 and the curtain . . . before the 'holy of holies' in the tabernacle as that which both separates and protects the people from the glory of God."

Anthropomorphic Vision—God's Veiled Holiness

Centuries later, Isaiah saw the Lord represented to him in a vision when he received his commission as prophet. Moses had seen the Lord's glory. Isaiah saw his holiness and cried out: "'Woe to me!' I cried. 'I am ruined! For I am a man of unclean lips, and I live among a people of unclean lips, and my eyes have seen the King, the LORD Almighty'" (Isa. 6:5). The Lord revealed himself to Isaiah in human categories, with similarity but punctuated with dissimilarity. Isaiah saw the Lord upon a throne, but what the prophet saw, though resembling an earthly throne room, was unlike any throne room he had seen. It was not only the seat of government; it was also the center of worship, for it was a temple. The Lord's throne was high and lofty, and the train of the Lord's robe filled the temple. There were royal attendants, too, but not like King Uzziah's, for there were six-winged seraphs hovering above the Lord as they covered their faces and feet with their other four wings. With voices that shook the doorposts and thresholds of this magnificent temple filled with smoke, they worshiped the Lord who sat upon the throne.

Isaiah's entire portrayal of heaven's throne room is anthropomorphic. God trades upon the splendor and royalty of the earthly kingship he established to reveal himself as the one true king. While sufficient similarities were present so that, in his vision, Isaiah recognized a regal throne room, dissimilarities abounded. Thus, when Isaiah prophesied to Israel, he highly exalted the Lord throughout his prophecy.

Anthropomorphic Prophecy—God's Veiled Eternity

Bruce Ware cogently demonstrates, from a sequence of passages in Isaiah 40–48, that God's knowledge of the future is a distinctive attribute of his deity that sets him apart from idols. Ware expands upon Stephen Charnock's argument concerning Isaiah 41:22b-23a—"Or declare to us the things to come, tell us what the future holds, so we may know that you are gods." Charnock says:

> Such a fore-knowledge of things to come, is here ascribed to God by God himself, as a distinction of him from all false gods; Such a knowledge, that if any could prove that they were possessors of, he would acknowledge them gods as well as himself: 'that we may know that you are gods.' He puts his Deity to stand or fall upon this account, and this should be the

point which should decide the controversy, whether he or the heathen idols were the true God; the dispute is managed by this medium,—He that knows things to come is God; I know things to come, *ergo* I am God; the idols know not things to come, therefore they are not gods.[76]

How does God make his case that he is God because he knows the future? He reveals himself anthropomorphically. Consider just one passage where the Lord speaks through Isaiah.

Remember this, fix it in mind,
  take it to heart, you rebels.
Remember the former things, those of long ago;
  I am God, and there is no other;
  I am God, and there is none like me.
I make known the end from the beginning,
  from ancient times, what is still to come.
I say: My purpose will stand,
  and I will do all that I please.
From the east I summon a bird of prey;
  from a far-off land, a man to fulfill my purpose.
What I have said, that will I bring about;
  what I have planned, that will I do. (Isa. 46:8-11)

The Lord's argument hangs upon the analogical relationship between God and man. The Lord calls upon humans to remember and to imagine, but he guides both. The command to remember calls upon Israel to take a proper theological view of their history, to understand the present and the future in view of the past, and to recognize "the continuity of action of the one God" whose love and provision for them never faltered.[77] The Lord calls Israel to remember how he provided for her from conception:

Listen to me, O house of Jacob,
  all you who remain of the house of Israel,
you whom I have upheld since you were conceived,
  and have carried since your birth.

---

[76] Stephen Charnock, *The Existence and Attributes of God*, reprinted from 1853 edition (Grand Rapids, Mich.: Baker, 1996), 431.

[77] J. Alec Motyer, *The Prophecy of Isaiah: An Introduction and Commentary* (Downers Grove, Ill.: InterVarsity Press, 1993), 370.

Even to your old age and gray hairs
  I am he, I am he who will sustain you.
I have made you and I will carry you;
  I will sustain you and I will rescue you. (Isa. 46:3-4)

The Lord's call to remember entails anthropomorphism, but God's speech accents lack of resemblance between himself and man: "I am God, and there is no other; I am God, and there is *none like me*" (v. 9). These words recall what the prophet had just said. "To whom will you compare me or count me equal? To whom will you liken me that we may be compared?" (v. 5). No idol sustained Israel. No idol will deliver Israel. The Lord's words express wry mockery:

Some pour out gold from their bags
  and weigh out silver on the scales;
they hire a goldsmith to make it into a god,
  and they bow down and worship it.
They lift it to their shoulders and carry it;
  they set it up in its place, and there it stands.
  From that spot it cannot move.
Though one cries out to it, it does not answer;
  it cannot save him from his troubles. (Isa. 46:6-7)

One may be an idolater without casting an icon from metal or without carving an image from wood or stone. Idolatry begins in the imagination by conceiving of God in one's own likeness. Therefore, the Lord guides proper imagination of his anthropomorphic self-disclosure by emphasizing dissimilarity: "I make known the end from the beginning, from ancient times, what is still to come." Clearly, these anthropomorphic disclosures of unlikeness guard us against placing human limitations upon God. Though we resemble God in that like him, we have "purposes" and "plans," God's purposing and planning are unlike ours, for his are *utterly expansive*—"I make known the end from the beginning, from ancient times, what is still to come." Furthermore, God's purpose is *wholly effective* and *never frustrated*—"My purpose will stand, and I will do all that I please." God *never falters;* he carries out his plan—"What I have said, that will I bring about; what I have planned, that will I do." He effectively accomplishes his purpose, even when it entails a man, even a king, the most powerful human—"From a far-off land, a man to fulfill my purpose" (a reference to Cyrus; 44:28–45:7). Imagine the vast difference between God and us. When we carry out our plans, especially plans that encompass other humans, because we are creatures we are restricted to two options: we may do so by persuasion or resort to coercion. Neither is necessarily effective. God is unlike us. Because God is the sovereign creator, and not a creature, he does not relate to his creatures as one creature relates to another. As the one who made us, he has his own divine ways to move us to do his bidding without violating our wills. God does not coerce his creatures, as open theism claims he must on occasions.[78] Also, God's persuasion is unlike ours, for all our persuasion is external but God's is not, because God turns the heart of the most powerful human as a human diverts a stream of water (Prov. 21:1).

Consider Boyd's explanation of Isaiah 46:10-11:

> Immediately after telling us that he declares "from ancient times things not yet done," the Lord adds, *"My purpose* shall stand, and *I will fulfill* my intention"* (Isa. 46:10b). The Lord is not appealing to information about the future he happens to possess; instead, he is appealing to *his own intentions* about the future. He foreknows that certain things are going to take place because he knows *his own purpose and intention* to bring these events about. As sovereign Lord of history, he has decided to settle *this* much about the future. . . . The Lord's announcement . . . tells us that he is talking about *his own* will and *his own* plans. He declares that the future is settled to the extent that he is going to determine it, but nothing in the text requires that we believe that *everything* that will ever come to pass will do so according to his will and thus is settled ahead of time.[79]

There are two things to observe concerning Boyd's comments. First, Boyd is correct when he says that God does not know the future by pre-observation; he knows the future because he has planned it. In this

---

[78] Boyd contends, "God's design to have creatures who are capable of *moral* decision making requires a sort of covenant of noncoercion with each of them. . . . This means that his response to their evil choices must, under ordinary circumstances, stop short of coercion" (*Satan and the Problem of Evil*, 183). He continues by saying, this "does not entail that God can *never* exercise coercive power in his interactions with free creatures. Nor does it entail that creatures have the power *eternally* to exercise an evil influence on the creation" (185). For a critique of Boyd's willingness to endorse coercion, see the chapter in this volume by Paul Kjoss Helseth.

[79] Boyd, *God of the Possible*, 30.

regard, we are like God. We do not anticipate future events by clair-
voyance. Anticipation of our relationship to tomorrow or next month
derives from our plans, ineffective as they are. Second, Boyd commits
the referential fallacy; he inverts the analogy implicit throughout Isaiah
46:8-11, by taking the analogue's knowledge as the measure of God's
knowledge. He has the analogy upside down. Instead, our knowledge
of the future is like God's knowledge. Of course, the dissimilarities
between our knowing and God's knowing are astronomical. His knowledge is sure, because his purpose is effective; our knowledge is uncertain
because our plans are ineffective. Therefore, to imagine God to have
knowledge of the future with human-like restrictions, when he speaks
of "my purpose" and "what I have planned," as Boyd contends, is to
turn on its head the Lord's words, "I am God, and there is none like me."
Isaiah seeks to shatter this icon. God's knowledge of the future is a distinctive attribute of deity that sets him apart from gods carved out in the
likeness of God's image, namely humans.

Incarnate Word—God's Glory Veiled in Flesh

"No one has ever seen God," the Fourth Gospel announces, alluding to
the time Moses saw the Lord's glory on the mountain (John 1:18; cf. Ex.
33:20). Nevertheless, the glory of the Lord, whose presence stood as a
pillar of cloud at the entrance of the "tent of meeting" where he spoke
face to face with Moses, came to reside among us in his "tent" of human
flesh (John 1:14).[80] The Word, who was with God in the beginning and
who was God, pitched his tent among us to reveal the Father. God's
unique and beloved Son, "who is in the bosom of the Father," emerged
from the cloud that veiled God's glory on Mount Sinai becoming the

---

[80] John 1:14 says, "The Word became flesh and *pitched his tent* [*eskēnōsen*] among us." John's
allusion to the *skēnē* may reference either the tabernacle called "the tent" (Ex. 26:7) where the
Lord would dwell (Ex. 25:8) or the "tent of meeting" located "outside the camp some distance
away" (Ex. 29:42-43; 33:7). The "tent of meeting" seems to have been a provisional tent of
meeting with God until the construction of the tabernacle (Ex. 36:8-38). After the Israelites
constructed the tabernacle, it seems the "tent of meeting" became another designation for the
tabernacle (Ex. 40:29, 34). Moses would enter the provisional tent to meet the Lord. The Lord
would signify his presence with the cloud's descent and station it at the door outside (Ex. 33:9-
10). Inside the tent, the Lord would speak with Moses face to face (33:11). This way the tent of
meeting functioned like the cleft of the rock in which the Lord placed Moses to preserve his life
as his glory passed by (Ex. 33:22-23). Later, the tabernacle would stand in the midst of the Israelite
camp, and the cloud of glory rested not outside the door but inside the tent, so at first Moses had
to stay outside (Ex. 40:34-35). Because the tent of meeting and the tabernacle merge as one, we
should hardly try to distinguish whether John 1:14 alludes to one or the other.

incarnate Word who makes God known (v. 18).[81] The Lord's symbolic manifestation as a cloud took on flesh in the Word. The Lord's anthropomorphic self-disclosure of his glory to Moses, whom he hid in the cleft of the rock on the mountain, now reveals himself as the Word incarnate. Long ago, the Lord said to Moses, "I will make all my goodness pass before you, and will proclaim before you the name, 'The LORD'; and I will be gracious to whom I will be gracious, and will show mercy on whom I will show mercy" (Ex. 33:19). At the close of his mission, the incarnate Word says, "I made your name known to them, and I will make it known" (John 17:26).

As if imitating the Word's glory veiled in flesh, John's Gospel provides semi-veiled verbal links to Exodus 33–34, that the Lord has answered Moses' request more fully—"Now show me your glory" (Ex. 33:18). "We have seen his glory, the glory of the One and Only . . . from the Father" (John 1:14, NIV).[82] This surely refers to John and other eyewitnesses of the incarnate Word. Yet, John does not attach glory to the Word's physical form but to his incarnate identity. He is the unique One who came from the Father, full of grace and truth. Whether John's adjective "full" (*plērēs*) refers to "the Word" or "glory" is not of great consequence, but it seems best to understand it as modifying "glory."[83] John saw the incarnate Word as "full of grace and truth," a description that corresponds to what the Lord revealed to Moses on the mountain when he said, "I will make all my goodness pass before you" (Ex. 33:19). God's glory is his goodness, more fully expressed as "full of grace and truth," the glory of the incarnate Word. John's prologue sustains reference to the theophany and giving of the Law on the mountain by saying, "For from his fullness we have received grace instead of grace. For the Law was given through Moses; grace and truth came through Jesus Christ" (John 1:16-17).[84] Then John closes his prologue with the profound declaration: "No one has ever seen God; the Unique

---

[81] John, referring to the Word, says, "that one *made him known* [*exēgēsato*]." D. A. Carson suggests, "Jesus is the exegesis of God" (*The Gospel According to John* [Leicester, U.K.: InterVarsity Press; Grand Rapids, Mich.: Eerdmans, 1991], 135).

[82] "Glory" (*doxa*) is the LXX rendering of Hebrew *kābôd*, used to signify visible manifestations of God's self-revelation in theophany (e.g., Ex. 33:22; Deut. 5:24).

[83] For discussion of how *plērēs* functions in John 1:14, see D. A. Carson, *Gospel According to John*, 129; and A. T. Hanson, *Grace and Truth: A Study in the Fourth Gospel* (London: SPCK, 1976), 5ff.

[84] On the phrase *elabomen kai charin anti charitos* (we have received grace instead of grace), see Carson, *Gospel According to John*, 131-132.

One, God, who is in the bosom of the Father, that One made him known" (v. 18). John's prologue emphasizes that revelation of the incarnate Word is the ultimate disclosure of God himself to humans. To look upon the Word is to look upon the face of God veiled in flesh.

In the upper room, sounding like Moses long ago, Philip petitioned Jesus, "Lord, show us the Father, and that will be enough for us" (John 14:8).[85] Philip's petition uncovers his ignorance but also his desire for direct access to and an unmediated display of God himself. Jesus does not offer Philip something more, as the Lord did for Moses on the mountain. Instead, he mildly rebukes him: "Have I been with you all this time, Philip, and you still do not know me? Whoever has seen me has seen the Father. How can you say, 'Show us the Father'?" Jesus could rebuke Philip, for he had instructed his disciples saying, "Everyone who has heard and listens to the Father comes to me. Not that anyone has looked upon the Father except the One who is from God; this one has looked upon the Father" (John 6:45-46). Furthermore, Jesus had already said, "The one who looks upon me looks upon the one who sent me" (John 12:45).[86] Therefore, Jesus asks, "Do you not believe that I am in the Father and the Father is in me?" Essentially, Jesus says, "You ask to see the Father. It is enough that you have seen me."

Though God's glory is manifest in all things he created, when God reveals his glory, in covenant, he does not do so indiscriminately or superficially. He veils his glory and goodness from all but those to whom he will show mercy and whose iniquities he will forgive with steadfast love and faithfulness. The Lord said to Moses on the mountain, "I hereby make a covenant. Before all your people I will perform marvels, such as have not been performed in all the earth or in any nation; and all the people among whom you live shall see the work of the LORD; for it is an awesome thing that I will do with you" (Ex. 34:10, NRSV). The majority of Israelites would not trust God, though they would see and experience his wonders.

When the Lord showed his glory to Isaiah, he commissioned the prophet to preach the people deaf, blind, and calloused:

---

[85] The LXX of Exodus 33:18 reads, *kai legei Deixon moi tēn seautou doxan.* John 14:8 reads, *legei autō . . . Kurie, deixon hēmin ton patera, kai arkei hēmin.*

[86] Cf. "Blessed are the pure in heart, for they will see God" (Matt. 5:8).

Go and say to this people:

> "Keep listening, but do not comprehend;
>   keep looking, but do not understand."
> Make the mind of this people dull,
>   and stop their ears,
>   and shut their eyes,
> so that they may not look with their eyes,
>   and listen with their ears,
> and comprehend with their minds,
>   and turn and be healed." (Isa. 6:9-10)

Isaiah's commission foreshadowed Jesus' mission. Of the incarnate Word, John announces, "We have looked upon his glory." Yet, not only human flesh veils the Word's glory; Jesus' signs also veil his glory. Simultaneously, the Word reveals and conceals his glory by his signs. Not all could perceive the Word's glory, even though they saw his signs in which he "revealed his glory" (John 2:11). At the wedding in Cana, "The servants saw the sign, but not the glory; the disciples by faith perceived Jesus' glory behind the sign, and they *put their faith in him.*"[87] By way of contrast, when Jesus was in Jerusalem, "many believed in his name because they saw the signs that he did" (John 2:23). Their faith was as superficial as their sight.

Jesus ended his public ministry by revealing, in a veiled manner, that his glory entails exaltation: "And I, if I be lifted up from the earth, I will draw all men to myself" (John 12:32; cf. Isa. 52:13). The crowd recognized his announcement as speaking of his death ("The Son of Man must be lifted up" [John 3:14; 8:28; 12:34]). Therefore, they rejected him, for they claimed the Law taught them that Messiah lives forever. Jesus called the crowd to "believe in the light, in order that you may become sons of the light" (12:36a). Then the incarnate Word dramatized God's rejection of them as "he departed and hid from them" (12:36b). The one who disclosed his glory in his signs hid his already veiled glory from the crowd. John explains,

---

[87] Carson, *Gospel According to John*, 175.

Now, though he had done so many signs in their presence, they did not believe in him, in order that the saying of Isaiah the prophet might be fulfilled, which says,

> "Lord, who believed our message?
> And to whom has the arm of the Lord been revealed?"

Because of this, they are not able to believe, for Isaiah said again,

> "He has blinded their eyes,
>   and he petrified their hearts,
> lest they look with their eyes
>   and understand with their hearts and turn and I heal them."

Isaiah said these things because he saw his glory, and he spoke concerning him. Even so, many of the rulers believed in him, but because of the Pharisees, they did not confess openly lest they be expelled from the synagogue, for they loved the glory of man more than the glory of God. (John 12:37-43)

John indicates that Jesus' mission fulfills the prophet's words of astonished lament over Israel's rejection of the Servant of the Lord (Isa. 53:1). As John uses the passage, the question, "To whom has the arm of the Lord been revealed?" refers to Jesus' signs and wonders. John understands Jesus' signs to function as God's judicial blinding and hardening of the Jews, for he explains, "Because of this, they are not able to believe." Even though John does not explicitly say that Jesus' ministry fulfilled Isaiah 6:10, he makes it clear that Isaiah's commission foreshadowed Messiah's. "Isaiah said these things because he saw his glory, and he spoke concerning him" (John 12:41).[88]

Incarnate Word—God's Eternity Veiled in Flesh

As Isaiah 40–48 repeatedly argues that God's sure knowledge of all the future is a distinctive attribute of his deity that sets him apart from idols, so John's Gospel explicitly links Jesus Christ's knowledge of future actions and events with his deity. On the evening of his betrayal, Jesus

---

[88] On linkages between Isaiah's commission (Isaiah 6) and the final Servant Song (Isa. 52:13–53:12), see ibid., 450.

specifically predicted, "I solemnly say, one of you will betray me" (John 13:21). He meant Judas (v. 26). Before he made the prediction, he announced, "From now on I am telling you before it occurs, in order that when it occurs you might believe that I am" (v. 19). Jesus' announcement echoes the Lord's challenge of Isaiah 43:9-10: "Which of them foretold this and proclaimed to us the former things? Let them bring in their witnesses to prove they were right, so that others may hear and say, 'It is true.' 'You are my witnesses,' declares the LORD, 'and my servant whom I have chosen, so that you may know and believe me and understand that *I am he.*'" The phrase, "I am he" of Isaiah 43:10, as in Isaiah 41:4, contains "the truth of the changeless self-consistency of the Lord and is resonant of the 'I am' of Exodus 3:14."[89] Likewise, the phrase *egō eimi*, in John 13:19, likely calls to mind the unspeakable name of God because of the allusion to Isaiah 43:10.[90] So, Jesus knew in advance that Judas would betray him, and his ability to predict with certainty is a mark of his deity.

Another passage in John's Gospel suffices to make the point that Jesus' knowledge of the future indicates his deity, not just that he was a great prophet. A detachment of soldiers (usually 600) and temple officials, guided by Judas, came to the garden to seize Jesus. John's narrative suggests that, rather than waiting for the soldiers to seize him with strength, Jesus seized control of the situation by initiating contact to surrender. "Therefore, Jesus, knowing all the things that were coming upon him, went and said to them, 'Whom do you seek?'" (John 18:4). The irony in this verse intensifies when read in view of open theism's claim that if God were to ask a question while knowing the answer, he would be disingenuous.[91] John specifically indicates that Jesus had full knowledge of everything that he would experience and that with this knowledge Jesus asked, "Whom do you seek?" They replied, "Jesus the Nazarene." Jesus startled the detachment of soldiers and temple officials by openly acknowledging, "I am!" John continues,

---

[89] Motyer, *Isaiah*, 334.

[90] Carson, *Gospel According to John,* 471.

[91] Cf. Boyd, *God of the Possible,* 58-59, 82. Reflect upon John 6:5-6: "When he looked up and saw a large crowd coming toward him, Jesus said to Philip, 'Where are we to buy bread for these people to eat?' He said this to test him, for he himself knew what he was going to do." Herman Ridderbos observes, "Here again the Evangelist appeals to Jesus' foreknowledge, which for Jesus always means action" (*The Gospel of John: A Theological Commentary,* trans. John Vriend [Grand Rapids, Mich.: Eerdmans, 1997], 575).

"Therefore, when he said, 'I am,' they stepped back and fell upon the ground."[92] Soldiers and religious officials came to seize Jesus by force, but he seized them with his reply, "I am," as he manifested his glory. He disclosed his identity to them and gave himself up to them as he laid down his own life (cf. 10:17-18).

Clearly, Jesus' question does not reveal ignorance. Furthermore, the fact that Jesus knew all that would happen to him did not render his question duplicitous when he stepped forward to ask, "Whom do you seek?" Jesus, in human flesh, spoke as a human. The incarnate Word embodied anthropomorphism. He spoke as God routinely spoke anthropomorphically through his prophets (Gen. 3:9, 11; Num. 14:11; 1 Kings 22:20; Job 1:7-8; Hos. 8:5). Humans routinely ask questions while knowing the answers, and they do so without duplicity. Likewise, Jesus did not ask his question because he was ignorant; he asked his question to take command of the situation.[93] God's knowledge of the future choices and actions of humans does not render his questions and actions disingenuous, whether in the flesh or in anthropomorphic self-revelation in the Old Testament.

Incarnate Word—Image of the Invisible God Veiled in Flesh

According to Scripture, it suffices that when we see Jesus Christ, we see as much of the invisible God as the pure in heart will see (cf. Matt. 5:8). To this end, Jesus instructed Philip, "Whoever has seen me has seen the Father." The remainder of the New Testament reinforces the fact that "no one can see God and live," but Jesus Christ, his Son, has made him known to us (John 1:18). God "alone possesses immortality, who inhab-

---

[92] Carson reasons, "we must not conjecture that Jesus' interlocutors fell back for no other reason than that Jesus uttered an expression that ought to be reserved for the Almighty alone." He suggests that if those who came to arrest him had understood Jesus' "I am" as a claim to deity, "their reaction would have mirrored that recorded in 8:58-59, where Jesus utters the same words without the covering ambiguity." He proposes that they were clumsy in the middle of the night on a sloping mountainside and that, "in the Evangelist's eyes, their physical ineptitude was another instance of people responding better than they knew" (*Gospel According to John*, 578). Carson's proposal is intriguing. However, John connects their falling back and to the ground with Jesus saying, "I am." To make the point more vivid, John narrates: "Therefore, again Jesus asked, 'Whom do you seek?'" The mob reiterated, "Jesus the Nazarene." Then Jesus repeats, "I told you, 'I am.'" It seems more likely that the soldiers and temple officials, some of whom may have been on the same mission earlier (7:45ff.), understood Jesus' "I am" as the divine name. It seems likely that John underscores the intractable hardness of those who came to arrest Jesus. See F. F. Bruce, *The Gospel of John* (Grand Rapids, Mich.: Eerdmans, 1983), 341.

[93] The verb *exēlthen* ("he went out," 18:4) fits Jesus' taking control of the situation. He did not wait to be seized. He revealed himself to those who would arrest him.

its unapproachable light, whom no one has seen or is able to see; to him be honor and eternal dominion. Amen" (1 Tim. 6:16). God invisible has made himself visible in the incarnate Son who is "the image of the invisible God" and in whom "the fullness of deity resides bodily" (Col. 1:15; 2:9; 1:19; cf. 2 Cor. 4:4). The Son "is the radiance of the Glory and the exact imprint of his very being" (Heb. 1:3). The Son became incarnate that he might be humiliated and then exalted (Phil. 2:6-9). The apostle John assures us that if we know the Son of God, we know the true God. "And we know that the Son of God has come and has given us understanding in order that we might know the one who is true; and we are in the true one, in his Son, Jesus Christ. This one is the true God and life eternal" (1 John 5:20).

Each New Testament writer searches God's ordered world for apt imagery to capture as well as possible the inexhaustible thought of deity incarnate. All are anthropomorphic, which means that God correlates his self-revelation to his own image imprinted upon us. We are like God; he is unlike us. Our similarity to God brings accessibility to true knowledge of God as Father and of Jesus Christ as his Son. God shows himself to be dissimilar to us by his awesomeness, his unique possession of immortality, his inhabiting unapproachable light, his invisible quality, and his glorious radiance. Our creator endowed us with imaginations capable of grasping the fact that our thoughts cannot grasp or apprehend God, for we intuitively know that we derive from God who made us.

We need to reject the conclusion Sanders draws from these passages on the premise of his posited "shared context" that God and humans inhabit together.[94] He reifies God's anthropomorphic revelation by emptying revelation of its essential anthropomorphic nature while calling it "anthropomorphism."[95] It is not surprising, then, that he pushes the incarnation of the Word beyond the limits of Scripture, as he forges a reified "God-in-the-flesh theology"—"If the incarnation is true

---

[94] Sanders, *The God Who Risks,* 24.
[95] "Apart from revelation we cannot know that anything exists beyond our boundaries, and if, by revelation, we are informed of a transcendent existence, we can only understand it by use of our conditions. . . . If we take our status as creatures seriously, then we shall have to content ourselves with knowing and speaking about God within the conditions of our createdness. In other words, we must understand the God-human relationship as taking place within a shared context, and so the use of metaphors and anthropomorphic language (in the broad sense) when speaking of God is necessary" (ibid., 37-38).

and the divine son experienced fully human life, then God in this way relates to the world in precisely the same way we do."[96] Bavinck is a more reliable guide:

> The *name* of God in Scripture does not designate him as he exists in himself, but in his manifold revelation and relation to the creature. Nevertheless, this name is not arbitrary, but God reveals himself as he *is*. Hence, God's name stands for his honor, glory, excellencies, revelation, and divine essence. . . . Moreover, whereas God's revelation in nature and Scripture is definitely directed to man, God uses human language to reveal himself and manifests himself in human forms. It follows that Scripture does not merely contain a few anthropomorphisms; on the contrary, *all* Scripture is anthropomorphic. From beginning to end Scripture testifies a condescending approach of God to man. The entire revelation of God becomes concentrated in the Logos, who became "flesh." It is as it were *one* humanization, *one* incarnation of God. If God were to speak to us in divine language, no one would be able to understand him; but ever since creation, he, in condescending grace, speaks to us and manifests himself to us in human fashion.[97]

IV. VEILED REVELATION—ANTHROPOMORPHISM AND OPEN THEISM

Open theism's simplistic interpretation of the Bible corresponds to its Enlightenment view of knowing God and his ways. Boyd summarizes open theism's interpretive principle: except in passages where "what is said about God is either ridiculous . . . or because the genre of the passage is poetic," open theists insist that God does not accommodate his

[96] Ibid., 26.
[97] Bavinck, *The Doctrine of God*, 85-86. Cf. A. Berkeley Mickelsen, *Interpreting the Bible*, 307-308. "To say that certain language is figurative does not mean that the event is unreal. In fact, when the language of the earthly realm . . . is used to describe the beginnings of all that exists and the climax of all that exists, the figurative language best conveys that which is most real, abiding, and certain. Earthly language from a known sphere of existence is used to describe what took place or will take place in a sphere of existence that no mere human creature has ever entered. God must attest to that which took place in creation and that which will take place in the climax. . . . God disclosed his truths in language taken from the life experiences of the Hebrews and the early Christians to describe for them that which far transcended all that they ever knew. . . . When we consider the materials in the light of all that the Scriptures have revealed about God, we are impressed even more with the use of figurative language. Without it, little or nothing could have been disclosed. With it God was able to indicate how much more there is yet to be known. Man now knows in part."

revelation to us but discloses himself to us as he is in himself.[98] Boyd also summarizes open theism's "naïve realist" view of knowledge, born out of the Enlightenment:

> Striving to have a plausible theology is necessary because, for many of us, the mind must be thoroughly convinced if the heart is to be thoroughly transformed. . . . [T]he open view of God and of the future makes more intellectual sense than the classical view. . . . It is the only view that allows us to affirm that the way things *appear* is basically the way things actually *are*. . . . The open view . . . has for many the "ring of truth" precisely because it is consistent with the way we experience the world and the way we experience ourselves as decision-making beings.[99]

Open theism's appeal to human reasoning as the final arbiter concerning knowledge of God shows rejection of analogical thinking and reasoning. Open theists do not believe God's revelation accommodates his created categories. Instead, they believe God reveals himself to us in human categories just as he truly is in his "very nature."[100]

Boyd's statements represent open theism's dual beliefs: (1) that God's self-revelation with human categories requires the categories to mean the same thing when used of God as when used of humans; (2) that if we do not know God as he *truly* is, then we do not *truly* know God. Follow Boyd's reasoning:

> However, there is nothing ridiculous or poetic about the way the Bible repeatedly speaks about God changing his mind, regretting decisions, or thinking and speaking about the future in terms of possibilities. . . . They only strike some as ridiculous because these readers bring to the text a preconception of what God *must* be like. . . . It is not at all on par with a figure of speech in which God has an outstretched arm or protecting wings.
>
> If the classical view is correct, we have to be willing to accept that God could in one breath say that the Israelites' behavior "did not enter my

---

[98] Boyd, *God of the Possible,* 118.
[99] Ibid., 90-91.
[100] Sanders, *The God Who Risks,* 38.

mind," though their behavior "was eternally in my mind." If this is not a contradiction, what is?

It is difficult to understand how God could have sincerely "sought for" someone to intercede if he was eternally certain that there would be no one. Could you genuinely look for a coin in your house that you always *knew* was not there?

We must wonder how the Lord could truly experience regret for making Saul king if he was absolutely certain that Saul would act the way he did. . . . Common sense tells us that we can only regret a decision we made if the decision resulted in an outcome other than what we expected or hoped for when the decision was made.[101]

Despite his claims to the contrary, Boyd's reasoning brings the Creator down to the creature's level, for he reasons, what is true for the creature must be true for the Creator. Strange as it may seem, open theists believe that classic Christian beliefs about God's knowledge of the future "bring the Lord down to our level."[102] At the same time, they chastise and mock

---

[101] Boyd, *God of the Possible*, 118, 62, 63, 56.

[102] Boyd reasons, "While it may be difficult to imagine ourselves carrying out a providential plan so masterfully without a meticulous blueprint ahead of time, there is no reason to bring the Lord down to our level. If we grant that God is all-powerful and infinitely wise, we should have no trouble seeing how he could weave free agents into his plan while allowing them to resolve for themselves a partly open future."

"Some scholars have argued that it is not possible for God to predestine an event without predestining or at least foreknowing the people who would carry out the event. There is no justification for limiting God in this fashion, however."

"In my view, every other understanding of divine providence to some extent diminishes the sovereignty and glory of God. It brings God's wisdom and power down to the level of finite human thinking. We would need to control or possess a blueprint of all that is to occur ahead of time to steer world history effectively. But the true God is far wiser, far more powerful, and far more secure than we could ever imagine."

"Isn't a God who is able to know perfectly these possibilities wiser than a God who simply foreknows or predetermines one story line that the future will follow? And isn't a God who perfectly anticipates and wisely responds to everything a free agent *might* do more intelligent than a God who simply knows what a free agent *will* do? Anticipating and responding to possibilities takes problem-solving intelligence. Simply possessing a crystal ball vision of what's coming requires none."

"If the classical view of divine foreknowledge is correct, there are positive things humans can do that God cannot do. . . . Though the Bible is explicit in ascribing many of these experiences to God . . . , the classical view rules them out. Is this not limiting God?" (Boyd, *God of the Possible*, 39, 45, 68, 127, 129).

belief that God accommodates himself to his creatures when he reveals himself. Calvin argued,

> The Anthropomorphites, also, who imagined a corporeal God from the fact that Scripture often ascribes to him a mouth, ears, eyes, hands, and feet, are easily refuted. For who even of slight intelligence does not understand that, as nurses commonly do with infants, God is wont in a measure to "lisp" in speaking to us? Thus such forms of speaking do not so much express clearly what God is like as accommodate the knowledge of him to our slight capacity. To do this he must descend far beneath his loftiness.[103]

The Anthropomorphite assumption seems to be that predications concerning God must apply to God in the same way they apply to humans, otherwise God's analogical self-disclosure tells us nothing about him. Therefore, if God's self-revelation is to bear genuine meaning or real significance and convey true truth to us, it cannot be truly analogical.[104] Anthropomorphites de-anthropomorphized anthropomorphisms. Open theists employ the same reasoning. To advance his own reification of God's anthropomorphic self-disclosure, Sanders objects to Calvin's argument against the Anthropomorphites. Sanders mocks,

> Of course, those making such a claim [that God "lisps"] were somehow able to transcend their finite minds in order to know what God is really like. That is, they seemingly believed they could observe God using both lisping and normal discourse and were consequently able to tell the rest of us which forms of discourse were accommodations and which were literal. Though I do not wish to deny that God is in certain respects beyond our comprehension, I do want to point out that lurking behind the notion of divine accommodation seems to be the idea that some people *know* for a fact what God is really like and are thus able to inform the rest of us . . . "duller folk" that we are mistaken.[105]

---

[103] The Anthropomorphites were a Syrian sect of Christians during the fourth century who followed the teachings of Audius, who held that God has a human form.

[104] The argument is similar to John Feinberg's: "Hence, for metaphors about God to make sense, I must know some things about him that are both literal and true" (*No One Like Him: The Doctrine of God*, Foundations of Evangelical Theology [Wheaton, Ill.: Crossway, 2001], 77).

[105] Sanders, *The God Who Risks*, 33-34. Boyd adopts the same argument in *Satan and the Problem of Evil*, 98.

Though he quotes Bavinck's words, *"all* Scripture is anthropomorphic," Sanders does not seem to understand that all God's revelation truly is analogical, including his negative assertions: "I am God, and there is none like me" (Isa. 46:9), or "God is not a man, that he should lie, nor a son of man, that he should change his mind" (Num. 23:19). Therefore, Sanders does not seem to realize that by rejecting God's accommodative and analogical self-revelation he has cast aside biblical restraints that would prevent him from becoming a full-fledged modern Anthropomorphite.[106]

Open theism's challenge has taken advantage of a fault in much of classical Christian theology. Correction of this fault is crucial for both the life and the doctrine of the church. If we suppress the anthropomorphic nature of God's Word, we do injury to the church's teachings and relationship with our God who relates to us in covenant, that is, analogically. We will tend to hyperbolize God's transcendence. We will tend to transform the Bible into a form we think is more manageable. God's Word will seem cold and systematic.[107] God will seem remote and aloof. If we fail to preach God's Word, as his veiled glory, as inherently analogical self-revelation, we cannot hope to correct any large-scale reification of anthropomorphism in passages contained within God's Word, as brought into the church by open theism. We will injure the church's relationship with God by exaggerating God's immanence. We will conceive of him as "one of us." Then, even though we may have an intuitive sense of its defect, we will have no adequate response to the pedestrianization of God such as expressed in the lyrics by Eric Bazilian

---

[106] Pinnock nudges closer to being a modern unqualified Anthropomorphite, for he says, "There is an issue that has not been raised yet in the discussion around the open view of God. If he is with us in the world, if we are to take biblical metaphors seriously, is God in some way embodied? Critics will be quick to say that, although there are expressions of this idea in the Bible, they are not to be taken literally. But I do not believe that the idea is as foreign to the Bible's view of God as we have assumed. In tradition, God is thought to function primarily as a disembodied spirit but this is scarcely a biblical idea. For example, Israel is called to hear God's word and gaze on his glory and beauty. . . . Perhaps God's agency would be easier to envisage if he were in some way corporeal. Add to the fact that in the theophanies of the Old Testament God encounters humans in the form of a man. They indicate that God shares our life in the world in a most intense and personal manner. . . . The only persons we encounter are embodied persons, and if God is not embodied, it may prove difficult to understand how God is a person. What kind of actions could a disembodied God perform?" (*Most Moved Mover: A Theology of God's Openness* [Grand Rapids, Mich.: Baker, 2001], 33-34).

[107] Systematic theology is vital to the church's life and doctrine. Systematic theology is crucial to check and correct our preaching and teaching. However, God calls us to proclaim his Word. See Goldsworthy, *Preaching the Whole Bible as Christian Scripture.*

and sung by Joan Osborne: "What if God was one of us, just a slob like one of us, just a stranger on a bus, trying to make his way home . . . ?"

It is insufficient for us simply to show that this passage or that passage in Scripture employs anthropomorphism. What we must demonstrate is that *all Scripture is anthropomorphic by God's design*. We need to show, from God's Word, that all our knowledge of God depends upon God's creational design that, as his analogues, our knowledge of him is analogical. Our concern is not pedantic or trivial. It has in view the life of the church, God's people. It concerns idolatry, not images graven in stone but formed in the imagination of our hearts. The First Commandment—"You shall have no other gods besides me" (Ex. 20:3)—addresses the heart first, for our hearts guide our hands. Thus, the Second Commandment states: "You shall not make for yourself an idol in the form of anything in heaven above or on the earth beneath or in the waters below" (v. 4). The apostle John's closing admonitions agree with this. "And we know that the Son of God has come and has given us understanding in order that we might know the one who is true, and we are in the true one, in his Son, Jesus Christ. This one is the true God and life eternal. Children, guard yourselves from idols" (1 John 5:20-21). John's warning is against wrongly conceiving of Jesus Christ, which amounts to idolatry. "The fundamental objection to idolatry is its confusion of creature and Creator, objects 'made with hands' with the divinely created image. There can be no *graven* image of God, not because God has no image but because he has already established his own, *human* image of himself."[108] Supreme among humans is one, Jesus Christ, "who is the image of God" and "in whom the fullness of deity dwells bodily" (2 Cor. 4:4; Col. 2:9).

If all God's Word is anthropomorphic in character, not just in its parts, how should we understand certain passages to which modern-day Anthropomorphites appeal to argue that God is like us? If all God's revelation comes to us analogically, as creatures made in his image, how should we understand God's self-disclosure as one who asks questions, who uses common human idioms, who regrets, who uses suppositional language? The essay has already commented on some of these, and I have addressed all of them elsewhere.[109] Brief comments on three kinds of passages must suffice.

[108] Green, *Imagining God*, 91-92.
[109] Caneday, "The Implausible God of Open Theism," 66-87.

Open theists want Christians to believe that God did not know that Judah would be unfaithful. They prove it by citing Jeremiah 3:19—"I thought you would call me 'Father' and not turn away from following me" (NIV). "If God tells us he thought something was going to occur while being eternally certain it would not occur, is he not lying to us?"[110] The prophet, speaking for the Lord, employs an idiom we humans use routinely. It does not express ignorance. It functions as a rebuke. In human terms, it is the Lord's idiomatic rebuke of Judah: "You did what was unthinkable!"[111]

Jeremiah speaks for the Lord and rebukes Judah for building altars to false deities, "which I did not command, nor did it come into my mind" (Jer. 7:31; 19:5; 32:35). Sanders claims, in passages such as this, "God is explicitly depicted as not knowing the specific future. God himself says that he was mistaken about what was going to happen."[112] Again, the Lord rebukes Israel anthropomorphically by using the common idiom: "It never entered my mind." As an idiomatic expression, it means something quite different from the individual meanings of its elements. It is not a confession of previous ignorance any more than the following idiom acknowledges possession of a poor memory—"For I will forgive their wickedness and *will remember their sins no more*" (Jer. 31:34). Because God speaks to us in human language, he also employs human idioms. Hyper-scrupulous minds may not use the expression— "it never entered my mind"—lest they lie, but this only betrays ignorance of the idiom's meaning.[113] It is an intensive idiom to express what is unthinkable.

Open theists quote passages such as 1 Samuel 15:11 as transparent proof that God does not know the future. "I regret that I made Saul king, for he has turned back from following me, and has not carried out my commands" (NRSV; see also 15:35). Though evangelicals have the right

---

[110] Boyd, *God of the Possible*, 60, 119. Even if we should take the Hebrew *ʾāmar* as "said," it is still anthropomorphism.

[111] For fuller consideration of Jeremiah 3, see Caneday, "The Implausible God of Open Theism," 75ff.

[112] Sanders, *The God Who Risks*, 74. Cf. Boyd, *God of the Possible*, 61.

[113] Open theists fail to recognize the idiomatic nature of this expression. If they insist that we must take the expression literally, then they have a problem, because they also claim that God knows all possibilities, yet here is something that did not enter God's mind. If that is the case, then he did not know this even as a possibility. Caird cleverly observes, "No doubt in any community there will be someone who takes everything literally, someone whose leg you dare not pull for fear that it will come away in your hands" (*The Language and Imagery of the Bible*, 184).

intuition, they may too easily dismiss the significance of 1 Samuel 15:11 by appealing to 15:29—"He who is the Glory of Israel does not lie or change his mind; for he is not a man, that he should change his mind" (NIV). Both passages use the Hebrew word *nāḥam*, translated "I regret" and "change his mind." However, if classical Christian theists wrongly suppress the anthropomorphism of 1 Samuel 15:11 by appealing to 15:29, open theists mishandle the meaning and significance of 15:29 in order to reify the figure of speech in 15:11. Sanders claims that 1 Samuel 15:29 and Numbers 23:19 simply assert "that God will not repent" with reference "to specific situations in which God refuses to reverse a particular decision."[114] It is true that Samuel declares to Saul that the Lord will not change his mind about tearing the kingdom from Saul. However, any fair reading of 1 Samuel 15:29 has to acknowledge that Samuel grounds God's irrevocable purpose in the character of God in contrast to human character. Otherwise, why characterize God by saying, "He who is the Glory of Israel does not lie or change his mind; for he is not a man, that he should change his mind"?[115] This passage no less portrays God anthropomorphically or analogically than does 1 Samuel 15:11. Whether Scripture says that God repents or that God does not repent, both are analogical, for both reference humans. God's character remains the same. God's set purpose does not alter. Then, how do the two verses correlate? What changes if God's character and purpose do not? First, the Lord speaks analogically to Samuel to reveal a change from his earlier revelation to anoint Saul over Israel (1 Sam. 15:1; 9:16; 10:1). God's revelation concerning Israel's kingship changed. Second, Samuel clearly recognizes that God has not altered either his character or his eternal purpose when he reminds Saul of the Lord's character (1 Sam. 15:29). If God had not disclosed to Samuel a change in his revelation concerning Saul, then Samuel would have had reason to doubt the Lord's unchangeable character. This is so, for Samuel had already announced to Saul the Lord's intention to end his kingship (1 Sam. 13:13-14).

If the Lord had not revealed to Samuel a change toward Saul because of his disobedience (1 Sam. 15:1-10), then Samuel would have

---

[114] Sanders, *The God Who Risks*, 69.

[115] Ibid., 70. Sanders's explanation is problematic, for he presents God as utterly arbitrary: "In its context the teaching is clear: God reserves the right to alter his plans in response to human initiative, and it is also the divine right not to alter an alteration."

had grounds for thinking that the Lord's character had truly changed. The biblical narrative of 1 Samuel 15 hardly brings into question the Lord's eternal purpose to raise up Israel's king from the tribe of Judah and not from the tribe of Benjamin (cf. Gen. 49:8-12). Rather, the narrative analogically discloses how the Lord brought about his prophetic word announced long ago through Jacob that the Messiah would descend from Judah.

V. CONCLUSIONS: CHASTENING AND CHIDING

Open theism challenges the ground of traditional Christian theology by contending that God does not know with certainty the future free decisions and acts of his creatures.[116] Open theism has gained popular reception by way of recent publications, denominational disputes, and published reports of discussion within the Evangelical Theological Society.[117] Its increased popularity has largely come about because open theists have shifted their approach from pedantic and philosophical discussions that kept the view rather esoteric, to books that attempt to demonstrate their view from the Bible. Understandably, then, biblically based responses to open theism have tended to demonstrate open theism's inadequate explanations of Scripture, passage by passage. This is noble and painstaking work. However, a more foundational work that

---

[116] See Bruce A. Ware, "Defining Evangelicalism's Boundaries Theologically: Is Open Theism Evangelical?" *JETS* 45 (2002): 193-212.

[117] Open theism has stirred controversy within at least four church denominations: the Baptist General Conference (BGC), the United Brethren in Christ (UBC), the Evangelical Free Church of America, and the Southern Baptist Convention (SBC). The controversy in the UBC focused upon Sanders's views on Christ's atonement and inclusivism. At the height of the conflict, several documents were posted on the UBC web pages (http://www.ub.org/otherstuff/theology/index.html) but no longer can be seen there. Concerning the conflict in the BGC, see Elesha Coffman, "Did Open Debate Help the Openness Debate?" *Christianity Today* 45, no. 3 (19 February 2001), 42; Edward E. Plowman, "Open and Shut: A Baptist Group Rejects 'Open Theology,' but Not Its Chief Advocate, While Presbyterians Debate Beliefs," *World* 15, no. 28 (22 July 2000): 26; and John Piper, "We Took a Good Stand and Made a Bad Mistake: Reflections on the Baptist General Conference Annual Meeting, St. Paul, June 25-28, 2000" (http://desiringgod.org/library/fresh_words/2000/070500.html). For the resolution passed overwhelmingly by the SBC, see www.sbc.net/resolutions/amResolution.asp?ID=574. For reports concerning the conflict raised by open theism within the Evangelical Theological Society, see David Neff, "Foreknowledge Debate Clouded by 'Political Agenda,'" 19 November 2001 internet posting at www.christianitytoday.com/ct/2001/147/13.0.html; idem, "Scholars Vote: God Knows Future," *Christianity Today* 46, no. 1 (7 January 2002): 21; Timothy C. Morgan, "Theologians Decry 'Narrow' Boundaries," *Christianity Today* 46, no. 7 (10 June 2002): 18; "The Buzz: ETS Votes to Reject Open Theology," *World* 16, no. 46 (1 December 2001): 10; R. Albert Mohler, "A New Low? 'The Word Made Fresh': Revisionist Theologians Offer Instead More Stale Liberalism," *World* 17, no. 13 (6 April 2002): 26; Doug Koop, "Evangelical Theological Society Moves Against Open Thests: Membership of Pinnock and Sanders Challenged by Due Process," 22 November 2002 internet posting at www.christianitytoday.com/ct/2002/145/54.0.html.

classical Christian theology needs to do is return to a pre-Enlightenment understanding of Scripture as inherently God's analogical revelation. This essay endeavors to do some of this biblical-theological work by showing, from Scripture, that God designed his creation to disclose his glory. In particular, God made man in his own image so that he integrated revelation of himself into our very being. Thus, all of God's revelation comes to us with reference to his likeness in us. All God's revelation is analogical. This means that the Bible does not simply contain anthropomorphisms and other figures of speech. The Bible itself *is* anthropomorphic, for it is God's speech to humans in human language.

This essay seeks to bring biblical correctives to both sides in the current controversy raised by open theism. Consideration of the Bible's own testimony concerning the manner of God's self-revelation should chasten classical Christianity's indebtedness to the Enlightenment's suppression of anthropomorphism in favor of philosophical abstraction. It should also chide open theism's indebtedness to the Enlightenment's exaltation of human autonomy as the final arbiter of what constitutes true knowledge, which has led open theism to reify God's anthropomorphic revelation and to court idolatry.

As we speak of God, whether or not we use images in the analogical verbal sense is not under dispute. We cannot avoid imagery, for our knowledge of God depends upon analogy, because God's Word is not only replete with verbal imagery; all God's revelation is, in its very nature, anthropomorphic. The conflict, stirred in the church by open theism, is not whether we should conceive of God with verbal imagery but how we are to understand the nature and function of biblical imagery. Open theists obscure the essential anthropomorphic character of God's revelation. The fact that God *speaks* to us in human language with categories from within his creation constitutes all God's revelation anthropomorphic. God's revelation is anthropomorphic, for it comes to us in the form of speech, whether the heavens' speech that translates itself, God's speech through his prophets, or his speech through the incarnate Word, it is all intrinsically anthropomorphic.

Analogy is intrinsic to God's creation, for God has left his fingerprints on everything he has made (Rom. 1:20ff). Analogy is inherent to God's design of us, creatures he made in his own image and likeness. All our thoughts about God are properly birthed with self-referential awareness that conceives of God analogically. Properly conceived, our thoughts about God openly confess that the analogical relationship between God and us does not begin with us and move to God, but begins with God and moves to us. God is not like us. We are like God. Therefore, right thinking about God begins with candid acknowledgment that we are God's reflection. As the image in a pond depends entirely upon the object casting the image, so we depend completely upon God who casts the image we are. Likewise, as the glory of the image in the pond is but a shadow of the object's glory, so whatever glory we bear as the image, only derives from the glory of God who cast the image. Thus, right thinking about God necessarily acknowledges that the analogical relationship between Creator and creature entails both similarities and differences. For the fact that the analogy runs from Creator to creature obligates us to acknowledge this with candor.

How we understand God's revelation, the Bible, is inseparable from how we believe we acquire true knowledge. The fact that God made us in his image, as his earthly analogues, and that the Creator reveals himself to us analogically in categories from within his creation, means that we acquire true knowledge of God by tracing the revelatory character of everything God created, including our own consciousness. We are like God, so our knowledge of him and of his creation is true. Because we are also unlike God, our knowledge of God and his creation can never be comprehensive. Our knowledge of God is derived and veiled. When the incomprehensible God reveals himself to us, he also veils his glory from us, so we cannot know God as he is fully and truly in himself. Were God to show himself fully as he truly is, he would consume us. Yet, to the degree God has pulled back the veil to make himself truly known, we can truly know God, and this is enough. Therefore, if classical Christian theology hopes to endure the present theological challenge incited by open theism, we will have to return to pre-Enlightenment Christian faith that is content to know God analogically and not yield to seducing philosophies that would have us think that we can speak of God as though we knew God as he truly is in himself. We cannot, for our only access to God is through his own revelation, and God reveals himself anthropomorphically in keeping with the image with which he invested us.

Whether we are classical Christian theists or open theists, we need to return to the Bible. We must all confess that the Enlightenment has influenced us more deeply than we may want to admit. True as it is that the Bible expresses timeless truths, Scripture is so much more. The Bible presents God's unfolding revelation along its own story line of God's redemptive purpose and deeds on behalf of his people. God is the principal actor in the story. Therefore, all God's revelation is analogical. If we are to read the Bible correctly, then, our minds need training to retain the proper reference point when thinking about God. Our concept of God needs to be governed by the fact that God made us in his image. God is not like us. We are like God. Maintaining this reference point has deep implications for all of our talk about God. Thus, when Scripture beckons us to speak of God as our Father, any human father is only a shadow of true fatherhood. God does not borrow the earthly category— father. Rather, he bestowed his category upon us, for the analogy moves from God the Father to the human earthly father. It is precisely because of this analogical arrangement God established by creating us in his image that God is pleased to reveal himself to us as our Father. He delights to make himself known as the Father of all who acknowledge that human fatherhood bears his imprint. Thus, when the psalmist says, "As a father has compassion on his children, so the LORD has compassion on those who fear him"(Ps. 103:13, NIV), the reason the analogy works is that God was pleased to invest earthly fatherhood with analogical significance that points away from itself to the one who stamped something of himself upon it.[118] Our heavenly Father, who has revealed himself to us and in us by imprinting something of himself upon us, by anthropomorphic imagery, and through his incarnate Son, mercifully veils his glory in created analogies lest he consume us.[119]

---

[118] See the discussion of this perspective with reference to biblical figures by Richard C. Trench, *Notes on the Parables of Our Lord* (London: Kegan Paul, Trench, 1889), 13ff.

[119] Martin Luther agrees, for he says, "God in his essence is altogether unknowable; nor is it possible to define or put into words what He is, though we burst in the effort. It is for this reason that God lowers Himself to the level of our weak comprehension and presents Himself to us in images, in coverings, as it were, in simplicity adapted to a child, that in some measure it may be possible for Him to be known by us" (*Lectures on Genesis: Chapters 6–14*, 45). Cf. Walter A. Maier III, "Does God Change His Mind? A Study of Genesis 6:6 and Exodus 32:14" (paper presented at the annual meeting of the Evangelical Theological Society, Colorado Springs, 14-16 November 2001).

6

HELLENISTIC OR HEBREW?
OPEN THEISM AND REFORMED
THEOLOGICAL METHOD

Michael S. Horton

The goal of this chapter[1] is to contrast Reformed theological method with that of open theism, in an effort to demonstrate that it is here, at the beginning, where the two theologies diverge. We will attempt this by briefly (I) analyzing the assumption that classical theology is "Hellenistic" rather than biblical; (II) marking out the key features of Reformed method; and (III) comparing and contrasting this method with open theism. We will limit our scope to John Sanders's *The God Who Risks*[2] and Clark Pinnock's *Most Moved Mover.*[3]

I. HELLENISTIC OR HEBREW?

The late nineteenth-century historical theologian Adolf von Harnack advanced his thesis that nearly everything we regard as Christian "orthodoxy"—"the Catholic element"—is in fact the result of "the

---

[1] An earlier version of this essay was published as Michael S. Horton, "Hellenistic or Hebrew? Open Theism and Reformed Theological Method," *Journal of the Evangelical Theological Society* 45 (2002): 317-341. Reprinted and revised with permission.

[2] John Sanders, *The God Who Risks: A Theology of Providence* (Downers Grove, Ill.: InterVarsity Press, 1998).

[3] Clark H. Pinnock, *Most Moved Mover: A Theology of God's Openness* (Grand Rapids, Mich.: Baker, 2001). Cf. Clark Pinnock, "Theological Method," in *New Dimensions in Evangelical Thought: Essays in Honor of Millard J. Erickson*, ed. David S. Dockery (Downers Grove, Ill.: InterVarsity Press, 1998), 197-208.

acute Hellenization of the church."[4] But Harnack could apparently relativize every period but his own, as the earliest and therefore most authentic elements of Christianity were curiously well-suited to the dynamic, Hegelian worldview of *fin-de-siècle* intellectual life in Germany.

But long before Harnack, the Socinians, according to Genevan theologian Francis Turretin, reproached classical theism on the same basis; viz., that "the whole doctrine is metaphysical" rather than biblical.[5] Responding, Turretin writes, "The necessity of the immutability we ascribe to God does not infer Stoic fate," since it neither imposes an internal necessity upon God nor interferes "with the liberty and contingency of things."[6] With Hegel's ghost looking over his shoulder, Harnack argued that traditional theism represented a static Stoic worldview, while the apocalyptic religion of the early Jewish and Christian believers reflected values strikingly familiar in modern society: individualism, enthusiasm, and a direct, unmediated experience with God.[7]

This thesis has underwritten a century of modern theology, not only in neo-Protestantism but in neo-orthodoxy and in the version of the "biblical theology" movement identified especially with G. E. Wright. According to Wright, the God of systematic theology was the deity of static order, while the God of biblical theology was always on

---

[4] Adolf von Harnack, *History of Dogma*, vol. 1, translated from the third German edition (Boston: Little, Brown, 1902), 48ff. A similar tack may be discerned in the Arian attack on the doctrines of the Trinity and deity of Christ. On the basis of a literalistic reading of Proverbs 8:22-23 (Wisdom personified speaking: "The LORD created me" and "before the ages established me"), Arius denied the Trinity of God and the deity of Christ. But, as Jaroslav Pelikan notes, it was exegesis "in the light of a particular set of theological a prioris which produced the Arian doctrine of Christ as creature" (*The Emergence of the Catholic Tradition (100–600)*, The Christian Tradition, vol. 1 [Chicago: University of Chicago Press, 1971], 194). Among those presuppositions was the mathematical oneness of God. Although this was itself a presupposition of Arius's Neoplatonism, many modern historical theologians have made Arianism into "'a final, mighty upheaval' of an angel Christology that had come down from late Jewish and early Christian apocalypticism and was making its last stand 'against the new, hellenized christology,'" although Pelikan rightly judges that this characterization is unsupported (ibid., 198).

[5] Francis Turretin, *Institutes of Elenctic Theology*, trans. George M. Giger, ed. James T. Dennison, Jr., vol. 1 (Phillipsburg, N.J.: Presbyterian & Reformed, 1992), 191.

[6] Ibid., 205-206.

[7] "The attempts at deducing the genesis of the Church's doctrinal system from the theology of Paul" or the analogy of Scripture, Harnack was convinced, "will always miscarry; for they fail to note that to the most important premises of the Catholic doctrine of faith belongs an element which we cannot recognise as dominant in the New Testament, viz., the Hellenic spirit" (Harnack, *History of Dogma*, 1:48). In the beginning, the church possessed a "sure consciousness of an immediate possession of the Divine Spirit, and the hope of the future conquering the present; individual piety conscious of itself and sovereign, living in the future world, recognizing no external authority and no external barriers" (ibid., 49).

the move.[8] But the twentieth century, especially through the work of Barth and Brunner, also witnessed the rehabilitation of the Reformers in this respect, shifting the blame for "Hellenistic" theology to their systematizing successors instead.[9]

More recently, however, this thesis has been unraveling. On the biblical-theological side, James Barr led the way to its demise,[10] and subsequent research has raised serious questions about its viability: in relation to Jesus (Hebrew) vs. Paul (Greek)[11] and the Reformers vs. the Protestant scholastics.[12]

In his chapter, "Overcoming a Pagan Influence," Pinnock takes this well-traveled road, but with the entire classical tradition from the church fathers to current orthodoxy dismissed in one stroke as hopelessly trapped in ancient paganism.[13] This does not keep Pinnock, any more

---

[8] G. E. Wright, *God Who Acts: Biblical Theology as Recital* (London: SCM, 1952). He speaks of "propositional dogmatics, the systematic presentation of abstract propositions or beliefs about God, man and salvation. The churches retain and encourage this conception in their liturgy and creeds. For example, every elder, deacon, commissioned church worker and minister in the Presbyterian Church (U.S.A.) is required to affirm when he or she is ordained that the confession of faith of that church contains 'the system of doctrine taught in the Holy Scriptures.' But does the Bible contain a *system* of doctrine?" (35). Therefore, "Biblical theology cannot be analyzed after the manner of propositional dogmatics because it rests on a living, changing, ever expanding and contracting attitude toward historical events" (81). Biblical theology is preferred to "the rubrics of systematic theology in the customary static and abstract form: i.e., the doctrine of God, the doctrine of man, the doctrine of sin, the doctrine of redemption, the doctrine of Christ, the doctrine of the Church, etc." (111).

[9] This was the working assumption of neo-orthodoxy (particularly evident in Brunner and Barth), in its attempt to rescue the Reformers while eschewing the systems of their successors. On the Reformed side, it is the controlling presupposition of T. F. Torrance, James B. Torrance, Michael Jinkins, Jack Rogers, B. A. Armstrong, R. T. Kendall, and others. It has proved so effective rhetorically that even many conservatives have assumed it in their work.

[10] James Barr, "The Old Testament and the New Crisis of Biblical Authority," *Interpretation* 25, no. 1 (January 1971): 24-40; cf. Barr, *The Semantics of Biblical Language* (Oxford: Oxford University Press, 1961); idem, *Biblical Words for Time* (London: SCM, 1962).

[11] Against the application of the Harnack thesis to the so-called "Jesus vs. Paul" antithesis, see the recent collection, Troels Engberg-Pedersen, ed., *Paul Beyond the Judaism/Hellenism Divide* (Louisville, Ky.: Westminster John Knox, 2001).

[12] For the criticism of the Luther/Calvin vs. Lutheranism/Calvinism version, see particularly Richard Muller, "Calvin and the 'Calvinists': Assessing Continuities and Discontinuities Between the Reformation and Orthodoxy," *Calvin Theological Journal* 30 (1995): 345-375; and 31 (1996): 125-160; cf. Robert Preus, *The Theology of Post-Reformation Lutheranism*, 2 vols. (St. Louis, Mo.: Concordia, 1970–1972). Articles and monographs by Willem van Asselt, David Steinmetz, Susan Schreiner, Irena Backus, and Robert Kolb, among others, have contributed significantly to this field.

[13] First, Pinnock does not seem to grant that in the Hellenistic world are many mansions: not only Parmenidean stasis, but Heraclitean flux. To reduce Hellenism to the Stoics and Plato is to ignore the fact that even Hegel et al. appealed to important streams of Greek thought (especially Aristotle, oddly enough). As we will see in this chapter, reductionism is a glaring weakness of many aspects of the open theism proposal. Second, the early Reformed tradition has usually related to the classical theological tradition in a sympathetically critical manner, suspicious of the Stoicism of Justin Martyr and Origen, the neo-Platonism of Augustine, the Aristotelianism (alleged and real) of Aquinas, late medieval nominalism, and the rise of rationalism evident in Socinianism. This

than Harnack, from reading Scripture through the lens of modern thought, especially Hegel, in addition to Teilhard and Whitehead, a debt that Pinnock readily identifies.[14] But in this case the philosophical debt is evidently justified, since "modern culture . . . is closer to the biblical view than classical theism."[15] Pinnock gives the impression in this book and elsewhere that the detection of unintended philosophical influence from the quarter of ancient philosophy disqualifies a theological model, while his own explicit dependence on modern philosophical trends is greeted practically as *praeparatio evangelica*. But Pinnock, Sanders, and their colleagues have yet to produce new evidence that might reopen this now widely discredited thesis.

II. SPEAKING OF GOD: REFORMED THEOLOGICAL METHOD

Heinrich Heppe started the rumor that predestination was the central thesis of Calvin and Calvinism.[16] However, this has been refuted by close attention to the primary sources: both Calvin and the Reformed scholastics.[17] From the beginning, with Melanchthon and Bullinger leading the way, covenant theology emerged as the very warp and woof of Reformed theology.[18] As we will see below, Calvin warned against speculating concerning eternal predestination, and the Reformed tradition reflects this caution, emphasizing the dynamic relationship and even partnership that obtains in the history of redemption through God's

suspicion has been just beneath the surface throughout the movement's career, as is evident in the works not only of the scholastics but of their British and Continental heirs. Cornelius Van Til, for example, in *A Christian Theory of Knowledge* (Phillipsburg, N.J.: Presbyterian & Reformed, 1969), 118-119, is sharply critical of Justin Martyr, Clement of Alexandria, Origen, and Augustine. He is able to show that while Augustine was "in some measure subject to the principles of Platonism and particularly neo-Platonism," his writings display an irreducibly biblical interest. So Van Til can critique Augustine's "rationalist-irrationalist" dialectic (dependent on Neoplatonism) while affirming the major thrust of his work as a distinctively Christian project.

[14] Pinnock, *Most Moved Mover,* 142ff., etc.

[15] Clark Pinnock, "From Augustine to Arminius: A Pilgrimage in Theology," in *The Grace of God and the Will of Man: A Case for Arminianism,* ed. Clark H. Pinnock (Grand Rapids, Mich.: Zondervan, 1989), 24.

[16] Heinrich Heppe, *Reformed Dogmatics,* trans. G. T. Thompson, rev. and ed. Ernst Bizer (Grand Rapids, Mich.: Baker, 1978).

[17] Both the notion of a "central dogma" (predestination) and the widely influential thesis of Perry Miller have been ably refuted by Richard Muller, in the article cited above ("Calvin and the 'Calvinists'") and also in his *Post-Reformation Reformed Dogmatics,* vol. 1 (Grand Rapids, Mich.: Baker, 1987); and *Christ and the Decree: Christology and Predestination in Reformed Theology from Calvin to Perkins* (Grand Rapids, Mich.: Baker, 1986).

[18] See, for instance, Heinrich Bullinger, *De testamento seu foedere Dei unico et aeterno* (1534); cf. Philip Melanchthon, *Loci communes* (1543), where the covenant concept repeatedly appears as a unifying factor.

covenantal dealings. Unlike Barth's overemphasis on divine transcendence, Reformed orthodoxy understood the Creator-creature relationship in covenantal terms even at the ontological level, which implied similarity as well as dissimilarity.[19] As a result, it advocated its own version of the doctrine of analogy. But before we describe that position, let us briefly explain the biblical assumptions upon which it rests.

A. The Creator-Creature Relationship

Contrary to popular caricature, Reformed scholasticism championed an anti-speculative and anti-rationalistic theological method based on the Creator-creature distinction. Turretin, for example, speaks for the whole tradition when he states,

> But when God is set forth as the object of theology, he is not to be regarded simply as God in himself . . . , but as revealed. . . . Nor is he to be considered exclusively under the relation of deity (according to the opinion of Thomas Aquinas and many Scholastics after him, for in this manner the knowledge of him could not be saving but deadly to sinners), but as he is our God (i.e., covenanted in Christ as he has revealed himself to us in his word) . . . [20]

Even *sola scriptura* is not some abstract notion of authority imposed on theology from without, but is the recognition that, as the Reformers so clearly warned, the knowledge of God in his blinding majesty is deadly, while the knowledge of God in his condescending self-revelation is saving. Turretin elaborates on the contrasting approaches:

> Thus although theology treats of the same things with metaphysics, physics and ethics, yet the mode of considering them is far different.

---

[19] Analogy and therefore similarity as well as dissimilarity are written into the very fabric of creaturehood. See, for instance, Cornelius Van Til, *The Defense of the Faith* (Phillipsburg, N.J.: Presbyterian & Reformed, 1979), especially 9-14, although it is a theme running throughout this work and Van Til's thought generally: "Man is created in God's image. He is therefore like God in everything in which a creature can be like God. He is like God in that he too is a personality." On the other hand, "Man can never in any sense outgrow his creaturehood. . . . He is like God, to be sure, but always on a creaturely scale. He can never be like God in God's aseity, immutability, infinity and unity." Man was created as a prophet "to interpret this world" and to both dedicate the world to God (priest) and rule over it for him (king), and his fall was at least in part the result of "a false ideal of knowledge." "Man made for himself the ideal of absolute comprehension in knowledge. . . . Man confused finitude with sin. Thus he commingled the metaphysical and the ethical aspects of reality" (13-15).

[20] Turretin, *Institutes of Elenctic Theology*, 1:16.

It treats of God not like metaphysics as a being or as he can be known from the light of nature, but as the Creator and Redeemer made known by revelation. . . . For theology treats of God and his infinite perfections, not as knowing them in an infinite but in a finite manner; nor absolutely as much as they can be known in themselves, but as much as he has been pleased to reveal them.[21]

In fact, Turretin offers a typical Reformed complaint concerning those such as

. . . Justin Martyr, Origen, Clement of Alexandria, and the Scholastics, whose system is philosophical rather than theological since it depends more upon the reasonings of Aristotle and the other philosophers than upon the testimonies of the prophets and apostles. . . . The Socinians of this day strike against the same rock, placing philosophy in the citadel as the foundation of faith and interpreter of Scripture.[22]

If Scripture's primacy is an implication of the Creator-creature distinction, what does Scripture say of this relationship? First, it is a relationship of communion as well as difference.[23] This is why covenant and not predestination is the organizing principle. As B. B. Warfield describes it, "The architectonic principle of the Westminster Confession is supplied by the schematization of Federal [covenant] theology, which had obtained by this time in Britain, as on the Continent, a dominant position as the most commodious mode of presenting the corpus of Reformed doctrine."[24] (Thus it is odd to claim, as Pinnock does, that when Reformed theologians turn to such notions as covenant to express the dynamic relationship, they are simply jumping on the open theist's bandwagon.[25]) We reach the doctrine of analogy from the Creator-creature relationship by way of four other sub-categories.

First: transcendence and immanence. Eschewing an abstract and

---

[21] Ibid., 17.

[22] Ibid., 44.

[23] Open theists sometimes appeal to Karl Barth's hyper-transcendence (viz., God as "wholly other"), as if the central dogma of Christianity is "the infinite qualitative distinction between God and man." But Barth's controversial account is hardly representative of the Reformed tradition—not only on the conservative side, but illustrated in the well-known debate with Emil Brunner over natural or general revelation.

[24] B. B. Warfield, *The Westminster Assembly and Its Work* (New York: Oxford University Press, 1931), 56.

[25] Pinnock, *Most Moved Mover*, 75-77.

static notion of these categories, which always ends up affirming some version of hyper-transcendence or hyper-immanence, Reformed theology insists that these can only be understood as analogies for non-metaphysical notions.[26]

The second corollary is the "hidden-revealed" distinction. "Truly, you are a God who hides yourself . . ." (Isa. 45:15, ESV). We are reminded in Deuteronomy, "The secret things belong to the LORD our God, but the things that are revealed belong to us and to our children forever, that we may do all the words of this law" (Deut. 29:29, ESV). God has his own independent intra-Trinitarian life apart from the creation, and this life is hidden from view and unknowable to creatures. Yet God has condescended not only to create and enter into a personal relationship with creatures, but to reveal his character insofar as it pleases him and benefits us. It does not benefit us to know the secret essence of God or to probe the hiddenness of his Trinitarian life, but it does benefit us to know that God the Creator is also our Redeemer in Jesus Christ.

The third corollary is the distinction between the eternal decree and its temporal (redemptive-historical) execution.[27] This is why Calvin, like other Reformers, insisted we were not to look for our election in the "naked God" (i.e., his hidden decree), but in Christ (i.e., the revealed promise of the gospel in the covenant of grace embraced by faith). Probing God's secret predestination is like entering a "labyrinth" from which we will never escape.[28] Those who seek God out in his hidden decree will eventually come to believe in a God of arbitrary freedom (the *potentia Dei absoluta*), rather than the God in whom they can trust because they have his revealed promise conferred and sealed in his ordinary ministry (the *potentia Dei ordinata*). Calvin attacked the "absolute power of God" asserted by late medieval accounts of predestination pre-

---

[26] God is clearly not spatially separated from us, since he is omnipresent. The context of Ecclesiastes 5:2—"for God is in heaven and you are on earth" (ESV)—indicates that we are not dealing here with univocal description as to God's whereabouts, but with a reminder that God is not a creature. "Far" and "near" in Scripture always refer either to the Creator-creature distinction, underscoring God's independence, or to the ethical distance between Yahweh's righteousness and the sinfulness of his fallen creatures.

[27] See Richard Muller, *Christ and the Decree.* This pattern is Muller's chief concern in this volume.

[28] In the *Institutes,* Calvin observes that the hiddenness of God's decree to us makes it not entirely wrong to think of certain events as "fortuitous" even though they are not beyond God's foreknowledge (John Calvin, *Institutes of the Christian Religion* [Philadelphia: Westminster, 1960], 1.16.9).

cisely because they substituted speculation for concentration on God's ordained power (i.e., the covenantal promise revealed). This emphasis on the absolute freedom of God, Calvin warned, would make us little more than balls that God juggles in the air.[29] "Omnicausality" is explicitly rejected by Calvin.[30] The truth of God's eternal decree (in both providence and election) is clearly revealed in Scripture and is comforting to believers in their trials: "Yet his wonderful method of governing the universe is rightly called an abyss, because while it is hidden from us, we ought reverently to adore it."[31] "Meanwhile, nevertheless, a godly man will not overlook the secondary causes."[32]

As a result of these distinctions, covenant theology therefore focuses on the dynamic outworking of God's redemptive plan in concrete history, taking very seriously the twists and turns in the road—including God's responses to human beings. But it does so without denying the clear biblical witness to the fact that God transcends these historical relationships. Transcendence and immanence are not antithetical categories for us, compelling us to choose one over the other. Neither Plato nor Aristotle; Kant nor Hegel; Kierkegaard nor Cobb gives us a biblical model for either transcendence or immanence.

The final corollary we will consider is the "archetypal-ectypal" distinction, the epistemological corollary of the ontological Creator-creature distinction. Although it had been a category in medieval system, Protestant dogmatics gave particular attention to this distinction and made it essential to their method. Just as God is not merely greater in degree (viz., *"supreme* being"), but in a class by himself ("life in himself," John 5:26, ESV), his knowledge of himself and everything else is not just quantitatively but qualitatively different from that of creatures. Theologians as diverse as Carl Henry and Langdon Gilkey have had trouble accepting this, claiming that it leads to irrationalism to say that God's knowledge of an object and our knowledge of an object are never

---

[29] Calvin, *Institutes*, 1.17.2, see especially footnote 7: "Cf. Calvin, *De aeterna Dei praedestinatione,* where he assails the 'Sorbonnist dogma that ascribes to God absolute power' dissociated from justice. . . . Similarly, in Sermons on Job lxxxviii, on Job 23:1-7: 'What the Sorbonne doctors say, that God has an absolute power, is a diabolical blasphemy which has been invented in hell' (CR XXXIV, 339f.)." Although open theism appears at times to separate God's love from his justice, Calvin will not allow that either God's love or his sovereignty is unhinged from his justice.

[30] Calvin, *Institutes*, 1.17.1.

[31] Ibid., 1.17.2.

[32] Ibid., 1.17.9.

identical at any point.[33] And yet affirmation of this distinction is essential if we are to affirm with Scripture that no one has ever known the mind of the Lord (Rom. 11:34, where the context is predestination); that his thoughts are far above our thoughts (Isa. 55:8-9); and that he is "above" and we are "below" (Eccles. 5:2)—if, in other words, we are to truly affirm the Creator-creature distinction.

B. Analogy

All of this leads us, finally, to the doctrine of analogy. When we assert certain predicates of God, based on God's own self-revelation, we use them in one of three senses: univocally, analogically, or equivocally. If we say that the predicate "gracious" means exactly the same thing, whether in God or in a creature, we are using "gracious" *univocally*. At the other end of the spectrum, if we say that by using that predicate we are ascribing something to God whose appropriateness is unknown to us, we are using it *equivocally*. If, however, God is said to be "gracious" in a way that is both similar and dissimilar to creatures, we say it is *ana-*

---

[33] Duns Scotus argued this point against Thomas Aquinas's doctrine of analogy, and in the modern era it is challenged on essentially the same basis (alleged irrationality/skepticism) by Gordon Clark, Carl F. H. Henry, Ronald Nash, Clark Pinnock, and John Sanders. Henry, for example, summarizes the Clark-Van Til debate over whether human and divine knowledge of the same object is quantitatively or qualitatively different, respectively. Against the doctrine of analogy, which he suggests leads to agnosticism, Henry cites Clark: "If no proposition means to man what it means to God, so that God's knowledge and man's knowledge do not coincide at any single point, it follows by rigorous necessity that man can have no truth at all," cited in *God, Revelation and Authority*, vol. 2 (Waco, Tex.: Word, 1976; reprint, Wheaton, Ill.: Crossway, 1999), 53-54. Aquinas's analogical method "seems therefore finally to channel into theological agnosticism. Protestant Christians are more at home with a natural theology less dependent upon Aristotelian concepts and not encumbered by the notion of analogical predication" (ibid., 115). Yet all the major dogmatic systems of Protestant orthodoxy were in fact explicit in their use of the analogical as opposed to univocal method. But Henry also misunderstands the classical doctrine of analogy: "To Thomas Aquinas, Christendom specially owes the emphasis that religious language does not state what is literally true of God but involves only analogical predication" (ibid., vol. 3, 336). Henry appears to confuse "literal" with "univocal," while those who appeal to analogy hold that predications of certain attributes in God are literal but analogical. This approach, says Henry, is "a futile attempt to explore a middle road between univocity and equivocity." However, "Only univocal assertions protect us from equivocacy; only univocal knowledge is, therefore, genuine and authentic knowledge" (ibid., 364). Not only does an analogical approach lead to skepticism, but (according to Henry) it is basically the same thing as a symbolic theology. This would make Aquinas a precursor of Protestant liberalism. Henry appears to be encumbered by a positivist view of language and propositional assertions. Theology, for instance, "consists essentially in the repetition, combination, and systematization of the truth of revelation in its propositionally given biblical form" (ibid., vol. 1, 238). Interestingly, both a liberal theologian such as Langdon Gilkey ("Cosmology, Ontology, and the Travail of Biblical Language," *Journal of Religion* XLI [July 1961]: 200) and a conservative such as Carl Henry (*God, Revelation and Authority*, vol. 1 [Waco, Tex.: Word, 1976; reprint, Wheaton, Ill.: Crossway, 1999], 237-238) erroneously link univocity to premodern, and analogy or equivocity to modern (liberal) moves. This is to miss a rather dominant strain of theological prolegomena running from the patristics to Aquinas to the Reformers and their successors.

logical. For instance, when we acknowledge that God is a "person," do we really mean to say that he is a person in *exactly* the same sense as we are? When we follow Scripture in using male pronouns to refer to God, do we really believe that he is male? Unless we are willing to ascribe to God (in a univocal sense) all attributes of human personhood, predications must be analogical.

Human language cannot transcend its finitude, so when God reveals himself in human language, he draws on human analogies to lead us by the hand to himself. It is correct description, but not univocal description. As we will argue below, the univocal approach to such language almost always tends toward rationalism and the suspicion of the mystery inherent in the Creator-creature distinction. And equivocal approaches, such as those adopted in some forms of mysticism and in the wake of Kant, denying any certainty about the truth of our predications, tend toward skepticism under the guise of God's mysterious incomprehensibility.[34]

Thus, Calvin and the Reformed do not use analogy as a fall-back strategy when they find something that does not fit their system. Rather, it is the warp and woof of their covenantal approach, a necessary implication of the Creator-creature relationship as they understand it. *All* of God's self-revelation is analogical, not just some of it. This is why Calvin speaks, for instance, of God's "lisping" or speaking "baby-talk" in his condescending mercy. Just as God comes down to us in the Incarnation in order to save us who could not ascend to him, he meets us in Scripture by descending to our weakness. Thus, not only is God's transcendence affirmed, but his radical immanence as well. Transcendence and immanence become inextricably bound up with the divine drama of redemption. Revelation no less than redemption is an act of condescension and grace.[35]

---

[34] In spite of significant differences, Gordon Kaufman and Wolfhart Pannenberg illustrate the post-Kantian difficulty with accepting biblical analogies as divinely authoritative. Both appeal to divine incomprehensibility to affirm an essentially equivocal stance, although Pannenberg argues that our frankly equivocal ascriptions of praise to God for specific attributes is justified by the proleptic anticipation of revelation at the end of history. See his chapter "Analogy" in *Basic Questions in Theology,* trans. George H. Kehm, vol. 1 (Philadelphia: Westminster, 1970), 211-238. It should also be pointed out that Calvin was hardly the inventor of this idea or, for that matter, of the notion of accommodation, which we find replete in the writings of the church fathers— Chrysostom and Athanasius as well as Augustine and Ambrose. It was abundant in apophatic theology and persisted through the Middle Ages, despite attempts to transgress the boundary of mystery in pursuit of the *Visio Dei.* According to the Fourth Lateran Council, in all analogies between God and the creature there is always more dissimilarity than similarity.

[35] For a brilliant treatment of this relationship, see Ronald Thiemann, *Revelation and Redemption* (Notre Dame, Ind.: University of Notre Dame Press, 1985).

Those who are uncomfortable with this analogical approach frequently betray an autonomous view of knowledge.[36] How can we know if the analogies fit? The assumption seems to be that unless one can stand outside of the analogy and its referent, one cannot compare the analogy for its accuracy. Many conclude that if the predicate "good" applied to both God and Sally does not mean exactly the same thing, then we are left in skepticism (equivocity). Either rationalism or irrationalism: that is the choice that an autonomous epistemology requires. But a Reformed analogical approach insists that because Scripture is God's own speech in human language, the analogies that *God* selects are appropriate whether *we* know the exact fit or not. We do not need that which we cannot possibly have—namely, archetypal knowledge.[37] Because creaturely knowledge is inherently ectypal, it is essentially analogical. Univocal knowledge is reserved for the Creator and his archetypal theology. But if God authorizes the analogies, they must be accurate descriptions even though they do not provide univocal access to God's being. Scripture is sufficient for the purposes God intended—to reconcile us to himself, not to satisfy our curiosity.

Once more, it was the Socinian and Remonstrant (Arminian) schools that strongly opposed this approach, raising reason and speculative deductions above clear scriptural statements and insisting upon univocal access to God's being. This is further evidence that Reformed theology is far from being a rationalistic system claiming to be a reproduction of the mind of God.[38] In fact, although the term "pilgrim theology" (*theologia viatorum*) was employed by Hilary of Poitiers (fourth century), it became the favorite phrase for Reformed and Lutheran systems.

---

[36] Pannenberg, "Analogy."

[37] Following Herman Bavinck, Van Til says that all revelation is not only analogical but anthropomorphic: "It is an adaptation by God to the limitations of the human creature. Man's systematic interpretation of the revelation of God is never more than an approximation of the system of truth revealed in Scripture, and this system of truth as revealed in Scripture is itself anthropomorphic. But being anthropomorphic does not make it untrue. The Confessions of the Church pretend to be nothing more than frankly approximated statements of the inherently anthropomorphic revelation of God" (*A Christian Theory of Knowledge*, 41).

[38] Bavinck displays this anti-speculative character, asserting that "God's being in the abstract is nowhere discussed" in Scripture. "The Hebrew word *tushiah* from the root *yashah*, to exist, to be . . ." indicates an enduring character (Job 5:12; 6:13; 12:16; 26:3; Prov. 2:7; 3:21; 8:14; Isa. 28:29; Mic. 6:9); "but in none of these passages does it signify the being of God." These passages give us something of God's "excellencies or virtues," but not access to his nature. "Scripture nowhere discusses God's being apart from his attributes" (*The Doctrine of God*, trans. and ed. William Hendriksen [Grand Rapids, Mich.: Eerdmans, 1951; Edinburgh: Banner of Truth, 1977], 114).

To cap off this trajectory, it is necessary to add the analogy of Scripture. If all language about God, including that which we find in Scripture, is analogical, we can never rest on one analogy and "translate" it into a univocal predicate. This translation error may be done by Calvinists as well as by open theists, as whenever God's simplicity is denied in favor of either his sovereignty or his love. When this occurs, the object of theology is no longer a personal God but an abstract attribute that is now said to be God's essence. An analogical approach, therefore, in order to work properly, must listen to the symphony of biblical analogies, knowing that none of the analogies by itself can be reduced to the whole (univocal) score.

III. Open Theism: Comparison and Contrast

John Sanders offers a refreshingly fair summary of the methodological approach we have considered:

> God is not knowable unless God makes himself known, and even then we do not possess a complete understanding of God. Barth goes on to say that this hiddenness is not due to the inadequacy of human language . . . and not because of any metaphysical distinction between the abstract and the sensual. Instead, the incomprehensibility of God is based on the Creator-creature distinction that comes to us from divine revelation.[39]

As we shall see, however, open theism and classical Reformed theology differ considerably on this question, at least in practice if not always in theory. We will follow the same outline as above in our comparison and contrast.

First, open theism claims to be biblical. But where Reformed theology recognizes Scripture alone as the source of theology, while experience, reason, and tradition are treated as significant influences, open theists adopt the so-called Wesleyan Quadrilateral, with Scripture as the first but not sole normative source.[40] In a previous work Pinnock

---

[39] Sanders, *The God Who Risks*, 20.

[40] "My approach to theological method is bi-polar," Pinnock announces, which is to say, faithful to the Christian message and the contemporary world. "As Paul Tillich put it, theology ought to satisfy two basic needs: to state the truth of the Christian message and to interpret the truth for every generation." This dialectical movement " . . . is not easy to balance . . ." (*Most Moved Mover*, 19). "To be more precise," Pinnock adds, "I adhere to the rule of Scripture within a trilateral hermeneutic. . . . I hold the Bible to be the primary norm for theology in the midst of the other sources" (ibid.).

reasoned, "Just as Augustine came to terms with ancient Greek thinking, so we are making peace with the culture of modernity."[41] Yet one
would be hard-pressed to find Augustine sharing Pinnock's assessment
of such direct dependence.[42] Pinnock writes, "As an open theist, I am
interested in such authors as Hegel, Pierre Teilhard de Chardin and
Whitehead because they make room in their thinking for ideas like
change, incarnation and divine suffering. . . ."[43]

A. The Creator-Creature Distinction

It is no secret that there are strong similarities between process thought
and open theism: both process and open theists have repeatedly
acknowledged these. However, they have also acknowledged important
differences even in these two works that we are citing.[44] Among these
differences, for instance, is the essential Creator-creature distinction.[45]

Yet, despite calls to trade abstract for concrete descriptions of God,
Pinnock does end up speaking of transcendence and immanence in quite
abstract, static, and general terms. They appear to be timeless ideas,
drawn from the familiar antitheses of ancient and modern dualism (and
dualistic monism), and this often leads to false dilemmas. Either we worship a God who does not want to "control everything, but to give the
creature room to exist and freedom to love," or " . . . an all-controlling

---

[41] Pinnock, "From Augustine to Arminius," 27.

[42] It is one thing to suggest that Augustine was influenced by Greek thought; quite another to
conclude that he was taking a posture of capitulation. Whether Pinnock concedes this in his case
with respect to the culture of modernity, it is certain that Augustine would not have recognized
himself as treating culture as a source of theology.

[43] Pinnock, *Most Moved Mover*, 142. So it is really not the case that Pinnock substitutes a frankly
biblical approach for an ostensibly pagan philosophical one, but that he more explicitly draws
upon secular thinking as a subordinate source. Pinnock even refers to Whitehead as a Christian,
although this would have been questioned as much by Whitehead, at most a Unitarian, as by
anyone. These writers treated the incarnation as an idea—an abstract, general concept. This is far,
it seems to me, from the Christian doctrine of the incarnation, which is hardly an instance of a
general type. It cannot be made into a general philosophical concept, whether of a Parmenidean-
Kierkegaardian or a Heraclitean-Hegelian form. Hegel, Teilhard, and Whitehead were as indebted
to Greek thought (the Heraclitean type) as their Stoic friends were devoted to Parmenides. In fact,
elsewhere Pinnock draws on Justin Martyr's formulation of the logos concept in his search for a
universal natural theology, even though the Stoic influence is well known.

[44] Ibid., 142-150; and Sanders, *The God Who Risks*, 161, 190, 207, 113. See also the new
collaborative volume, edited by Pinnock and John Cobb, Jr.: *Searching for an Adequate God: A
Dialogue Between Process and Free Will Theists* (Grand Rapids, Mich.: Eerdmans, 2000).

[45] Pinnock insists, "God has no need of an external world to supply experiences of relationality
because God experiences it within himself apart from any world." Creation " . . . is not something
God needs but something he wants" (*Most Moved Mover*, 29). There is no panentheism in his
remark, "God enjoys the world; it means something to him as an expression, but it is not an
essential element of his self" (30).

despot who can tolerate no resistance (Calvin),"[46] giving the false impression that Calvin actually held this position attributed to him. Further, we must choose between a God who is "immobile" (a "solitary monad") and the "Living God" who is dependent on the creation for his happiness.[47] But who really believes the former? That is important, since the very title of Pinnock's book suggests that the position he is criticizing is little more than a religious gloss on Aristotle's "Unmoved Mover." He calls it "the immobility package."[48] But if there is no such thing, it would seem that the options are not as extreme as some would have us believe. Since Pinnock repeats this charge, a brief response will illustrate my larger point.

Pinnock and his colleagues conflate immutability and immobility. But this misses a crucial step; namely, that of determining whether the tradition did in fact adopt Aristotle's doctrine. As Richard Muller points out, "The scholastic notion of God as immobile does not translate into English as 'immobile'—as one of the many cases of cognates not being fully convertible—but as 'unmoved.'"[49] However much in this respect the Christian doctrine sounds similar to Aristotle's "Unmoved Mover," the differences are greater. Since Old Princeton is often targeted as the bastion of classical theism, let us listen to its most illustrious systematician, Charles Hodge. Christians maintain that God is immutable:

> [B]ut nevertheless that He is not a stagnant ocean, but an ever living, ever thinking, ever acting, and *ever suiting his action to the exigencies of his creatures, and to the accomplishment of his infinitely wise designs.* Whether we can harmonize these facts or not, is a matter of minor importance. We are constantly called upon to believe that things are, without being able to tell how they are, or even how they can be. Theologians, in their attempts to state, in philosophical language, the doctrine of the Bible on the unchangeableness of God, are apt to confound immutability with immobility. In denying that God can change, they seem to deny that He can act.[50]

---

[46] Ibid., 4.

[47] Ibid., 6.

[48] Ibid., 78.

[49] Richard Muller, "Incarnation, Immutability, and the Case for Classical Theism," *Westminster Theological Journal* 45 (1983): 27.

[50] Charles Hodge, *Systematic Theology*, vol. 1 (Grand Rapids, Mich.: Eerdmans, 1946), 390-391, emphasis added.

Immutability must not be confused with immobility, and there is unanimity here among the various Reformed dogmatics.[51]
In a similar vein, Van Til writes,

> Surely in the case of Aristotle the immutability of the divine being was
> due to its emptiness and internal immobility. *No greater contrast is
> thinkable than that between the unmoved* noesis noeeseoos *of Aristotle
> and the Christian God.* This appears particularly from the fact that the
> Bible does not hesitate to attribute all manner of activity to God. . . .
> Herein lies the glory of the Christian doctrine of God, that the
> unchangeable one is the one in control of the change of the universe.[52]

Yahweh is therefore not a solitary monad preoccupied with himself, a
Buddha-like figure who closes his eyes to the world in order to contemplate his own bliss. But he is also not a creature contained in and
circumscribed by the reality that he has created apart from himself. Not
surprisingly, the classical prohibition of univocal access to God's being
is motivated by the Creator-creature distinction. While open theists have
serious difficulties with this *epistemological* boundary, they affirm the
ontological distinction.[53]

B. Analogy

Analogy is ideally suited to the biblical understanding of the God-world
relationship. While equivocity is a mark of hyper-transcendence and its
concomitant skepticism, univocity is a mark of hyper-immanence and its
concomitant rationalism. An equivocal approach to religious language

---

[51] Ibid., 392. Here Hodge criticizes in particular some statements of Augustine to that effect,
charging that he speculated beyond the limits of exegesis. But modern theology is far more
indebted to philosophical assumptions, he charges: "We must abide by the teachings of Scripture,
and refuse to subordinate their authority and the intuitive convictions of our moral and religious
nature to the arbitrary definitions of any philosophical system." Bavinck concurs: "The fact that
God is immutable does not mean that he is inactive: immutability should not be confused with
immobility" (Bavinck, *The Doctrine of God*, 151).

[52] Emphasis added. Cited by Muller, "Incarnation, Immutability, and the Case for Classical
Theism," 30.

[53] Of course, the Creator-creature distinction is affirmed, but what makes it difficult right up front
is that we have not yet agreed on definitions for the debate. Pinnock asserts, "All of us hold to the
fundamentals of orthodox theism, e.g., the immanent Trinity, the God-world distinction, God's
actions in history, the goodness, unchangeableness, omnipotence, and omniscience of God, and
the atoning death and resurrection of Jesus Christ" (*Most Moved Mover*, 11). Yet in the same
book Pinnock admits that his proposal is an alternative to "orthodox theism"; the status of the
immanent/economic Trinity distinction is ambiguous, and "unchangeableness, omnipotence, and
omniscience" are affirmed by Pinnock only at the cost of redefining these terms.

champions difference at the expense of similarity, while a univocal approach offers a reverse sacrifice. But analogies assume both difference and similarity. It is therefore less reductive than either univocal rationalism or equivocal irrationalism. It is not just that some scriptures (viz., that represent God as repenting) are treated as analogical or anthropomorphic, while others (viz., that represent God as never changing) are treated as univocal. All of this language is analogical, the result of God's self-condescension and accommodation. Human beings, "when they indulge their curiosity, enter into a labyrinth," Calvin warned.[54] Far safer, then, to let God descend to us.[55]

In an ironic move for those who accuse Calvin and the tradition generally of being held hostage to reason, Pinnock and Sanders complain that such strong affirmations of divine incomprehensibility and mystery can only lead to skepticism. Scripture declares, "To whom will you liken me and make me equal, and compare me, as though we were alike?" (Isa. 46:5, NRSV; cf. 55:8-9; Num. 23:19; 1 Sam. 15:29; Hos. 11:9). But such texts, Sanders says, "are often understood as biblical warrant for the disparagement of anthropomorphism."[56] But does that really meet its mark? How is one *disparaging* anthropomorphism simply by treating it *as* anthropomorphic? Is it not those who demand that anthropomorphism and analogy be translated into univocal predicates who are scandalized by the former? From our perspective, Scripture is no less analogical when it says that God does not repent than when it represents him as doing just that.

Despite his incomprehensibility, God wills to enter into a relationship with his creatures. The covenant is the context in which that becomes possible. Let us turn for a moment to examples of this covenan-

---

[54] Calvin, *Institutes*, 1.16.9.

[55] In the *Institutes*, for instance, the Genevan reformer appeals to analogy to challenge the anti-Trinitarianism of some of his critics. Note the anti-speculative intent of this appeal:

> Here, indeed, if anywhere in the secret mysteries of Scripture, we ought to play the philosopher soberly and with great moderation; let us use great caution that neither our thoughts nor our speech go beyond the limits to which the Word of God itself extends. For how can the human mind measure off the measureless essence of God according to its own little measure, a mind as yet unable to establish for certain the nature of the sun's body, though men's eyes daily gaze upon it? Indeed, how can the mind by its own leading come to search out God's essence when it cannot even get to its own? Let us then willingly leave to God the knowledge of himself (*Institutes*, 1.13.21).

[56] Sanders, *The God Who Risks*, 20.

tal (analogical) discourse, particularly as touching on this debate. We will treat classes or types rather than offering exegesis of specific passages. The obvious examples have to do with God relenting and repenting. Both, open theists contend, demonstrate that God is *not* immutable, independent, or omniscient—at least as these terms have been historically understood. We know the passages, but what do we do in such instances? Occurring as they do in the dramatic narrative of God's covenant dealings with his people, we know that we are not in the realm of God's hiddenness, "God-in-himself," the eternal decree of the immanent Trinity. Rather, we are in the realm of God's revelation, "God-for-us," the historical outworking of that eternal plan. On one hand, we are to take seriously the dynamic relationship of covenant partners (1 Sam. 15:11), yet without translating them into univocal descriptions that lead us to conclude that God does in fact change his mind (v. 29). The same is true in Malachi 3:6: "'For I am the LORD, I do not change; therefore you are not consumed, O sons of Jacob'" (NKJV). Neither God's nature nor his secret plan changes, and this is why believers can be confident that "if we are faithless, he remains faithful—for he cannot deny himself" (2 Tim. 2:13, ESV). So what changes if not his secret plans? It is his revealed plans that change: the judgment that he has warned that he will bring upon the people is averted—precisely as God had predestined before the ages. The dynamic give-and-take so obvious in the history of the covenant must be distinguished from the eternal decree that Scripture also declares as hidden in God's unchanging and inaccessible counsel (Eph. 1:4-11).

These are not two contradictory lines of proof-texts, one line pro-openness; the other pro-classical theism. Rather, they are two lines of analogy acting as guardrails to keep us on the right path. There is real change, dynamic interaction, and partnership in this covenant (*Deus revelatus pro nobis*). At the same time, God is not like the human partner in that he does not repent the way the latter repents: God transcends the narrative (*Deus absconditus in se*). With Scripture, we speak on one hand of our existence after the fall in terms of not being as God intended things, and yet recognize that even this is part of God's eternal plan to display his glory. We are not denying the analogy or failing to take it seriously, but we are refusing to take it univocally. Theologians and preachers in the Reformed tradition have not had difficulty with the "repentance" passages the way open theists seem, by their troubling silence, to be burdened by the "non-repentance" passages. That may be due in part to the fact that the tradition does not reduce everything to either the eternal decree of the hidden God or the historical covenant of the revealed God.[57]

One of the marks of a strong theory is that it is able to make sense of the greatest amount of its appropriate data. Open theism has still not provided a serious exegetical account of the passages that clearly indicate that God does not change, does not repent, does not depend on the world for his happiness, and passages that do affirm God's knowledge of and sovereignty over all contingencies of history to the last detail. On the other hand, an analogical account provides a paradigm in which both may be seriously affirmed without resolving the mystery in a false dilemma.

This point comes into sharper focus in open theism's treatment of the classical doctrine of divine impassibility, which it incorrectly defines as the inability to experience or feel emotion. (By the way, *passio*, in Latin, means "suffering," not "feeling" or "experiencing.") If God were exactly identical to every representation we come across in Scripture, could we not justly conclude that he is, for instance, capricious: "Kiss the Son, lest he become angry and you perish in the way, *for his wrath can flare up in an instant*" (Ps. 2:12, author's translation)? In this Psalm, God is depicted as mocking his enemies with sardonic laughter. But do we really want to ascribe this univocally to God's being rather than recognizing it as a sober portrait of a great king undisturbed by the pretenses of human power? We have yet to discover among open theists an argument in favor for God's rage being understood in the same univocal terms as his repentance.[58]

---

[57] Pinnock and his colleagues may not approve the Reformed account of double agency, but their repeated misrepresentation of this tradition as "omnicausality" and the elimination of human partnership in the covenant is a perennial weakness of their rhetoric. This notion of double agency is not the incursion of philosophy, but is a good and necessary inference from such numerous passages. In the familiar Joseph narrative, the same event—Joseph's cruel treatment by his brothers—has two authors with two distinct intentions: "You meant it for evil, but God meant it for good" (see Gen. 50:19-20). Peter offers precisely the same rationale for the crucifixion: "You with your wicked hands. . . . [But] he was delivered up according to God's foreknowledge" (see Acts 2:23).

[58] Further, there is enough similarity to what we experience as love to say "God is love" (1 John 4:8), but love is obviously different in the case of the one who loves in absolute freedom than for creatures whose experience of love is always related to some form of dependence and reciprocity. This very point seems implied in the same chapter: "In this is love, not that we loved God but that he loved us and sent his Son to be the atoning sacrifice for our sins. . . . We love because he first loved us" (1 John 4:10, 19, NRSV). In other words, here God's love is the ultimate reality and human loves analogies. We will never know exactly how God's loving and creaturely loving compare, but we have seen God's love in the face of Christ and that is sufficient for eternity. Think of the numerous passages narrating God's impatience with Israel's unfaithfulness in the wilderness,

Surely this dialectic play of analogies is comparable to the narrative representation of God as repenting and yet affirming, "I am not a man that I should repent" (see 1 Sam. 15:29).[59] Sanders judges,

> The desire not to speak about God anthropomorphically simply seems correct. After all, just about everyone takes the biblical references to the "eyes," "arm" and "mouth" (anthropomorphisms proper) of God as metaphors for divine actions, not assertions that God has literal body parts. But some go further, claiming that the anthropopathisms (in which God is said to have emotions, plans or changes of mind) are not actually to be attributed to God.[60]

First, as we have insisted, "the desire not to speak about God anthropomorphically" is far from our contention. But further, why would we make an arbitrary distinction between analogies of being and analogies of feeling? If all predicates applied to God and creatures must be regarded as analogical, that would include references to God's sardonic laughter at his enemies in Psalm 2 or his grief at the disobedience of covenant partners. Perhaps, to attain consistency, an open theist would want to agree with Moltmann that God somehow does actually cry real tears.[61] Pinnock does in fact take this next logical step, speculating con-

---

threatening to destroy them. Although God is frequently represented in narrative texts as impatient (Gen. 18:22ff; Ex. 32:9-14), he also passed before Moses proclaiming his name: "The LORD, the LORD, the compassionate and gracious God, *slow to anger . . .*" (Ex. 34:6, NIV). "Slow to anger" is as analogical as the impatience discerned in the narrative.

[59] So are open theists consistent in their denial of impassibility? Is "impatience" in God the same as our impatience? It would appear that there are only two options. On one hand, one can say that God can just as easily be overwhelmed with impatience or vengeance as he can be with love. In this case, we can be confident that for the time being at least God has not rejected us, but we cannot be absolutely certain about tomorrow. Univocal interpretations of divine suffering cut both ways. The other interpretive strategy is to recognize that while God is not affected or changed by creatures, expressing his interaction with creatures in redemptive history cannot help but rely on analogies that, by definition, break down. Because God is essentially good, loving, just, righteous, and merciful, and not essentially impatient and vengeful (or repentant and sorrowful), he is unlike the idolatrous projections of the human imagination. Our God is reliable. This, in fact, is the very logic of Malachi 3:6: "For I am the LORD, I do not change; *therefore you are not consumed, O sons of Jacob*" (NKJV).

[60] Sanders, *The God Who Risks*, 20.

[61] Some advocates of divine suffering verge on caricaturing their own position when they criticize the traditional view, as Moltmann does, as holding that "[God] cannot weep, for he has no tears" (Jürgen Moltmann, *The Crucified God* [New York: Harper & Row, 1974], 222). Does Moltmann believe that God possesses tear ducts? Or is he anthropomorphic as the texts he cites for his position? Is the next step to deny God's spirituality as yet another relic of Platonic dualism that will have to give way in the light of so many biblical representations of God in physical terms? It would seem that panentheism of some sort is the necessary consequence of open theism's critique. And any divine transcendence, including omnipresence or divine spirituality, would appear just as threatened as the other incommunicable attributes we have considered.

cerning God's embodiment beyond the Incarnation.[62] This is a good example of how distinctions collapse in open theism. Even Jesus' assertion that "God is spirit" could conceivably be surrendered as one more incursion of Greek philosophy. Pinnock cites Mormon theologian David Paulsen, among others, for support[63] and appeals to Mormon criticisms of divine incorporeality as well as other classical attributes.[64] Is it not open theism, then, that disparages anthropomorphism and cannot live with analogies *as* analogies?

But short of making this move to affirm divine corporeality, there seems to be no theoretical reason to separate attributions of particular emotions from attributions of particular limbs and organs.[65] We do not have the space here to pursue this important point further.[66] Nevertheless, renewed attention to this particular formulation of divine impassibility would seem to be called for on both sides of this debate. B. B. Warfield's treatment of divine emotion contrasts sharply with the picture that one obtains from Pinnock's caricature.[67]

At the end of the day, Sanders is worried that an analogical approach will leave us with agnosticism (equivocity), citing John Macquarrie's con-

---

[62] Pinnock, *Most Moved Mover*, 33-34.

[63] Ibid., 35 n. 31.

[64] Ibid., 68 n. 11.

[65] Marylin Adams has observed, in a written response as part of a seminar with Professors Nicholas Wolterstorff and Marylin Adams on Divine Impassibility at Yale University in 1997: "It seems to me that human suffering could be a reason for Divine compassion without being an efficient cause of it." Adams captures what is really at stake here: "If something other than God causally affects God, however, God can't be the first cause of every change, unless Divine passibility is just an indirect approach to Divine self-change. . . . If God could be totally or even nearly overcome by grief within God's Divine nature, God would not only fail to have an ideal Stoic character (which those of us who flirt with passibility can live with), God's providential control might be jeopardized. Do crucifixion, earthquakes, and eclipses signal that God has 'lost it' in Divine rage and grief?"

[66] See Paul Helm, "The Impossibility of Divine Passibility," in *The Power and Weakness of God*, ed. Nigel M. de S. Cameron (Edinburgh: Rutherford, 1990), 123, 126: "Aquinas, for example, does not object to some of what are affections in human beings being a part of God's character [*Summa contra gentiles* I.90], he only objects to those affections which, if they are had by anything, require that individual to be passive and to be in time. So that if there are attributes which, though they in fact carry such implications when possessed by human beings, do not when possessed by God, then Aquinas is ready to recognize the possibility of such in God. And clearly there are such— love, joy, delight, care and grace, for example. God has each of these with the greatest possible intensity and power."

[67] B. B. Warfield, *The Person and Work of Christ*, ed. Samuel G. Craig (Philadelphia: Presbyterian & Reformed, 1970), 570-571:

Men tell us that God is, by the very necessity of His nature, incapable of passion, incapable of being moved by inducements from without; that He dwells in holy calm and unchangeable blessedness, untouched by human sufferings or human sorrows for ever,—haunting

cern that without a "univocal core," theology "lapses into agnosticism."[68] Macquarrie and other liberal or existentialist theologians have reason to worry about agnosticism, however, only because they do not accept the authority of Scripture to deliver *trustworthy* analogies. But if God has authorized these analogies, why should we feel anxious?

Similar to Pannenberg's criticism of analogy above,[69] Sanders seems to assume a faulty (autonomous) standard for what counts as real knowledge. He must *see* the fit between language and reality in order to know with apodictic certainty that it is accurate: "If one suggests that there is an infinite difference between the analogates when speaking of God and humanity, then the doctrine of analogy fails to give us any knowledge of God."[70] We must see the fit ourselves in order to judge it (univocity) or else know nothing concretely about God (equivocity) only if God has not spoken (analogy).[71]

Here the analogy of Scripture becomes essential. We might even call

---

> The lucid interspace of world and world,
> Where never creeps a cloud, nor moves a wind,
> Nor ever falls the least white star of snow,
> Nor ever lowest roll of thunder moans,
> Nor sound of human sorrow mounts to mar
> His sacred, everlasting calm.

Let us bless our God that it is not true. God can feel; God does love. We have Scriptural warrant for believing that, like the hero of Zurich, God has reached out loving arms and gathered into His own bosom that forest of spears which otherwise had pierced ours. But is not this gross anthropomorphism? We are careless of names: it is the truth of God. And we decline to yield up the God of the Bible and the God of our hearts to any philosophical abstraction. . . . We may feel awe in the presence of the Absolute, as we feel awe in the presence of the storm or of the earthquake. . . . But we cannot love it; we cannot trust it. . . . Nevertheless, let us rejoice that our God has not left us by searching to find Him out. Let us rejoice that He has plainly revealed Himself to us in His Word as a God who loves us, and who, because He loves us, has sacrificed Himself for us.

I am grateful to Professor John Frame for pointing out this reference.

[68] Sanders, *The God Who Risks,* 25.

[69] Note 34.

[70] Sanders, *The God Who Risks,* 286 n. 43. Sanders adds, "Furthermore, thinkers as diverse as John Duns Scotus, William of Ockham, George Berkeley, William Alston, Richard Swinburne, Thomas Tracy, and Paul Helm all agree that there must be a 'hard literal core' or 'univocal core' to our talk about God. There must be some properties that are used of God in the same sense that they are used of things in the created order. *Otherwise we will be back in the cave of agnosticism.* Anthropomorphic language does not preclude literal predication to God" (25, emphasis added).

[71] It is worth pondering whether the dominance of the "mirror" as a root metaphor for the relationship of language and reality is at bottom a rationalist presupposition, in contrast to the biblical emphasis on "hearing" the (analogical) word. This is a point I develop at length in *Covenant and Eschatology: The Divine Drama* (Louisville, Ky.: Westminster John Knox, 2002). For a helpful description of the career and influence of the "mirror" epistemology, see Richard Rorty, *Philosophy and the Mirror of Nature* (Princeton, N.J.: Princeton University Press, 1979).

it, somewhat awkwardly, the analogy of analogy. No single analogy, abstracted from the rest, adequately represents God's character. Only taken together as one multifaceted self-revelation do the analogies effectively render a sufficient knowledge of God. (The analogy of Scripture applied to theology proper, it should be noted, is the corollary of the doctrine of divine simplicity, which open theism also rejects, reducing the diverse divine attributes to one: love.)

To summarize thus far, open theism affirms the Creator-creature distinction at least in principle, distinguishing it from process thought. Furthermore, it tries to affirm the correlative distinctions between God's being-in-himself and his being-for-us, and affirms the role of analogies. But does it succeed in maintaining these in actual practice? This is where Pinnock and Sanders appear to be tentative at best.

Methodologically, theological proposals must do more than offer an alternative to a dominant position that nobody actually holds. For Pinnock, it is either "libertarian freedom" or despotic "omnicausality," not even recognizing that Reformed theology (like other traditions) affirms a fairly well-developed and well-known account of double agency. Calvinism, according to Pinnock, envisions God as "the sole performer who cannot make room for significant human agents."[72] It may be that Pinnock thinks that this is what Calvinism amounts to, but the official confessions and catechisms of the Reformed and Presbyterian family explicitly affirm double agency and stridently reject any suggestion of the sort alleged by Pinnock.[73] Perhaps he thinks that since his position is beyond Arminianism he must render his nemesis something beyond Calvinism.

Related to the biblical confession that "God is in heaven and we are on earth" (again, not a spatial announcement, but an analogical way of stating the Creator-creature distinction) is the insistence of historic Christian theology that we know God "not as he is in himself but by his works," a formula found as early as Chrysostom, among others.[74]

---

[72] Pinnock, *Most Moved Mover*, 158.

[73] Although he sometimes cites the first part of the Westminster Confession 3.1 ("God from all eternity did by the most wise and holy counsel of his own will, freely and unchangeably ordain whatsoever comes to pass"), he has not yet, by my reckoning, quoted the entire statement: " . . . yet so as thereby neither is God the author of sin, nor is violence offered to the will of the creatures, nor is the liberty or contingency of second causes taken away, but rather established."

[74] John Chrysostom, "Homilies on John," in *A Select Library of the Nicene and Post-Nicene Fathers of the Christian Church*, ed. Philip Schaff, vol. 14 (reprint, Edinburgh: T & T Clark, 1989), 7: "And if these instances are not sufficient fully to explain the whole matter, marvel not,

Contrary to the antitheses of modern theology, which led Nietzsche to reject the Creator in favor of the creation, it is striking that in the Mars Hill speech, for instance, Scripture does not present the false choice offered by secular notions of transcendence and immanence. God does not have to "make space" for others, as open theists repeatedly express it, by limiting his own freedom.[75] Paul's speech simply does not assume the transcendence-immanence problem that has plagued ancient and modern metaphysics.

Among the ironic similarities between the methodological approach of open theism and hyper-Calvinism is the fact that both are apparently impatient in the face of mystery. Demanding univocal knowledge, both reflect a rationalistic streak that cannot live without the final resolution of the divine sovereignty-human freedom mystery into one or the other.[76] But analogies of transcendence and immanence must never become translated into univocity. Otherwise, the next move may be the denial of divine omnipresence. According to this attribute, God's "filling all things" disallows any notion of his being wholly contained or circumscribed in one place.[77]

---

for our argument is God, whom it is impossible to describe, or to imagine worthily; hence this man nowhere assigns the name of His essence (for it is not possible to say what God is, as to essence), but everywhere he declares Him to us by His workings. . . . In short, one name is not sufficient, nor two, nor three, nor more, to teach us what belongs to God. But we must be content to be able even by means of many to apprehend, though but obscurely, His attributes."

[75] It is not in some reality above or beyond God, shared by the creature, that humans have freedom—an area of autonomous freedom. Rather, it is in God's sovereign reign that creatures have creaturely freedom in the first place. Like transcendence and immanence, freedom is not an abstract philosophical concept, but is at least for Christians defined by God as its source and therefore as the one who normatively defines it. Freedom is not autonomy, but faithful existence in God's *ex nihilo* created space. Paul regards God's sovereignty, independence, and freedom as the very environment in which freedom for others is possible. He moves effortlessly from the statement that God has "determined the times set for [human beings] and the exact places where they should live" to the announcement, "'For in him we live and move and have our being'" (Acts 17:26-28, NIV). Here God's sovereign freedom comprehends both his immanence and his transcendence, not favoring one to the neglect of the other.

[76] Pinnock sees Thomism and Calvinism as "threatening the reality of creaturely actions. . . . It is the model in which the omnicausality of God is central and in which God is seemingly the solo performer" (*Most Moved Mover*, 8). This may be a hunch, but if Pinnock had tested it, he would have found himself quite alone among historical theologians. "When the covenant between God and humankind is stressed, the element of partnership comes to the fore and works against determinism in the system" (8). And yet, "I do not presume to judge what Calvin really meant . . ." (9). This appears to me to be another instance of Pinnock's hit-and-run policy.

[77] When we read that God is "near" his people—for instance, in the cloud, the tabernacle, and the temple, or even in Jesus Christ—this cannot be used to cancel his omnipresence. Instead of being cashed out in univocal spatial terms, we recognize that "nearness" has to do with God's presence for us (*pro nobis*). To be near his people is to be reconciled to them. Is open theism willing to treat as univocal those passages that represent God as changing locations, thereby surrendering also divine omnipresence and spirituality? As we have observed, this is a very real question. If not, however, the burden would seem to be on open theists to demonstrate how changing locations differs from changing attitudes and plans.

While open theism affirms the God-world distinction, the corollary distinctions we have considered fray to the point of threatening to unravel that commitment. John Sanders is aware of these classic distinctions that have played such an important role especially in Protestant systems, and he is not ready to be wholly rid of them.[78] But Sanders sees classical theology as privileging the hidden God over the revealed God. As a result of this fear, in actual practice at least, these distinctions play little or no role in the open theism proposal.[79]

Reformed theology is chided by Sanders, like Pinnock, for "claiming that it [the relation of sovereignty and responsibility] is simply a 'mystery beyond human understanding.' The subject simply transcends human reason."[80] He challenges Packer and the following quote from D. A. Carson: "For us mortals there are no rational, logical solutions to the sovereignty-responsibility tension."[81] On one hand, Reformed theology is berated for denying mystery in the headlong pursuit of a logical and rationalistic system; on the other, for affirming mystery too strongly. We have difficulty being satisfied with analogies just as the frail humanity that hid the blinding majesty of the God-man may lead us to miss the paradox of God's glory hidden under the cross. Ironically similar to a hyper-Calvinist, Pinnock rejects the notion of "mystery" in the

---

[78] Sanders: "Those scandalized by anthropomorphism align themselves with the tradition elevating the hidden God above the revealed God and attempt to discover the face of God behind the mask. This maneuver today elicits a strong reaction that God does not wear a mask. Rather, the God who reveals himself to us is the same God who remains hidden. Thus it is not surprising to find those who follow 'Rahner's rule' that the economic Trinity is the immanent Trinity and vice versa or that God pro nobis (for us) is the God in se (in himself) and vice versa. In my opinion, though the notion of the hidden God has been abused, it should not be completely rejected, for the reason that it is one way of affirming that God has being apart from the world and does not need the world in order to be fulfilled. . . . All that is possible for us to know is what God is like in relation to us" (30). Here we find a willingness to at least consider the abiding significance of these distinctions, and Sanders is certainly correct in his observation that this is less radical than the move that has been made not only by Rahner but by Moltmann, Pannenberg, and probably the broad consensus of leading theologians at present. As a less radical break, this constitutes a real point of potential agreement between our camps that deserves further conversation.

[79] In practice, it seems that the incarnation ends up being not only the climax of God's self-revelation but the only self-revelation. Instead of God the Son becoming flesh, we detect Hegelian hints of the incarnation serving as cipher for an abstract description of God's being-in-himself. Although we cannot pursue the point in this chapter, I have for some time wondered whether open theism shares with some abstract versions of classical theism an underdeveloped Christology that requires the concept of God-in-himself to do all of the duty that God-for-us, namely, the incarnate God-man, does in our understanding of the humanity of God. This is the perennial problem, as I see it, in Hegelian metaphysics leading through Teilhard de Chardin and Whitehead. The incarnation becomes the paradigm through which all divine existence and action is interpreted, as if the triune Godhead just is inherently kenotic. Again, doesn't such a "static" notion of "incarnation" subvert the "dynamic" incarnation of our Lord in first-century Palestine?

[80] Sanders, The God Who Risks, 35.

[81] Ibid.

relationship of divine sovereignty and human freedom. One of them simply has to go to resolve the tension: "All-controlling sovereignty is not taught in Scripture. There may be mysteries that go beyond human intelligence but this is not one of them." Perhaps anticipating the likely objection, Pinnock simply asserts, "The Bible, not rationalism, leads to this solution,"[82] but this is more easily asserted than demonstrated.

Open theism, in practice if not always in intent, makes ectypal knowledge archetypal; analogical language univocal; God's being for us is his being in and for himself; the hidden decree is swallowed up in the history of redemption; eternity is engulfed by time.[83] Pinnock counters what he describes as Calvinism with a dynamic emphasis on covenant:

> History is a drama with profound risks and enormous dynamics. God goes in for partnerships where the junior partners make a real contribution. It is a covenantal-historical way of understanding based on mutual vows and obligations. It is not the situation of omnicausalism where even the input of the creature is already predetermined.[84]

Pinnock nowhere (that I have located) allows that there is such a thing as Reformed covenant theology, in which double agency is a celebrated mystery, even though the likes of Pannenberg and Moltmann have self-consciously drawn on Reformed "federal" or covenant theology to emphasize the dynamic element.[85] Like some hyper-Calvinists, he sees

---

[82] Ibid., 55.

[83] The result is that God's accommodated self-revelation is no longer treated as such, but is regarded in a literalistic manner as providing direct access to the being of God, as if God were standing naked, unveiled, before us. Colin Gunton has addressed the problem of immediacy in modern theology (*A Brief Theology of Revelation* [Edinburgh: T & T Clark, 1995]). If I am not mistaken, this tendency that has plagued both fundamentalism and liberalism is all too apparent in the proposal of open theism: Whatever their material differences in this debate, Carl Henry and Clark Pinnock agree that univocity is the only way forward and that analogy necessarily degenerates into irrational skepticism.

[84] Pinnock, *Most Moved Mover*, 36.

[85] Johannes Cocceius (1603–1669) was among the first to develop a concentrated focus on the dynamic history of redemption within the context of Reformed (covenant) theology (see especially his *Summa doctrinae de foedere et testamento Dei*, 1648). This perspective has been reawakened in the Dutch/Dutch-American "biblical theology" movement, which includes Geerhardus Vos, Herman Ridderbos, Meredith Kline, and Richard Gaffin, Jr. The rise of federal theology in the sixteenth and seventeenth centuries has had a tremendous influence beyond its familiar borders and is often cited by contemporary theologians as a major resource for the recovery of eschatological reflection. Rather than seeing the Bible simply as a sourcebook for timeless truths, it was regarded as a covenant between God and God's people, orienting it to history and dramatic events interpreted by the primary actor in those events. Jürgen Moltmann observes, "This new historic understanding of revelation had its ground in the rebirth of eschatological millenarianism in the post-reformation age. It was the start of a new, eschatological way of thinking, which called

only two options: open theism or "omnicausalism"; but Reformed theology—with the "covenantal-historical way of understanding based on mutual vows and obligations" at its heart—provides an alternative to both that has yet to be considered by open theists.

"We must take seriously how God is depicted in these stories and resist reducing important metaphors to mere anthropomorphic or accommodated language," Pinnock insists, assuming that ("mere") accommodated language equals nonserious language. But he does not seem to have an alternative method, conceding, "God's revelation is anthropomorphic through and through. We could not grasp any other kind. We must take it all seriously, if not always literally."[86] And he even recognizes the danger to which his criticism of "mere analogy" opens himself:

> The open view of God proposes to take biblical metaphors more seriously and thereby recover the dynamic and relational God of the gospel, but in doing so it runs the risk of being too literal in its interpretation. . . . It could give the impression that God fumbles the ball just like we do or that God is limited as to place and knowledge (cf. Gen. 18:16-33, where God says he has to go over to Sodom to find out just how wicked these people are). We must avoid presumption in the matter of our speech about God whose reality transcends whatever we wish to say about him. Purely affirmative theology, without the check of negative theology, may make God the creature of our intellect as the Eastern traditions have reminded us.[87]

But once Pinnock has conceded that God does not fumble the ball *just like we do* and is not limited *in the ways we are,* he has already thrown into question the univocal approach he has assumed in treating his favored passages.[88] We hear the frustration in Pinnock's challenge: "How often have we heard reasoning like this: the Bible may say that

to life the feeling for history" (*Theology of Hope* [Minneapolis: Fortress, 1993], 70). In fact, he specifically refers to Johannes Cocceius. Wolfhart Pannenberg has recently written, "Only in the federal theology of Johannes Cocceius does the kingdom of God come into view again as a dominant theme of salvation history and eschatology . . ." (*Systematic Theology*, vol. 3 [Grand Rapids, Mich.: Eerdmans, 1998], 530).

[86] Pinnock, *Most Moved Mover*, 20.

[87] Ibid., 61.

[88] Richard Rice writes, "If human beings and God have nothing whatever in common, if we have utterly no mutual experience, then we have no way of talking and thinking about God and there

God repents but, being infinite, he doesn't really. . . . Why can't we allow such passages to speak?"[89] And of course he has a point. In cases where the accommodated, analogical, covenantal, "God-for-us" language is not allowed to have its say and is not taken seriously, only one type of analogy (viz., "I do not change") is allowed to dominate. But why do open theists not allow the "other passages" to speak, many interesting passages that he and other open theists have not attended to in their exegesis? Further, what does it mean to accuse critics of asserting that "the Bible may say that God repents but, being infinite, he doesn't really," when he has himself already conceded that God is not limited and does not "fumble the ball" exactly the way we do? Has he not conceded an analogical answer to that question?

We must let *all* of the passages speak, recognizing that they are all delivered in the analogical mode. This approach hardly stifles the Bible, as Pinnock suggests, but recognizes (as Pinnock claims to recognize at various points) the rich diversity of metaphors that God uses to accommodate to our condition.[90] In our account, analogical language, divinely revealed and sanctioned, provides just the sort of certainty that Sanders correctly insists upon, but without surrendering the kaleidoscopic analogies to a single univocal picture. The certainty comes from knowing that God has selected the appropriate reference-range, not from our own God's-eye view of the fit. To adapt a phrase from Rorty, "It's analogy all the way down."

However much Pinnock and Sanders might wish to accept the distinctions undergirding the Creator-creature distinction, it seems that whenever we meet in church history a strong affirmation of the mystery of God, Sanders detects the fingerprints of Hellenism.[91] As if

---

is no possibility of a personal relationship with him" ("Biblical Support for a New Perspective," in Clark Pinnock, et al., *The Openness of God: A Biblical Challenge to the Traditional Understanding of God* [Downers Grove, Ill.: InterVarsity Press, 1994], 35). This assumes, however, that there is a general space or reality that is not created by God, an autonomous, neutral reality that comprehends both God and creatures. Fearful of irrationalism, open theism risks collapsing into a rationalism that denies the Creator-creature distinction in practice if not always in principle.

[89] Pinnock, *Most Moved Mover*, 61.

[90] Part of the confusion may be due to regarding analogy and literal predication as mutually exclusive. Figures as diverse as Langdon Gilkey and Carl Henry have similarly misunderstood the doctrine of analogy in this direction. At least as formulated by the Reformed, to say that "God is Lord" is both an analogy and literally true. Modern (especially positivistic) views of language have tended to relegate analogy, metaphor, parable, and the like to the hinterlands of unreality. But our understanding of analogical revelation coheres perfectly with Sanders's description of "literal" when he writes, "What I mean by the word *literal* is that our language about God is reality depicting (truthful) such that there is a referent, an other, with whom we are in relationship and of whom we have genuine knowledge" (*The God Who Risks*, 25).

[91] Ibid., esp. 26-38.

there were no exegetical warrant, Sanders equates the suspicion of univocal knowledge of God with Philo of Alexandria: "The philosophical and theological attack on anthropomorphism assumes that we cannot know the essence of God."[92] Do we or do we not know God's essence, then? Sanders cannot seem to decide. Further withdrawing whatever allowance he has given to these distinctions, Sanders later adds,

> If the qualitative difference between God and humanity is absolutely infinite, then there is no correspondence between God and the creation, and this will preclude any notions of creation or revelation. . . . If "the finite cannot comprehend the infinite," then all revelation of God in history, any incarnation, the possibility of a personal relationship with God and all knowledge of God within our existence are ruled out. The concept of God becomes Teflon to which no predicates will stick.[93]

But once more, such fears assume that analogical knowledge is not true or accurate knowledge; that the inability of creatures to comprehend (i.e., "fully contain") the infinite, necessarily entails no apprehension of God on his own terms (i.e., revelation).[94]

This false choice offered by modernity should be resisted. It is neither the case that God is "wholly other" nor that he is "wholly like" anything in creation apart from the incarnate person of Jesus Christ. We do not believe that God is *completely* ineffable," because he has revealed himself in Scripture and supremely in his Son.[95]

---

[92] Ibid., 27.

[93] Ibid., 29.

[94] At the end of the day, the very distinctions Sanders has struggled to affirm fall under the weight of this false alarm: "Feuerbach's criticisms are devastating at this point. He says that what is completely ineffable lacks predicates and what has no predicates has no existence: 'The distinction between what God is in himself, and what he is for me destroys the peace of religion, and is . . . an untenable distinction. I cannot know whether God is something else in himself or for himself than he is for me'" (ibid., 30).
But, I would submit, the very opposite is the case. Kant denied any constitutive knowledge of God—univocal or analogical. Rationalism, on the other hand, has maintained the possibility of a pure intellectual vision of eternal forms. The result was that analogies and anthropomorphisms were often ascribed univocally, which Feuerbach correctly took to be nothing more than a projection of human attributes onto a non-existent referent. Is this not precisely what open theism tends toward?

[95] Furthermore, we are created in God's image and even in our suppression of the truth in unrighteousness are witnesses to his invisible attributes in creation (Romans 1 and 2). We trust the apostolic testimony, confirmed by the Holy Spirit, that God has given the world his supreme self-revelation in Christ, whose Godhead remains incomprehensible even in the incarnation. See the Chalcedonian Creed in John H. Leith, ed., *Creeds of the Churches* (Atlanta: John Knox, 1982), 34-36. Also, it seems that Sanders is requiring nothing less than what Feuerbach demanded: If I cannot have univocal (autonomous) knowledge of the fit between predicates and reality; if I must rely on

CONCLUSIONS

Notwithstanding arguments to the contrary, in truth God remains a *mysterium tremendum*—truly given in, yet transcending, his own self-revelation. In Scripture we are introduced to a divine drama in which God is tacitly recognized as the playwright but is focally known as the central, though not sole, actor. Pinnock demands, "Why does it seem as if they are suppressing these dimensions of the text or, at best, making the story sound dynamic when it really isn't?"[96]

But once again I am left wondering who might be the target of his criticism. The discipline of biblical theology, which stresses the dynamic element of redemptive history and refuses to reduce the Bible to a mere collection of timeless truths, was pioneered by Reformed theology. Its recent interpreters, like Geerhardus Vos, Herman Ridderbos, Richard Gaffin, and Meredith Kline, have stressed this dynamic and interactive quality of the biblical drama.[97] And yet, all of these figures staunchly affirm at the same time God's eternal decree and his unchangeable plan and will known only to him. It is never the "naked God," but the "revealed God" who clothes himself in our weakness and simplicity.

Pinnock and Sanders do not seem to think that they are standing before this mask or that they are being hidden in the cleft of the Rock while the backward parts of God pass by. In short, theirs is a univocal model. Pinnock defends his approach: "The model takes Scripture very seriously, especially the dynamic, personal metaphors, while our critics seem to consider it beneath them. Embarrassed by biblical anthropomorphisms, they are inclined to demythologize and/or deliteralize them."[98] But not only

---

the God who is hidden in incomprehensible majesty to condescend to address me, I cannot have true knowledge. The significant difference between Sanders and Feuerbach is that the latter surrendered belief in God altogether, while the former surrenders the distinction between God's archetypal knowledge (known intuitively) and our ectypal knowledge (mediated through Scripture). Both views rest on the assumption that only if one possesses a God's-eye perspective himself or herself is one entitled to claim epistemic certitude. This is the tragic legacy of the Enlightenment.

[96] Pinnock, *Most Moved Mover*, 62.

[97] For instance, Ridderbos: "It is this great redemptive-historical framework within which the whole of Paul's preaching must be understood and all of its subordinate parts receive their place and organically cohere" (*Paul: An Outline of His Theology*, trans. J. R. DeWitt [Grand Rapids, Mich.: Eerdmans, 1975], 39); cf. Richard B. Gaffin, Jr., *Resurrection and Redemption: A Study in Paul's Soteriology* (Phillipsburg, N.J.: Presbyterian & Reformed, 1978): "Revelation never stands by itself, but is always concerned either explicitly or implicitly with redemptive accomplishment. God's speech is invariably related to his actions. . . . An unbiblical, quasi-gnostic notion of revelation inevitably results when it is considered by itself or as providing self-evident general truths. . . . In a word, the concept of theology is redemptive-historically conditioned" (23-24).

[98] Pinnock, *Most Moved Mover*, 62.

have we shown that the tradition has taken anthropomorphism and analogy *more* seriously, one detects in Pinnock a reticence to wholly embrace his own method.

At the same time, there is a Scylla and Charybdis to be negotiated. On the one hand, there is the danger of missing the truth of the metaphors. What are the texts of divine repentance telling us? What is it that God's suffering implies? On the other hand, we do not have to be crassly literal. There is not always a one-for-one correspondence in texts that tell us important things. In any analogy there is something literal about reality that we don't want to miss and, at the same time, something different. We need to avoid both literalism and agnosticism. The way forward is to work with the diversity of metaphors and follow the grain of them. For example, God repents, but not as humans do; God suffers, but not exactly as we do; God works out his purposes in time, but not subjected to the ravages of time as we are.[99]

Such reservations make it difficult to determine whether open theism is really convinced of its own methodological position.[100] It does not deny outright the Creator-creature distinction or its corollaries, but it appears suspicious of them (at least as traditionally employed) and seems uncomfortable with their regulative function in developing their proposal.

In this brief space we have attempted to exchange straw men for the actual arguments, presuppositions, and methods of Reformed system.

---

[99] Ibid.

[100] Everything stated in the paragraph above would be heartily affirmed by Reformed theology—although we would say that there is *never* a one-for-one correspondence (not just "not always"). But why does Pinnock seem to refuse to "work with the diversity of metaphors," instead privileging a certain important but by no means exclusive type?

I must confess that at the end of the day I am not exactly sure what method open theism is pursuing. On one hand, Pinnock criticizes classical theism in general and Reformed theology in particular for appealing to analogy. Yet, "The problem with the tradition is not that it takes the biblical language metaphorically rather than literally but that it bypasses truths conveyed by it. . . . Metaphors have meaning and traditionalists owe an explanation as to what they think the meaning is. For example, what does it mean for God to grieve, to interact, to weep, to cry out, to respond to prayer?" (*Most Moved Mover*, 63).

Of course, the tradition *has* given an explanation, from the church fathers to the present. It is in every commentary, every dogmatics, every handbook of theology under the locus "providence." Pinnock just does not like the answer. He is free to hold that opinion, of course, but Pinnock and his colleagues often write as if classical theology in general and Augustinian-Reformed theology in particular had no theoretical account of double agency, prayer, or God's responsive concern. He and his colleagues offer sweeping indictments without the slightest serious engagement with the tradition any more than with the biblical passages upon which the tradition has relied. What does Pinnock make of Augustine's *Confessions*? Calvin's lengthy treatment of prayer in the *Institutes*? These writers sometimes give the impression that Augustinians do not believe in divine response to prayer, evangelism, or missions, which is contrary to the facts of both the written record and the practice that has dominated such communities.

We have demonstrated that we do not deny the knowability of God but the comprehensibility (that is, exact, archetypal knowledge) of God. In contrasting our theological methods, we have shown that, despite the serious misunderstandings of the tradition often assumed by open theism's advocates, classical Reformed theology has proposed a theological method that has yet to be refuted. While the classical theological tradition of Roman Catholic, Orthodox, and Protestant communions may be influenced in its formulations by alien philosophical perspectives, the distinctions so central to its method are ultimately due to the biblical emphasis on the Creator-creature distinction and not to a capitulation to pagan thought. It is hoped that after serious conversation begins here, at the beginning, we may at least arrive at the place where our genuine differences may be fruitfully explored.

A POSTSCRIPT FOR FURTHER DISCUSSION

To conclude this chapter, I would like to offer two practical methodological conclusions suggesting a way forward in this debate.

The first has to do with the level and tone. We are not interested in assessing the intentions of open theism advocates, even if that were possible. I do not doubt that these writers want to be biblical. If they were persuaded that their view is not biblical, I have every confidence that they would abandon it. As it is, however, they feel compelled to embrace open theism precisely because they believe that it better explains the biblical data. Classical theists, Reformed included, must take advantage of the challenges posed by open theism to reassess their own method and conclusions in the light of exegesis, always prepared to conform their system to God's revelation. The recent revival of biblical theology in Reformed circles, where the discipline was born, promises to open new vistas to the dynamic nature of redemptive history that a one-sided emphasis on systematic theology does not always display.

I would hope that, given the highly emotional and exaggerated charges of some leading proponents of open theism, they too would stop trying to divine the motives and intentions of their critics and hold out some hope that perhaps the latter are as concerned to faithfully represent biblical teaching. Pinnock, for instance, reduces the debate to a face-off between "pilgrims" like himself "who are comfortable with change, and others" who "are more like settlers who find change difficult."[101] Taking that moral high ground, it is fairly easy then to dismiss quite historic positions with caricatures that, although largely untrue, suit the "gut" instincts of those who do not hold those positions. Those who go on defending things that have been defended for a very long time are by definition "settlers" rather than "pilgrims." Like a somewhat cantankerous grandfather, the "settler" can tell stories of "the good old days," but cannot be expected to generate new contributions to the family.

Therefore, Pinnock can take the most extreme examples of criticism of his position and paint as malicious all but apparently one critic of his view.[102] Hostility to his position simply reflects "the scandal of the evangelical mind," with "many examples of ignorance, malice, and poor taste."[103] Referring to a theologian who was not most representative of the Reformed theological tradition, Pinnock complains, "Boettner was the type of Calvinist who [sic] I term paleo-Calvinist because he had not moved beyond the Westminster Confession."[104] If that is the case, any Reformed or Presbyterian person who signs the confessional standards in good faith is necessarily dismissed as a "paleo-Calvinist"—the cranky grandfather who cannot seem to realize that his number is up. But this is bullying, not arguing.

Pinnock adds, "Openness theology must be opposed more radically because it poses much more of a threat [than mere free will theism]. (I actually agree with the paleo-Calvinists about that.) As in politics, where winning however you do it is the only goal, so in this context the gatekeepers of orthodoxy will resort to anything," including "scare tactics and lying."[105] "The attacks and hostility never seems to end."[106] This is theology by pathos and it is beneath theologians of Pinnock's stature.

If it is wrong to dismiss open theism as simply a revival of Socinianism or a lackey of process theism, it is just as erroneous to conclude that open theism represents a noble stream of Christian thought. No group generally recognized as "orthodox" or "catholic" (Eastern or Western)—that is, belonging to the mainstream Christian tradition—has

---

[101] Pinnock, *Most Moved Mover*, xii.
[102] Ibid., 11.
[103] Ibid., xiii.
[104] Ibid., 14.
[105] Ibid., 15.
[106] Ibid., 16.

ever denied God's exhaustive foreknowledge, atemporality, aseity, simplicity, or immutability, as those terms have been historically understood.[107] None of this should be treated by openness theologians as uncharitable, since Pinnock himself recognizes and even frequently revels in the radical character of his proposal, characterizing his earlier book as a "bombshell on the theological playground (to recall Barth's expression)."[108] After all, "it waved a red flag in their faces." "I have to be sanguine, how could one expect those, who have only recently come to tolerate Arminian thinking, to stomach a more radical version of it. . . . The fact is that the openness model diverges from historic Protestant and Catholic thought at several points and inevitably becomes a target for criticism."[109]

If Calvinism represented even in broad terms the description given to it especially by Pinnock, it could hardly have unleashed the energies for dynamic Christian action in missions, social compassion, education and the arts, vocation, and countless other enterprises which it has in fact unleashed. Many of us fail to recognize Reformed theology in his polemical descriptions of it. Even when he attempts to recognize that Calvinists sometimes affirm the correct beliefs, he can only credit this to their "trying to work such [open theist] themes into their work." In fact, they are seeking to "co-opt them," he suggests, " . . . taking advantage of the rhetoric of the open view of God, which Bible readers find compelling, and are trying to work it into their own language."[110] He ignores the criticism within the Reformed tradition of various aspects of traditional formulations and seems to advocate the astonishing thesis that covenant theology was launched in 1994 with the publication of *The Openness of God.*

Recent wrestling within traditional Christian reflection on the divine attributes among evangelical theologians Pinnock can only see being "half-hearted,"[111] revealing that they "lack the courage to challenge the conventional thinking head-on."[112] But couldn't it simply reflect the

---

[107] To be sure, some evangelical theologians critical of open theism have themselves offered slight revisions in how these attributes are articulated, but without a denial of the traditional predicates.

[108] Pinnock, *Most Moved Mover*, xi.

[109] Ibid.

[110] Ibid., 75.

[111] Ibid., 77.

[112] Ibid.

struggle that all responsible theology must experience when attempting to formulate and systematize the fruit of exegesis?

It is quite possible that this recent debate and similar proposals from mainline theologians have highlighted certain traditional problems. It is undoubtedly true that conservative theologies in the last two centuries have often been uncritical of inherited categories and formulations, a fact that stands in sharp contrast to the Reformation and post-Reformation dogmatic tradition. We do need to always be evaluating our formulations in the light of God's Word. But Pinnock seems to work in azure isolation. He speaks a great deal about his personal struggle, but does not seem to appreciate that Christian theologians, especially since the Reformation, have been struggling with the problems of the medieval synthesis well before the advent of open theism.

Orthodox Christians are bound by their affirmation of the absolute normativity of Scripture above tradition to allow for the possibility of having gotten their doctrine of God wrong—even for a very long time. Helped by the communion of saints throughout all times and places, we cannot be otherwise than suspicious of heterodoxy, but "orthodoxy" is defined ultimately by its faithfulness to Scripture. On that much we can certainly agree.

PART FOUR

What Is at Stake in the Openness Debate?

7

WHAT IS AT STAKE IN THE OPENNESS DEBATE?
THE INERRANCY OF SCRIPTURE[1]

Stephen J. Wellum

When one thinks of the topics that create friction among Christians, the subject of divine sovereignty is probably high on the list. We all have experienced heated discussions over the nature of divine sovereignty, especially as it relates to the issues of divine election and salvation. Many Christian people, even seminary students, have expressed to me time and again that they wish the subject would somehow disappear. But that is hardly likely since the subject of divine sovereignty is so foundational to one's entire theology and praxis.

In fact, within evangelical theology today, the perennial polemics over divine sovereignty-human freedom are heating up more than ever given the rise of the view known as open theism. At the heart of the openness proposal is a reformulation of the doctrine of divine sovereignty and omniscience that has massive implications for how we

---

[1] Major portions of this chapter were previously published as "Divine Sovereignty-Omniscience, Inerrancy, and Open Theism: An Evaluation," *Journal of the Evangelical Theological Society (JETS)* 45 (2002): 257-277. However, in this chapter I have made two significant additions. First, I have added a section outlining what was assumed in the previous article, namely, a historic view of Scripture. My reason for doing so was to add completion to the argument. It is important to understand what Scripture is claiming for itself before we contrast that view with the openness proposal. As the reader will discover, it is my conviction that the openness proposal is *not* able to substantiate what the Bible claims for itself, and as such, for biblical Christians, it must then be rejected as unwarranted and unbiblical. Second, I have especially interacted with Greg Boyd's recent views on "neo-Molinism" and the nature of human freedom, as well as some of his responses to critics of open theism, in *Satan and the Problem of Evil: Constructing a Trinitarian Warfare Theodicy* (Downers Grove, Ill.: InterVarsity Press, 2001), which I was not able to consider in the previous article. Both of these additions, then, add completion to the argument.

think of God and his relation to the world.[2] That is why, given the recent trends, it seems unlikely that discussion over the sovereignty-freedom relationship or foreknowledge-freedom tension will fade into the background. Instead, the subject, because it is so critical, must be revisited once again with a renewed sense of vigor and determination as we seek to test our proposals, whether new or old, against the standard of God's Word.

The goal of this chapter is to do just that, but not in the typical way of evaluating this issue. Often our discussions of divine sovereignty, omniscience, human freedom merely collapse into the age-old debates over divine election, free will, and the nature of human depravity—soteriological issues. No doubt these debates are important and they must be handled with care and faithfulness to the biblical text. However, what is sometimes lost in these discussions is the fact that one's view of God and his relation to the world has massive implications for one's *whole* theology, not simply for issues of soteriology. Theology, as J. I. Packer reminds us, is a "seamless robe, a circle within which everything links up with everything else through its common grounding in God."[3] Theological doctrines, in other words, are much more organically related than we often realize, and that is why a reformulation in one area of doctrine inevitably affects other areas of our theology. This is important to remember, especially in evaluating old and new proposals regarding the doctrine of God, and in particular open theism.

In this regard, there are at least two complementary ways to evaluate theological proposals. First, does the proposal do justice to *all* of Scripture? Is it biblical? After doing all the hard exegetical work and seek-

---

[2] The literature on "open theism" is growing by the month. For some helpful statements of the view see Clark Pinnock, et al., *The Openness of God: A Biblical Challenge to the Traditional Understanding of God* (Downers Grove, Ill.: InterVarsity Press, 1994); David Basinger, *The Case for Free Will Theism: A Philosophical Assessment* (Downers Grove, Ill.: InterVarsity Press, 1996); John Sanders, *The God Who Risks: A Theology of Providence* (Downers Grove, Ill.: InterVarsity Press, 1998); Gregory A. Boyd, *God of the Possible: A Biblical Introduction to the Open View of God* (Grand Rapids, Mich.: Baker, 2000); and *Satan and the Problem of Evil*; and Clark H. Pinnock, *Most Moved Mover: A Theology of God's Openness* (Grand Rapids, Mich.: Baker, 2001). For a sympathetic yet critical summary of open theism, see Terrance Tiessen, *Providence and Prayer: How Does God Work in the World?* (Downers Grove, Ill.: InterVarsity Press, 2000), 71-118. For various critiques of open theism, see Bruce A. Ware, *God's Lesser Glory: The Diminished God of Open Theism* (Wheaton, Ill.: Crossway, 2000); and John M. Frame, *No Other God: A Response to Open Theism* (Phillipsburg, N.J.: Presbyterian & Reformed, 2001).

[3] J. I. Packer, "Encountering Present-Day Views of Scripture," in *The Foundation of Biblical Authority*, ed. James M. Boice (Grand Rapids, Mich.: Zondervan, 1978), 61.

ing to relate texts with other texts into a coherent reading of the canon, any theological proposal may be evaluated as to whether it does justice to all of the textual data. But there is also a second and complementary way to evaluate theological proposals: Is the proposal, along with its implications and entailments, consistent with other theological doctrines, especially with those doctrines that we consider more central to our theological system? If the answer is yes to both of these ways of evaluation, then we may be assured that our theological proposal is on track and warranted. However if our answer is negative on both counts, then it should encourage us to reject our proposal or, at least, rethink it through very carefully before embracing it as a correct view. In this chapter, I want to apply the latter option to the theological proposal of open theism. Specifically, I want to investigate whether the open theist construal of the divine sovereignty-omniscience and human freedom relationship will be able to support a high view of Scripture as reflected in the doctrine of inerrancy. In other words, granting the open theist's construal of divine sovereignty and omniscience, what, then, are the logical entailments of such a position for our belief in the inerrancy of Scripture? Will the openness proposal, at the end of the day, uphold or undermine our view that Scripture is nothing less than God's Word written?

How do I propose to carry out my investigation? In three main steps. First, I will briefly outline the doctrine of Scripture in terms of what the Bible says about itself in regard to authority, inspiration, and inerrancy. Second, I will outline and describe the open theist construal of divine sovereignty, omniscience, and human freedom. Third, I will attempt to evaluate whether the openness proposal is supportive of or detrimental to the doctrine of Scripture, and in particular inerrancy, in relation to the specific issues of a concursive theory of inspiration and the phenomena of predictive prophecy. I will then finish with three concluding reflections.

I. WHAT EXACTLY IS THE BIBLE? THE DOCTRINE OF SCRIPTURE

Biblical Christianity has affirmed throughout the ages that Scripture is nothing less than God's Word written, the product of God's action through the Word and by the Holy Spirit whereby human authors freely

wrote exactly what God intended and without error.[4] Christians have
affirmed this view due to their conviction that Scripture itself teaches this
view. This affirmation of Scripture's own self-witness is important for at
least two reasons. First, we do not approach the Bible and make it something that it does not claim to be. We do not confer upon it an authority
that it does not claim for itself. Rather, it comes to us, bearing its own
self-witness or self-attestation, that is, that it is nothing less than God's
Word written, and as God-given, it not only bears the marks of divine
origin, but it is also completely authoritative, sufficient, and reliable. Of
course, one is free either to accept or reject such a claim. But if one does
reject it, then one must also state the basis on which one does so.[5]

Second, as with any doctrine of the Christian faith, including our
doctrine of Scripture, we must substantiate it by an appeal to Scripture.
No doubt, this leads to a kind of "circularity" in our formulation of our
doctrine of Scripture, but that should not surprise us. When it comes to
ultimate criterions and highest authorities in anyone's worldview, an
argument of this sort is quite unavoidable.[6] For, as already stated,
Christian theology is like a seamless robe or an organic whole, rooted

---

[4] Kevin J. Vanhoozer has called this view the "Received View." See his, "God's Mighty Speech-
Acts: The Doctrine of Scripture Today," in *A Pathway into the Holy Scriptures*, ed. Philip E.
Satterthwaite and David F. Wright (Grand Rapids, Mich.: Eerdmans, 1994), 143-181. Until
recently, conservatives and non-conservatives alike have agreed that the witness of church history
has favored a high view of Scripture including its inerrancy. But in recent years this view has been
challenged by a revisionist historiography. A new generation of historians is arguing that the
modern conservative position on Scripture is something of an aberration that owes its impetus in
part to scholastic theology of the post-Reformation period and in part to the Princetonians,
especially Charles Hodge, A. A. Hodge, and B. B. Warfield. Probably the best-known work to
espouse this view is that of Jack B. Rogers and Donald K. McKim, *The Authority and
Interpretation of the Bible* (San Francisco: Harper & Row, 1979). Rogers and McKim's thesis is
that the historic position of the church only maintains the Bible's authority in areas of *faith and
practice* (understood in a restrictive sense), *not* its reliable truthfulness in every area on which it
chooses to speak. This proposal has been shown to be seriously flawed. For a critique of this
viewpoint, see John D. Woodbridge, *Biblical Authority: A Critique of the Rogers/McKim Proposal*
(Grand Rapids, Mich.: Zondervan, 1982); and Paul Kjoss Helseth, "Re-Imagining the Princeton
Mind: Postconservative Evangelicalism, Old Princeton, and the Rise of Neo-Fundamentalism,"
JETS 45 (2002): 427-450. See also the historical essays in the following works: D. A. Carson and
John D. Woodbridge, eds., *Scripture and Truth* (Grand Rapids, Mich.: Zondervan, 1983); idem,
Hermeneutics, Authority, and Canon (Grand Rapids, Mich.: Zondervan, 1986); Norman L.
Geisler, ed., *Inerrancy* (Grand Rapids, Mich.: Zondervan, 1979); Earl D. Radmacher and Robert
D. Preus, eds., *Hermeneutics, Inerrancy, and the Bible* (Grand Rapids, Mich.: Zondervan, 1984);
and John D. Hannah, ed., *Inerrancy and the Church* (Chicago: Moody, 1984).

[5] For more on this, see John M. Frame, "Scripture Speaks for Itself," in *God's Inerrant Word*, ed.
John W. Montgomery (Minneapolis: Bethany, 1974), 178-181.

[6] On the issue of "circularity," see John M. Frame, *Apologetics to the Glory of God* (Phillipsburg,
N.J.: Presbyterian & Reformed, 1994), 9-14; idem, *The Doctrine of the Knowledge of God*
(Phillipsburg, N.J.: Presbyterian & Reformed, 1987); and D. A. Carson, "Approaching the Bible,"
in *New Bible Commentary: Twenty-first Century Edition*, ed. G. J. Wenham, et al. (Downers
Grove, Ill.: InterVarsity Press, 1994), 9-10.

and grounded in our view of God. Since the God of the Bible, the sovereign-personal triune Lord, is nothing less than the final court of appeal (cf. Heb. 6:16-18), it should not surprise us that his Word, by its very nature, is self-attesting, and that our view of Scripture is made by appeal to that very same Word. In other words, God's Word of necessity must be our *ultimate* criterion and authority for justifying any theological doctrine, including our doctrine of Scripture.[7]

An important entailment of this, of course, is that given such a view of God and his Word, biblical authority and inerrancy necessarily follow. For how can Scripture serve as its own self-attesting authority—as God's Word—by which we evaluate all theological proposals, if it is not fully authoritative and inerrant? How can we affirm and confirm any doctrine simply on the Bible's own say-so—which is the very nature of self-attestation—unless Scripture is fully authoritative, trustworthy, and reliable? In this sense, as theologians have argued repeatedly, biblical authority and inerrancy is of epistemological necessity if we affirm that Scripture alone (*sola scriptura*) is ultimately the necessary and sufficient condition to warrant and justify any theological proposal.[8] Another way of stating this, in more philosophical language, is to say that the authority and reliability of Scripture is the *transcendental* condition for the very possibility of doing Christian theology in any kind of normative fashion. Is it any wonder that our view of Scripture is so crucial to the entire theological enterprise? Without the living God who discloses himself in an

---

[7] Of course, this whole discussion has a bearing on apologetic methodology. For a helpful discussion of this applied to apologetics, see Frame, *Apologetics*, 1-88; and Greg L. Bahnsen, *Van Til's Apologetic: Readings and Analysis* (Phillipsburg, N.J.: Presbyterian & Reformed, 1998).

[8] The epistemological argument for inerrancy has often been misunderstood, yet it is an important argument. For example, Stephen T. Davis, *The Debate About the Bible: Inerrancy Versus Infallibility* (Philadelphia: Westminster, 1977), 66-82, helpfully distinguishes various forms of this argument, but then reduces the argument to the claim that if the Scripture is errant at any point, then *all* statements of Scripture are in fact false. Obviously, this is a fallacious argument. For example, a telephone book may be generally reliable, but it still may contain errors; in a similar manner one could argue the same thing for the Bible. It must be granted that general reliability does not entail that *all* statements of Scripture are false. However, this is not the argument that I am alluding to here. Rather, I am asserting that if the Bible is errant, it raises the possibility that *any* statement of Scripture may be false. And if *any* statement of Scripture may be false, then one would need an independent criterion to justify one's theological proposals—a way of distinguishing the errant statements from the inerrant ones. In this sense, then, one could not use Scripture *alone* as a self-attesting authority, as the sole criterion by which theological proposals are justified, unless it was inerrant. But this also raises a further question for those who deny inerrancy: if I need independent criterions to justify theological doctrines since the Bible alone cannot be appealed to, then what are those criterions? Human reason? Religious experience? The assured results of biblical scholarship? And then a further question would need to be asked: What, then, justifies human reason, religious experience, and so on? As one can see, the epistemological necessity of inerrancy for Christian theology is no small matter.

authoritative and reliable Word-revelation, theology loses both its *identity* and its *integrity* as a discipline and is set adrift, forever to be confused with psychology, sociology, philosophy, anthropology, and the like.[9]

Now with that said, we must briefly turn to the Bible's witness regarding itself. What does Scripture say about itself, and thus what should we affirm about the nature and authority of the Bible? Given the constraints of this chapter, I propose to address these questions by highlighting three important matters regarding the Bible's self-witness: the pervasive nature of this witness, and some comments regarding the doctrines of inspiration and inerrancy.

1. The Pervasiveness of Scripture's Claim for Itself[10]

From the outset, it is important to stress that the Bible's witness to itself is not limited merely to a few texts scattered throughout the Bible such as 2 Timothy 3:16 and 2 Peter 1:21. If that were the case, then liberal scholars, such as James Barr, would have a point when they dismiss the conservative claim that the Bible has a view of itself.[11] Instead, what we discover is that when we read the Bible on its own terms there is, in the words of Sinclair Ferguson, a "canonical self-consciousness" from Genesis to Revelation. From what we witness of God's activity in

---

[9] The philosophical term "transcendental" comes from the thought of Immanuel Kant. It refers to the task of discovering the preconditions for something to be possible. In the case of Kant, he was attempting to discover the transcendental conditions for the possibility of knowledge. In the context of this chapter, the term is being used to state that the necessary precondition for the possibility of a normative, truth-telling theology, and the knowledge of God is the self-disclosure of the triune God in Scripture. For more on this discussion, see Kevin J. Vanhoozer, "Christ and Concept: Doing Theology and the 'Ministry' of Philosophy," in *Doing Theology in Today's World: Essays in Honor of Kenneth S. Kantzer*, ed. John D. Woodbridge and Thomas E. McComiskey (Grand Rapids, Mich.: Zondervan, 1991), 99-145. On the nature of "transcendental arguments," see the discussion in Bahnsen, *Van Til's Apologetic*, 496-529.

[10] In what follows I am highly indebted to and dependent upon the discussion in Sinclair B. Ferguson, "How Does the Bible Look at Itself?" in *Inerrancy and Hermeneutic*, ed. Harvie M. Conn (Grand Rapids, Mich.: Baker, 1988), 47-66; Frame, "Scripture Speaks for Itself," 178-200; Wayne Grudem, "Scripture's Self-Attestation and the Problem of Formulating a Doctrine of Scripture," in *Scripture and Truth*, 19-59; and B. B. Warfield, *The Inspiration and Authority of the Bible*, ed. Samuel G. Craig (Phillipsburg, N.J.: Presbyterian & Reformed, 1948).

[11] See James Barr, *Fundamentalism* (London: SCM, 1977), 78. Barr writes: "According to conservative arguments, it is not only Jesus who made 'claims'; the Bible made 'claims' about itself. The Book of Daniel 'claims' to have been written by a historical Daniel some time in the sixth century B.C.; the Book of Deuteronomy 'claims' to have been written by Moses; and more important still, the Bible as a whole 'claims' to be divinely inspired. All this is nonsense. There is no 'the Bible' that 'claims' to be divinely inspired, there is no 'it' that has a 'view of itself.' There is only this or that source, like 2 Timothy or 2 Peter, which makes statements about certain other writings, these rather undefined. There is no such thing as 'the Bible's view of itself' from which a fully authoritative answer to these questions can be obtained. This whole side of traditional conservative apologetic, though loudly vociferated, just does not exist; there is no case to answer."

redemptive history, it is evident that God intends to rule his people, whether in the Old Testament or New Testament era, through a book, a written constitution, that is nothing less than *his* Word.[12] Ferguson nicely lays out the evidence for this assertion in four propositions.[13]

First, the Old Testament displays a canonical self-consciousness; a recognition that what is written is given by God to rule and direct his people. That is already indicated, as Meredith Kline has demonstrated, by the fact that written documentation accompanies the covenant relationship between God and his people and is intended to rule and direct their lives (see Deut. 5:22, 32; 29:9; 30:9-10, 15-16; 31:24-29; Josh. 1:7-8; 8:34).[14] As Ferguson rightly notes, it is from this fact that the rest of the books of the Old Testament are written, in various ways, in exposition of this authoritative, canonical, covenantal word. He states:

> The Old Testament grows from this root. Out of this flows, in part, the Chronicler's covenantal, canonical interpretation of history and the confidence of the prophetic "This is what the Sovereign Lord says." New Scripture is written in the confidence that it is "Scripture" only because of its inherent relationship to what God has already given.[15]

Second, there is, in the New Testament, the clear recognition of the

---

[12] For a development of this idea, see Frame, "Scripture Speaks for Itself," 181-192; see also E. J. Schnabel, "Scripture," in *New Dictionary of Biblical Theology*, ed. T. Desmond Alexander and Brian S. Rosner (Downers Grove, Ill.: InterVarsity Press, 2000), 34-43; and Carson, "Approaching the Bible," 1-19.

[13] See Ferguson, "How Does the Bible Look at Itself?" 50-54.

[14] See Meredith G. Kline, *The Structure of Biblical Authority* (Grand Rapids, Mich.: Eerdmans, 1972), 21-68; cf. Frame, *Apologetics to the Glory of God*, 122-128. Kline rightly argues, and Frame following him, that the covenant relationship of the Old Testament is patterned after the "suzerainty treaty" in the ancient Near East. What is significant about this point, for our purposes, is that the written document is not at all peripheral to the covenant; it is central to it. To violate the document is to violate the covenant, and vice versa. In terms of the Old Testament, the king who enters into covenant relationship with Israel is nothing less than the God of creation and providence. And in entering into covenant relationship with Israel, God gives the people *his* Word. And in that document, God speaks as author, giving his own name in the usual location for the name of the great king (see Ex. 24:12; 31:18; 32:15-16; 34:1, which, in the strongest of terms, emphasizes God's authorship of the document). Furthermore, as redemptive history unfolds, God constantly and consistently brings his people back to his covenantal Word (see Deuteronomy 32). It becomes God's song of witness (Deut. 31:19) against the nation. It is regarded as holy, because it is God's own Word. It is for that reason alone that no one may add to or subtract from its words (see Deut. 4:2; 12:32; cf. Josh. 1:7; Prov. 30:6; Rev. 22:18-19). And as redemptive history unfolds, from time to time God adds new words to this covenant document, the canon of Scripture (see Deut. 18:14-22; Isa. 8:1; 30:8ff; 34:16-17; Jer. 25:13). In the Old Testament, then, given the very nature of the covenant, there is a God-given canonical self-consciousness that is pervasive. God rules and governs his people by *his* Word, a Word that is fully authoritative, trustworthy, and true.

[15] Ferguson, "How Does the Bible Look at Itself?" 50.

divinely given canon we now know as the Old Testament. Evidence for this is abundant. Such expressions as "Scripture," "law and the prophets," "it is written," "God said," and "Scripture says" prove this very point. In addition, as John Wenham has shown, both Jesus and the apostles use Scripture in a normative, canonical way.[16] For Jesus, his very life, death, and resurrection is to *fulfill* Scripture. For our Lord, as well as for the apostles, an appeal to the Old Testament settles the matter because it is nothing less than God's Word (see Matt. 4:4; 5:17-19; Acts 15:12-29). In fact, when Jesus makes belief in Moses the prerequisite to belief in his own word (John 5:46) and when he denies that Scripture should ever be broken (John 10:33-36), he is adding his witness to the Old Testament. Or, when Paul speaks in 2 Timothy 3:16, he is referring to the Old Testament, that which he assumes is normative and binding because as Ferguson states, "To the authors of the New Testament, the Old Testament is God's Word."[17]

Third, there is, in the New Testament, a consciousness among the authors that the authority of their own writing is on a par with that of the Old Testament and that the content of the revelation given to them is, in some sense, superior to it, not in terms of inspiration but in the clarity and progress of the revelation recorded (see Eph. 3:2-6). This consciousness in the apostolic writings, as Ferguson notes, is "tantamount to a deliberate addition to the canon in order to bring it to completion in the light of Christ's coming"[18] as well as an inscripturation of that canon, parallel to the written nature of the old covenant. In this sense, the New Testament canon is virtually demanded by the coming of Christ (see Heb. 1:1-2) since the older revelation pointed beyond itself to the "last days" inaugurated by the Son.[19] Furthermore, when it comes to the "Son revelation" (*en huiō*)—his person and words, along with the words of his apostles, like those of old, must be believed and obeyed.[20]

Fourth, in the New Testament writings, we also notice that some sources express a sense not only of their own canonical character but of

---

[16] See John Wenham, *Christ and the Bible*, 3rd ed. (Grand Rapids, Mich.: Baker, 1994).

[17] Ferguson, "How Does the Bible Look at Itself?" 50.

[18] Ibid., 51.

[19] For this same point, see Carson, "Approaching the Bible," 1-3.

[20] For a sample of such texts, see Matt. 7:21-29; Mark 8:38; Luke 8:21; 9:26ff; John 6:63, 68-69; 8:47; 12:27ff; 14:15, 21, 23-24; 15:7, 10, 14; 17:6, 17; Rom. 1:16-17; 2:16; Col. 4:16; 1 Thess. 4:2; 5:27; 2 Thess. 3:14; 1 Tim. 6:3; 2 Pet. 3:16; Rev. 12:17; 14:12.

the existence of a class of literature sharing that status. No doubt, we do not expect to see this phenomenon fully developed since the New Testament canon was still being written. However, the fact that it does surface is adequate warrant for believing that it reflects a wider church consciousness that God was giving a new canon of Scripture tied to the coming of the Son (Heb. 1:1-2) and the new covenant era. In particular one thinks of 1 Timothy 5:18 (which quotes from both Deut. 25:4 and Luke 10:7) and 2 Peter 3:16 (which refers to Paul's writings), both of which refer to New Testament writings as "Scripture."[21]

No doubt, much more could be said, and I refer the reader to the literature in the footnotes for further reflection, but it should be noted that it is no small matter to speak of "Scripture's view of itself." Scripture comes to us as nothing less than God's Word written. To be sure, it is written by human authors carried along by the Holy Spirit, but one must never forget that the primary emphasis of Scripture is that it is God's own Word, given to rule his people and, ultimately, to lead them to salvation in Christ Jesus (see 2 Tim. 3:15-17). Scripture views itself as supremely authoritative speech and writing precisely because it is *his* Word. Thus, one can rightly say: what Scripture says, God says; what God says, Scripture says. That is why to disbelieve or disobey any word of Scripture is to disbelieve or disobey God, and the only proper response to God's Word is to believe, trust, and obey (Isa. 66:2).

2. The Inspiration of Scripture

Scripture bears witness that it is God's authoritative Word through the agency of human authors. But how are we to explain or account for the relation between God's Word and the words of the human authors? The theological term that has been used to explain this relation is "inspiration."[22] Thus, to speak of the "inspiration" of Scripture is to

---

[21] One can also see this canon-consciousness emerge in the opening and closing sections of the book of Revelation. It is assumed that it will be read in public to the church (1:3). Both reader and hearer are promised "blessing," i.e., divine, covenantal blessing. Furthermore the book ends with a warning not to add or subtract from it (22:18-19) which echoes God's same warning in the Old Testament (Deut. 4:2; 12:32). In this sense, these final words reflect the apex of canon-consciousness in the New Testament that links it with God's covenantal Word of the Old Testament. For more on this, see Ferguson, "How Does the Bible Look at Itself?" 52.

[22] The term "inspiration," especially in our day, is misleading. Often we think of artists or writers who were "inspired" or who are "inspiring." In this sense, it refers to either the greatness of their work or the effect they have upon us to think or act in a different way. However, that is not the theological meaning of the term inspiration. In biblical thinking, inspiration refers neither to the

affirm two biblical emphases simultaneously, namely that Scripture is God's Word due to his action by the Spirit first, in and upon the human authors (2 Pet. 1:20-21) and, second, in the nature of the resulting "God-breathed" (*theopneustos*) text (2 Tim. 3:16-17). Hence, a working definition of the term may be stated as follows: "inspiration is that supernatural work of the Holy Spirit upon the human authors of Scripture such that their writings are precisely what God intended them to write, and as such, are completely trustworthy and authoritative."[23]

Now what is important about this definition is that it attempts to do justice to the Bible's own self-witness that *all* of Scripture, not just certain parts of it, are both the words of human authors and the Word of God. This point is well illustrated by how the New Testament quotes from the Old Testament. Some have estimated that the New Testament quotes some 300 texts and makes at least 1,500 allusions to the Old Testament. This is significant, as Ferguson reminds us, because "the random, rather than selective, use of Scripture is manifest. If any part is God-breathed, then the whole is God-breathed."[24] Theologians have sought to capture this *all-ness* of inspiration by the words "verbal" and "plenary." "Plenary" stresses the fact that *all* of Scripture is God's breathed-out Word. "Verbal" emphasizes that inspiration is not limited merely to Scripture's teaching or to particular doctrines but extends even to the very words and sentences.[25] In this sense, Scripture perfectly reflects, through human authors, what God intended to have communicated and written—Scripture is *his* Word.

But, many a critic has legitimately asked, how is it logically possible to affirm this high view of inspiration? How is it that God can *guarantee* that through the agency of human authors what he intends to communicate is actually written? After all, if human authors freely com-

---

common conception of it nor to the "in-breathing" of God (either into the authors or into the text of Scripture), but to the "God-breathed" character of the product of the author's writing. In this sense, what is stressed is *not* the manner of Scripture's coming into being, *but its divine source.* Just as God has created the universe by his own "breathed out word," so he has "breathed out" Scripture.

[23] For a similar definition as well as a detailed exegetical discussion of 2 Timothy 3:16-17, see B. B. Warfield, *The Inspiration and Authority of the Bible,* 131-166; Paul D. Feinberg, "The Meaning of Inerrancy," in *Inerrancy,* ed. Geisler, 277-287; and Ferguson, "How Does the Bible Look at Itself?" 54-56.

[24] Ferguson, "How Does the Bible Look at Itself?" 57.

[25] Verbal inspiration does *not* mean that we should treat the Bible as a dictionary of theological terms since inspiration extends to words of Scripture, somehow divorced from sentences, paragraphs, and genres. Rather, it is affirming that the words, sentences, and genres are there because God intended them to be there through the agency of the human authors.

pose their writings, must not some kind of error creep in so that the biblical documents, though they might reflect God's Word in some general sense, could never be exactly what God intended to have written? Even more: if we continue to affirm such a high view of inspiration, does it not entail that we must affirm some kind of dictation view?[26] Why? Because, as the critic argues, it is only if God dictates the text and removes the freedom of the human authors that God could provide such a *guarantee* in regards to Scripture. But, as the critic continues, to affirm a dictation theory is disastrous since the phenomena of the text will not allow it. It is quite evident that as we read Scripture, the human authors do not give the impression that they are stenographers; rather they write freely, utilizing their own gifts and abilities. It seems, as the critic points out, it is hard to account for this high view of inspiration and, more importantly, what Scripture claims for itself. Two points need to be made in reply.

First, the critic is correct in observing that Scripture gives no evidence for a dictation view of inspiration, except in a few places. The human authors give abundant evidence of freely exercising their gifts and abilities to write what they wrote.[27] From an examination of Scripture, we discover that God used a variety of *modes* in giving us Scripture. Some texts are the result of dreams; others are the product of historical research and thoughtful interpretation (see Luke 1:1-4; Chronicles); others still, the result of direct revelation from the Lord (Exodus 20). That is why biblical Christianity has argued for a "concursive theory of inspiration." This view attempts to do justice to the biblical data by insisting both that the human authors freely exercised their gifts and abilities to write what they wrote and that God so superintended the process of composing the Scriptures that the end result was nothing less than his guaranteed divine intention. B. B. Warfield nicely summarizes it this way:

---

[26] The charge of dictation is a common one. See the discussion in the following resources that refute such a charge: Carl F. H. Henry, *God, Revelation and Authority*, 6 vols. (Waco, Tex.: Word, 1976–1983; reprint, Wheaton, Ill.: Crossway, 1999), 4:138; J. I. Packer, *"Fundamentalism" and the Word of God* (London: InterVarsity Fellowship, 1958), 78-79; B. B. Warfield, "Inspiration," in *Selected Shorter Writings*, ed. John E. Meeter, 2 vols. (Phillipsburg, N.J.: Presbyterian & Reformed, 2001 [4th printing]), 2:614-636.

[27] For a discussion as to why the dictation theory of inspiration is contrary to the biblical evidence and thus why it should be rejected, see I. Howard Marshall, *Biblical Inspiration* (Grand Rapids, Mich.: Eerdmans, 1982), 32-33.

The fundamental principle of this conception [concursus] is that the whole of Scripture is the product of divine activities which enter it, however, not by superseding the activities of the human authors, but confluently with them; so that the Scriptures are the joint product of divine and human activities, both of which penetrate them at every point, working harmoniously together to the production of a writing which is not divine here and human there, but at once divine and human in every part, every word and every particular. According to this conception, therefore, the whole Bible is recognized as human, the free product of human effort, in every part and word. And at the same time, the whole Bible is recognized as divine, the Word of God, his utterances, of which he is in the truest sense the Author.[28]

Second, however, the critic is incorrect in drawing the conclusion that the Bible's view of inspiration is logically incoherent. No doubt, Scripture never explains how God sovereignly superintended the writing of the human authors so that their texts are nothing less than what God intended to be written, but it does affirm that it is so. But, interestingly, the critic has observed something important in biblical Christianity's view of inspiration, and it is namely this: one's view of God's sovereignty and human freedom underlies one's view of inspiration. In this sense, there is a close relationship between the nature of inspiration and divine providence.[29] Both are attempting to do justice to the divine sovereignty-human freedom relationship. And a traditional view of inspiration affirms both the sovereign action of God and the freedom of the human authors in such a way that God is able to *guarantee* exactly what he intends to communicate through the human authors of Scripture. Of course, it is this exact point that needs to be investigated in terms of the "new" proposal of open theism. Given its understanding of the sovereignty-freedom relationship, will it be sufficient to substantiate biblical Christianity's view of divine inspiration? But that is still to come.

---

[28] Warfield, "The Divine and Human in the Bible," in *Selected Shorter Writings,* 2:547.

[29] For a further discussion of the close relationship between one's view of Scripture and one's view of divine providence, see Vanhoozer, "God's Mighty Speech-Acts," 143-181; and Edward Farley and Peter Hodgson, "Scripture and Tradition," in *Christian Theology,* ed. Peter C. Hodgson and Robert H. King, 2nd ed. (Philadelphia: Fortress, 1985), 61-87.

3. The Reliability and Inerrancy of Scripture

The reliability and inerrancy of Scripture is really a consequence of its verbal-plenary inspiration. Scripture is free from error in all its teaching and affirmation because it is, in its entirety, the product of a sovereign-personal, omniscient God who cannot err. The evidence for this has been marshaled elsewhere and I refer the reader to those resources.[30] No doubt, our understanding of inerrancy must be carefully formulated. It must do justice to the actual material of Scripture, including phenomenological matters, human author's idiosyncrasies, unique grammatical constructions, issues of precision in recording that reflect the times and culture of the Bible, genre issues, and so on. But when all is said and done, Paul Feinberg has captured well a fine working definition of inerrancy when he writes: "Inerrancy means that when all the facts are known, the Scriptures in their original autographs and properly interpreted will be shown to be wholly true in everything that they affirm, whether that has to do with doctrine or morality or with the social, physical, or life sciences."[31]

One further note: It must be stressed that our belief in inerrancy does not imply, and has never implied, that we know how to resolve every prima facie inconsistency in Scripture. In fact, we are not under any obligation to do so in order to believe in inerrancy. To be sure, we must attempt to resolve difficulties where possible, convinced that when all the facts are known, Scripture will be shown to be wholly true. However, we affirm the doctrine of inerrancy, not because we can answer all the difficulties, but because our belief rests on the Bible's own self-testimony and we realize that without God's Word, ultimately we would have no basis for the doing of theology in any normative fashion.[32] Of course, this brings us full circle to where we began this discussion, stressing the fact that Scripture, given who God is, is our ultimate authority and criterion for our theology. Scripture, in other words, is foundational and central to the Christian worldview. It is grounded in the biblical conception of God as the self-authenticating Lord. And it is necessary if we are to know God in any true sense of the word, living not only as his creatures but also as his fallen creatures, who need, more than anything else, a sure,

[30] See the books listed in the above footnotes.
[31] Feinberg, "The Meaning of Inerrancy," 294.
[32] For a further discussion of this point, see Ferguson, "How Does the Bible Look at Itself?" 61-65.

reliable, true, and trustworthy Word-revelation from our Creator-Redeemer God.

With that sketch of the doctrine of Scripture before us, let us now turn to the openness proposal of the divine sovereignty-omniscience and human freedom relationship so that we may better discern whether their proposal will be able to support and uphold what the Scripture claims for itself, namely, that it is nothing less than God's Word written.

II. THE OPENNESS PROPOSAL

What exactly is the openness proposal in regard to the relationship between divine sovereignty, omniscience, and human freedom? Probably the best place to begin is to define clearly what open theists mean by human freedom, before we turn to how they view the divine sovereignty-omniscience and human freedom relationship.

1. Human Freedom[33]

In the current philosophical and theological literature there are two basic views of human freedom which are primarily discussed and adopted—an indeterministic notion referred to in various ways such as libertarian free will or incompatibilism, and a deterministic notion referred to as compatibilism or soft determinism.[34] Open theism strongly endorses the former rather than the latter. It is important to be clear as to what this view of freedom is since, as we shall see, it has dramatic implications for how the open theist construes the divine sovereignty-omniscience and human freedom relationship.

What, then, do philosophers and theologians mean by the concept of a libertarian view of freedom? Simply stated, the basic sense of this view is that a person's act is free if it is not causally determined. For

---

[33] For a more detailed discussion of the debate surrounding the nature of human freedom, see Mark R. Talbot, "True Freedom: The Liberty That Scripture Portrays as Worth Having," chapter 3 in this volume.

[34] Scripture does not precisely define the nature of human freedom, but philosophers and theologians discuss it. As stated, there are two main notions of freedom—libertarianism and compatibilism. These two conceptions of human freedom clearly contradict one another, but both are possible views of freedom in the sense that there is no logical contradiction in affirming either view. Supporting the notion that both views of freedom are coherent and defensible is Thomas Flint, "Two Accounts of Providence," in *Divine and Human Action,* ed. Thomas V. Morris (Ithaca, N.Y.: Cornell University Press, 1988), 177-179. Ultimately the view of freedom that one ought to embrace should be the view that best fits the biblical data, not our preconceived notions of what human freedom is or ought to be.

libertarians this does not mean that our actions are random or arbitrary. Reasons and causes play upon the will as one chooses, but none of them is *sufficient* to incline the will decisively in one direction or another. Thus, a person could always have chosen otherwise than he did. David Basinger states it this way: for a person to be free with respect to performing an action he must have it within his power "to choose to perform action A or choose not to perform action A. Both A and not A could actually occur; which will actually occur has not yet been determined."[35]

This view of freedom is set over against a compatibilist or soft determinist view.[36] In a compatibilist approach, human actions are viewed as causally determined yet free. In other words, in contrast to a libertarian view, a compatibilist view of freedom perceives the human will as decisively and *sufficiently* inclined toward one option as opposed to another, yet it is still free as long as the following requirements are met: "(1) The immediate cause of the action is a desire, wish, or intention internal to the agent, (2) no external event or circumstances compels the action to be performed, and (3) the agent could have acted differently if he had chosen to."[37] If these three conditions are met, then even though human actions are determined, they may still be considered free. John Feinberg summarizes this view well when he states, "If the agent acts in accord with causes and reasons that serve as a sufficient condition for his doing the act, and if the causes do not force him to act contrary to his wishes,

---

[35] David Basinger, "Middle Knowledge and Classical Christian Thought," *Religious Studies* 22 (1986): 416. See also William Hasker, *Metaphysics* (Downers Grove, Ill.: InterVarsity Press, 1983), 32-44; Ledger Wood, "Indeterminism," in *Dictionary of Philosophy*, ed. Dagobert Runes (Savage, Md.: Rowman & Littlefield, 1983), 159; Michael Peterson, et al., *Reason and Religious Belief* (New York: Oxford Press, 1991), 59-61; and Thomas Talbott, "Indeterminism and Chance Occurrences," *The Personalist* 60 (1979): 254.

[36] Even though compatibilism or soft determinism is a view of human freedom that fits under the broad category of determinism, it is important to distinguish it from the concept of "hard" determinism found in the natural sciences and from the concept of fatalism. For more on these distinctions, see John S. Feinberg, "God Ordains All Things," in *Predestination and Free Will*, ed. David Basinger and Randall Basinger (Downers Grove, Ill.: InterVarsity Press, 1986), 21-26; idem, *No One Like Him: The Doctrine of God*, Foundations of Evangelical Theology (Wheaton, Ill.: Crossway, 2001), 625-642; and Richard Taylor, "Determinism," in *The Encyclopedia of Philosophy*, ed. Paul Edwards (New York: Macmillan, 1967), 2:359-373. For more on compatibilism in general, see Paul Helm, *Eternal God* (Oxford: Clarendon, 1988), 157-158; and *The Providence of God* (Downers Grove, Ill.: InterVarsity Press, 1994). An excellent biblical case for compatibilism is found in John M. Frame, *The Doctrine of God*, A Theology of Lordship (Phillipsburg, N.J.: Presbyterian & Reformed, 2002), 119-159.

[37] Peterson, et al., *Reason and Religious Belief*, 59. See also Feinberg, "God Ordains All Things," 26-28.

then a soft determinist would say that he acts freely."[38] Open theists reject this view of freedom and they do so quite strongly.[39]

---

[38] John S. Feinberg, "Divine Causality and Evil: Is There Anything Which God Does Not Do?" *Christian Scholar's Review* 16 (1987): 400.

[39] See for example, Sanders, *The God Who Risks*, 220-224; and Basinger, *The Case for Free Will Theism*, 21-37. In the open theist literature, the only exception I can see to this almost universal rejection of compatibilism is the interesting recent proposal of Greg Boyd. In *Satan and the Problem of Evil*, Boyd argues that God has given all human beings the irrevocable gift of libertarian freedom, or, in his words, "self-determining freedom" (see 50-84, 178-185). Similar to most libertarians, Boyd argues that the very nature of human freedom is the "ability to do otherwise" and that "in light of all influences and circumstances, agents ultimately *determine themselves*" (56). This view of freedom, he argues, is "the one presupposed in Scripture and the one required if love is to be possible for contingent creatures" (57). Furthermore, Boyd is emphatic that "self-determining freedom" must be set over against "compatibilistic freedom." He understands "compatibilism" to be the view that "agents are free if there is nothing that constrains them from doing what they want. But they need not be—and, most would argue, cannot be—free to determine *what they want*" (58). Thus, in contrast with libertarianism, he understands the compatibilist to argue that factors outside the agent are not merely influential but also *coercive* (see 56, 60). However, even though he thinks that compatibilism renders moral responsibility unintelligible and intensifies the problem of evil (see 59-61), he then turns around and argues that libertarian freedom is *not* an end in itself, but instead probationary, leading to a "higher form" of freedom, namely compatibilism! (see 189-190). He states, "Our libertarian freedom is the probationary means by which we acquire compatibilistic freedom either for or against God. So long as we possess self-determining freedom we possess the power to do otherwise. But this power is provisional. It diminishes over time until our *doing* has determined our *being*. It is at this point no longer true that we *could be* other than we are" (189). Boyd's position is that as we choose certain options utilizing our libertarian freedom (i.e., self-determining acts), those choices lead to a "self-determined character," for good or ill, that is *irreversible* and compatibilistic (see 185-206). And thus, explains Boyd, given the fact that we have made choices that have solidified our characters (*habitus acquires*), God is now morally able not only to predestine certain acts of wicked individuals without impugning his character but also to *know* what certain individuals *will do* in certain situations, given the kind of character a person has irreversibly chosen (see 121-129). It is by this explanation that Boyd thinks he can "make sense of the certainty of God's ultimate victory" (190) and decrease the amount of risk that God takes in the world. What are we to think of such a view? A number of preliminary points need to be stated in terms of response. First, Boyd, as far as I know, is the only open theist who argues such a position. It will be interesting to see how other open theists respond to it. Second, Boyd misunderstands compatibilism. As stated above, compatibilism does not argue that the human will is *sufficiently* inclined in a *coercive* manner; rather it is quite the opposite (see above discussion). Third, given Boyd's view of "neo-Molinism," that is, that God knows both would- and might-counterfactuals (see 127-129), he believes that God, from all eternity, is able to know "*if* agent *x* freely follows a certain possible life-trajectory, he will *become* the kind of person who would do *y* in situation *z* (*habitus acquirus* [*sic*])" (128). With this belief, he thinks he has answered the notoriously difficult "grounding-objection" of *would*-counterfactuals in Molinism and thus made a strong case for an open view of God being able to *know* large amounts of the future, even though some elements of the future are still open. However, given his commitment to libertarianism, there are two problems in terms of the coherency of this explanation. The first problem centers on how God in fact does *know* when a person's character has become so irreversibly set. Given libertarianism, it might look as if a person's character is being set in a certain direction, but is it not possible for the person to surprise even God by doing otherwise? And, in addition, how *would* God *know* this from all eternity? Knowing possible scenarios (might-counterfactuals) is hardly the same as *knowing* actualities (would-counterfactuals). Fourth, even if we grant that libertarianism may lead to compatibilism, given Boyd's understanding of compatibilism, would not this person whose character is irreversibly set be more robotic than free? And if, as Boyd argues, libertarianism is required for love to be real and genuine in order to do justice to God's creation project, then would a person with compatibilistic freedom, given Boyd's understanding of it, be a person who is incapable of fulfilling the divine project? At the heart of Boyd's creative proposal seems to be an inherent incoherency, especially given his prior commitment to self-determining freedom and his definition of compatibilism. I am not convinced he has made his case in the least. For a more thorough critique of Boyd's view, see Paul Kjoss Helseth, "The Trustworthiness of God and the Foundation of Hope," chapter 8 in this volume.

2. Divine Sovereignty and Human Freedom

How, then, does open theism conceive of the divine sovereignty-human freedom relationship, given its commitment to libertarianism? How do open theists view the relationship between a libertarian view of human freedom and God's sovereign rule over the affairs of humanity? Most open theists, if not all of them, tend to "limit" God's sovereignty in some sense. Now it must quickly be added that by the use of the word "limit" I am not necessarily using the word in a pejorative or negative sense. Instead, it is being used in the sense that God freely chooses to limit himself by virtue of the fact that he has chosen to create a certain kind of world, that is, a world that contains human beings with libertarian freedom. In this sense, then, "limit" does not refer to a weakness or imperfection in God; rather it refers to a self-imposed limitation that is part of his plan, not a violation of it.[40]

But it must still be asked: how does God's creation of people with libertarian freedom limit his sovereignty? What exactly is the nature of God's sovereign rule according to open theism? David Basinger states the limitation well when he acknowledges that open theists are quite willing to admit that a sovereign God "cannot create a co-possible set of free moral agents without also bringing about the possibility that states of affairs will occur which God does not desire but cannot prohibit."[41] In other words, this particular proposal of the nature of divine sovereignty entails that God cannot guarantee that what he decides will be carried out. Of course, the important word here is *guarantee*. Given the open theist's view of human freedom, it is not possible to affirm "that the exercise of the gift of freedom is *controlled* by God."[42]

---

[40] On the issue of "limit" in regard to divine sovereignty, see Frame, "The Spirit and the Scriptures," in *Hermeneutics, Authority, and Canon,* ed. Carson and Woodbridge, 217-235. For an example of the outworking of this view in relation to divine sovereignty and libertarianism, see Jack Cottrell, "The Nature of Divine Sovereignty," in *The Grace of God and the Will of Man: A Case for Arminianism,* ed. Clark H. Pinnock (Grand Rapids, Mich.: Zondervan, 1989), 108-110.

[41] David Basinger, "Human Freedom and Divine Providence: Some New Thoughts on an Old Problem," *Religious Studies* 15 (1979): 496.

[42] William Hasker, "God the Creator of Good and Evil?" in *The God Who Acts: Philosophical and Theological Explorations,* ed. Thomas F. Tracy (University Park, Pa.: Pennsylvania State University Press, 1994), 139. As noted in note 39, an exception to this conclusion in open theism is Greg Boyd. In *Satan and the Problem of Evil,* Boyd thinks that it is logically and morally possible for God to control the free actions of human beings, even predestining certain acts of wicked individuals, as long as this predestining did not occur before these individuals had freely resolved their own characters. As he states, "God would be morally culpable if he predestined people to carry out wicked acts prior to their birth. But he is not morally culpable if he chooses to direct the path of people who have already *made themselves* wicked" (122). As to the validity of such reasoning,

Pinnock states it this way: "What God wants to happen does not always come to pass on account of human freedom. . . . There is no blueprint that governs everything that happens, it is a real historical project that does not proceed smoothly but goes through twists and turns. . . . There is no unconditional guarantee of success because there are risks for God and the creature."[43]

At this point, it might be helpful to illustrate the openness proposal of divine sovereignty by referring to the work of Pinnock. He admits that, as creator, God is unquestionably the superior power. For example, God has the power to exist and the power to control all things. But almightiness, according to Pinnock, is not the whole story. As he states,

> Though no power can stand against him, God wills the existence of creatures with the power of self-determination. This means that God is a superior power who does not cling to his right to dominate and control but who voluntarily gives creatures room to flourish. By inviting them to have dominion over the world (for example), God willingly surrenders power and makes possible a partnership with the creature.[44]

Thus, due to God's own free choice to create creatures with libertarian freedom, God limits himself. But, as Pinnock states, this is not to be seen as a limitation "imposed from without"; it is a self-limitation.[45] In fact, Pinnock does not view this self-limitation of God as a "weakness" since, as he argues, it requires more power to rule over an undetermined world than it does to rule over a determined one. However, even though God's own self-limitation is not to be viewed as a weakness, it should still be viewed as entailing a risk view of divine sovereignty.

What exactly does this mean? In the end it means that God must respond and adapt to surprises and to the unexpected. As Pinnock states, "God sets goals for creation and redemption and realizes them ad hoc in

---

which I do not think will work, I refer the reader back to my comments in note 39. But I am pleased to see that Boyd is at least taking seriously biblical teaching centered around biblical prophecy regarding the certainty of God's predictive Word involving the free actions of such people as Josiah, Cyrus, Judas, and Peter. However, I am convinced that the explanation for this is found in a biblical compatibilism, not open theism. For further literature on a biblical compatibilism, see note 36.

[43] Pinnock, *Most Moved Mover*, 44-45.

[44] Pinnock, "Systematic Theology," in Pinnock, et al., *The Openness of God*, 113.

[45] Ibid.

history. If Plan A fails, God is ready with Plan B."[46] Thus, says Pinnock, because of God's creation of human beings with libertarian freedom, the sovereign God delegates power to the creature, making himself vulnerable. Sovereignty does not mean that nothing can go contrary to God's will, but that God is able to deal with any circumstances that may arise. As Pinnock asserts, "By his [God's] decision to create a world like ours, God showed his willingness to take risks and to work with a history whose outcome he does not wholly decide."[47] Hence, to a large extent, reality is "open" rather than closed. For Pinnock and other open theists this ultimately means that "genuine novelty can appear in history which cannot be predicted even by God. If the creature has been given the ability to decide how some things will turn out, then it cannot be known infallibly ahead of time how they will turn out. It implies that the future is really 'open' and not available to exhaustive foreknowledge even on the part of God."[48] This last observation leads us to our next point of discussion, namely that of the openness view of divine omniscience.

3. Divine Omniscience and Human Freedom

Traditionally, Christian theologians and philosophers have sought to maintain that God has complete and infallible knowledge of everything past, present, and future and necessarily so. As Thomas Morris states,

> Not only is God omniscient, he is *necessarily omniscient*—it is impossible that his omniscience collapse, fail, or even waver. He is, as philosophers nowadays often say, omniscient in *every possible world*. That is to say, he is actually omniscient, and there is no possible, complete and coherent story about any way things could have gone (no "possible world") in which God lacks this degree of cognitive excellence.[49]

However, as has long been discussed in the history of theology, this view of God's omniscience seems to generate a very thorny problem, namely,

[46] Ibid. For a further development of this theme of divine risk taking, see Sanders's *The God Who Risks*.

[47] Pinnock, "Systematic Theology," 116.

[48] Pinnock, "God Limits His Knowledge," in *Predestination and Free Will,* 150.

[49] Thomas Morris, *Our Idea of God* (Downers Grove, Ill.: InterVarsity Press, 1991), 87. Morris clarifies what he means by this on page 88. He argues that to say "God is omniscient" does not merely assert a necessity *de dicto,* i.e., God knows all true propositions and none that are false, but also a necessity *de re,* i.e., God has perfect personal knowledge of all things. In other words, "not only is omniscience necessary for divinity, divinity is a necessary or essential property of any

how can we possibly be thought to be free in our actions if God knows exactly how we will act on every occasion in the future? Morris poses the problem in this way: "If God already knows exactly how we *shall* act, what else can we possibly do? We must act in that way. We cannot diverge from the path that he sees we shall take. We cannot prove God wrong. He is necessarily omniscient. Divine foreknowledge thus seems to preclude genuine alternatives, and thus genuine freedom in the world."[50] This is what is known as the foreknowledge-freedom problem.[51]

Now it is at this point that open theists offer a solution to the foreknowledge-freedom problem that is logically consistent yet is a departure from traditional Christian belief. Their view is known as "presentism." Presentism strongly insists that God knows everything there is to know—God is truly omniscient.[52] But then presentism adds this very critical point: it is precisely future free actions of people that are impossible to know. Given libertarian freedom, they insist, it is impossible for anyone, including God himself, truly to know what people will do since there are no antecedent sufficient conditions which decisively incline a person's will in one direction over another. Thus, in upholding a libertarian view of human freedom, open theism denies that God can know the future free actions of human beings.[53]

---

individual who has it . . . the property of being God is best thought of as a necessary or essential property. An individual who is God does not just happen to have that status. It is not a property he could have done without. . . . Omniscience is thus not only a necessary condition of deity, it is a necessary or essential property for any individual who is God. No literally divine person is even possibly vulnerable to ignorance."

[50] Ibid., 89.

[51] For the basic argument of the foreknowledge-freedom problem, see ibid., 91:
  (1) God's beliefs are infallible. Thus,
  (2) For any event x, if God believes in advance that x will occur, then no one is in a position to prevent x.
  (3) For any event x, if no one is in a position to prevent x, then no one is free with respect to x.
  (4) For every event x that ever occurs, God believes in advance that it will occur. Therefore,
  (5) No one distinct from God is free with respect to any event. And so,
  (6) Human free will is a complete illusion.

[52] In this regard, listen to the definition of omniscience given by Richard Swinburne, a proponent of present knowledge, when he states, "omniscience is knowledge of everything true which is logically possible to know" (*The Coherence of Theism* [Oxford: Clarendon, 1977], 175).

[53] For a further description of "presentism," see William Hasker, "A Philosophical Perspective," in Pinnock, et al., *The Openness of God*, 136-138 and 150-151; and *God, Time, and Knowledge* (Ithaca, N.Y.: Cornell University Press, 1989), 186-190; as well as the article by Pinnock, "God Limits His Knowledge," 143-162; and Richard Rice, *God's Foreknowledge and Man's Free Will* (Minneapolis: Bethany, 1985). See also David Basinger, "Divine Control and Human Freedom: Is Middle Knowledge the Answer?" *JETS* 36 (1993): 55-64.

What are some of the implications of such a view? As has already been stated, the God of open theism is a risk taker.[54] Accordingly, the implication is not only that God lacks exact and infallible knowledge of the contingent future but also that, as David Basinger argues, "It can no longer be said that God is working out his ideal, preordained plan. Rather, God may well find himself disappointed in the sense that this world may fall short of that ideal world God wishes were coming about."[55]

Does this then mean that open theists also believe that God's *ultimate* plans will not come to pass? The answer is no. Open theists argue that even though God does not have exhaustive knowledge of future contingents, he is still God. And given his familiarity with present causal tendencies and his clear grasp of his own providential designs, God is almost "sure" about how the future will turn out even though the future remains open. Richard Rice explains it this way:

> God's future thus resembles ours in that it is both definite and indefinite.[56] But it differs greatly from ours in the extent to which it is definite. Since we are largely ignorant of the past and present, the future appears vastly indefinite to us. We know very little of what will happen because we know and understand so little of what has already happened. God, in contrast, knows all that has happened. Therefore a great deal of the future that appears vague and indefinite to us must be vividly clear to Him.[57]

---

[54] For examples of this kind of language from those who defend present knowledge, see Pinnock, "God Limits His Knowledge," 143-162; Hasker, *God, Time, and Knowledge,* 186-205; and J. R. Lucas, "Foreknowledge and the Vulnerability of God," in *The Philosophy in Christianity,* ed. Godfrey Vesey (Cambridge: Cambridge University Press, 1989), 119-128.

[55] Basinger, "Divine Control and Human Freedom," 58.

[56] See Boyd, *God of the Possible,* 21-87; and *Satan and the Problem of Evil,* 123-129, who also makes this same point especially by his appeal to "neo-Molinism." For Boyd, the traditional Molinist view wrongly assumed that counterfactuals were exclusively about what agents would or would not do. But, argues Boyd, this does not exhaust the logical possibilities of counterfactual propositions. Instead, we should also think of counterfactuals as "might or might not do-counterfactuals" that also have an eternal truth value that is known by God. Thus, the determinate aspects of any possible world, including worlds that include true might-counterfactuals, are grounded in God's decision to create such a world, and in such a world they will come to pass. On the other hand, the openness of the future is linked to God creating a world in which some might-counterfactuals are true. Furthermore, as Boyd contends, there is no problem accounting for the eternal facticity of what libertarian agents *will* do or *would* do in other circumstances because "the actions of these agents flow either from the character God has given them (*habitus infusus*), in which case they are not morally responsible for them, or from the character they will freely acquire (*habitus acquirus*) [sic] if they pursue a certain possible course of action, in which case they are responsible for them" (128). For a brief response to Boyd's proposal, see note 39.

[57] Rice, *God's Foreknowledge and Man's Free Will,* 55-56. Peter Geach in a very similar way argues that the indeterminacy of the future does not mean that God's ultimate plans will not come to pass. In his book (*Providence and Evil* [Cambridge: Cambridge University Press, 1977], 40-66), Geach views God as a "Grand Chess Master" who is simultaneously playing

But, it must be quickly added, even after all the caveats have been factored in, open theists must affirm that a God with only present knowledge must take risks. For if God makes decisions that depend for their outcomes on the responses of free creatures in which the decisions themselves are not informed by knowledge of the outcomes, then creating and governing such a world is, in the words of William Hasker, "a risky business."[58]

III. The Openness Proposal and the Doctrine of Scripture

We now turn to investigate whether the open theist construal of the divine sovereignty-omniscience and human freedom relationship has any logical bearing on the doctrine of Scripture. Is the openness proposal able to uphold a high view of Scripture or will it undermine it? Given the openness proposal of God's relation to the world, does it have any bearing on what we may or may not affirm about Scripture? It is to these questions that we now turn. I will attempt to address these questions in two steps. First, I want to think through the open theist's view of the divine sovereignty-freedom relationship as it relates to the doctrine of inspiration. Second, I want to investigate the openness proposal regarding divine omniscience in relation to the subject of predictive prophecy.

1. Divine Sovereignty, Human Freedom, and the Concursive Theory of Inspiration

Does the openness proposal regarding the sovereignty-freedom relationship make any difference in what we may affirm about Scripture? An excellent place to begin our evaluation is with a short but very insightful article by David Basinger and Randall Basinger entitled "Inerrancy, Dictation, and the Free Will Defence."[59] What is significant about this arti-

---

several games of chess. He has everything under control even though some of the players are consciously trying to hinder his plan, while others are trying to help it. But whatever the finite players do, God's plan will be executed because as the Grand Master he cannot be surprised, thwarted, cheated, or disappointed.

[58] Hasker, *God, Time, and Knowledge,* 197.

[59] David Basinger and Randall Basinger, "Inerrancy, Dictation, and the Free Will Defence," *Evangelical Quarterly* 55 (1983): 177-180. See also the exchange of articles that the Basingers' article has generated between themselves and Norman Geisler. See Norman Geisler, "Inerrancy and Free Will: A Reply to the Brothers Basinger," *Evangelical Quarterly* 57 (1985): 349-353; Basinger and Basinger, "Inerrancy and Free Will: Some Further Thoughts," *Evangelical Quarterly* 58 (1986): 351-354; and Geisler, "Is Inerrancy Incompatible with the Free Will Defense?" *Evangelical Quarterly* 62 (1990): 175-178.

cle, at least for our purposes, is the Basingers' argument—"one cannot consistently affirm the total inerrancy of Scripture and yet *also* utilize the Free Will Defence as a response to the problem of evil."[60] Now at first sight this argument might seem somewhat removed from our investigation regarding whether the open theist construal of divine sovereignty makes any difference in what one may affirm about Scripture, but it is really not. In fact, if we carefully unpack the Basingers' argument, we will soon discover that it has a direct bearing on our investigation.

The Basingers begin by observing, as I also noted in the previous discussion of the doctrine of inspiration, that "one of the stock arguments employed by the challenger to the inerrancy position is that inerrancy implies a dictation theory of inspiration."[61] That is, in order to obtain a verbally inspired and inerrant Scripture, one must affirm, so says the critic, that the human authors were reduced to impersonal instruments, and as such, in the writing of Scripture their freedom was taken away.

In response to the critics, the Basingers rightly acknowledge that modern proponents of inerrancy emphatically deny that dictation is necessary in order to accept the inerrancy position. In reply, proponents of inerrancy insist that the reason one can affirm verbal inspiration and inerrancy is precisely because the scriptural writers' "thinking and writings were *both* free and spontaneous on their part *and* divinely elicited and controlled."[62] In fact, it is for this very reason that proponents of a traditional view of Scripture have argued for a *concursive* theory of inspiration, in contrast to a dictation theory. The rationale for this, as we have seen, is to emphasize that both God and the human author are active in the process, thus guaranteeing that what God intended through the human authors was written.

Now at this point, the Basingers insist, in order for the proponents of inerrancy to succeed in their reply to the critics, they must accept as true the following proposition: "Human activities (such as penning a

---

[60] Basinger and Basinger, "Inerrancy and Free Will: Some Further Thoughts," 351.

[61] Basinger and Basinger, "Inerrancy, Dictation, and the Free Will Defence," 177. For two contemporary examples of the charge of dictation, see William Abraham, *The Divine Inspiration of Holy Scripture* (Oxford: Oxford University Press, 1981), 28-38; and James Barr, *Fundamentalism* (London: SCM, 1981), 290-293.

[62] Packer, *"Fundamentalism" and the Word of God,* 80. See also John Jefferson Davis, *Foundations of Evangelical Theology* (Grand Rapids, Mich.: Baker, 1984), 174-176; Gordon R. Lewis, "The Human Authorship of Inspired Scripture," in *Inerrancy,* ed. Geisler, 227-264; and A. N. S. Lane, "B. B. Warfield on the Humanity of Scripture," *Vox Evangelica* 16 (1986): 77-94.

book) can be totally controlled by God without violating human freedom."[63] If this proposition is accepted, maintain the Basingers, then the
argument for a high view of Scripture must look something like this:

(1) The words of the Bible are the product of free human activity (are human utterances).

(2) Human activities (such as penning a book) can be totally
controlled by God without violating human freedom.

(3) God totally controlled what human authors did in fact
write.

(4) Therefore, the words of the Bible are God's utterances.

(5) Whatever God utters is errorless (inerrant).

(6) Therefore, the words of the Bible are errorless (inerrant).[64]

But, contend the Basingers, there is a major problem with this argument.
The problem is not so much with the argument itself, but with its implications. For example, if one accepts premise (2), then major implications
follow for one who attempts to answer the problem of evil along the
lines of the famous Free Will Defense (FWD). In fact, the Basingers argue
that the acceptance of (2) is incompatible with the FWD. Why is this the
case? Because, as the Basingers correctly point out, in order for the FWD
to be successful, it must assume a specific conception of human freedom,
namely libertarianism.[65] The Basingers state it this way:

> The assumption behind this argument [FWD] is the belief that God *can-
> not* both create free moral creatures and still bring it about (infallibly
> guarantee) that they will perform the specific actions he desires. For
> once it is assumed that God *can* control the actions of free creatures, it
> follows immediately that God could have created a world containing
> free moral agents but absolutely no moral evil—i.e. God could have
> brought it about that every individual would always freely choose in
> every situation to perform the exact action God desired. But if God
> could have brought it about that every instance of moral evil was freely
> not performed, then we must conclude that God is directly responsible

---

[63] Basinger and Basinger, "Inerrancy, Dictation, and the Free Will Defence," 178.

[64] Ibid.

[65] Ibid., 179. In the contemporary literature, no one has done more to develop and defend the FWD
than Alvin Plantinga in *God, Freedom, and Evil* (New York: Harper & Row, 1974; reprint, Grand
Radids, Mich.: Eerdmans, 1978).

for each instance of moral evil in the world and the free will defence fails. In short, the free will defence can only work—i.e. divine responsibility for the actuality of moral evil in the world can only be absolved—by denying that God can totally control free creatures, that is, by denying premise (2).[66]

Given the fact that the FWD is linked to an acceptance of libertarianism (and its particular construal of divine sovereignty), it should now be evident why an adoption of FWD is incompatible with (2). Premise (2) assumes God can infallibly *guarantee* that humans will perform the specific actions he desires without violating their freedom, whereas libertarianism denies this possibility. Thus, the Basingers conclude with the following dilemma: either affirm (2) and thus inerrancy, but at the cost of making God responsible for all the moral evil in the world; or adopt the use of the FWD, thus absolving God of any responsibility for evil, but at the cost of rejecting (2) and thus being "left with the seemingly impossible task of showing how God could perfectly control what the biblical writers uttered without removing their freedom."[67]

How are we to evaluate the Basingers' argument? Two points need to be emphasized. First, the Basingers' argument is reductionistic. Why? Because there are more options available to us than what they seem to allow. For example, the FWD is *not* the only way to absolve God of the responsibility for evil in the world. No doubt, for a person who embraces a libertarian view of human freedom, the FWD is a logically consistent and attractive option. Nonetheless, it is not the only defense available to a libertarian, nor is it the only defense that is available to other theological viewpoints that do not embrace libertarianism.[68] Moreover, along a similar line and more importantly for our purposes, the Basingers are reductionistic in presenting libertarianism as the only option for a defender of inerrancy. Even though it is outside the purpose

---

[66] Basinger and Basinger, "Inerrancy, Dictation, and the Free Will Defence," 179. On this same point cf. Alvin Plantinga, *The Nature of Necessity* (Oxford: Clarendon, 1974), 166-167.

[67] Basinger and Basinger, "Inerrancy, Dictation, and the Free Will Defence," 180.

[68] On other ways to solve the problem of evil from a commitment to libertarian freedom, see John S. Feinberg, *The Many Faces of Evil* (Grand Rapids, Mich.: Zondervan, 1994), 111-123. However, regardless of which way a libertarian attempts to solve the problem of evil, it is still true that if one adopts libertarianism, there is a problem with holding premise (2). On other ways to solve the problem of evil from a non-libertarian view, see Feinberg's defense of a compatibilistic theological position in *The Many Faces of Evil*, 124-155. On this latter point see also Frame, *Apologetics*, 149-190; idem, *Doctrine of God*, 160-182; and Greg L. Bahnsen, *Always Ready* (Texarkana, Tex.: Covenant Media Foundation, 1996), 163-175.

of this paper, I would argue that a person such as myself, who adopts a view of divine sovereignty that incorporates a compatibilistic understanding of human freedom, is able to affirm premise (2) without contradiction, and thus, defend a high view of Scripture.

Second, I do think that their argument, however, does have important implications for open theism. Why? Because given open theism's understanding of the sovereignty-freedom relationship, it would seem that it must reject premise (2). But with the rejection of premise (2) there is a very serious entailment, namely, that the theological underpinnings for a high view of Scripture have been greatly weakened. Why? Because if God cannot infallibly *guarantee* that what the human authors freely wrote was precisely what he wanted written, without error, then it seems difficult to substantiate the traditional view of Scripture at this point.[69] In fact, most defenders of a high view of Scripture have viewed premise (2) as intimately connected with a proper defense of inerrancy. As E. J. Young wrote many years ago, "inspiration is designed to *secure* the accuracy of what is taught and to keep the Lord's spokesman from error in his teaching. . . . inspiration is designed to *secure* infallibility . . ."[70] But with the undermining of premise (2), open theism greatly weakens the theological defense for an infallible and inerrant Bible.

But does this then entail that the person who adopts open theism or a libertarian view of freedom cannot *logically* affirm inerrancy? In terms of logical possibility, the answer is no. It is logically possible to affirm that the biblical authors "just happened" to write everything that God wanted them to write, without God *guaranteeing* it.[71] For it is true, as Norman Geisler contends in his response to the Basingers, that, "it is not essential (necessary) for humans to err whenever they speak or write . . . human free choice only makes error *possible*, not necessary."[72] But even

---

[69] I am assuming in the following discussion that the dictation theory of inspiration is not an option. No doubt, one could always defend inerrancy and libertarianism by affirming that in the special case of Scripture God took away the freedom of the authors and dictated the text. This would certainly be a logical explanation. However, for anyone who takes the phenomena of the Scripture seriously, this is not really a viable option.

[70] E. J. Young, *Thy Word Is Truth* (Grand Rapids, Mich.: Eerdmans, 1957; reprint, Edinburgh: Banner of Truth, 1997), 41-42, emphasis added.

[71] The Basingers admit this possibility as a mere possibility, but then correctly argue that if (2) is false then "God can never *guarantee* that any human will freely do what he wants" ("Inerrancy and Free Will: Some Further Thoughts," 354).

[72] Geisler, "Inerrancy and Free Will: A Reply to the Brothers Basinger," 350.

though it is logically possible to affirm libertarianism and inerrancy, it must be acknowledged that it is highly improbable. For without an infallible *guarantee*, given the diversity of the biblical authors and the nature of the content of Scripture, the probability that the biblical authors just happened to get everything correct, thus resulting in an infallible and inerrant text, is indeed very, very low.

Moreover, a commitment to open theism and a libertarian view of freedom also raises an important epistemological issue. What happens when we find an apparent error or contradiction in Scripture? What should our attitude be toward the Bible? Should we seek to resolve it because we are convinced that Scripture is inerrant? And if we are so convinced, from whence does this conviction come? For if God *cannot* guarantee that what he wanted written was written, then our conviction on these matters certainly does not stem from the view that the Scriptures were "divinely elicited and controlled, and what they [biblical writers] wrote was not only their own work but also God's work."[73] On the other hand, when we do come across an apparent contradiction or problem in Scripture, do we then admit that it is an error? For after all, given libertarianism, it may be true that it is logically possible to affirm inerrancy, but the probability of it is so low that we have no overwhelming reason to think that the apparent problem is not really an error after all. And if we move in this direction, can Scripture then serve as its own self-attesting authority by which we evaluate all theological proposals? Or are we driven always to confirm Scripture at point after point, on independent grounds whatever they may be, and not to receive Scripture on its own say-so?

Indeed, these are serious implications for one's view of Scripture given open theism's understanding of the sovereignty-freedom relationship. But, someone might object, could not this challenge also be raised against other evangelicals who hold to a view of divine sovereignty that incorporates a libertarian view of human freedom, and not just the viewpoint of open theism? Is it only the open theist who succumbs to this kind of problem? Do not all those who affirm libertarianism also face this same dilemma? And thus, are you not indicting other evangelicals who reject open theism but affirm libertarianism? My answer is both yes and

---

[73] Packer, *"Fundamentalism" and the Word of God*, 80.

no. Yes, in the sense that it is very difficult for any libertarian position to argue consistently how God can *guarantee* that what he wants written is written freely by human authors. But no, in the important sense that traditional evangelicals who are committed to libertarianism are also committed to exhaustive divine foreknowledge of future free human actions, which allows them to maintain simultaneously libertarian freedom and the *guarantee* necessary in order to uphold a high view of Scripture. An excellent example of this approach is that of William Craig.

In a recent article, Craig appeals to the theory of middle knowledge as the means by which he reconciles his commitment to libertarianism and the doctrine of inerrancy.[74] Even though I do not adopt this approach and instead opt for a compatibilist solution, Craig does demonstrate cogently that there is a way to reconcile libertarianism and inerrancy.[75] But it is important to stress that this is *not* an option "open" to open theists. And thus, the openness proposal faces some serious problems, especially in regard to how God can *guarantee* what he intends to be written, through the free agency of human authors. How, in the end, is open theism able to explain rationally and coherently how both God and the human author are active in the process of inspiration and that the final result is exactly what God intended?[76] It would seem

---

[74] William L. Craig, "'Men Moved by the Holy Spirit Spoke from God' (2 Peter 1:21): A Middle Knowledge Perspective on Biblical Inspiration," *Philosophia Christi* 1 (1999): 45-82.

[75] The problem I have with middle knowledge is that I do not think it can get off the ground in terms of an explanation. Middle knowledge depends upon the notion that God knows what we *would* freely do, not just could do, and were we placed in different circumstances, and on the basis of that knowledge, God then freely decides to actualize one of those worlds known to him through this middle knowledge. But given *libertarianism,* I do not see how God can *know,* even counterfactually, what we *would* do if we can always choose otherwise. Hence, in the end, I do not think middle knowledge will be able to deliver what it promises. For similar critiques of middle knowledge at this point, see Helm, *The Providence of God,* 55-61; J. A. Crabtree, "Does Middle Knowledge Solve the Problem of Divine Sovereignty?" in *The Grace of God, the Bondage of the Will,* ed. Thomas R. Schreiner and Bruce A. Ware, 2 vols. (Grand Rapids, Mich.: Baker, 1995), 2:429-457; and Feinberg, *The Many Faces of Evil,* 89-90.

[76] One answer to this charge that may be possible for an open theist is the proposal of Boyd in his recent work, *Satan and the Problem of Evil.* In arguing that libertarian freedom is the probationary means by which we acquire compatibilistic freedom by our own self-determining acts, is it not possible to conclude that in the case of Scripture God can *guarantee* that his purposes will be accomplished since he is working alongside authors whose characters have been established in such a way that they follow the leading of the Holy Spirit in their writing? After all, given the fact that Boyd thinks that this explanation accounts for how God can predestine the wicked acts of such individuals as Cyrus or Judas, why is it not possible to think that God can *control* the good actions of individuals whose characters have been set in a compatibilistic direction by their own free will? In this sense, an open theist may be able to affirm that God can *guarantee* that what he wants written is actually written through the free agency of human authors. In response to this potential solution, I first refer the reader to my discussion of the coherency, or in my view, the incoherency of this view in note 39. I do not think it will work. But even if we grant Boyd's proposal for sake of argument, given his understanding of compatibilistic freedom, I do not see how a person who

that the openness proposal, at least at this point, undermines the doctrine of inerrancy and has a difficult time accounting for the confluent authorship of Scripture.[77]

Interestingly, Pinnock, in response to an article of mine on this subject, basically admits this point but then appeals to the "interplay of divine initiative and human activity."[78] He goes on to explain that God is overseeing the process but human authors are also active in the process as well. He states, "God is always present, not always in the mode of control, but often in the manner of stimulation and invitation. God works alongside human beings in order to achieve by wisdom and patience the goal of a Bible that expresses his will for our salvation."[79] True enough, but given the openness proposal regarding the sovereignty-freedom relationship, how is this explanation a rational accounting for the *guarantee* that seems to underpin the doctrine of inerrancy? It seems to me that open theists must resort to some kind of fideistic explanation at this point, unless they want to appeal to a dictation theory of inspiration, something that I have never seen them do. However, the

---

has the kind of freedom Boyd describes is truly free. No doubt, Boyd's proposal would fit well with a dictation theory of inspiration, but it does not cohere well with a concursive theory which argues that both God and the human author are active in the *same* act, by which the final result is a God-breathed-out text. This last observation is strengthened, especially when one considers that in order for Boyd to buttress our confidence that God can actually guarantee that what he wants is accomplished, God must occasionally intervene unilaterally in the world, even sometimes in a coercive manner (see 185-186). But once again, when applied to Scripture, this might make sense of a dictation theory, but not a traditional view of inspiration and Scripture.

[77] In this regard, it is interesting to compare the early Pinnock with the current Pinnock. The early Pinnock, by his own admission, was a strong advocate of both inerrancy and a Calvinistic view of divine sovereignty. The current Pinnock, now an advocate of open theism with its weakened view of divine sovereignty, has also shifted to a weakened view of inerrancy. The early Pinnock maintained that the concept of confluent authorship is intelligible only within the context of biblical theism. By this he meant, "God and man can both be significant agents simultaneously in the same historical (Acts 2:23) or literary (2 Pet 1:21) event. The Spirit of God worked concursively alongside the activity of the writers, Himself being the principal cause and they the free instrumental cause. The result of this concursive operation was that their thinking and writing were both free and spontaneous on their part and divinely elicited and controlled, and what they wrote was not only their own work, but also God's work. There is a monotonous chorus of protest against the biblical concept of inspiration on the grounds that it involves mechanical dictation. The only way to explain the repetition of this false charge is to recognize the sad eclipse of biblical theism today. Men seem unable to conceive of a divine providence which can infallibly reach its ends without dehumanizing the human agents it employs. According to the Bible, the sovereignty of God does not nullify the significance of man" (*Biblical Revelation* [Phillipsburg, N.J.: Presbyterian & Reformed, 1985 (1971)], 92-93). However, the current Pinnock views the traditional emphasis on *concursus* as suggesting total divine control, tantamount to saying God dictated the text (see *The Scripture Principle* [New York: Harper & Row, 1984], 100-101).

[78] Pinnock, *Most Moved Mover*, 129. For my article see Stephen J. Wellum, "The Importance of the Nature of Divine Sovereignty for Our View of Scripture," *The Southern Baptist Journal of Theology* 4, no. 2 (Summer 2000): 76-90.

[79] Pinnock, *Most Moved Mover*, 129.

problem with fideistic explanations is that, at the end of the day, they force us to believe in logically contradictory states of affairs and leave us with no satisfying rational explanation regarding the sovereignty-freedom and Scripture relationship, thus undermining our confidence in the doctrine of inerrancy.[80]

2. Divine Omniscience, Human Freedom, and Predictive Prophecy

We now turn our attention to the implications of the openness proposal regarding divine omniscience and the phenomena of predictive prophecy. At the outset it would seem that an adoption of the openness proposal at this point would have some serious entailments for an evangelical view of Scripture. Why? Because it seems highly improbable for a God who does not have exhaustive knowledge of future contingents to be able to predict accurately what will come to pass. If Scripture contains predictions and prophecies about the future, which most evangelicals admit, then how is God able to *guarantee* that these predictions will come to pass as he has predicted?[81] God might be able to give us a Scripture that includes his guesses, expert conjectures, or even adept hypotheses of how he expects his plan for the world to unfold. But this is certainly a far cry from God being able to give us *infallible* and *inerrant* knowledge of these matters.[82] For it would seem that if God's knowledge of future contingents is not exhaustive, then he is only able, at best, to make intelligent conjectures about what free persons

---

[80] No doubt, it must be admitted that all of us, no matter what our theological convictions are, have to appeal to "mystery" in speaking of the sovereignty-freedom relationship and its application to the doctrine of Scripture. However, my point is that the open theist proposal is not merely appealing to "mystery"; it is also attempting to reconcile a view of sovereignty-freedom that is fundamentally at odds with the doctrine of inerrancy and a concursive theory of inspiration, at least in terms of rational accounting for and theological explanation of it.

[81] William Craig nicely states what most evangelicals admit about Scripture, namely that it contains various predictions and prophecies about the future. He states, "God's knowledge of the future seems essential to the prophetic pattern that underlies the biblical scheme of history. The test of the true prophet was success in foretelling the future: 'When a prophet speaks in the name of the Lord, if the word does not come to pass or come true, that is a word which the Lord has not spoken' (Deut 18:22). The history of Israel was punctuated with prophets who foretold events in both the immediate and distant future, and it was the conviction of the New Testament writers that the coming and work of Jesus had been prophesied" (*The Only Wise God* [Grand Rapids, Mich.: Baker, 1987], 27). Craig goes on to give numerous other examples of the kinds of predictions that are found in Scripture (ibid., 27-30).

[82] By the term "knowledge" I am referring to what epistemologists have defined as "justified true belief." See John L. Pollock, *Contemporary Theories of Knowledge* (Savage, Md.: Rowman & Littlefield, 1986), 7-10.

might do. But does this not imply that God, in fact, is ignorant of vast stretches of forthcoming history since, as William Craig rightly contends, "even a single significant human choice could turn history in a different direction, and subsequent events would, as time goes on, be increasingly different from his expectations. At best, God can be said to have a good idea of what will happen only in the very near future."[83] And if God is ignorant of vast stretches of forthcoming history, then how can any of the predictive prophecies in Scripture be anything more than mere probabilities?[84]

In addition, given the fact that prophecies have taken place, then, given the claims of Scripture, they must necessarily come to pass and thus be true. But, once again, if one denies that God is able to know future contingents, then how does one explain how God can *know* that these prophecies will truly come to pass? Would it not be more consistent to affirm that God possibly has erred or might err on these matters? But if one were to admit that, then how would one also affirm that Scripture is an infallible and inerrant revelation on all areas that it touches, including the prophetic realm? It seems that the openness proposal faces a serious dilemma. Either reject the inerrancy of Scripture and admit that God can only give us probabilities about the future, or reject the openness proposal regarding divine omniscience for the traditional view of

---

[83] Craig, *The Only Wise God*, 39. See also Morris, *Our Idea of God*, 101; and Basinger, "Middle Knowledge and Classical Christian Thought," 409.

[84] Francis J. Beckwith, in a very helpful article ("Limited Omniscience and the Test for a Prophet: A Brief Philosophical Analysis," *JETS* 36 [1993]: 357-362) defends the same conclusion. Working from a commitment to inerrancy, Beckwith asserts that one of the tests for a true prophet is given in Deuteronomy 18:22: "If what a prophet proclaims in the name of the LORD does not take place or come true, that is a message the LORD has not spoken. That prophet has spoken presumptuously. Do not be afraid of him" (NIV). From this criterion, Beckwith forms the following argument (A):

(1) If X speaks for God about the future in any possible world, then necessarily in any possible world X is correct about the future when he speaks for God about the future.
(2) It is not the case that X is correct about prophecy Y.
(3) Therefore X does not speak for God (358).

Of course, bound up with the construal of presentism is the view that God is not able to know future contingents. As such, when it comes to predictive prophecy, it is within the realm of possibility that God could make a mistake about the future. In other words, as Beckwith notes, (a) in some possible world God makes a mistake in predicting the future (359). But once this is accepted, when (a) is applied to argument (A), we get the following result (A₁):

(1) If X speaks for God about the future in any possible world, then necessarily in every possible world X is correct about the future.
(2) In some possible world (Z), X is God and his prediction about the future is incorrect (which is a possible world for the limited omniscience defender).
(3) Therefore in some possible world God does not speak for God (359).

God's exhaustive knowledge of the future and retain the doctrine of inerrancy. At least on the surface, there seems to be no other option.[85]

Of course, many non-evangelical theologians do not have a problem with this conclusion.[86] But for many open theists who want to maintain both the doctrine of inerrancy and their view of divine omniscience, this poses a serious dilemma. Indeed, William Hasker admits that one of the major obstacles to the acceptance of their view is that of predictive prophecy. As Hasker asks, "if God does not *know* what the future will be like, how can he *tell* us what it will be like?"[87] How, then, do open theists respond? Generally, there are three responses that all center on their understanding of biblical prophecy—an understanding of which does not entail divine foreknowledge of future contingents. Let us look at each in turn to discover whether the attempt to reconcile a high view of Scripture with the openness proposal is successful or not.

First, there is a kind of conditional prophecy which does not require a detailed foreknowledge of what will actually happen since the purpose of it is to call God's people back to covenant faithfulness and repentance.[88] In fact, conditional prophecy assumes that "what is foretold may *not* happen."[89] Second, many prophecies are "predictions based on

---

[85] In fact, Pinnock seems to adopt the first option when he states: "We may not want to admit it but prophecies often go unfulfilled—Joseph's parents never bowed to him (Gen. 37:9-10); the Assyrians did not destroy Jerusalem in the eighth century (Mic. 3:9-12); despite Isaiah, Israel's return from exile did not usher in a golden age (Is. 41:14-20); despite Ezekiel, Nebuchadnezzar did not conquer the city of Tyre; despite the Baptist, Jesus did not cast the wicked into the fire; contrary to Paul, the second coming was not just around the corner (1 Thes. 4:17); despite Jesus, in the destruction of the temple, some stones were left one on the other (Mt. 24:2). God is free in the manner of fulfilling prophecy and is not bound to a script, even his own. The world is a project and God works on it creatively; he is free to strike out in new directions. We cannot pin the free God down" (*Most Moved Mover*, 51 n. 66).

[86] James Barr is a good example. He thinks the prophetic element in Scripture has been greatly exaggerated. In fact, one of his main criticisms against the traditional view of Scripture is that it has treated the Bible as only one kind of literature—prophetic literature, or what he calls the "prophetic paradigm." As such, Barr believes that the prophetic paradigm stands at the very center of the traditional view's doctrine of inspiration: the authors speak not their own words but those given them by God. Barr believes that there are two results which follow from the prophetic paradigm: (1) the prophetic paradigm is extended to all of Scripture; (2) the prophetic paradigm conveys implications of the sort of truth that must reside in Scripture—verbal, supernatural, inerrant, and infallible. See his book, *Beyond Fundamentalism* (Philadelphia: Westminster, 1984), 20-32. For a similar criticism of the traditional view, see John Barton, *People of the Book* (Louisville: Westminster/John Knox, 1988), 71. For a response to James Barr's charge, see Vanhoozer, "God's Mighty Speech-Acts," 154-156.

[87] Hasker, *God, Time, and Knowledge*, 194.

[88] Ibid. For these same three responses, see also Pinnock, "God Limits His Knowledge," 158; idem, *Most Moved Mover*, 50-53; Rice, *God's Foreknowledge and Man's Free Will*, 75-81; Sanders, *The God Who Risks*, 129-137; and Boyd, *Satan and the Problem of Evil*, 93-100.

[89] Hasker, *God, Time, and Knowledge*, 194.

foresight drawn from existing trends and tendencies" which do not require God to have foreknowledge of future contingents in order to give us predictions.[90] As Hasker reminds us, "even with our grossly inadequate knowledge of such trends and tendencies, we invest enormous amounts of energy trying to make forecasts in this way; evidently God with his perfect knowledge could do it much better."[91] An example of such a prophecy is God's prediction to Moses about the hardness of Pharaoh's heart. Richard Rice suggests that "the ruler's character may have been so rigid that it was entirely predictable. God understood him well enough to know exactly what his reaction to certain situations would be."[92] Third, many prophecies include things that are foreknown because it is God's purpose or intention to bring them about irrespective of human decision. After all, God is God, and if he intends to accomplish a certain task, he does not have to foresee it before he can know about it; he can simply declare it so, and it will be accomplished. Thus, as Richard Rice explains, "if God's will is the only condition required for something to happen, if human cooperation is not involved, then God can unilaterally guarantee its fulfillment, and he can announce it ahead of time. . . . God can predict his own actions."[93] Most of the events of redemptive history—the prediction of the incarnation, the cross, and the second coming—are all placed in this last category by open theists.[94]

Now, of course, the major question in this explanation is whether

---

[90] Ibid.

[91] Ibid., 194-195.

[92] Rice, "Biblical Support for a New Perspective," in Pinnock, et al., *The Openness of God*, 51. Pinnock adds the further point that many of these prophetic forecasts based on present situations are also quite imprecise, so imprecise that many of these prophecies go unfulfilled. Does this then mean that the prophecies were *wrong?* No, Pinnock states, "God is free in the manner of fulfilling prophecy and is not bound to a script, even his own. The world is a project and God works on it creatively; he is free to strike out in new directions. We cannot pin the free God down" (*Most Moved Mover*, 51 n. 66). But what exactly does this mean? It is hard not to think that Pinnock is attempting to find a way to maintain biblical prophecy in such a way that does not require complete accuracy.

[93] Rice, "Biblical Support for a New Perspective," 51.

[94] In regard to the cross, open theists argue that God did not foresee it; instead "he declared that it was going to happen, because he fully intended to bring it about" (Hasker, *God, Time, and Knowledge*, 195). However, open theists do not all agree on the timing of this intention. Boyd, for example, argues that "it was certain that Jesus would be crucified, but it was not certain from eternity that Pilot [*sic*], Herod, or Caiaphas would play the roles they played in the crucifixion" (*God of the Possible*, 45). Sanders, on the other hand, does not even view the cross as planned from the creation of the world. For him, it only comes about as late as Gethsemane, as Jesus wrestles with the will of his Father and comes to the conclusion that he must now go to the cross (see *The God Who Risks*, 98-104).

the above strategy will work, given the parameters of the doctrine of inerrancy. Let us look at each of the steps of this strategy in turn and ask whether it actually delivers what it promises.

First, no one denies that the prophets' role was primarily to call the covenant people back to obedience. In this regard, many prophecies were and are conditional, but certainly not all of them. For example, what about the prophecies which refer to the specific place of Christ's birth, the fact that our Lord would be virgin born, or even the fact that our Lord would ultimately be rejected and crucified? What about prophecies regarding the second advent of Christ? Certainly these are not conditional. No doubt, open theists admit that these latter kinds of prophecies, especially those centered in the coming of our Lord Jesus Christ, are not conditional. That is why they place such prophecies under category 3. But as I will argue below, I think there are some problems with this as well.

Second, the suggestion that many of the non-conditional prophecies can be explained in terms of predictions based on foresight drawn from existing trends and tendencies does not help us either. Given a libertarian view of free will, how is it that God can make any predictions based on existing trends? There is simply no way God can *guarantee* the fulfillment of any prediction, even if it is only based on existing trends and tendencies, since the agent could always do otherwise. Unless, of course, what you mean by "prediction" is that God makes guesses, conjectures, and expert hypotheses. But this is a far cry from what a high view of Scripture asserts, namely that God has made prophecies and predictions of the future and as such, he *guarantees* that they will come true.

Hasker, in fact, basically admits this fact. He argues that God's purpose and superior strategy will *not* enable him to foresee *everything* that will happen, but, he says, "the central point is that God is able to carry out his overall plan despite whatever resistance may be offered by human beings."[95] That view might be acceptable for other views of Scripture that deny inerrancy, but it is not acceptable for a view that does not. A high view of Scripture requires that unless God is able to foresee and know everything that will happen, then he cannot *guarantee* that

---

[95] Hasker, *God, Time, and Knowledge*, 196.

predictive passages of Scripture will be an *infallible* and *inerrant* revelation of his will.

In this regard it is interesting to note a footnote of Richard Rice in his article "Biblical Support for a New Perspective." In the article, Rice chides Francis Beckwith for criticizing the view of presentism in light of a single "biblical test of a prophet," namely, the ability to predict the future accurately. Rice complains that Beckwith equates an "unfulfilled prophecy" with a "false prediction" and then argues that unless a prophet is correct about the future in every possible world the prophet does not speak for God. Rice is disturbed that Beckwith ignores what he calls "the texture and complexity of biblical prophecy." Moreover, Rice goes on to state that Beckwith fails to consider other kinds of prophecy such as conditional prophecies, and as such, Beckwith presents only a one-sided picture of biblical prophecy.[96]

The problem, however, with Rice's analysis is that it misses the point. I am sure that Beckwith would agree with Rice that there are different types of prophecies in Scripture and one of those types contains conditional prophecies. But Beckwith's main intent is not to analyze "the texture and complexity of biblical prophecy," but to take a legitimate biblical criterion—a criterion, we must emphasize, that is bound up with a high view of Scripture—and to demonstrate that given the model of presentism, it is impossible to uphold this criterion. For if it is possible for God to make a mistake in predicting the future, a possibility that presentism must allow, then it is not only impossible to uphold the biblical criterion of a test of a true prophet, but it is also impossible to maintain that God can *guarantee* that his promises and predictions will come to pass. No doubt, one could still argue that it is possible that God "just happened" to predict everything correctly and that the biblical authors just happened to write everything that God wanted them to write. But that appeal is certainly quite different than asserting that God can *guarantee* that what he predicts will come true.

Third, it must be admitted that in some cases God does unilaterally act irrespective of human decision. However, there are a good number of prophecies that are neither conditional nor mere predictions based on foresight drawn from existing trends, but prophecies that are uncondi-

---

[96] See Rice's criticisms of Beckwith's article in, "Biblical Support for a New Perspective," 181 n. 76.

tional, that convey God's intentions of what will certainly occur through the means of future human choices and actions. And it is precisely in these kinds of prophecies that God most clearly demonstrates himself to be the Lord over history (see Isaiah 40–48). Certainly the major redemptive events of Scripture, such as the death of Christ, involved both the free actions of individuals to crucify Jesus and the sovereign predetermination and foreknowledge of God (see, e.g., Acts 2:23; 4:23-30).[97] It will hardly do to reduce these events either to a conditional category or merely to God's purposes and intentions irrespective of human actions. Yes, God declared that Jesus was going to die, but he also declared the manner of his death and the intricate details concerning all those humans who would freely be a part of his death in the precise fulfillment of Old Testament Scripture. In the case of the cross, it requires much more than God's general knowledge and strategies of the future. Instead it requires nothing less than God's detailed foreknowledge.[98] But how

---

[97] Boyd, *Satan and the Problem of Evil*, attempts to respond to some of these challenges, particularly the issues of the foreordination of the cross (Acts 2:23; 4:28) and predictions centered around such people as Josiah (1 Kings 13:2-3), Cyrus (Isa. 45:13), Judas (John 6:64, 70-71; 13:18-19), and Peter (Matt. 26:34). As we have already stated, Boyd appeals to his development of "neo-Molinism" and his proposal of the probationary period of libertarian freedom producing a kind of compatibilistic freedom, due to our choices, that leads to a self-determined character. Thus, for example, in terms of the cross, "*that* Jesus would be killed was predetermined. *Who* would do it was not . . . there is no contradiction in claiming that an event is predestined while affirming that the individuals who carry it out are not" (121). The problem, however, is that Acts 4:28 is much more specific than this. "They did" (*poiēsai*), that is, specific individuals mentioned in the text—Herod and Pontius Pilate—"what your power and will had predestined should happen." Furthermore, even Boyd has to admit that in a few cases, such as Josiah, Cyrus, Judas, and Peter, the prophecies are very specific indeed. How does he handle these predictions? He asserts that either God exerted "whatever influence was necessary to accomplish these tasks through these individuals" so much so that he restricted their libertarian freedom (121 n. 7), or God predestined certain acts of individuals after their characters were set in a certain direction, such as in the case of Judas and Peter (see 122-123; 130-133). But the problem with this explanation is that the individuals in question are *not* presented in Scripture as having their freedom restricted, *nor* is this explanation doing justice to the details of the text. For example, in the case of Peter, it is one thing for Jesus to say that he knows Peter will disown him because his character is solidified in a certain direction; it is quite another to predict that Peter will do it three times *and* before the rooster crows! This is much more than character assessment. This kind of prophecy is right down to the very details. And, even more, though Peter heard the prediction and denied he would do it, he did it anyway, and then after he did it, he remembered what the Lord had said. Moreover, at the conceptual level, Boyd's explanation of such texts depends upon a proposal that it is very difficult to make coherent. On this last objection see my comments in note 39.

[98] D. A. Carson states it this way: "It will not do to analyze what happened as an instance where wicked agents performed an evil deed, and then God intervened to turn it into good, for in that case the cross itself becomes an afterthought in the mind of God, a mere reactive tactic. All of Scripture is against the notion. The Biblical theology of sacrifice, the passover lamb, the specifications for *yom kippur*, the priestly/sacrificial system—all together anticipate and predict, according to the New Testament authors, the ultimate sacrifice, the sacrifice of the ultimate lamb of God. But neither will it do to reduce the guilt of the conspirators because God remained in charge. If there is no guilt attaching to those who were immediately responsible for sending Jesus to the cross, why should one think that there is guilt attaching to *any* action performed under the

can God predict such an event, given the intertwined views of libertarianism and presentism?[99]

What, then, should we conclude about the relationship between the openness proposal regarding divine omniscience and the doctrine of Scripture? Does the proposal uphold or undermine a high view of Scripture, or does it have very little impact? It would seem that the openness proposal does have some very significant implications for one's doctrine of Scripture. Two points need to be made in this regard. First, even though it is *logically* possible for someone to affirm simultaneously an openness view of divine foreknowledge and the doctrine of inerrancy by believing that God, as well as the biblical authors, "just happened" to get everything right, it is certainly highly improbable. In fact, I see no explanation forthcoming as to how open theists are able to affirm that God can *guarantee* that what he predicts will in fact come true.

Second, even if one desired to affirm the doctrine of inerrancy and open theism at this point of predictive prophecy, how would one attempt to do so? Inductively, one could not now make the affirmation that Scripture is inerrant since there would be no way to *know* until the eschaton whether God and the biblical authors just happened to get it right. Deductively, one could not now make the affirmation either since not one of us could say with assurance that God is able to *guarantee* that all of his promises and predictions will come to pass given the openness view of divine foreknowledge. Thus, even though it is logically possible to affirm open theism and inerrancy in regard to predictive prophecy, similar to its implications with the doctrine of inspiration, it is highly improbable that such a view will yield an inerrant set of passages that predict future events.

---

sovereignty of God? And in that case, of course, we do not need any atonement for guilt: The cross is superfluous and useless" ("God, the Bible, and Spiritual Warfare: A Review Article," *JETS* 42 [1999]: 263).

[99] William Craig has some helpful comments on this point. He states, "Explanation (1) [the idea that prophecy can be explained in terms of God's announcement of what he intends to do] is useful only in accounting for God's knowledge of events which he himself will bring about. But the Scripture provides many examples of divine foreknowledge of events which God does not directly cause, events which are the result of free human actions. And even in prophecies concerning God's own actions, foreknowledge of free human actions is sometimes presupposed. For example, when God speaks of using Cyrus to subdue the nations (Isa 44:28–45:1), God's intention presupposes his foreknowledge that such a person shall in fact come to exist at the proper time and place and be in a position to serve as God's instrument. To respond that God brings about all these details as well would be to deny the very human freedom which the view we are discussing wants to affirm" (*The Only Wise God*, 43-44). On some similar points, see the helpful discussions in Frame, *No Other God*, 198-203; and Feinberg, *No One Like Him*, 767-775.

IV. CONCLUDING REFLECTIONS

What, then, shall we conclude about our investigation as to the relationship between the openness proposal on divine sovereignty-omniscience and the doctrine of Scripture? I offer three brief concluding reflections.

First, open theists must seriously reconsider their proposal on the relationship between divine sovereignty-omniscience and human freedom because it leads to insurmountable problems for a high view of Scripture, particularly the doctrine of inerrancy. No doubt, the openness proposal does allow for open theists logically to affirm inerrancy even though it would be highly improbable. But more importantly, the openness proposal undermines: (1) any kind of *guarantee* that either the human authors will freely write precisely what God wanted written, or that what God predicts will in fact come to pass; and (2) a strong epistemological grounding to our belief in and defense of the inerrancy of Scripture.

Second, if open theists want to maintain and defend a high view of Scripture along with the theological underpinnings of that view, they need to surrender their open view of God.[100] I do not see how any coherent and rational defense of an inerrant Scripture can be made on the foundation of open theism.

Third, open theists should not be surprised that other evangelicals find their views unacceptable and outside the limits of biblical orthodoxy. Evangelicals are willing to think through theological matters time and time again in light of Scripture. But when proposals arise that have implications that undermine the very basis for an authoritative and inerrant Bible, it should come as no surprise that many of us will find these proposals problematic, unwarranted, and unbiblical. The price is too great. Open theism must be rejected, at least on this count: it undercuts that which is foundational to Christian theology—the sovereign, self-attesting triune God who speaks with all authority, knowledge, and wisdom, through human authors, in a true, faithful, and inerrant manner.

---

[100] On this point, see the wise observation of J. I. Packer: "The customary apologetic for biblical authority operates on too narrow a front. As we have seen, faith in the God of Reformation theology is the necessary presupposition of faith in Scripture as 'God's Word written,' and without this faith *sola scriptura* as the God-taught principle of authority more or less loses its meaning.... we must never lose sight of the fact that our doctrine of God is decisive for our concept of Scripture, and that in our controversy with a great deal of modern theology it is here, rather than in relation to the phenomena of Scripture, that the decisive battle must be joined" ("'Sola Scriptura' in History and Today," in *God's Inerrant Word,* ed. Montgomery, 60).

8

WHAT IS AT STAKE IN THE OPENNESS DEBATE?

THE TRUSTWORTHINESS OF GOD AND THE FOUNDATION OF HOPE[1]

Paul Kjoss Helseth

I. INTRODUCTION

Throughout the history of the Christian church, orthodox theologians have claimed that God is an omniscient being who has exhaustive knowledge of the whole scope of cosmic history. God's knowledge is exhaustive, they argue, because he knows all true propositions about everything that has been, is, and will be, and he does so in a manner that extends to the minutiae of past, present, and future reality. But if it is indeed true that God knows everything there is to know about the whole scope of cosmic history, then how are we to conceive of the relationship between divine omniscience and creaturely freedom? Must we conclude that human and angelic beings are less than significantly free because God knows everything there is to know about what has been, is, and will be—including the future free decisions of his creatures? Or, must we

---

[1] Selected portions of this chapter were published previously in slightly different form in Paul Kjoss Helseth, "On Divine Ambivalence: Open Theism and the Problem of Particular Evils," *Journal of the Evangelical Theological Society (JETS)* 44 (2001): 493-511. While my *JETS* article remains a valid critique of openness theologians who are consistently opposed to the viability of any form of compatibilism, it does not address more recent developments in the open view of the future, including those that have to do with what Gregory Boyd calls "neo-Molinism." This chapter represents my attempt to wrestle with Boyd's more fulsome exposition of the open view in general and the open view of evil in particular in *Satan and the Problem of Evil: Constructing a Trinitarian Warfare Theodicy* (Downers Grove, Ill.: InterVarsity Press, 2001). Portions that were published previously are used with permission.

rather acknowledge that God is less than exhaustively omniscient because morally responsible beings in fact are significantly free?

Whereas orthodox theologians have historically maintained that the perceived tension between divine omniscience and creaturely freedom can be satisfactorily explained by conceiving of omniscience in any one of several ways that neither undermine the authenticity of human and angelic freedom nor compromise the scope of God's sovereign knowledge, a number of contemporary theologians would have us believe that such conceptions no longer pass muster.[2] New interpretations of the relationship between divine omniscience and creaturely freedom are in order, they argue, not only because classical interpretations are lacking in exegetical precision but also because traditional interpretations are no longer existentially satisfying to philosophically astute theologians living at the beginning of the twenty-first century. Interpretations that see "all things as coming from God's hand"—including "all the nightmares of the world"[3]—must be rejected or at least significantly revised, these theologians argue, not only because they impose an "existential drag" on the ordinary believer,[4] but more importantly because they reduce the God of Scripture to "the enemy" of agents who might otherwise "partner" with him in actualizing his loving purposes for the created order.[5]

How, then, do these theologians suppose that we should conceive of the relationship between divine omniscience and creaturely freedom? And what, moreover, are the implications of their conception for the perennially thorny problems of moral evil and human suffering? In this

---

[2] For an overview of the various ways in which the relationship between divine omniscience and creaturely freedom can be conceived of, see John Sanders, "Mapping the Terrain of Divine Providence" (paper presented at the Wheaton Philosophy Conference, 27 October 2000); William Hasker, "A Philosophical Perspective," in Clark Pinnock, et al., *The Openness of God: A Biblical Challenge to the Traditional Understanding of God* (Downers Grove, Ill.: InterVarsity Press, 1994), 126-154; William C. Davis, "Does God Know the Future? A Closer Look at the Contemporary Evangelical Debate," *Modern Reformation* 8, no. 5 (September/October 1999): 20-25; and idem, "Does God Know the Future via 'Middle Knowledge'?" *Modern Reformation* 8, no. 5 (September/October 1999): 24-25.

[3] Boyd, *Satan and the Problem of Evil*, 163 n. 27.

[4] Clark H. Pinnock, *Most Moved Mover: A Theology of God's Openness* (Grand Rapids, Mich.: Baker, 2001), 23.

[5] Boyd, *Satan and the Problem of Evil*, 163 n. 27, 105. Boyd argues that "If God, not Satan, is behind all the nightmares of the world, then far from trusting God we should rather follow the advice of W. Robert McClelland and consider it our moral obligation to 'rage' against God as our 'enemy.' . . . From the blueprint model of providence McClelland draws the logical conclusion that God can only be understood in the midst of suffering as 'the enemy.' . . . If one grants McClelland's omnicontrolling view of God . . . everything he says about God follows" (ibid., 163 n. 27). Frankly, these kinds of comments make it rather difficult to take Boyd seriously when he says that the open view of the future "is not an issue over which Christians should divide" (ibid., 87).

chapter I examine and critique the resolutions to these questions proposed by openness theologians, and I do so through an analysis of
selected works by Gregory Boyd, the contemporary standard-bearer for
the open view of evil.[6] My thesis is that despite the creative yet remarkably conventional nature of Boyd's recent attempts to render the open
view of evil plausible, the open view remains "deeply flawed"[7] not only
because it is essentially incoherent but more importantly because it
undermines the believer's confidence in precisely that which it purports
to champion, namely the love of God for his creatures.

II. THE OMNISCIENCE OF GOD, CREATURELY FREEDOM, AND THE PROBLEM OF EVIL: THE OPENNESS SOLUTION

The Redefinition of Omniscience

Open theists insist that the perceived tension between the omniscience
of God and the freedom of contingent beings can be resolved only by
redefining the precise nature of God's omniscience. Genuine creaturely
freedom and the omniscience of God can be reconciled, they argue, only
when we acknowledge that there are some things that even an omniscient God simply cannot know. While God can know all true propositions about the past and present and can, on the basis of that knowledge
and his knowledge of his own future activity, know a good deal about
future reality, his omniscience does not extend to the details of future
reality in an exhaustive, definite fashion. Why? The following quotation
by Boyd articulates the typical answer. "In the Christian view God
knows all reality—everything there is to know. But," Boyd argues,

> to assume He knows ahead of time how every person is going to
> freely act assumes that each person's free activity is already there to
> know—even before he freely does it! But it's not. If we have been
> given freedom, we create the reality of our decisions by making
> them. And until we make them, they don't exist. Thus, in my view

---

[6] I recognize that Boyd does not speak for all open theists, and that the approach of openness theologians to the problem of evil is not monolithic. Nevertheless, as far as I can tell, Boyd is the movement's most nuanced and compelling advocate on this issue, particularly on the specific issue being addressed in this chapter. Note how even Clark Pinnock points to Boyd's work when discussing the problem of evil and the trustworthiness of God (cf. *Most Moved Mover*, 132 n. 34). For a discussion of John Sanders's view of evil, see the chapter in this volume by Mark R. Talbot.

[7] Bruce A. Ware, *God's Lesser Glory: The Diminished God of Open Theism* (Wheaton, Ill.: Crossway, 2000), 26.

at least, there simply isn't anything to know until we make it there
to know. So God can't foreknow the good or bad decisions of the
people He creates until He creates these people and they, in turn, create their decisions.[8]

Since the future is composed in part of possibilities having to do with the
free decisions of responsible moral agents, openness theologians conclude
that God's knowledge cannot extend to the minute details of future
reality simply because the free decisions yet to be made do not constitute
a part of what can be known presently. Like square circles or two-sided
triangles, future free decisions cannot be known because they simply do
not exist; they do not constitute a part of knowable reality.

The Openness Justification

But how can openness theologians justify such assertions? Why do they
suppose, in other words, that God "can't know future free actions before
they are resolved for the same reason he can't know the weight of a rock
he cannot lift"?[9] They do so, in short, for two reasons. In the first place,
they are convinced that a literal reading of Scripture leaves them with
no other alternative.[10] In an article published in the *Clarion*, the student
newspaper of Bethel College and Seminary, Boyd writes:

> The belief of mine which has caused such a stir is called "the Open
> view of God," though I prefer to call it "the Open view of the future."
> In a word, this view states that the future is not entirely settled. It partly
> consists of open possibilities. Since God knows reality perfectly, He

---

[8] Gregory Boyd, in Gregory A. Boyd and Edward K. Boyd, *Letters from a Skeptic: A Son Wrestles with His Father's Questions About Christianity* (Wheaton, Ill.: Victor, 1994), 30; cf. idem, *God of the Possible: A Biblical Introduction to the Open View of God* (Grand Rapids, Mich.: Baker, 2000), 16-17. Throughout his writings Boyd is eager to affirm that he is in no way challenging the orthodox commitment to the omniscience of God. God's knowledge, he argues, is "coterminous with reality." What Boyd *is* challenging, however, is "the ontological status of the future in the present." See, for example, Gregory A. Boyd, *God at War: The Bible and Spiritual Conflict* (Downers Grove, Ill.: InterVarsity Press, 1997), 304 n. 33. See also Clark Pinnock, "Systematic Theology," in Pinnock, et al., *The Openness of God*, 123; William Hasker, *God, Time, and Knowledge* (Ithaca, N.Y.: Cornell University Press, 1989), 73-74, 188-205; David Basinger, *The Case for Freewill Theism: A Philosophical Assessment* (Downers Grove, Ill.: InterVarsity Press, 1996), 39-40; and John Sanders, *The God Who Risks: A Theology of Providence* (Downers Grove, Ill.: InterVarsity Press, 1998), 194-200.

[9] Gregory A. Boyd, "The Open-Theism View," in *Divine Foreknowledge: Four Views*, ed. James K. Beilby and Paul R. Eddy (Downers Grove, Ill.: InterVarsity Press, 2001), 43.

[10] See A. B. Caneday's discussion in chapter 5 of this volume of how openness theologians equivocate on the word "literal."

knows the future perfectly, *just as it is;* partly as settled, partly as open. So, some things about the future are a "maybe," not a "certainty," even to God.

Why do I believe this? Because I simply can't make sense of the Bible without it. Yes, the Bible clearly reveals that God is certain of many things that are going to take place ahead of time. But the Bible also reveals that some things about the future are open possibilities, even to God.[11]

Openness theologians deny the exhaustive, definite foreknowledge of God, then, because they are convinced that faithfulness to Scripture demands it. They do so as well for philosophical reasons, for they are persuaded that traditional resolutions of the omniscience-creaturely freedom problem are untenable philosophically. Why? To begin with, openness theologians believe, much like Aristotle before them, that if the propositions that God believes about future contingents have truth-value—if, in other words, the propositions that God believes about future free actions convey what must in fact happen—then the consequence of that knowledge is fatalism.[12] The consequence, in other words, is that human and angelic beings are reduced to robots that lack the ability to engage in significantly free activity.[13] To avoid this conclusion, and to preserve the notion that morally responsible beings are truly "*self*-determining" agents, openness theologians therefore maintain that propositions about future contingents *are* neither true nor false, but rather *become* true or false when agents with self-

---

[11] "Boyd Summarizes Open View, Responds to Recent Dialogue," *Clarion: The Newspaper of Bethel College 75*, no. 4 (13 October 1999): 3. For a devastating critique of Boyd's exegesis and interpretive method, see A. B. Caneday, "The Implausible God of Open Theism: A Response to Gregory A. Boyd's *God of the Possible*," *Journal of Biblical Apologetics* 1 (2000): 66-87. Pinnock insists that the open "model" of God is "more biblical" than the traditional model (*The Openness of God*, 101-125). See also David Basinger, "Can an Evangelical Christian Justifiably Deny God's Exhaustive Knowledge of the Future?" *Christian Scholar's Review* 25 (1995): 133-145; and Richard Rice, "Biblical Support for a New Perspective," in Pinnock, et al., *The Openness of God*, 11-58. For an incisive response to Rice's contention that "*love* is the first and last word in the biblical portrait of God" (ibid., 18), see Mark R. Talbot, "God's Vocation, Our Vocation," *Modern Reformation* 8, no. 3 (May/June 1999): 15-20. Like Jonathan Edwards before him, Talbot persuasively argues that "God's 'vocation' . . . is to manifest his own glory" (ibid., 19).

[12] Cf. *Aristotle's Categories and Propositions (De Interpretatione)*, translated with Commentaries and Glossary by Hippocrates G. Apostle (Grinnell, Ia.: The Peripatetic Press, 1980), 113-117. I am indebted to Ronald Nash for pointing out the connection between Aristotle and open theism.

[13] Thus, according to the open view, classical Arminianism is just as susceptible to the charge of fatalism as is Calvinism, a point that seems lost on ostensibly "irenic" Arminians who are "open to openness."

determining freedom make free decisions.[14] Since propositions about future contingents exist only as possibilities until they are actualized through the free agency of agents possessing self-determining freedom, openness theologians conclude that it is logically impossible to know such propositions, for such propositions, being neither true nor false, are merely possible objects of knowledge and not the objects of knowledge *per se.* According to Ronald Nash, a forceful critic of open theism,

> The relevance of Aristotle's position for resolving the omniscience-[creaturely] freedom problem should be obvious. If propositions about future, free . . . actions have no truth value, then they cannot be known by anyone, including an omniscient God. God's inability to know the future should not count against his omniscience, since the power to know is constrained only in cases where there is something to know. But if no propositions about future, free actions can be true, they can-

---

[14] Boyd, *God of the Possible,* 137. Boyd is convinced that moral agents are genuinely free only when they possess *self-*determining freedom. The essential characteristic of *self-*determining freedom, he contends, is the "power to do otherwise." According to Boyd, "This conception of freedom affirms that 'given the same causal conditions, [free agents] could have chosen or done otherwise than we did.'" To put it differently, "In this view . . . the total set of antecedent causes does not determine a truly free action. While factors outside the agent are *influential* in every decision an agent makes, such factors are never *coercive* when the decision is in fact free. Thus, appealing to factors external to the agent can never *exhaustively* explain the free choice of the agent. In light of all influences and circumstances, agents ultimately *determine themselves*" (*Satan and the Problem of Evil,* 56). On the basis of this conception of freedom, Boyd argues that for freedom to be anything more than a robotic "charade," human beings must be "autonomous, self-determining, morally responsible agents" (*God of the Possible,* 134, 136). They must possess, in other words, the authentic ability "to choose between . . . possibilities" that really matter, and those choices must not be "pre-settled" in any significant sense (ibid., 122, 126). Note that Boyd is convinced that this understanding of freedom—which is based upon "the concept of indeterministic causation," the notion that an event or a decision can be caused yet not irresistibly determined or necessitated by a set of antecedent conditions (*Satan and the Problem of Evil,* 73; cf. Boyd's discussion of "A Theology of Chance," ibid., 386-393)—is supported by Scripture, reason, "our experience of ourselves as self-determining agents" (ibid., 83), and contemporary science, especially quantum mechanics. For a critical assessment of Boyd's understanding of quantum mechanics, particularly the concept of causation that informs his understanding of "the complementarity of determinism and indeterminism" (cf. ibid., 151-155); cf. John C. Beckman, "Quantum Mechanics, Chaos Physics and the Open View of God," *Philosophia Christi* 4 (2002): 203-214. Note as well that there is a significant distinction in Boyd's thought between "self-determining freedom" and "self-determined acts." "Self-determining freedom" is the same thing as "libertarian" or "incompatibilistic" freedom, and as such it is "incompatible with any form of determinism" (cf. *Satan and the Problem of Evil,* 52 n. 3, 423). The class of "self-determined acts," on the other hand, includes acts performed with "self-determining freedom" *as well as* acts that flow out of self-determined characters. It is important to note that these latter kinds of acts—those that flow out of self-determined characters—*can be foreknown and even determined by God* if God so desires. For more on this critical distinction, see the forthcoming discussion. For more on what it means to say that an agent is "*self*-determining," see note 27 below. For a brief discussion of the rather clever role that "our experience/perception" plays in Boyd's thought, see note 39 below. Finally, note how Boyd's understanding of self-determining freedom equates determinism with coercion. This point will be important in the discussion that follows.

not be the object of knowledge for anyone, including God. God cannot know the future because there is nothing for him to know.[15]

If openness theologians advance a revised interpretation of omniscience on the one hand because it allows them to maintain that agents with self-determining freedom are the ones who render "indefinite possibilities . . . into definite realities" that can be known,[16] they do so on the other because it suggests a solution to the problem of evil that they suppose absolves God of culpability for the horrendously wicked aspects of reality that offend our moral sensibilities. While classical solutions allegedly make God culpable for "the terrifying dimensions of our experience"[17] by presuming that there is "a specific providential purpose being served" even by horrifying evils, the openness solution attempts to isolate God from culpability for evil by insisting that "the ultimate cause of any particular evil is the free agent, human or angelic, who produced it."[18] Open theists are convinced that when we approach the problem of evil with the awareness that we live in "a relational cosmos" in which love "cannot be coerced" but "must be freely chosen,"[19] we recognize that evil exists because agents with self-determining freedom "have significant power to thwart God's will and inflict suffering on others."[20] According to Boyd, God rules the created order through a "sovereignty of love" rather than a "sovereignty of control," and though "the one thing he *really* wants" is for moral agents to freely choose "to participate in his triune love," that participation cannot be controlled or it will be violated and undermined by the control that brings it

---

[15] Ronald Nash, *Life's Ultimate Questions: An Introduction to Philosophy* (Grand Rapids, Mich.: Zondervan, 1999), 319.

[16] Boyd, *Satan and the Problem of Evil*, 428; cf. 126, 375.

[17] Boyd, *God at War*, 141-142.

[18] Boyd, *Satan and the Problem of Evil*, 14, 429.

[19] Ibid., 239, 52.

[20] Boyd, *God at War*, 141-142; cf. 290-293. Boyd is convinced that, "At its heart the trinitarian warfare theodicy is simply an expansion and fleshing out of the free will theodicy that Arminians have always appealed to. The question of the openness of the future, then, is an in-house Arminian discussion on how to render the freewill defense most coherent, biblical and credible" (*Satan and the Problem of Evil*, 87). On freewill theism and evil, see also Basinger, *The Case for Freewill Theism*, 87-89; Hasker, "A Philosophical Perspective," 152; idem, *God, Time, and Knowledge*, 186-205; idem, "The Necessity of Gratuitous Evil," *Faith and Philosophy* 9 (1992): 23-44; idem, "Providence and Evil: Three Theories," *Religious Studies* 28 (1992), 101-105; idem, "Suffering, Soul Making, and Salvation," *International Philosophical Quarterly* 28 (1988): 15-19; Michael Peterson, *Evil and the Christian God* (Grand Rapids, Mich.: Baker, 1982), 102-107, 122-125; Sanders, *The God Who Risks*, 251-268; and R. K. McGregor Wright, *No Place for Sovereignty: What's Wrong with Freewill Theism* (Downers Grove, Ill.: InterVarsity Press, 1996), 177-203.

about.[21] Thus, God's extending of his love is an inherently risky endeavor, for it can be and often is rejected, and it is in this rejection that evil finds its true genesis. Since "the possibility of love among contingent creatures . . . entails the possibility of its antithesis, namely, war," it follows that the possibility of evil is "implied" in God's risky decision to create a world "in which love is possible. It is, in effect, the metaphysical price God must pay if he wants to arrive at a bride who says yes to his triune love."[22]

III. MORAL CHARACTER, COMPATIBILISTIC "FREEDOM," AND THE "INFINITELY INTELLIGENT" LORD OF HISTORY

Open theism's resolution of the perceived tension between divine omniscience and creaturely freedom certainly appears to be satisfying on one level. It guarantees that a fashionable understanding of creaturely freedom will not be compromised, and it then utilizes that understanding in an attempt to isolate God from being tarnished by the problem of evil.[23] But can the proposed resolution stand careful scrutiny? In the remainder of this chapter I suggest that it cannot. Though I recognize that the following discussion is far from exhaustive, my purpose is simply to suggest that the revision put forward by openness theologians actually raises far more serious questions about the character of God than do the traditional interpretations that it claims are less than compelling.

Standard Philosophical Critiques of the Open View of the Future

The most incisive philosophical critiques of open theism that have been offered to date focus primarily on two distinct yet interrelated shortcom-

---

[21] Boyd, *God of the Possible*, 148, 134.

[22] Boyd, *Satan and the Problem of Evil*, 16-17, 52-53.

[23] Millard Erickson argues that on openness terms God is "at least partially and indirectly culpable" for the problem of evil because he chose to limit himself "by creating free human beings" (*The Evangelical Left: Encountering Postconservative Evangelical Theology* [Grand Rapids, Mich.: Baker, 1997], 106). See Boyd's response, *God of the Possible*, 135-136. This chapter builds upon yet goes beyond Erickson's critique by suggesting, among other things, that the problem of evil establishes that the God of open theism is in many respects an ambivalent and arbitrary being. Indeed, he could intervene to prevent the pain and suffering that are associated with particular evils but he does not, not because his nonintervention is governed by a larger purpose, but rather because, in the end, he just does not want to. For a critical discussion of the concept of libertarian freedom and its foundational significance to the open view of the future, see the chapter in this volume by Mark R. Talbot.

ings of the openness program. In the first place, critics contend that the solution put forward by openness theologians is not necessary to resolve the perceived tension between divine omniscience and creaturely freedom because it is possible to conceive of creaturely freedom in compatibilist terms. It is possible to conceive of creaturely freedom, in other words, in terms that recognize that God's exhaustive and even determinate knowledge of the future is compatible with genuine creaturely freedom in some significant sense.[24] As such, many critics reject open theism because openness theologians endorse an understanding of omniscience that these critics suppose has been vitiated by the conviction that genuine creaturely freedom necessitates the indeterminacy of the will, or what incompatibilists like Boyd call a "power to do otherwise."[25] While many critics would no doubt agree that God *cannot* foreknow future free actions if genuine creaturely freedom is incompatible with determinism of "any" kind,[26] they nonetheless reject the openness solution because they are convinced that foreknown actions can be both determined and genuinely free in some real sense, though beyond our full explanation. It is simply not necessary to equate genuine creaturely freedom with a libertarian understanding of the will, they argue, and thus it is wrong for open theists to argue as if it is, particularly when, as we shall see, the concept of compatibilistic freedom is gaining strange new respect in openness circles.[27]

---

[24] It goes without saying that not all incompatibilists endorse the open view. See, for example, Thomas C. Oden, "The Real Reformers Are Traditionalists," *Christianity Today* 44, no. 2 (9 February 1998): 46; Robert E. Picirilli, "Foreknowledge, Freedom, and the Future," *JETS* 43 (2000): 259-271; and William Lane Craig, "Middle Knowledge, A Calvinist-Arminian Rapprochement?" in *The Grace of God and the Will of Man: A Case for Arminianism*, ed. Clark H. Pinnock (Grand Rapids, Mich.: Zondervan, 1989; Minneapolis: Bethany, 1995), 141-164.

[25] Boyd, *Satan and the Problem of Evil*, 189. See note 14 above.

[26] Ibid., 423. According to incompatibilists like Boyd, "creaturely freedom is incompatible with any form of determinism."

[27] Please note that compatibilists do *not* concede that God is working in a coercive fashion when he moves individuals to act by moving with, rather than against, their character. Also note that compatibilists do *not* believe that God accomplishes his sovereign purposes by moving against, rather than with, the character of the acting agent. Finally, please note that compatibilists do *not* deny that human beings make free decisions, that these decisions really matter, and that they are responsible for the decisions they make. What they deny is the notion that genuine freedom necessitates the autonomy of the will. In this regard, note the distinction that compatibilists make between "self-determination" and the "self-determination of the will"; they affirm that moral agents are self-determining, but deny that the "will" itself (as if the "will" were a faculty that can operate in isolation from the "whole man") is self-determining. See, for example, Charles Hodge, *Systematic Theology*, 3 vols. (1871–1873; Grand Rapids, Mich.: Eerdmans, 1989), 2:294-295. Whereas Boyd talks about *self*-determination, what he clearly has in mind is the self-determination of the "will." This is why God's reign of love is risky; not because agents are free, but because the "will" itself is free. See, for example, *God of the Possible*, 111, 134-135. Obviously, percolating beneath the debate over open theism are many concerns relating to the issue of free will, all of which are of critical importance to evangelical theology. In this respect, it is interesting to note

If critics are convinced that the openness program is suspect in the first place because it restricts the class of genuinely free acts to those acts that presume a "power to do otherwise," they are so in the second because they are persuaded that the distinction between classes of future events that allegedly flows out of this restriction approaches incoherence. Critics contend that the distinction between a class of future events that can be known and a class of future events that cannot be known cannot be consistently maintained because it presumes on the one hand what it denies on the other.[28] It presumes that God not only can but must know *something* about future free creaturely activity, but at the same time it denies that he can in fact know *anything* about future free creaturely activity, and in so doing it renders "the biblical portrait of God as the sovereign Lord of history" virtually unintelligible.[29] "How," Nash asks, "can God know what he is going to do in the future, when God's own future acts are a response to future . . . free actions that he cannot know?"[30] Given what we have been led to believe by the advocates of open theism to date, the answer, it would seem, is that God can know what he is going to do in the future and thus can retain "significant providential control"[31] over the flow of history either because he can, after all is said and done, know at least some future contingents, or because he knows what he is going to do in the future irrespective of the genuinely free decisions of responsible moral agents.

---

that the current debate in the evangelical camp over open theism is very similar to the debate in the nineteenth century between Old and New School Presbyterians over the precise nature of imputation. In both cases, controversy over an issue that some regard as peripheral is informed by doctrinal differences that get to the heart of what it means to be an evangelical. In fact, some might go so far as to say that many of the same issues that were driving the debate in the nineteenth century are driving the openness debate today. On this possibility, see how Boyd discusses acquired character traits (*Satan and the Problem of Evil*, 122, 189-190). On the dispute between Old and New School Presbyterians in the nineteenth century and on the implications of this dispute for the character of American evangelicalism, see David Wells, "Charles Hodge," in *The Princeton Theology*, ed. David Wells (Grand Rapids, Mich.: Baker, 1989), 39-62; and George Marsden, *The Evangelical Mind and the New School Presbyterian Experience* (New Haven, Conn.: Yale University Press, 1970).

[28] The future is partly open because God cannot know with certainty the future libertarianly free decisions or actions of his creatures, and it is partly closed because God can know all true propositions about the past and present and can, on the basis of that knowledge and his knowledge of his own future activity, know some aspects of future reality.

[29] Boyd, *Satan and the Problem of Evil*, 120.

[30] Nash, *Life's Ultimate Questions*, 320-321.

[31] Boyd, *Satan and the Problem of Evil*, 130.

The Rather Dated Nature of the Standard Philosophical Critiques

Such answers can no longer be universally justified, however, because they betray an understanding of the open view of the future that must be significantly revised in light of Boyd's more fulsome exposition of the open view in his recent book, *Satan and the Problem of Evil: Constructing a Trinitarian Warfare Theodicy*. While my fellow critics and I have carefully argued that the distinction between two classes of future events cannot be sustained if the self-determining freedom of contingent beings is regarded as "an [unlimited] end in itself,"[32] what we must now consider more carefully is that openness theologians have remained more or less undaunted by our arguments because many, in fact, are willing to acknowledge the coherence of at least some form of compatibilism. Boyd, for example, is eager to affirm that God can retain "significant providential control" over the flow of history, simply because he can, in fact, have "a significant role in steering human choices."[33] But how can this be? How can theologians whose entire theological program to date seems to have been based upon a rejection of compatibilism now be willing to sanction a form of compatibilism? In the paragraphs that follow I endeavor to answer these questions by unfolding a number of Boyd's more significant arguments in *Satan and the Problem of Evil*, for these arguments represent the most ambitious and creative attempt to render the open view of the future intelligible. What the reader must note from the start is that Boyd's proposals, although not entirely new, move the openness debate into a realm heretofore unimagined by the critics of open theism.[34] For what Boyd makes clear is that the openness debate has moved beyond the question of whether or not God *can*, in fact, foreknow the future actions of responsible moral agents, to the question of the *kinds* of responsible moral actions that God, in fact, can foreknow.

---

[32] Ibid., 190. See, for example, Nash, *Life's Ultimate Questions*, 320-321; Ware, *God's Lesser Glory*, 216; and Helseth, "On Divine Ambivalence," 497-510. Note that these critiques remain valid critiques of openness theologians who are consistently opposed to all forms of compatibilism.

[33] Boyd, *Satan and the Problem of Evil*, 123. As we shall see, this steering activity can involve God's foreknowing and even determining of the future decisions and actions of responsible moral agents.

[34] It is important to note that most of Boyd's proposals in *Satan and the Problem of Evil* are not new, but involve more fulsome explanations of commitments that, in retrospect, were largely assumed in his earlier writings. For an example of an earlier discussion that is easier to understand in light of the material presented in *Satan and the Problem of Evil*, see *Letters from a Skeptic*, 41-43.

The Sovereign Lord of History and the Balanced Oversight of Established and Yet-to-Be-Established Characters

How, then, can the God of open theism retain "significant providential control" over the flow of history if it is logically impossible for him to foreknow the libertarianly free decisions of responsible moral agents? How, in other words, can his providential control of history really involve anything more than mere "guesswork about the future" if future contingents, in fact, do not exist to be known by anyone, including God?[35] The answers to these questions, as we shall shortly see, are to be found in God's balanced oversight of the kinds of activity that are associated with established and yet-to-be-established characters. While actions that flow from established characters can be foreknown and even determined, thus affording God "significant providential control" over the flow of history, those that flow from yet-to-be-established characters can be neither foreknown nor determined, for the agent who is performing them retains self-determining or libertarian freedom, and thus has "the power to do otherwise."[36]

According to Boyd, it is reasonable to suppose that when God creates moral agents, he gives each agent a "domain of irrevocable freedom"[37] and then "binds himself to interact with [them] in ways that honor that [gift of] self-determination."[38] While the extent and duration

---

[35] Boyd, *Satan and the Problem of Evil*, 123.

[36] The two kinds of activity that God weaves together into the unfolding story of history must be understood in light of what Boyd calls "neo-Molinism." In the paragraphs that follow, I discuss the affirmations of neo-Molinism that allegedly explain how God can retain "significant providential control" over the flow of history without undermining the genuine freedom that is necessary for love. For Boyd's more technical discussions of neo-Molinism, cf. ibid., 116-133; idem, "An Open-Theism Response [to William Lane Craig]," in *Divine Foreknowledge: Four Views*, ed. Beilby and Eddy, 144-148; and, "Neo-Molinism and the Infinite Intelligence of God" (paper presented at the annual meeting of the Evangelical Theological Society, Colorado Springs, 15 November 2001). Boyd's most concise definition of neo-Molinism reads as follows: "Classical Molinism . . . affirms that God has significant control over the world even though agents possess libertarian freedom because God knows what agents would do in every conceivable situation. . . . The open view substantially agrees with this position but asserts, in contrast, that God also knows what agents might do in certain situations. In otherwords [*sic*], classical Molinism errs in limiting God's counterfactual knowledge to *would*-counterfactuals instead of including *might*-counterfactuals. In the neo-Molinist view God knows what agents *might* do insofar as agents possess libertarian freedom. And God knows what agents *would* do insofar as they have received from God and through circumstances or acquired for themselves determinate characters. God knows both categories of counterfactuals as they pertain to every possible subject in every possible world throughout eternity. As in classical Molinism, God creates the world (or better, the set of possible worlds) that best suits his purposes" (*Satan and the Problem of Evil*, 425).

[37] Ibid., 182; Boyd also refers to this "domain" of freedom as an agent's "quality of freedom" (cf. 182, 428).

[38] Ibid., 183 n. 6. God's self-imposed commitment not to undermine the self-determining freedom of genuinely free agents is captured in what Boyd calls his "covenant of noncoercion" (cf. 420).

of the "domain of freedom" that is given varies from agent to agent and is thus in principle unknowable to the contingent observer,[39] what remains constant (at least in theory) is God's commitment "not to micro-control a free agent he has created" until that agent either oversteps "the parameters of the gift of freedom God has given," or "solidifies" his character through the use of his self-determining freedom.[40] Until agents with self-determining freedom either go beyond the established bounds of their domain of freedom or their free choices "become crystallized in the form of an irreversible character," God "cannot *by his own choice* coerce [or determine their] decisions."[41] Indeed, God's "integrity" demands that he "honor" the gift of self-determining freedom that he has given, for if he does not, he "undermines the authenticity of both freedom and moral responsibility," and thereby establishes that the

---

[39] Boyd is convinced that it is our ignorance of the innumerable contingent variables that condition God's interaction with the world—variables that are directly related to the inscrutable domains of freedom that he gives to every moral agent—that accounts for the apparent arbitrariness of life. "Life lacks rhyme or reason," he contends, "not because God is arbitrary . . . [but] because *our perspective on reality is so myopic.* We experience the effects but can never comprehensively discern the causes [of what happens in history]." Note that it is this appeal to creaturely ignorance that also plays a critical role in Boyd's Trinitarian Warfare Theodicy. The impenetrable mystery of evil is emphatically *"not about God's character or plan,"* Boyd contends, but about *"the complexity of creation."* There is, he argues, "an element of impenetrable mystery surround[ing] every particular contingent feature of our world. Everything ultimately influences everything else, and . . . there is an element of spontaneity at every level of being. Thus an exhaustive explanation of anything would ultimately require an exhaustive explanation of everything, and even then we would have to acknowledge that things could have happened differently. Only the omniscient God can be certain of why particular events happen precisely as they do." Since the created order is "so complex," contingent beings who "observe God's interactions with free subjects from the outside" must recognize that they "are simply not in a position to know most of the relevant facts that would explain the specifics of his interaction in any given situation." Although they can know "some of the principles on which God operates," they are largely ignorant of the innumerable contingent variables that condition his providential guidance of the world. In light of the fact that contingent beings simply cannot know everything that goes on "behind the scenes," they must trust God "despite appearances," believing that if "[they] saw what God sees, [they] would understand why God did what he did and [they] would see that he is always concerned with maximizing goodness and minimizing evil" (ibid., 386, 215-216, 216, 196, 203, 200, 204).
    Please note the rather predictable and convenient role that "our experience/perception" plays in Boyd's thought. Boyd uses "our experience/perception" to justify his take on the *coherence* of self-determining freedom (cf. ibid., 78, 83), the *incoherence* of an Augustinian understanding of sovereignty (cf. ibid., 37 n. 13), and the *untenability* of "the mechanistic, deterministic worldview of Newton" (cf. ibid., 153-155). "Our experience/perception" is completely disregarded, however, when it challenges a critical component of his theodicy. While "in our experience" God's "mode of operation certainly appears arbitrary," in reality it is not, for God is not an arbitrary being. In short, we must trust that the God of open theism is not arbitrary despite the appearance that he is (ibid., 196, 200). It goes without saying that one can only wonder what larger hermeneutical principle, if any, guides Boyd's reliance upon "our experience/perception." Without such a principle, it is reasonable to conclude that his employment of "our experience/perception" in one way and then another is ultimately informed by little more than a rather nuanced form of special pleading.

[40] Ibid., 420, 191, 188.

[41] Ibid., 427, 183 n. 6.

gift of self-determining freedom was never genuinely given in the first place.[42]

When an agent has exhausted the gift of self-determining freedom that God gave him, however, God is then "under no obligation to refrain from intervening on [that] agent's freedom,"[43] for that agent has established his free choices in the form of an "eternalized"[44] character that is "irrevocably open or irrevocably closed to God's love."[45] Indeed, it is no longer possible for that agent to be anything "other than [he is]," for his self-determining freedom, which was the "probationary means" to establishing the "kind of eternal being" he would irreversibly become, has given way to a "self-determined character"[46] that is defined in its "essence"[47] by a kind of moral orientation that is compatibilistically inclined "either for or against God."[48] Since "self-determining acts lead to a self-determined character" and "libertarian freedom [thus] becomes

---

[42] Ibid., 191, 60, 182. It is important to note that the domain or quality of freedom that the God of open theism gives to moral agents *does not extend* to those solidified character traits that are the targets of compatibilistic manipulation. While it is certainly true that the God of open theism does infuse "basic characteristics" (ibid., 128) into moral agents when he creates them, he does not "preordain" that particular individuals will have the solidified traits that render their activity certain when manipulated compatibilistically. Rather, moral agents *themselves* establish the character traits that make them susceptible to compatibilistic exploitation (ibid., 122 n. 8).

[43] Ibid., 191; cf. 171 n. 42.

[44] Boyd, *Letters from a Skeptic,* 42.

[45] Boyd, *Satan and the Problem of Evil,* 190.

[46] Ibid., 189, 188, 122 n. 8; cf. 171 n. 42.

[47] Gregory A. Boyd, "Christian Love and Academic Dialogue: A Reply to Bruce Ware," *JETS* 45 (2002): 242.

[48] Boyd, *Satan and the Problem of Evil,* 189. Boyd refers to the period of time in which agents possessing self-determining freedom are determining their *own* characters as a "probationary period" (cf. 171 n. 42, 188-189, 427). Note that during this period God cannot work in a deterministic fashion without revoking the irrevocable gift of freedom that he has given to moral agents. Note as well that during this time moral agents are determining not only their whole characters as either for or against God but also those individual character traits that eventually become the targets of compatibilistic exploitation. According to Boyd, *"We tend to become the decisions we make.* The more we *choose* something, the more we *become* that something. We are all in the process of solidifying our identities by the decisions we make. With each decision we make, we pick up momentum in the direction of that decision. . . . So it is, I believe, in every area of our lives. The more we choose something, the harder it is to choose otherwise, until we finally are solidified—eternalized—in our decision. The momentum of our character becomes unstoppable. We create our character with our decisions, and our character, in turn, exercises more and more influence on the decisions we make. It's in the nature of free, created beings, and I don't see how it could be otherwise. Life, I guess, is like the proverbial snowball rolling down the hill" (*Letters from a Skeptic,* 41-42). For confirmation that individual character traits—and not just entire characters—are solidified through the use of libertarian freedom, see, for example, Boyd's discussion of Peter's cowardice in *Satan and the Problem of Evil,* 130-133. For examples of other character traits becoming established through the use of libertarian freedom, see *Letters from a Skeptic,* 41, 42; and *Satan and the Problem of Evil,* 122-123, 188-189.

compatibilistic freedom,"[49] it follows that there are two kinds of "free" activity for which acting agents are morally responsible and which we must factor into our understanding of the open view of the future. Contingent beings are morally responsible for what they do, Boyd argues, not only when they *could* do otherwise in a particular situation given their retention of the gift of self-determining freedom but also when they *could not* do otherwise in a particular situation given the characters they acquired for themselves by the use of their self-determining freedom.[50] "We must remember," Boyd notes in a passage that is critically important for understanding his exposition of the open view,

> that moral responsibility applies to the acquired character of self-determining agents even more fundamentally than it applies to the particular decisions agents make which reflect and reinforce their character. Traditionally theologians have distinguished the character a person receives from God (*habitus infusus*) from the character they freely acquire (*habitus acquirus*) [*sic*]. *There is no contradiction in the claim that a person is morally responsible for an act even though they could not have done otherwise, so long as the character that now rendered their action certain flowed from a character they themselves acquired. It was not "infused" into them by God.* . . . *Hence, if God decides that it fits his providential plan to use a person whose choices have solidified his character as wicked, God is not responsible for this person's wickedness.*[51]

In light of the fact that morally responsible actions can be foreknown and even determined if those actions flow from self-determined characters, it follows that openness theologians like Boyd feel justified in affirming that the future is both partly open and partly closed because they view the future as an unfolding story involving God's balanced oversight of both determined and yet-to-be-determined components. Whereas the unfolding story is open and unknowable to the extent that moral agents retain

---

[49] *Satan and the Problem of Evil*, 122 n. 8. According to Boyd, it is the *self*, not God, who gives *determinateness* to character. Once this determinateness has been acquired God is then free to work compatibilistically with the agent, and to do so with integrity (cf. ibid., 375).
[50] Ibid., 392-393.
[51] Ibid., 122, emphasis added; cf. Boyd, "Neo-Molinism and the Infinite Intelligence of God," 7; and idem, "An Open-Theism Response [to William Lane Craig]," 148.

self-determining or libertarian freedom, it is settled and knowable to the extent that actions flow from self-determined characters that are allowed to act spontaneously or are manipulated compatibilistically. As the author of an unfolding story involving agents who possess self-determining freedom, God thus retains "significant providential control" over the story not only because he knows how particular moral agents with established characters will act in particular situations if the contingents of history unfold in a certain fashion. He does so, moreover, because he can, if he chooses, have a more direct role in the steering of history by interacting compatibilistically with moral agents who have solidified their own characters through the use of their self-determining freedom. Indeed, God can accomplish his loving purposes for the created order not only by pre-destining and foreknowing events without ordaining from eternity who will carry out those events, but he can also orchestrate circumstances that exploit the character traits of compatibilistically free yet susceptible moral agents so that those predestined events are actualized in time.[52] Scripture suggests, for example,

> that the Messiah's betrayal was predestined and Jesus foreknew that Judas would betray him (Jn 6:64, 70-71; 13:18-19). These contentions do not contradict the view that morally responsible, self-determining actions cannot be predestined or foreknown as long as Judas was not *in particular* chosen to carry out this deed before Judas had *made himself* into the kind of person who *would* carry out this deed. After Judas unfortunately hardened himself into this kind of person, God wove his character into a providential plan. God thus used evil for a higher good (cf. Gen 50:20). Jesus could therefore foreknow that Judas would be the one to betray him. But nothing suggests that it was God's plan *from eternity* that Judas would play this role. . . . [As such,] there is no difficulty in understanding how God could predestine and thus

---

[52] Boyd, *Satan and the Problem of Evil*, 122 n. 8. Boyd is convinced that objections to the notion that events can be ordained without ordaining the particular people who will carry out those events are ultimately based upon the presupposition of "a *mechanistic worldview*. . . . That is, if a one-to-one relationship between causes and effects is assumed, then a particular effect cannot be determined without its antecedent causes also being determined. But this assumption is not necessary. To the contrary, this assumption is at odds with the general direction most fields of science took throughout the twentieth century. In a multitude of differing ways we have discovered that reality is constituted as a balance between determinism and freedom, stable laws and chance, regularity and spontaneity, general predictability and an element of unpredictability about specifics" (ibid., 121). For a discussion of how Boyd's own assumptions might be coloring his reading of the scientific literature, cf. Beckman, "Quantum Mechanics, Chaos Physics and the Open View of God," 203-214.

foreknow that Jesus would be betrayed and crucified by wicked people without predestining or foreknowing who specifically would betray and crucify him. God orchestrated events to the extent that certain wicked people (and certain wicked spirits, Jn 13:27; 1 Cor 2:8) acted out their self-acquired characters and did what they wanted to do in conformity with his plan to have his Son betrayed and crucified. But they are still responsible for what they did, for they are responsible for the kind of agents they had freely become. God was simply employing their sinful intentions to his own end.[53]

Divine Coercion: The Key to the Continuity of History

In the end, then, openness theologians like Boyd can affirm that the future is both partly open and partly closed and that God "is intelligent and powerful enough to . . . accomplish all his objectives"[54] only because they are willing to sanction a form of compatibilism that, ironically, regards compatibilistically free acts as coerced or determined acts for which the acting agent is morally responsible. God is the sovereign Lord of history, openness theologians argue, not only because he is "an infinitely intelligent chess player" who is able "to anticipate *every* possible move and *every* possible combination of moves, together with *every* possible response he might make to each of them, for *every* possible agent throughout history."[55] He is so, moreover, because he will act unilaterally or coercively when necessary, as David Basinger says, in order "to keep things on track."[56] He will ensure that his purposes for

---

[53] Boyd, *Satan and the Problem of Evil*, 122-123. As this text makes clear, Boyd clearly endorses some form of the "greater good" argument (see also ibid., 19, 396-397). Note, however, that these "greater goods" are not ordained from before the foundation of the world, as in more traditional theodicies, but as the narrative of history unfolds; God works these "greater goods" into his providential plans in time rather than before time, as moral agents solidify their characters and thereby acquire compatibilistic freedom.

[54] Ibid., 130.

[55] Boyd, *God of the Possible*, 127.

[56] David Basinger, "Practical Implications," in Pinnock, et al., *The Openness of God*, 159; see Basinger's extended discussion of this point in, "Can an Evangelical Christian Justifiably Deny God's Exhaustive Knowledge of the Future?" 136-139. In *The Case for Freewill Theism*, 32-36, Basinger notes that while "Freewill theists believe that God does unilaterally control some things," they nonetheless insist "that God, *as a general rule*, must allow choice to be voluntary in the sense that it is free from coercive divine manipulation." In other words, God, as a general rule, must allow history to unfold without "overrid[ing] or withdraw[ing] freedom of choice" ("Can an Evangelical Christian Justifiably Deny God's Exhaustive Knowledge of the Future?" 138). On the sporadic nature of God's unilateral/coercive involvement in creaturely affairs, see also Hasker, "A Philosophical Perspective," 142; Pinnock, "Systematic Theology," 194 n. 49; and Sanders, *The God Who Risks*, 257-261. See Steven R. Tracy's incisive discussion of this point, "Theodicy, Eschatology, and the Open View of God" (paper presented at the annual meeting of the Evangelical Theological Society, Danvers, Mass., November 1999), 14-29.

the created order are accomplished, in other words, in part by acting in ways that "override or withdraw [genuine] freedom of choice," i.e., that empty future creaturely actions of their uncertain or contingent nature.[57]

IV. THE INCOHERENCE OF THE OPEN VIEW OF THE FUTURE

The Revocable Nature of the Irrevocable Gift of Self-Determining Freedom

What, then, are we to make of the willingness of openness theologians like Boyd to sanction the unilateral or coercive activity of God in the lives of particular moral agents? Does their qualified endorsement of a form of compatibilism present any serious difficulties for the rest of the openness program? In addition to undermining their stated concern for the inherently contingent nature of "genuine creaturely freedom," it presents serious difficulties, I would argue, for at least three reasons.[58] In the first place, it demonstrates that the foundational convictions of even Boyd's more fulsome exposition of the open view cannot be consistently applied to the analysis of the flow of history. Openness theologians like Boyd

---

[57] Basinger, "Can an Evangelical Christian Justifiably Deny God's Exhaustive Knowledge of the Future?" 138. Bruce Ware correctly notes that, "At the heart of the openness proposal is the desire to uphold the *real* relationship that exists between God and others" (*God's Lesser Glory*, 43). Openness theologians are convinced that real relationships are not possible when God deals with contingent beings in a compatibilistic fashion, for compatibilistic interaction, they argue, compromises genuine reciprocity by negating the freedom of the will. While committed compatibilists would certainly challenge this presumption, note that it is *not* they who have a problem with coercion, but those who insist that genuine freedom presupposes the indeterminacy of the will. Charles Hodge, for example, is by no means guilty of reducing the Spirit's sovereign work in regeneration to what John Sanders calls, in a particularly uplifting example of irenic scholarship, the "divine rape" of the soul (*The God Who Risks*, 238-240), for Hodge insists that regeneration involves a moral change that takes place "in a manner perfectly congruous to the nature of a rational and active being." It takes place, in other words, "without any violence being done to the soul or any of its laws," for the Spirit's activity, "though immediate, is not compulsive," but "'according to reason, and the natural motion of the creature; the understanding proposing and the will embracing; the understanding going before with light, the will following after with love'" ("Regeneration, and the Manner of Its Occurrence," *Biblical Repertory and Princeton Review* 2 [1830]: 255-261). In the case of a compatibilist like Hodge, therefore, the Spirit's sovereign activity in regeneration ought not be cited as evidence of what Sanders calls "nonconsensual control" (*The God Who Risks*, 238-240), for the supernatural influence by which he works in the elect both to will and to do his good pleasure "[does] the soul no more violence than demonstration does the intellect, or persuasion the heart" ("Regeneration, and the Manner of Its Occurrence," 255-261).

[58] Note that these points both echo and build upon the conclusions of scholars who are troubled by the apparently arbitrary nature of the God of open theism's unilateral activity in creaturely affairs, particularly as this activity relates to moral evil and human suffering. See especially Tracy, "Theodicy, Eschatology, and the Open View of God," 13-29; and Edward Wierenga, review of *The Openness of God*, by Pinnock, et al., in *Faith and Philosophy* 14 (1997): 248-252. See also Ware, *God's Lesser Glory*, 207-211; Erickson, *The Evangelical Left*, 105-106; and Alfred J. Freddoso, review of *God, Time, and Knowledge*, by William Hasker, in *Faith and Philosophy* 10 (1993): 105-106.

would have us believe that the future is open to God as well as to contingent beings because the "ultimate purpose [of God] includes having free agents"[59] whose self-determining freedom is "irrevocable."[60] While the God of open theism can steer agents who have established their own characters through the use of their self-determining freedom, his integrity demands that he refrain from determining the decisions of agents who have yet to establish their own characters.[61] The willingness of openness theologians to allow for God to work in a fashion that violates the self-determining freedom of moral agents jettisons the coherence of the openness program, then, for it establishes that God cannot accomplish his ultimate purpose without violating a significant component of that purpose. Indeed, it establishes that God cannot accomplish his purpose for the created order without moving beyond the realm of what we might call "soft" coercion—working compatibilistically with agents who have established their own characters—into the relentlessly robotic realm of "hard" coercion—compelling agents to do what they otherwise might not do given their retention of the gift of self-determining freedom.[62]

Consider Boyd's treatment of Peter's denial of Jesus. Boyd says, "it should be clear that this episode poses no significant problem for the open view of the future."[63] I, on the other hand, contend that it undermines the coherence of his entire program. As we have seen, openness theologians like Boyd are convinced that there is such an intimate relationship between established moral character and moral activity that when self-determined individuals are "squeezed" in the correct fashion, their behavior is not only "predictable," it is "certain."[64] It is no longer contingent, in other words, but settled because it flows out of the very nature of the acting agent, and for this reason the agent retains responsibility for performing the event. It is the exploitation of character in this particular sense, then, that Boyd suggests is manifest in the case of Peter's "divinely orchestrated lesson."[65]

---

[59] Boyd, *Letters from a Skeptic*, 47.

[60] Boyd, *Satan and the Problem of Evil*, 181-184.

[61] Remember that the domain or quality of freedom that the God of open theism gives to moral agents *does not extend* to those specific character traits that are the solidified targets of compatibilistic exploitation.

[62] Note that even if we grant that "soft" coercion is compatible with open theism, "hard" coercion still presents insurmountable difficulties for the openness program.

[63] Boyd, *Satan and the Problem of Evil*, 131.

[64] Boyd, *God of the Possible*, 33-35.

[65] Ibid., 36.

"God," Boyd argues, "knew and perfectly anticipated (as though it was the only possible outcome) that if the world proceeded exactly as it did up to the point of the Last Supper, Peter's character would be solidified to the extent that he would be the kind of person who would deny Christ in a certain situation. . . . On the basis of this knowledge and his sovereign control as Creator, God decide[d] at some point to providentially ensure that just this situation would come about,"[66] and then actualized the event by orchestrating "highly pressurized circumstances" that "squeezed" Peter's cowardly character out of him three times.[67]

Even if we grant, for the sake of argument, that what we are calling "soft" coercion is compatible with the foundational assumptions of the openness program,[68] the case of Peter's denial of Jesus still presents insurmountable difficulties for the openness program because it establishes, despite what openness theologians like Boyd would have us believe, that the God of open theism is willing to violate the self-determining freedom of contingent beings in order to bring about states of affairs that he really wants to bring about. Remember, openness theologians insist that when God creates moral agents, he gives each agent the gift of self-determining freedom "and binds himself to interact with [them] in ways that honor that [gift of] self-determination."[69] In other words, he covenants not to "coerce [their] decisions" until they have "spent"[70] their gift of self-determining freedom and their self-determined decisions have given way to a self-determined character that is compatibilistically free and inclined either for or against God.[71] What Boyd's

---

[66] Boyd, *Satan and the Problem of Evil*, 131. Boyd's comments on character solidification in this quotation are vague. When he says, "solidified to the extent that," does he mean "irreversibly" established and "permanently" or "unalterably" acquired (ibid., 189)? Or, does he really mean something less than "irreversibly" established and "permanently" or "unalterably" acquired? If "solidified to the extent that" really means something less than *really* "solid," then how are we to avoid the conclusion that we are all compatibilistically free, even with regard to those character traits that have yet to be "permanently" fixed or settled? Are not *all* of our character traits solidified to one extent or another? What, then, does it really mean to say that a character trait is solidified "to the extent that" it serves as a legitimate candidate for compatibilistic exploitation, particularly when that character trait changes when it is manipulated compatibilistically?

[67] Boyd, *God of the Possible*, 35-37.

[68] For a thoughtful analysis of "neo-Molinism" that refuses to grant that compatibilism and open theism are compatible in any way, see the chapter in this volume by Bruce A. Ware.

[69] Boyd, *Satan and the Problem of Evil*, 183 n. 6.

[70] Ibid., 183 n. 6, 191; cf. 171 n. 42.

[71] Cf. ibid., 122 n. 8, 189. Again, the domain or quality of freedom that the God of open theism gives to moral agents *does not extend* to those character traits that are the solidified targets of compatibilistic exploitation. The God of open theism, in other words, does not "preordain" that certain individuals will have the solidified traits "that would render some of their behavior certain" (ibid., 122 n. 8), for moral agents acquire those traits for *themselves* through the use of their libertarian freedom.

treatment of Peter in fact establishes, however, is that God worked coercively with Peter *before* Peter's character became "crystallized in the form of an irreversible character."[72] Indeed, Boyd contends that God's compatibilistic manipulation of Peter was the "loving but necessarily harsh" means by which Peter's character "was permanently changed,"[73] thereby conceding that Peter's character was never irreversibly established or "eternalized" in the first place.[74] What the case of Peter really suggests, then, is both the coherence of a more full-bodied form of compatibilism—one that recognizes that genuinely free actions can be foreknown and even determined even if the character of the acting agent has yet to be "solidified" or "established"—and the utter untrustworthiness of the God of open theism. Since the God of open theism coerced Peter *before* Peter's character was "unalterably"[75] acquired, it is reasonable to conclude that the God of open theism is a covenant breaker who could accomplish his purposes only by revoking the "irrevocable" gift of self-determining freedom that he gave to Peter.

The God of Open Theism: The Occasional Author of Sin

In the second place, the willingness of openness theologians to allow for God to work in a coercive fashion makes it much more difficult for them to maintain consistently that "the ultimate cause [and explanation] of any particular evil is the free agent, human or angelic, who produced it."[76] Consider again Boyd's treatment of Peter's denial of Jesus. The case of Peter establishes that the God of open theism does in fact know what particular moral agents will do in the future, for he *knew* that Peter would betray Jesus if his character were "squeezed" in the correct fashion. God, Boyd tells us, "saw past Peter's false bravado and *knew* the effect Jesus' arrest would have on him."[77] In light of the fact that God "squeezed" Peter *before* Peter's character was irreversibly established, Boyd must either concede that the "God of the possible" can know what openness theologians contend it is logically impossible to know, namely

---

[72] Ibid., 427.
[73] Ibid., 133, 132.
[74] Boyd, *Letters from a Skeptic*, 42; cf. *Satan and the Problem of Evil*, 122 n. 8, 132.
[75] Ibid., 189.
[76] Ibid., 429.
[77] Boyd, *God of the Possible*, 36, emphasis added.

the future free decisions of agents possessing self-determining freedom, or he must acknowledge that God *knew* what Peter would do because God *knew* that he would orchestrate circumstances that would *compel* Peter to betray Jesus, in which case God forced Peter to sin.

While the critic might respond that such an acknowledgement would undermine the foundational assumptions of the openness program, open theists like Boyd apparently do not share this concern, for this is precisely the kind of acknowledgement he appears to make in his remarkable discussion of Genesis 45:5 and 50:20. Of these passages, Boyd argues that he is "largely in agreement" with compatibilists who insist that this text "illustrate[s] that God ordains evil actions for greater good."[78] The passage "seems to indicate," he concedes, "that God intentionally orchestrated the evil intentions of the brothers in order to get Joseph into Egypt."[79] But while Boyd agrees with compatibilists "that this text shows that God *may decide* to orchestrate evil actions according to his sovereign will, [he] den[ies] that this passage supports the conclusion that *all* evil actions occur in accordance with God's eternal, sovereign will."[80] Why? Of the three reasons that Boyd cites in his discussion of these texts, the second is most relevant to the question of who is ultimately responsible and therefore culpable for the evil actions that God actualizes through compatibilistic interaction. If we take Genesis 45:5 and 50:20 "as evidence of how God always operates," Boyd argues,

> we must accept the consequence that this passage always minimizes the responsibility of human agents. This is the conclusion Joseph himself draws from his observation that God used his brothers to send him to Egypt. "Do not be distressed, or angry with yourselves," he tells them, "for God sent me." If this text is taken as evidence of how God *always* controls human action—if God is involved in each kidnapping and murder the way he was involved in the activity of Joseph's brothers—we must be willing to console every murderer and kidnapper with Joseph's words: "Do not be distressed, or angry with yourself . . . for God kidnapped and murdered your victims." We cannot universalize

---

[78] Boyd, *Satan and the Problem of Evil*, 396.
[79] Ibid.
[80] Ibid., 397.

the mode of God's operation in this passage without also universalizing its implication for human responsibility.[81]

When we consider Peter's "divinely orchestrated lesson" in light of this rather strained caricature of compatiblism,[82] we are, it seems, left with two options, neither of which speaks very highly of the openness program: Either God *knew* that Peter would deny Jesus because he *knew* a future contingent (which for an open theist is a bit like saying that God can make a square circle), or, more likely, he *knew* that Peter would deny Jesus because he *knew* that he would remove Peter's self-determining freedom and *make* him deny Jesus (which calls God's sinless perfection into question, given the presumption that genuine creaturely freedom is incompatible with any form of determinism). What the case of Peter establishes, then, is that openness theologians can rescue God from the charge of being the author of coerced sins only by advancing the *ad hoc* hypothesis that some instances of compatibilistic activity—even some that involve what we referred to earlier as "hard" coercion—are intransitive. Apparently, in some cases, causing or determining an event does not entail responsibility for the event.

The God of Open Theism: An Ambivalent and Arbitrary Warrior

Finally and most importantly, the willingness of openness theologians to sanction coercion is problematic because it makes it much more difficult to rescue God from being tarnished by the problem of evil. Why? Before we consider the utterly vacuous nature of the open view of evil in the forthcoming section, note that openness theologians would have us

---

[81] Ibid., 396-397.

[82] Compatibilists endorse the doctrine of "concurrence" and thus believe that the same event is both fully caused by God and fully caused by the creature who performed it. Although the divine and creaturely causes "work in different ways," the doctrine nonetheless affirms "that God *directs*, and *works through*, the distinctive properties of each created thing, so that these things themselves bring about the results that we see. In this way, it is possible to affirm that in one sense events are fully (100 percent) caused by God and fully (100 percent) caused by the creature as well" (Wayne Grudem, *Systematic Theology: An Introduction to Biblical Doctrine* [Grand Rapids, Mich.: Zondervan, 1994], 319). Boyd, however, appears to believe that when God is active, the agent is passive, and when the agent is active, God is passive. Thus he conceives of responsibility like a pie; the more pieces God gets, the less the agent has, and *vice versa*. Note that if what Boyd says elsewhere about the moral responsibility of agents who have allegedly acquired compatibilistic freedom is to be believed (cf. Boyd, *Satan and the Problem of Evil*, 122-123), this caricature of compatibilism ironically supports the contention that Peter's character was *not* irreversibly established when God forced him to betray Jesus.

believe that their view of evil is superior to classical views not only because it helps us understand that evil in general and specific evils in particular are simply the unfortunate consequences of free decisions to reject the love of God, but also because it helps us understand why "the all-powerful Creator of the world" does not prevent certain events "he wishes would not take place."[83] Whereas classical views presume that there is "a *specific* divine reason for each *specific* evil in the world" and that all evils thus occur because they are part of an inscrutable divine plan, the open view insists that certain evils occur because God simply cannot with integrity prevent them without revoking the irrevocable gift of freedom that is necessary to love.[84] Indeed, while it is certainly true that the God of open theism is always doing everything he can "to further good and hinder evil," what he in fact can do in each particular situation is "determined" less by what "God would desire" than it is by the "innumerable [contingent] variables that constitute the 'givens' of [that] situation."[85] God can prevent some evils but not others, in short, neither because he lacks omnipotence nor because he is an inherently arbitrary being, but because the "nonnegotiable givens" of some situations prevent him from intervening in a fashion that does not compromise "the domain of irrevocable freedom that he has given to agents."[86] Thus, since it is impossible for contingent beings to know all of the variables that impact God's interaction with free agents in various situations,[87] they must simply trust that he is always doing everything he can to maximize good and minimize evil "given the situation he must work with."[88] They must trust,

---

[83] Ibid., 16.

[84] Ibid., 429; cf. 16, 423.

[85] Ibid., 203, 391, 392, 389 n. 3; cf. 212-213, 232-233. "The metaphysical principles that condition God's interaction with free agents . . . together with all the particular decisions and chance occurrences that influenced history to arrive at just this situation, constitute the 'givens' of a particular situation. The givens constitute that which God is up against in responding to a situation" (ibid., 422).

[86] Ibid., 196, 231. One of the key differences between open theism and process thought is found at this point. While the God of process theism "can *only* act in response to decisions of free agents and he must respond in accordance with metaphysical principles governing both him and creation," the God of open theism can intervene in a unilateral fashion if that intervention will not compromise the restrictions that he has placed on himself. Thus, whereas in process thought God exerts "the same influence at all times and in all places," in the open view of the future God can work in an exceptional fashion if he decides that he can do so in a particular situation with integrity, i.e., without undermining the self-determining freedom that he has given to moral agents (ibid., 229).

[87] Cf. ibid., 196-197.

[88] Ibid., 422, cf. 196; 204, 212-213.

in other words, "that when the Father tolerates wickedness, he does so out of his integrity. When he puts an end to it, he does this out of his integrity as well. Whatever good he can do, he does. Whatever evil he can prevent, he prevents. Whatever he must out of integrity allow, he allows."[89]

What, then, are we to make of the assertion that God can intervene to prevent evil in some cases but not in others because his integrity prevents him from compromising the "say-so" that is "the key to morally responsible personhood"?[90] Can we really rescue God from being tarnished by the problem of evil simply by insisting that he intervenes in one situation and not in another because "the complex constellation of contingent variables that collectively constitute a particular situation" allows him to intervene without rendering the gift of self-determining freedom "disingenuous"?[91] What I intend to establish in the remainder of this chapter is that we cannot. Since God can and does work unilaterally from time to time to bring about certain states of affairs, and since this coercive involvement can entail, as it did in the case of Peter, real violations of the gift of self-determining freedom given to moral agents, we simply cannot say that God is always doing "all he could do"[92] to prevent evil and promote good when what he is doing falls short of a violation of the covenant that he has established with free agents. Recall again that God worked compatibilistically with Peter *before* Peter's character was unalterably acquired, thus establishing that covenant infidelity is an option available to the God of open theism.[93] But how and on what basis does the God of open theism decide when he is going to violate his covenant vows? How does he determine, in other words, which aspects of the future he is going to leave open and which aspects he is going to close when the stated mechanism for making this determination does not obtain in all circumstances? Without a satisfactory answer to these questions—which, I submit, open-

---

[89] Ibid., 200. On the very real likelihood that Boyd's employment of "our experience/perception" ultimately reduces to a sophisticated form of special pleading, see note 39 above.

[90] Ibid., 232-233.

[91] Ibid., 422, 215.

[92] Ibid., 214.

[93] That the God of open theism violated his covenant of noncoercion with Peter is established by the fact that Peter's character in fact *did* change; God's coercion of Peter was the means by which Peter became a "new" man, "a man willing to lay down his life for the lambs the Master entrusted to him" (ibid., 133). Note that this conclusion is sound only because the domain or quality of freedom that the God of open theism gives to moral agents *does not extend* to those character traits that are the solidified targets of compatibilistic interaction. It is sound, in other words, only because the God of open theism did *not* ordain before the foundation of the world that certain individuals would have the solidified character traits that would render some of their activity certain.

ness theologians simply *cannot* coherently provide—we can only conclude that the God of open theism is an ambivalent and arbitrary warrior who cannot be trusted to rule in every situation in a way that maximizes good and minimizes evil for his creatures.

V. THE OPEN VIEW OF EVIL: UTTERLY VACUOUS

The Open View of Evil Summarized

In his book *God of the Possible,* Boyd sets up the problem of evil and the resolution proposed by openness theologians by revisiting a question that he addressed in one of his earliest works, *Letters from a Skeptic:*[94]

> A number of years ago, my agnostic father and I were conversing by letter about the problem of how an all-good, all-powerful God could allow nightmarish suffering to occur in his creation. In one correspondence, my father asked me why God would allow Adolf Hitler to be born if he foreknew that this man would massacre millions of Jews. It was a very good question. The only response I could offer then, and the only response I continue to offer now, is that this was not foreknown as a certainty at the time God created Hitler.
>
> If you claim that God foreknew exactly what Hitler would do and created him anyway, it's hard to avoid the conclusion that the world must somehow be better with Hitler than without him. Think about it. If God is all good and thus always does what is best, and if God knew exactly what Hitler would do when he created him, we must conclude that God believed that allowing Hitler's massacre of the Jews (and many others) was preferable to his not allowing it. If you accept the premises that God is all good and that he possesses exhaustively settled foreknowledge, the conclusion is difficult to avoid.[95]

While Boyd acknowledges that "the classical theology of the church has not shied away from this conclusion," he makes it clear that it is a conclusion he cannot endorse because it places the onus for evil on God rather than on "the nature of free will."[96] In his thinking, the open view presents a more promising solution to the problem of evil because it "allows us to say consistently in unequivocal terms that *the ultimate*

---

[94] Cf. Boyd, *Letters from a Skeptic,* 21-48, especially 29-31.
[95] Boyd, *God of the Possible,* 98-99.
[96] Ibid., 99.

source for all evil is found in the will of free agents rather than in God."[97]
Evil incidents occur, he argues, not because they were ordained by a God
of "dubious character" for some ultimately good but mysterious purpose, but rather because "Humans and fallen angels can—and do—
thwart God's will for their own lives and interfere with God's will for
others."[98] Although Boyd acknowledges that the open view of evil might
seem "scary" to some,[99] he nonetheless insists that it is more comforting than classical views not only because it declares that God is an
"unambiguously loving" being who is able to bring "a redemptive purpose" out of even the vilest of circumstances, but more importantly
because it affirms that God can anticipate evil and do something about
it.[100] What can he do? Among other things, he "can be trusted to inspire
us to avoid certain future possibilities he sees coming."[101] He can, in
other words, "sovereignly alter what otherwise would come to pass" by
working with us "to truly change what *might* have been into what
should be."[102] "Only if God is the God of what *might be* and not only
the God of what *will be*," he insists, "can we trust him to steer us away
from what *should not be* and in the direction of what *should be*."[103]

The God of Open Theism Cannot Be Rescued from the Problem of Evil

But if it is indeed true that "the 'God of the possible' is prepared for and
capable of responding to every contingency, however improbable, that
might arise,"[104] and if it is also true that God reserves the right to coerce
the wills of contingent beings despite the "givens" that obtain in particular situations, then how can we rescue God from the problem of evil
when the prevention of evil is within his power and there is sufficient

---

[97] Ibid., 102, emphasis added. It is not immediately clear how this statement can be reconciled with Boyd's comments on Genesis 45:5 and 50:20.

[98] Ibid., 156, 147.

[99] Ibid., 153. "It's true," Boyd concedes, "that according to the open view things can happen in our lives that God didn't plan or even foreknow with certainty (though he always foreknew they were possible). . . . This, it must be admitted, can for some be a scary thought."

[100] Ibid., 153, 155, 152.

[101] Ibid., 152.

[102] Ibid., 152, 18.

[103] Ibid., 153. This is an example of another comment from an earlier publication that is easier to understand in light of Boyd's more fulsome exposition of the open view in *Satan and the Problem of Evil*.

[104] Boyd, *God of the Possible*, 169.

precedent for his unilateral activity?[105] Take the example of the
Holocaust. If God in fact knew "from all eternity"[106] that the Holocaust
would become reality if particular states of affairs were actualized at significant points in the outworking of history, then why did he not work
his providential wonders at those moments to prevent the Holocaust
from becoming reality, especially when the horrors of the Holocaust
would in no way advance the realization of his loving purposes? Why,
for example, did God allow the German high command to appoint
Alexander von Kluck to the generalship of the German First Army just
prior to the outbreak of the First World War? According to political
philosopher Frances Fukuyama, who argues that, "The great events that
shape our time often spring from very small causes that one could easily imagine having happened differently," it was von Kluck's "hapless"
leadership in the first battle of Marne (September 1914) that led to the
conflict that is now known as World War I.[107] Had the German First
Army been commanded by a different general, or had von Kluck
attempted to take Paris by sweeping around the French left rather than
around the French right, it is entirely possible, Fukuyama contends, that
the history of the twentieth century would have unfolded in a radically
different fashion. It is within the realm of possibility, he argues, that had
the Germans been victorious in the first battle of Marne, the First World
War would not have occurred, and the historical circumstances that gave
rise to Hitler, National Socialism, and thereby to much of the unfath-
omable suffering of the twentieth century, would never have been actualized. "It is worthwhile thinking through," Fukuyama maintains in
what he acknowledges is an ultimately meaningless exercise in historical speculation,

> what might have happened had the Germans won in early September.
> They most likely would have swept on to Paris by the end of the

---

[105] Again, remember that God coerced or rendered Peter's activity certain *before* Peter's character
was irreversibly established. This is significant because the "givens" that obtain in particular
situations *include* the "metaphysical principles" that "condition" God's interaction with contingent
beings (Boyd, *Satan and the Problem of Evil*, 422). Among these "metaphysical principles" is God's
covenant promise *not* to intervene in the free activity of responsible moral agents until those agents
have established their *own* characters as either for or against God. Obviously, the case of Peter calls
the negotiability of this "nonnegotiable given" into question since he was not eternalized as a
particular kind of person when God manipulated him compatibilistically.
[106] Boyd, *God of the Possible*, 127.
[107] Frances Fukuyama, "It Could Have Been the German Century," *The Wall Street Journal* (31
December 1999), A10.

month, forcing a capitulation by the French government (as happened in the Franco-Prussian War of 1870-71, and again in May 1940). A quick German victory would have left unimpaired the cultural self-confidence of 19th-century European civilization. The 8.5 million casualties of World War I would not have spawned a radical revolutionary movement in Russia called Bolshevism. With no German humiliation there would have been no occasion for rabble-rousing on the part of an unemployed painter named Adolf Hitler, and therefore no National Socialism. . . . [Moreover,] no Russian Revolution and Nazism means there would have been no World War II, no Holocaust, no Cold War and no Chinese or Vietnamese revolutions. Decolonization and the emergence of the Third World might have taken place much later absent the exhaustion of the British Empire after two world wars and the rise of radical revolutionary movements in Eurasia. And the U.S., which came of age as a great power due to the world wars, may have remained the isolationist paradise fondly remembered by Patrick Buchanan.[108]

So what is the point? It is simply that openness theologians should not presume to have anything approaching a solution to the problem of evil until they have wrestled with the implications of God's alleged willingness to intervene in human history in a coercive fashion.[109] If God in fact knows all possibilities exhaustively and eternally, and if God in fact is willing to intervene coercively in human history in "soft" and even "hard" fashions despite his covenant promise not to compromise the self-determining freedom of moral agents, then God could have prevented untold suffering in the twentieth century alone had he merely been inclined to act on a particularly fragile fault line of history (which he knew was fragile because of his exhaustive knowledge of the present and of all future possibilities). Had he simply ensured that a different commander was appointed to the generalship of the German First Army, or had he merely "squeezed" von Kluck into sweeping left rather than right, it is conceivable, at least to political theorists like Fukuyama, that the twentieth century could have been the German and not the American century, a century without the Holocaust, without the torture

---

[108] Ibid.

[109] Hasker has the integrity to acknowledge that "some difficulty" for the open view of evil "still remains so long as we hold that God had the power to intervene to prevent these evils but did not do so" ("A Philosophical Perspective," 198 n. 50).

of little girls by Nazi storm troopers, and without the ethnic and ideo-
logical purges of tyrants like Stalin, Mao Tse-tung, and Pol Pot.[110]

Given God's exhaustive and eternal knowledge of all possibilities,
and given his willingness to act unilaterally in human affairs when it
accords with his purposes, I would therefore suggest that if the problem
of evil is a problem for anybody, it is a problem for those who insist that
it is acceptable for God to coerce the will in order to "keep things on
track," but who do not seem to appreciate that it is precisely God's
alleged willingness to coerce the will when he wants to that makes his
reluctance to do so in the cases of the German high command and von
Kluck so damning. Not only does his ignorance of future reality empty
pain, suffering, and evil of purpose and meaning, but his reluctance to
prevent the pain and suffering that he has always known was possible
raises questions about the love of God that are far more serious than any
of the questions that can be directed against compatibilists.[111] Why?
Because when push comes to shove, people suffer in the open view neither because the gift of self-determining freedom is "irrevocable" nor
because their suffering was ordained from before the foundation of the
world for a greater good, but rather because God simply was not
inclined to intervene at a particular point in the historical past or present. Like the pampered child whose every move is motivated by the
whims of self-interest, he could have intervened to prevent the suffering
that breaks his heart, but he did not, not because his nonintervention
was governed by a larger, albeit mysterious, purpose, but rather because
he, well, just did not feel like it.

---

[110] While it is certainly true that responsibility for horrendous evils like the Holocaust is
"widespread," since, "Evil on a grand scale always involves cooperation on a grand scale," it is also
true that the God of open theism could prevent these evils if he really wanted to not only because he
is willing and able to steer agents who possess compatibilistic freedom but more importantly because
this steering activity can involve, as it did in the case of Peter, real violations of the gift of self-
determining freedom given to responsible moral agents. Since God has both the wherewithal and the
willingness to do to all agents involved in a particular evil or set of evils what he did to Peter, the
attempt to absolve God of responsibility for horrendous evils by pointing to the "shared nature of
moral responsibility" (Boyd, *Satan and the Problem of Evil*, 174) simply will not wash.

[111] For an examination of how compatibilists deal with the problem of pain, cf. D. A. Carson, *How
Long, O Lord? Reflections on Suffering and Evil* (Grand Rapids, Mich.: Baker, 1990); idem,
"How Can We Reconcile the Love and the Transcendent Sovereignty of God?" in *God Under
Fire: Modern Scholarship Reinvents God*, ed. Douglas S. Huffman and Eric L. Johnson (Grand
Rapids, Mich.: Zondervan, 2002), 279-312; John M. Frame, *The Doctrine of God*, A Theology
of Lordship (Phillipsburg, N.J.: Presbyterian & Reformed, 2002), 119-182; and John S. Feinberg,
No One Like Him: The Doctrine of God, Foundations of Evangelical Theology (Wheaton, Ill.:
Crossway, 2001), 625-796; and Mark R. Talbot's chapter in this volume.

The Problem of Particular Evils

It follows, therefore, that the God of open theism is not only an ambivalent being, but he is an arbitrary being as well, for without "a specific divine purpose for every specific event"[112]—without, in other words, what Boyd derisively calls the "cruel" and "ridiculous" notion of an "all-encompassing divine blueprint"[113]—there can be no rhyme or reason to his unilateral activity. Please note that I am not suggesting that the God of open theism is universally or globally arbitrary. I recognize that according to the open view, evil exists (at least in theory) not because God never feels like intervening in human affairs but rather because his decision to create a universe populated with free agents who have the ability to thwart his loving purposes necessitates that he do nothing to compromise the self-determining freedom of the will. Thus, I recognize that in one sense it really does not matter what God feels like doing, for his nonintervention is required by the nature of the sovereignty that he has chosen to exercise.[114] But the fact remains that the God of open theism is willing to violate the self-determining freedom of contingent beings in order to bring about states of affairs that he really wants to bring about, and this fact presents a serious challenge to the open view of evil. Why? Because it suggests that *particular* evils cannot be accounted for solely by appealing to the self-determining freedom of wicked moral agents, for the genuine freedom that is presumed to be the ultimate source of evil can be overridden by the unilateral activity of God when he so desires. What I am suggesting, therefore, is that without an exhaustive plan that determines which particular evils will be tolerated and which ones will not be, God's toleration of one particular evil and not another becomes entirely arbitrary. To put it differently, without an "overarching divine purpose"[115] and plan that

---

[112] Boyd, *God of the Possible*, 99.

[113] For example, see Boyd, *God at War*, 43, 302 n. 18.

[114] Ware correctly notes that, "The sense in which the God of open theism is 'unable to intervene' . . . must be understood clearly. For openness proponents, surely God *could* intervene if he wished to violate creaturely freedom. And this is always the case. But the fact that God has chosen to create creaturely libertarian freedom and to respect its use leaves him in a position in which the integrity of that very freedom is jeopardized by his interference with it. The minute God starts to micromanage human affairs by canceling either the exercise or consequences of libertarian freedom in an ad hoc manner, the whole structure of his 'creation project' is imperiled. For this reason, God puts himself in the position where he accepts massive amounts of immoral and despicable, even fully pointless and gratuitous, free creaturely choices (witness the Holocaust, for example) in which he is 'unable to intervene' and still honor the freedom he has bestowed on his creation" (*God's Lesser Glory*, 197 n. 3; see also 56 n. 33).

[115] Boyd, *God of the Possible*, 153.

establishes when his intervening mercies will be extended and when they will be withheld, his extension of those mercies becomes subject to the vicissitudes of the moment, and suffering—i.e., the result of the instantaneous decision to withhold intervening mercies—becomes truly pointless. While openness theologians would have us believe that they have a viable solution to the problem of evil in *general*, they in fact can only hope that those who have been traumatized by *particular* evils do not find out that their troubles could have been prevented if God had simply been inclined to act in their case as he often does in others, namely coercively.[116]

VI. CONCLUSION: THE GOD OF OPEN THEISM IS A COSMIC SUGAR DADDY

D. A. Carson has wisely counseled that when all is said and done we must acknowledge that there is mystery in the problem of evil. We must acknowledge, in other words, that the problem of evil is beyond our capacity to understand exhaustively because God is beyond our capacity to understand exhaustively. He concludes, therefore, that we must repudiate any attempt to resolve the problem of evil in a manner that either compromises God's nature or undermines his sovereign purpose to work all things—including evil—for the good of his children and the glory of his name.[117] While some with openness leanings will no doubt insist that Carson's counsel is evidence of nothing less than "a piously confused way of thinking,"[118] we must ask what the alternative is. If nothing else, when we consider the pain and suffering that exist in the world in light of the willingness of the God of open theism to work coercively in order to bring about states of affairs that he really wants to bring about, it becomes immediately clear that the God of open theism cannot really be trusted. For he is little more than a cosmic sugar daddy whose affections are now hot and now cold, but never constant. He wants loving relationships with his creatures and to that end he reigns through a "sovereignty of love" rather than a "sovereignty of control."

---

[116] Note that this is an aspect of God's sovereignty that Boyd apparently did not discuss with "Suzanne" (ibid., 103-106). A whole new line of questioning would have presented itself to her if she had only realized that God could have ensured that her marriage was preserved and her suffering averted if that was the state of affairs that he really wanted to see realized. On pointless evil and suffering, see ibid., 98-103, 135-136, 153-156; and Sanders, *The God Who Risks*, 262.

[117] D. A. Carson, "God, the Bible and Spiritual Warfare: A Review Article," *JETS* 42 (1999): 267-268.

[118] Boyd, *Letters from a Skeptic*, 47.

But in the end his reign is administered only haltingly, for not all of his creatures are the recipients of his intervening mercies. While openness theologians would have us believe that the open view of evil offers "a psychological, as well as theological, benefit,"[119] the very opposite seems to be the case. After all, there is nothing particularly reassuring about a being who could prevent the pain and suffering that he claims to hate but who does not prevent it, either because he is not a good enough chess player, or because he is, at bottom, an untrustworthy being who is indifferent to the plight of his creatures. It goes without saying, then, that an arbitrary God who cannot be trusted to honor his covenant promises and whose very actions (or lack thereof) undermine the foundation of the believer's hope, is not the God of the Bible, but an illegitimate imposter who should be rejected by those who recognize that nothing—especially an implied character flaw in the one in whom "there is no variation or shadow of turning" (James 1:17, NKJV)—"shall be able to separate us from the love of God which is in Christ Jesus our Lord" (Rom. 8:39, NKJV).

---

[119] Basinger, "Practical Implications," 171.

9

WHAT IS AT STAKE IN THE OPENNESS DEBATE?
THE GOSPEL OF CHRIST[1]

Bruce A. Ware

The gospel of Jesus Christ may be summarized as follows: God, in eternity past, foresaw the future sin and consequent just damnation (apart from his grace) of the human race that he would create, and he planned then and there to save lost, helpless, and hopeless sinners. Though all deserved his eternal condemnation, he graciously chose people who would comprise a great host—it would include, in the end, men and women from every tribe, tongue, people, and nation!—and he set out, in love, to save them from their sin. To accomplish their salvation, he chose his very own Son to enter human existence as the incarnate God-man, to live a perfect life, and to offer himself as a sinless sacrifice for the sins of others, paying the penalties that each of them owed as their sin was imputed to him in his death on the cross. By his resurrection from the dead, God vindicated his Son as the victor over sin and death. And, through repentance of their sin and faith alone in this conquering Savior, all who so savingly believe may be justified before their righteous God, be assured of God's presence with them through all of life now, and in the end receive eternal life through his name.

I have endeavored to state this summation of the gospel in a way acceptable to Arminians and Calvinists. What we—and the whole

---

[1] This chapter is dependent upon and is a significant expansion of a portion of my essay, "Defining Evangelicalism's Boundaries Theologically: Is Open Theism Evangelical?" *Journal of the Evangelical Theological Society (JETS)* 45 (2002): 193-212. Responses to this article by Clark Pinnock, John Sanders, and Gregory Boyd, along with a rejoinder by this author, are also published in the same issue of this journal. Material from my *JETS* article is used with permission.

Protestant Christian tradition—hold in common is that in eternity past, God knew the future sin of humankind, he made a deliberate and decisive choice to save sinners,[2] and he formulated then a definitive and fixed plan by which he would succeed in bringing about their future, certain salvation. According to this saving purpose and plan, devised and fixed in eternity past, God would send his Son to die in the place of sinners to pay the penalties of their sin, and he offers freely the gift of justification and eternal life through faith alone in Christ alone.[3]

Yet upon reflection, it is also clear that the openness view, with its denial that God can know the future free decisions and actions of moral beings, simply cannot hold the gospel in this same way. Much of the gospel, for open theism, is God's contingency plan for the human race, not his set plan, determined in eternity past, by which the future sin of humans, and the future redemption from sin in Christ, are eternally set verities.

Just how compromised is the gospel if one holds an openness view? This chapter proposes to address this question and to demonstrate, in the end, that open theism is an unacceptable and nonviable view for Christians who desire to remain biblically faithful, in part because it fails to account for necessary elements of the glorious gospel of Jesus Christ, the gospel that is at the heart of the Christian faith itself. Consider with me, then, four broad areas in which the gospel is unavoidably compromised by open theism's denial of God's exhaustive, definite knowledge of all that will take place in the future.

I. THE GOSPEL'S DESIGN IN ETERNITY PAST

According to biblical teaching, as understood uniformly in the Protestant tradition, God possessed meticulous knowledge of every detail of the future of the world he would create, and he knew this in eternity past before he spoke into being the creation that he designed. This knowledge included his knowing about the sin that Adam and his wife would commit in the garden; it included knowledge of every single

---

[2] While Arminians understand God's election of sinners whom he would save to be conditioned on his eternal foreknowledge of just who would savingly believe when presented the gospel, and Calvinists hold that God's election to salvation was unconditional, yet both agree that God elected some to be saved in eternity past, before he created the world (Eph. 1:4).

[3] While Arminians and some Calvinists differ fundamentally over the extent of the atoning death of Christ, both agree that in eternity past God devised this saving plan by which Christ would die a substitutionary death on the cross for sinners, through which they may be saved, as they place their faith alone in Christ alone.

person who would ever be conceived, along with knowing every facet of their future lives, from conception to death; it included knowing all those who would savingly believe; and it included the certainty of the ultimate salvation of believers and the certain future condemnation of all those outside of Christ.

But in open theism, none of this massive reservoir of future knowledge can be known by God. Because each aspect of this future knowledge is attached to libertarian free choices (as openness advocates insist), it is impossible for God to *know* prior to their obtaining (as we shall see) just *who* will exist throughout history and, of course, *what free choices* they will make, along with all the *consequences* that flow from just these particular choices and not others. Thus, it certainly is the case that it is impossible, before creation, for God to *know* the future salvation of sinners, contrary to what orthodoxy has claimed. How is the gospel's eternal design and purpose affected, then, if the openness denial of God's exhaustive definite foreknowledge is accepted? Please consider the following three implications.

1. Open theism's denial of God's exhaustive definite foreknowledge precludes the possibility of God's knowing from eternity past whether sin would enter his created world.

Clark Pinnock writes that when God created free creatures, he "accepted a degree of risk with the possibility, not certainty, of sin and evil occurring."[4] For Sanders, sin was not only not foreknown, its occurrence in the garden was, to God, "implausible."[5] However, if God did not know that sin would occur, he could not predetermine to save, prior to the creation of humans and the actual sinful action they commit. At best, God could have a contingency plan in the event that sin occurred. But consider 1 Peter 1:19-20: we were redeemed "with the precious blood of Christ, like that of a lamb without blemish or spot. *He was foreknown before the foundation of the world,* but was made manifest in the last times for your sake."[6] And however Revelation 13:8 is translated (either

---

[4] Clark H. Pinnock, *Most Moved Mover: A Theology of God's Openness* (Grand Rapids, Mich.: Baker, 2001), 42.

[5] John Sanders, *The God Who Risks: A Theology of Providence* (Downers Grove, Ill.: InterVarsity Press, 1998), 45-46.

[6] All Scripture quotations in this chapter are from the English Standard Version of the Bible.

the saints' names are written from the foundation of the world, or Christ was slain from the foundation of the world), God's eternal purpose has been to save sinners. Surely the gospel is not God's *ad hoc* plan B; but if sin is a mere possibility, perhaps even an implausibility before Genesis 3, then no set plan would already be in place. The gospel, however, announces God's eternal and set purpose to save, which means he *knows* the sin that will occur and he has *already planned* for our rescue before he even creates.

2. *Open theism's denial of God's exhaustive definite foreknowledge precludes the possibility of God's knowing from eternity past just what persons would actually be conceived and born, at any and every point, throughout the history of humankind. That is, exactly who, how many, and obviously, anything about any of them, would be completely and fully unknown to God.*

Consider your own existence. Could God have known from eternity past that *you* would exist? On openness grounds, absolutely not. Consider the contingencies. Your parents decide to marry—yes, that particular man and woman, not another pair (which God could not have known in advance). And, they decide whether to have children, whether to use birth control or not, how many children to have, and in all this the genetic combinations vary for each possible conception. *None of this God can know ahead of time.* What is true of you is, of course, true also for each of your parents, and their parents, and so on all the way back to the garden. The fact is, God can no more know *now* who will be born a year from right now than you or I can.

This startling fact is not in the least ameliorated when openness proponents announce with such confidence that their God knows all future *possibilities.* On analysis, all this shows is truly how great is their God's ignorance of what *will* be. Imagine all the possible states of affairs that could be but will not be. And, of all of those, God does not know the one actual state of affairs which will obtain out of the infinite number of possible states of affairs that could be. By analogy, if one is working on a mathematics problem, how will it help to know all the *possible* answers that might be given—*all* of which are wrong, *save one*—yet not know which answer, of that infinite list of possible answers, is the correct answer? The incredible fact is, then, that the God of open theism cannot know any facts about the future that are tied to future free choices and actions.

Given the fact that, in principle, God simply could not know who would exist at any point in the future history of humankind (however long it might be, with whatever collection of people that might exist at any given time, and with all the massive number of free decisions and choices that they will make), it is inconceivable that God could elect to save some from their sin. As mentioned previously, he first would not know that sin would occur. But furthermore, he would not know who would exist, by which he could elect some to salvation. It is evident that the eternal plan and design of the gospel, if open theism is accepted, must be strictly a contingency plan. Consider the difficulty God faces: *If* sin occurs, then I'll know that I'll need to save, God must reason. Further, *when* people (beyond the initial pair) come into existence, then I'll know whether these particular individuals might possibly be subjects of my salvation. Of course, since I don't know how long they will live, or what choices they will make, I will only "choose" to save them at the moment that they trust in My Son, for only then will I *know* they exist *and* believe.

The sheer "naked" future of the human race, from God's vantage point in eternity past, is a startling implication of the open view's denial of God's exhaustive foreknowledge. How much of God's plans must now be seen not as certain, wise, and dependable, but as contingent, probabilistic (at best), and subject to massive revision and possible failure. If God cannot know future free choices and actions, there is virtually nothing about the future of humankind he could know prior to creation. This implication is staggering, and is contrary to Scripture's teaching of God's set purpose and plan, in eternity past, to choose and save fallen people through his Son's future definite act of redemption.

3. Open theism's denial of God's exhaustive definite foreknowledge renders it impossible for God to have foreknown and chosen those who would be saved in Christ—in either the Calvinist or Arminian understandings of these doctrines—before the foundation of the world.

As indicated above, this is so, in part, because God could not have known then even *who would exist*. The specific individuals who will populate human history along with any and all of their future choices and actions cannot be known by God in advance of their actual existence. He cannot have known "you" until you are actually conceived. But notice in Romans 8:29-30 that Paul uses a relative pronoun "whom" to indicate the objects of God's foreknowledge: "*those whom* he foreknew he also predestined . . . , and *those whom* he predestined he also called," etc. And Ephesians 1:4-5 says that God chose and predestined *us* in Christ before the foundation of the world. Whether this is corporate or individual, it refers to a specific group comprised of those who will be saved. God knows who we will be before he creates, and he knows whether we will be among those saved.

Boyd attempts to account for God's election as taught in Ephesians 1:4. He writes that,

> when Paul says that God "chose us in Christ before the foundation of the world," he immediately specifies that this predestination was for us "to be holy and blameless before him in love" (Eph. 1:4). Note, Paul does *not* say that we were *individually* predestined to be "in Christ" (or not). Scripture elsewhere tells us that if it were up to God alone, he would save everyone (1 Tim. 2:4; 2 Peter 3:9). But it is not up to God alone; God gave humans free will. What Paul says in this verse is that *whoever chooses* to be "in Christ" is predestined to be "holy and blameless before him in love."[7]

Boyd's exegesis and explanation are both problematic. Consider first, that for God to predestine us to be holy and blameless, it would require that God knew, before the foundation of the world, either that (1) *we* would be, or at least that (2) *some sinners or other* would be, who would believe and so be elected to be holy and blameless. But of course, the first option is impossible, since God cannot possibly know even now, at this moment, who will exist one year from now, and much less can he have known from eternity past who would exist through the history of the human race. On first glance, the second option seems plausible, but on further analysis, it too falters. If God knows from before the foundation of the world that *some sinners or other* will exist, this requires that God will have known before the foundation of the world that *sin itself* will

[7] Gregory A. Boyd, *God of the Possible: A Biblical Introduction to the Open View of God* (Grand Rapids, Mich.: Baker, 2000), 46-47.

enter the world. But, of course, the only way God can know that sin will occur is if that first sinful choice and action is not (libertarianly) free. If the first sin is free, God (in principle, by openness standards) cannot have known it would occur. But then, he cannot have known that there will be sinners. But then, he cannot have elected *some sinners or other* to be holy and blameless.[8]

Second, Boyd's insertion of the notion, "whoever chooses," into Ephesians 1:4 is simply invalid. His statement, "What Paul says in this verse is that *whoever chooses* to be 'in Christ' is predestined to be 'holy and blameless before him in love,'" adds a concept to this verse that simply is not there. What Paul says is that God "chose us." Boyd fails to account for the direct object of the choosing, and he illegitimately adds the notion of "whoever chooses," and he thereby distorts the verse. Furthermore, as pointed out above, God cannot have predestined "whoever chooses" to believe in Christ to be holy and blameless, because this would require that he know that people will, in their sin, need to choose Christ to be saved. But since he cannot have known that there would be sinners, he cannot have known that any would need to choose Christ to be saved. Strictly speaking, *some sinners or other choosing Christ to be saved* can be known to God, before the foundation of the world, only as a *possibility*. But this mere possibility is an insufficient basis for *predestining* (i.e., in which their future destiny is certain) them to be holy and blameless, i.e., delivered from the sin which he could not have known that they would have. The open view is, then, fully unacceptable, because it simply denies what Scripture affirms is true, viz., that God knows the actual individual persons whom he has chosen to save in his Son.

II. The Gospel's Expression in Old Testament Life and Theology

As we move forward in redemptive history, it becomes clear that not only is the certainty and specificity of the eternal gospel plan of God rendered impossible by the open view, but aspects of its expression in God's dealings with Israel, prior to Christ's coming, are also irreparably damaged. As we shall see, from the covenant promise of God to save a

---

[8] See the discussion below regarding whether Boyd's appeal to neo-Molinism on such issues may be of any help. It will be argued that no help to Boyd is forthcoming.

people to the glory of his name, to the actual saving acts of God throughout Old Testament history, the very gospel realities that Scripture emphasizes are unavoidably undercut by the openness denial of God's exhaustive, definite foreknowledge. Consider three aspects of the gospel in Old Testament life and theology, all central to Old Testament teaching and to redemptive history, that are rendered unattainable in the open view.

1. Open theism's denial of God's exhaustive definite foreknowledge renders unsure God's own covenant promise to bring blessing and salvation to the nations through the seed of Abraham.

Open theists take the test of Abraham in Genesis 22 as what they call a *real test,* i.e., a test with uncertain results, presumably, one Abraham could fail, thus disqualifying him from being the covenant partner through whom God would bring blessing to the world.[9] Concerning this test, Sanders writes, "God needs to know if Abraham is the sort of person on whom God can count for collaboration toward the fulfillment of the divine project. Will he be faithful? Or *must God find someone else* through whom to achieve his purpose?"[10] But if so, how shall we understand God's promise to Abraham in Genesis 12:2-3: "And I will make of *you* a great nation, and I will bless *you* and make *your name* great, so that *you* will be a blessing. I will bless those who bless *you,* and him who dishonors *you* I will curse, and in *you* all the families of the earth shall be blessed"? If *this* covenant could be fulfilled through another, then what does God's word mean? Furthermore, if Abraham fails this test, what assurances can we have that another, and then another, and then another, might not also fail?

Once again, it is staggering simply to consider seriously the implications of the open view when placed alongside a passage as central to all of biblical theology and redemptive history as Genesis 12:1-3. If, as God speaks forth this covenant promise, God is wondering whether Abraham really will be the person through whom the nations will be blessed, how can the language of this passage be understood? Its unconditional nature assures us that God knows and will ensure that

---

[9] Sanders, *The God Who Risks,* 52-53; and Boyd, *God of the Possible,* 64.
[10] Sanders, *The God Who Risks,* 52-53, emphasis added.

through Abraham and his offspring (cf. Gen. 12:7) the promised blessing will come. Certainly the Genesis narrative that follows is only meant to confirm this understanding, for here we see Sarah, then Abraham, unable to parent children, bringing them and the fulfillment of God's covenant promise to a point of crisis. Surely then, the miraculous conception of Isaac in Genesis 21 is intentionally designed to demonstrate the power of God *to keep his word and do just as he has promised*. But that's just it: on the open view, God's promise *cannot* be assured because God *cannot know* what Abraham and Sarah will do, and hence, God cannot have asserted with certainty in Genesis 12 that *Abraham* (and no one else) would be the one through whom the promised blessing to the nations would come. But since God did so assert Abraham as the provider of the promised offspring of blessing, the open view simply fails.

The problem does not end with Abraham, however. Many generations separate Abraham from the ultimate fulfillment in the seed who would come as the blessing to the nations, Jesus the Christ. What are we to say of this succession of seed-bearers, as we might call them, who are conceived and born, generation by generation, in the line of Abraham? Given God's total inability to know, for any time future, just who would be conceived and born, how long they would live, what actions and choices might make up their lives—how remarkable that God could predict in Genesis 12 that Abraham's seed would remain, and that the Messiah would come in his very line. Given the variables over roughly 2,000 years of human history that stand between Abraham and Christ, given God's total ignorance of the totality of future free choices and actions in human history at any and every time future, and given God's inability to control or regulate the free choices and actions of his human creatures, one can only marvel at the promise of God in Genesis 12 and stand incredulous before the question of how God could have pulled this off. Is the openness interpretation of this (and so many more!) promise satisfying? Does it account for the theology and history of Scripture? Surely this promise is a witness, not to God's ignorance of so much of the future as demanded by the open view, but to his full knowledge and accurate predictions of all that would take place.

2. Open theism's denial of God's exhaustive definite foreknowledge jeopardizes the legitimacy of God's justification of Old Testament saints by faith (e.g., Gen. 15:6).

Recall that in Romans 3:25-26 we are told that God passed over sins previously committed for the *demonstration of his righteousness at the present time.* So, what grounds the legitimacy of God's justification of Old Testament believers is, not their sacrifices, not their faith *per se,* but the *future payment of Christ's death* on the cross, by which God demonstrates *now, in Christ,* that he is righteous in having forgiven those he did (as well as forgiving others yet future). But herein lies the problem: For God to extend justification to Old Testament saints, apart from *knowing* their sin *would be paid* by a subsequent death for sin, would be to extend what was in fact a groundless and unjustified justification.

Perhaps an analogy might help. If I go shopping with my wife and we purchase a chair for the living room, I may "pay" for the chair by charging it to my credit card. Now, what makes this a legitimate and legal transaction is the obligation that I have accepted to cover the charged amount through monies I have in my bank account. If, when I placed the price of the chair on my credit card, I knew that I did not have the money in the bank to pay for it, and I did not know with certainty whether I would have that money, the transaction could later be viewed as illegal.

In other words, for God to *declare Abraham righteous* in his sight, as he did in Genesis 15:6, God must have known that the payment for Abraham's sin, by which he could be justified by faith, would surely and certainly be made by his Son. If God did not *know* whether the payment would be made, his *declaration* that Abraham *was righteous* was a legal sham. But how can the open view avoid this problem? After all, as we have seen, many variables separate Abraham from the coming of Messiah, and God cannot know what will take place during the intervening years, who will exist, what they will do, and what will occur. More particularly, on strict openness criteria of libertarian freedom,[11] God could not know that Christ would come as the incarnate God-man, nor whether he would obey perfectly and go to the cross to make his

---

[11] See discussion below, where Boyd proposes an alternative understanding, albeit with its own set of unique problems.

substitutionary payment for Abraham's (and others') sin. [12] Therefore, in the open view, when God declared Abraham righteous, he was doing so with less than full legal backing, for the possibility existed that Abraham's sin would never be atoned, and that the supposed basis for the declaration of his righteousness would never come to be. Only if God *knows with certainty* that future full and real atonement *will occur* can God declare, 2,000 years before the legal basis of the payment is made, that Abraham is justified and saved.

3. Parallel to the previous point: Open theism's denial of God's exhaustive definite foreknowledge renders illusory the salvific value of Old Testament atoning sacrifices for the forgiveness of sin.

In similar fashion, the type/antitype reality in the Old Testament sacrificial system requires the certainty of the future death of Christ, i.e., the *"Lamb of God, who takes away* the sin of the world" (John 1:29). But, of course, since God cannot have known whether his Son would freely offer himself as the once-for-all atonement for sin, God's institution of the sacrificial system was, strictly, a legal fiction. There was then no basis in the Old Testament period itself by which God could forgive sins through those sacrifices. Only if God *knows with certainty* that sin's debt *will be paid* in the future death of Christ can those Old Testament sacrifices function as types by which God can genuinely forgive.

What is clear, then, is that both the plan and promise of God to bring about salvation through the seed of Abraham, and the actual saving actions of God in his justification of sinners and through the sacrificial system's atoning efficacy, are undercut and shown to be strictly impossible if the open view is accepted. What massive gospel harm is done in the Old Testament period itself when it is denied of God that he can know the future free choices and actions of moral beings. Neither those free choices and actions of Abraham, Sarah, Abraham's line over 2,000 years, nor of Christ himself, could be known; and hence, no promise of salvation or any saving activity itself could be grounded and secured. Only when God knows the full future of human action and

---

[12] See discussion below of Sanders's statement, *The God Who Risks*, 100: "The path of the cross comes about only through God's interaction with humans in history. Until this moment in history other routes were, perhaps, open."

choice can God secure these realities in ways that accord clearly with Old Testament theology and history, as Scripture would have us believe and affirm.

III. The Gospel's Accomplishment in the Atoning Death and Resurrection of Christ

As we move yet further in the line of redemptive history, we come now to the centerpiece in the fulfillment of God's glorious and eternal purpose to save fallen sinners. The coming of Christ into the world expresses, at once, the love and the wrath of God toward sinners. To his very Son, God imputes our sin; and in his Son, God makes payment for our sin. In this, God's wrath is satisfied, and his inexpressible love for us is demonstrated. What glorious truth is the gospel!

Yet, once again, the glory of this gospel truth begins to diminish greatly when the life, ministry, death, and resurrection of Christ are examined within the strictures given us by open theism. What compromises to this central gospel reality do we encounter here? Consider the following four problems.

1. Open theism's denial of God's exhaustive definite foreknowledge renders uncertain the execution of God's plan of salvation through the delivering up of his Son by crucifixion on the cross; or, if God foreknows and predestines the death of Christ, then, by openness standards of freedom and morality, it renders Christ's obedience and offering himself up to be crucified to be the determined, constrained, and morally vacuous actions of a divinely engineered robot. We'll consider each possibility in order.

First, while it is harmful enough to the surety of God's covenant commitment to say, as Sanders has, that had Abraham not obeyed, God might seek another through whom to fulfill his covenant promise to bless the nations; it is altogether more devastating to the truthfulness of God's longstanding salvific covenant pledge to suggest that Christ, as a free agent, might not have chosen to go to the cross. Sanders writes, "Although Scripture attests that the incarnation was planned from the creation of the world, this is not so with the cross. The path of the cross comes about only through God's interaction with humans in history. Until this moment in history other routes were, perhaps, open."[13] Though startling, does not the open view require this possibility? If Christ is a moral agent and if his actions are free, it follows that Christ could choose to be given over or not, and then it follows that God cannot have known, prior to his choice, just what Christ would do. In light of Psalm 22; Isaiah 52:13–53:12; Acts 2:23; 4:27-28; and 1 Peter 1:20, this implication of the open view contradicts precious biblical teaching while it undercuts the certainty and surety of God's eternal saving promise and purpose.

But second, some may be aware that Boyd asserts a different position from Sanders on this point, claiming that "Scripture portrays the crucifixion as a predestined event" even if "it was not certain from eternity that Pilot [*sic*], Herod, or Caiaphas would play the roles they played in the crucifixion."[14] Boyd explains, "Since God determines whatever he wants to about world history, we should not find it surprising that the central defining event in world history—the crucifixion—included a number of predestined aspects. It seems that the incarnation and crucifixion were part of God's plan from 'before the foundation of the world.'"[15] Of course, holding this position has the advantage of avoiding the implication just noted, viz., of the uncertainty of the cross if God cannot know in advance what Christ will choose to do. But I am startled and incredulous that any open theist would want to solve this problem by asserting that the event of the crucifixion was divinely foreknown and predestined. After all, even if God may not know the roles that Pilate or Herod might play, if the event of the crucifixion is predestined, must God not know, at bare minimum, that his Son *will choose* to go to the cross?[16] But just call to mind the strong and emotionally charged language open theists regularly offer

---

[13] Sanders, *The God Who Risks*, 100.

[14] Boyd, *God of the Possible*, 45.

[15] Ibid., 44-45. Boyd's full last paragraph of this discussion reads, "While Scripture portrays the crucifixion as a predestined event, it never suggests that the individuals who participated in this event were predestined to do so or foreknown as doing so. It was certain that Jesus would be crucified, but it was not certain from eternity that Pilot [*sic*], Herod, or Caiaphas would play the roles they played in the crucifixion. They participated in Christ's death *of their own free wills*" (ibid., 45, emphasis added). But when Boyd says that the events of the crucifixion are not predestined, presumably this cannot include the one, central event, viz., the choice of Christ to obey the Father and go to the cross. If we are to see "the crucifixion as a predestined event," then, for Boyd, the bare minimum of what must be predestined, it would seem, is the actual choice of Christ to be crucified. If this is not the case, in what meaningful sense could we see "the crucifixion as a predestined event"?

[16] It seems that Boyd must allow for this. See note 15 above.

to the notion that God can fore*know* what creatures *freely* do. If God knows what they will do, their actions cannot genuinely be free; rather, they are robots, and there can be no true love, no true moral action, and no true relationship between the constrained agent and God. In fact, some open theists go so far as to call God's predetermination of future actions, carried out in a nonconsensual manner, instances of divine rape![17] What can save Boyd's position from being charged with entailing, on openness grounds, that the crucifixion of Christ, as predetermined by God, constituted the most egregious act of divine coercion perpetrated in the history of the universe?

Furthermore, if the event of the crucifixion was predestined, does this not require that every act of Christ's earthly obedience was also constrained, since what was predestined was (obviously) an *efficacious* crucifixion, i.e., the crucifixion of a *truly sinless* atoning sacrifice? But, if Christ's life of obedience and crucifixion were constrained, are they not, on openness grounds, morally vacuous, and is not the cross, then, worthless? And further yet, if the event of the crucifixion was predestined "before the foundation of the world," does this not entail God's foreknowledge of sin? How could God *predestine* a crucifixion to save from sin if sin is not certain? But if sin is certain, what then of human freedom and moral responsibility in choosing originally to rebel against God?

Boyd has offered a response to these criticisms in which he seeks to affirm that God fully knew and determined the crucifixion of Christ *and* Christ went to the cross freely. For those acquainted with openness literature, it is astonishing to find an open theist making such an assertion. If anything is clear from the openness critique of classical theism, it is that (in their view) God's *certain knowledge* of a future choice or action, and that choice or action being done *freely,* are strictly incompatible. For if God knows some action in fact will occur in the future, then when that moment arrives, it will not be possible for that action to fail to occur or for some different action to occur instead, or else God did not in fact *know* it. Choices and actions may be genuinely free (among other conditions) only insofar as they are not foreknown.[18] But now Boyd tells us that he envisions another possibility as it pertains to Christ. He writes:

[17] See, e.g., Sanders, *The God Who Risks*, 240.

[18] For fuller explanation of this openness contention, see my *God's Lesser Glory: The Diminished God of Open Theism* (Wheaton, Ill.: Crossway, 2000), 35-36.

While space restrictions prevent me from fleshing out my own Christology at this point, let me simply go on record as saying that I, for one, hold that Jesus possessed compatibilistic freedom. In my view, Christ was humanity *eschatologically defined*. He was the "already" entering into the "not-yet." He was what we shall be when perfected. The whole purpose of libertarian freedom, in my view, is to become what the God-man was from the start: humans who are defined *in their essence* by openness to God. Being contingent beings who are semi-autonomous from God, we must go through a probationary period, utilizing libertarian freewill, to becoming open (or closed) in our essence toward God. But Jesus, being God, was never on probation and hence did not possess libertarian free will (with regard to his openness to God).[19]

This is nothing short of a shocking proposal. Innovative? Yes. Creative? Yes. But also shocking. And the reason is simple. Given the complete derision that open theists have shown for the Calvinist notion of freedom, called compatibilist freedom, the reader may excuse this writer for showing a bit of amazement that now, in the singularly most significant human life ever lived, compatibilist freedom is lauded. Not only this, but in Boyd's view, compatibilist freedom is the kind of freedom that one day we (God's redeemed) shall all have. Far from sneering at this notion of freedom (as is customary among openness writers), Boyd here gives it pride of place as the "perfect" freedom possessed by Christ and by those in Christ when they are glorified.

But will this solution to the question of the determination of the cross work? Consider these difficulties. First, I am highly skeptical that Boyd will find an excited following for this proposal among his open theist colleagues. One major shift this makes is that it proposes that compatibilist freedom, evidently, is a legitimate conception of freedom—and not only legitimate, but superior, in some important sense of the term. But does Boyd really intend us to see "compatibilist freedom" as a kind of "genuine freedom"? If so, will this be acceptable to those committed to libertarian freedom? Or, does Boyd use the term "compatibilist freedom" to describe a kind of deterministic action which is not "really" free? It appears to me that he intends the former, but if so, much previ-

---

[19] Gregory A. Boyd, "Christian Love and Academic Dialogue: A Reply to Bruce Ware," *JETS* 45 (2002): 242.

ous work by open theists will have to be redone, in which libertarian freedom is currently expressed as the only "real," or "genuine" freedom that there is. And surely if it is, the Calvinist claim that compatibilist freedom is an altogether legitimate understanding of genuinely "free" moral action will have to be given a fresh hearing by those prone, previously, to reject it altogether.

Second, and more to the point, if Christ lived the whole of his life, obeyed the Father, and went to the cross, as God had fully, precisely, and accurately *foreknown*, then certainly it seems that God would, of necessity, know other human actions and choices that connect necessarily with those choices and actions of Christ's, foreknown by God. For example, if God precisely and accurately foreknows now that tomorrow at 10:00 A.M. my neighbor will choose to give me a ride to the emergency room to attend to a serious injury I incurred while repairing the shingles on my roof, consider all of the attending human choices, actions, and events that God would also have to know *besides knowing* (merely) that my neighbor would choose to take me to the hospital. In other words, how reasonable is it to say that Christ lived his (solitary) life with compatibilist freedom, that he went to the cross by the exercise of compatibilist freedom, and so *God knew precisely his life and choices and actions*—yet, all those around him, with libertarian freedom, did what they did, chose what they chose, and acted in relation to Christ as they freely willed, and God *did not and could not foreknow what their lives and choices and actions would be?*

Can Boyd's recent appeal to what he calls "neo-Molinism" address this problem? I don't believe so. To see this, consider briefly what Boyd means by his term "neo-Molinism." According to Boyd, besides there being "would-counterfactuals" as proposed in Molinism,[20] there are also "might-counterfactuals" that an omniscient being would know. He explains:

> Between God's precreational knowledge of all logical possibilities and God's precreational knowledge of what will come to pass is God's "middle knowledge" of what free agents *might or might not do* in certain situations as well as of what free agents *would do* in other situa-

---

[20] But, as explained below, the Molinist and neo-Molinist understandings of "would-counterfactuals" are significantly different.

tions. If it is true that agent *x* might or might not do *y* in situation *z*, it is false that agent *x* would do *y* in situation *z*, and vice versa.[21]

And in the glossary of his *Satan and the Problem of Evil*, he defines neo-Molinism, saying:

> In the neo-Molinist view God knows what agents *might* do insofar as agents possess libertarian freedom. And God knows what agents *would* do insofar as they have received from God and through circumstances or acquired for themselves determinate characters. God knows both categories of counterfactuals as they pertain to every possible subject in every possible world throughout eternity.[22]

What shall we say of this proposal? First, it appears to me that Boyd has proposed a category of God's knowledge, i.e., knowledge of "might-counterfactuals," which is both unnecessary and misleading. It is *unnecessary* because all such "might-counterfactuals" are about logically possible states of affairs in which an agent with libertarian freedom *might* or *might not* perform *x*, but then since God already knows all logical possibilities, he already knows such "might-counterfactuals" as part of his knowledge of these possible states of affairs. Boyd's so-called "might-counterfactuals" are merely a subset of God's exhaustive knowledge of all logically possible states of affairs, which knowledge includes everything (logically possible) that all possible (libertarianly) free agents might or might not choose to do. Or, more simply, "might-counterfactuals" comprise the subset of logically possible states of affairs, all known by God, in which libertarian freedom may be exercised so as to choose or refrain from choosing in some logically possible situation. Giving this subset of God's knowledge of possible states of affairs the name "might-counterfactuals" may sound impressive, but it advances our understanding of God's knowledge not at all.[23]

Boyd's category of "might-counterfactuals" is *misleading* for at least two reasons. First, by his assertion of the *logical possibility* of might-

---

[21] Gregory A. Boyd, *Satan and the Problem of Evil: Constructing a Trinitarian Warfare Theodicy* (Downers Grove, Ill.: InterVarsity Press, 2001), 126.

[22] Ibid., 425.

[23] Please understand that God does not necessarily know the *truthfulness* of these might-counterfactuals; he merely knows them as *logical possibilities*. The importance of this observation will be made clear in the discussion that follows.

counterfactuals, Boyd simply denies (without proof) that God *can know* what a *libertarianly free* creature *would* do, and that God *can have* exhaustive definite foreknowledge. That is, when Boyd asserts that it is logically possible for God to know what free creatures might or might not do, he intends to say that whenever God knows such might-counterfactual knowledge, he cannot also know what those same free creatures *would* do or *will do* in those same states of affairs. These are mutually exclusive realities. Recall his words above, "If it is true that agent *x* might or might not do *y* in situation *z*, it is false that agent *x* would do *y* in situation *z*, and vice versa."[24] And, while Boyd is correct about the mutually exclusive nature of God's knowing, for any particular action *y* by agent *x* in situation *z*, *either* what the agent might or might not do *or* (but not *and*) what the agent would or would not do, Boyd nonetheless does not prove that God *in fact* has such might-counterfactual knowledge *in regard to the real world*. He seems to think that if such knowledge is *logically possible*, then God must know the world *in fact* to be this way. But this clearly is not the case. Does not God know the *logical possibility* of unicorns while also knowing *in fact* that they do not exist? So, Boyd is false and misleading when he asserts, "Indeed, the very fact that might-counterfactuals are not self-contradictory (necessarily false) proves that God does not by definition have exhaustively definite foreknowledge."[25] This is a *non sequitur*, to be sure. While God may know as a *logical possibility* all might-counterfactuals within all possible worlds where God would neither determine all that would be nor have would-counterfactual knowledge (i.e., he knows what free creatures might or might not do in all worlds where might-counterfactual knowledge pertains), he may also know *in fact* and *exhaustively* what all free creatures would do and will do in this, the actual world. Essentially, Boyd misleads his readers into thinking that if might-counterfactuals are logically possible, God must know these to be true *about the actual world*. However, as we know, this is not the case for unicorns, and it is also not necessarily the case for might-counterfactuals.

Another way to see this is to ask, Is it logically possible for God to create a world in which he determines definitely and exhaustively all that will be? I'm not aware of any openness proponent who would answer no.

---

[24] Boyd, *Satan and the Problem of Evil*, 126.
[25] Ibid., 127.

And regardless, this obviously is a logically possible state of affairs. But then, should we make the reverse point from Boyd's, and claim that 'the very fact that exhaustive definite foreknowledge is not self-contradictory (necessarily false) proves that God does not by definition have might-counterfactual knowledge'? Of course not, because we recognize that *some* possible worlds are ones where God has might-counterfactual knowledge, and *others* are ones where God has exhaustive definite foreknowledge. Therefore, to assert that the *mere logical possibility* of might-counterfactual knowledge proves God does not have exhaustive definite foreknowledge is misdirected. The logical possibility of might-counterfactual knowledge (or of exhaustive definite foreknowledge) offers no proof whatsoever for God's in fact having might-counterfactual knowledge (or exhaustive definite foreknowledge) in this, the actual world. The fact is, both kinds of divine knowledge are possible, and so which is true in relation to the real world must be determined by looking elsewhere, and presumably the most important place to look is what God reveals about the nature of his own knowledge as given us in Scripture.[26]

Consider yet another way to see this point. Is it logically possible for God to lie? We must be careful how we answer this question. Clearly it is *impossible* for God to lie (e.g., Titus 1:2; Heb. 6:18), but is this impossibility a *logical* impossibility? No, the reason God cannot lie is not that it is logically impossible for him so to do, but rather that his character and nature are such that God is always truthful. So, the impossibility of God's lying is not logical but ontological.[27]

Now, what if this is also the case with God's omniscience? What if it is *logically possible* for God to know might-counterfactuals, but it is *ontologically necessary* that God (as omniscient) know what free creatures actually would and will do? More simply, what if God, as God (i.e., *qua* omniscient), simply must know the future definitely and exhaus-

[26] For recent biblical defenses of God's exhaustive and definite knowledge of the future that are cognizant of open theism's denial of this doctrine, see Ware, *God's Lesser Glory*, 99-141; John S. Feinberg, *No One Like Him: The Doctrine of God*, Foundations of Evangelical Theology (Wheaton, Ill.: Crossway, 2001), 299-320; John M. Frame, *No Other God: A Response to Open Theism* (Phillipsburg, N.J.: Presbyterian & Reformed, 2001), 191-203; idem, *The Doctrine of God* (Phillipsburg, N.J.: Presbyterian & Reformed, 2002), 479-505; and William Lane Craig, "What Does God Know?" in *God Under Fire: Modern Scholarship Reinvents God*, ed. Douglas S. Huffman and Eric L. Johnson (Grand Rapids, Mich.: Zondervan, 2002), 137-156.

[27] This is much the same reason why it is impossible for human beings, unassisted, to breathe underwater, or fly to the tops of trees, or run the mile in fifteen seconds—none of these is logically impossible, but all are ontological impossibilities for human beings, given the natures we have.

tively? If so, while God may know might-counterfactuals as a *logical possibility* (much as he knows 'God lying' as a logical possibility), God also must possess exhaustive definite foreknowledge by virtue of the nature of his omniscience, i.e., as an *ontological necessity*. Boyd's assertion that "the very fact that might-counterfactuals are not self-contradictory (necessarily false) proves that God does not by definition have exhaustively definite foreknowledge" simply does not follow. All that Boyd has shown by "might-counterfactuals" is that since these are logically possible states of affairs (much like "unicorns existing" or "God lying" are logically possible states of affairs), God knows these as *logically possible*. What Boyd fails to show is that (1) in fact God possesses such might-counterfactual knowledge regarding the real world, or that (2) possessing knowledge of might-counterfactuals as *logically possible* precludes God's also possessing exhaustive definite knowledge about the real world as factually true or, stronger, as an *ontological necessity* of his omniscient divine nature. Boyd's discussion misleads the reader to think that might-counterfactual knowledge as logically possible entails God's actual knowledge of might-counterfactuals in the real world and the actual denial of God's exhaustive definite foreknowledge. Boyd's argument here is simply mistaken.

Second, Boyd's discussion of might-counterfactuals is misleading insofar as it gives the appearance of providing God with some additional basis by which he can better regulate the future states of affairs that obtain throughout time. For instance, Boyd writes that, "because God possesses infinite intelligence, his knowledge of might-counterfactuals leaves him no less prepared for the future than his knowledge of determinate aspects of creation."[28] But how is this so? After all, since God knows by "might-counterfactuals" the myriad of possible choices that might or might not be made, but since he cannot know from "might-counterfactuals" just what choices will be made and what consequences will follow from them, he still must wait until libertarian free choices are made to know what actual choices are made and actual actions performed. So, how will such might-counterfactual knowledge help God? Boyd assures us that since God has infinite intelligence, he is able to attend to every possibility "as though it was the only possibility he had

---

[28] Boyd, *Satan and the Problem of Evil*, 128-129.

to consider."[29] While this is meant to be reassuring, I fail to see how it is. After all, God still must rely on contingency plans in the event that libertarian freedom is used in ways he doesn't want, or doesn't expect, and he still faces situations which are incalculably awful and over which (due to libertarian freedom) he has no control. Although God has given infinite attention to each and every possible eventuality, he still is faced with creaturely free decisions that are tragically contrary to his purposes and which result in no immediate or ultimate good.

When I read Boyd's triumphalism regarding any possible future decision, that "from all eternity God was preparing for just this possibility," and that God "is as perfectly prepared for the improbable as he is for the probable,"[30] I cannot help but bring to mind actual horrors and evils that have happened in history. On openness grounds, how does this rhetoric apply when asking how God's knowledge and infinite intelligence "perfectly prepared" him for dealing with the unfolding horrors of the Holocaust? How well does God's prior infinite attention work when assessing God's preparation to handle the circumstances in Warsaw that day when Zosia's eyes were cruelly plucked out, as Boyd describes in his *God at War?*[31] Or, I cannot help but wonder how this will reassure the woman, Suzanne, whose sad and gripping story of betrayal and desertion by her "Christian" husband, Boyd also tells us.[32] In other words, what practical benefit does this category of "might-counterfactual" knowledge give God in guiding the history of this world he has made, the one in which he is "perfectly prepared" for every possibility? It seems to me that infinite intelligence and "might-counterfactual" knowledge notwithstanding, open theism presents us with a God who watches in absolute horror and utter dismay as unspeakably evil situations unfold, over which he is unable (due to libertarian freedom) to exercise control. Despite Boyd's claim that it is "altogether unfounded"[33] to describe the God of open theism as wringing his hands in the face of unwanted yet relentlessly unfolding evils, I see no other way to understand this God,

---

[29] Ibid., 129.
[30] Ibid.
[31] Gregory A. Boyd, *God at War: The Bible and Spiritual Conflict* (Downers Grove, Ill.: InterVarsity Press, 1997), 33-34.
[32] Boyd, *God of the Possible*, 103-106.
[33] Boyd, *Satan and the Problem of Evil*, 128.

and Boyd's reassurances of God's infinite intelligence and might-counterfactual knowledge help his God out not one whit.

Second, within Boyd's conception of this so-called neo-Molinist middle knowledge is also his novel understanding of knowledge of "would-counterfactuals." These refer to future actions or choices which a person would or would not do, but (for Boyd, and contrary to Molinism) this requires that such future actions are done from one's nature in such a way that they are performed *without libertarian freedom,* i.e., they *could not* have been done differently. But given all that open theists (and other advocates of libertarian freedom) have said about the moral bankruptcy of actions performed that could not have been different, I fail to see how Boyd finds this a helpful category (within his openness structure). Do not the actions to which would-counterfactuals refer reduce to determined actions? If so, and given the rhetoric of libertarianism, how does moral accountability attach to them?

For example, when Boyd applies this understanding to Peter's denial of Christ, Boyd suggests that Peter made (libertarianly) free choices that led to his having a character of a certain kind such that "he would be the kind of person who would deny Christ in a certain situation."[34] On this basis, God *knew* that Peter *would* deny Christ. But, one must wonder how this differs from determinism. If Peter, because of previous free choices (in which he could have chosen differently), now is faced with a situation in which he cannot but make this one choice, on what grounds (on standards of libertarian freedom) does Boyd suggest we should hold Peter accountable for what he does in this moment? And how does this appeal to a crystallized character in Peter account for Jesus telling Peter that after his denials, "when you have turned again, strengthen your brothers" (Luke 22:32), since evidently Peter is only "the kind of person who would deny Christ" at one moment, but later he has changed? Furthermore, what happens to the notion that people can perform totally *unexpected actions* or make *shocking decisions,* as when we speak of someone "acting out of character"? It appears that again here, Boyd has delivered less than his rhetoric might suggest. What his "would-counterfactuals" turn out to be is simply a microcosm of determinate actions and choices, whether these are determined by God or by

---

[34] Ibid., 131. For detailed interaction with Boyd's proposal, see chapter 8 in this volume.

the person's character being such that he *will* make only this decision and not another. So, in the end, Boyd's "might-counterfactuals" are merely a subset of God's knowledge storehouse of all logically possible states of affairs, and Boyd's "would-counterfactuals" are merely a subset of previously determined actions and choices. It appears that nothing has been gained by appeal to these notions, and certainly they cannot help deal with God's regulation of the world.

Returning now to the question of whether Boyd's appeal to neo-Molinism can assist in explaining the certainty of the cross, it seems that no help can be given. God's knowledge of so-called might-counterfactuals only provides a divine understanding of the full array of possible actions and choices done by possible persons (recall, God cannot know in eternity past just *who* will exist), but it can provide him no knowledge of how Christ will be treated or how people will respond to him. And, by appeal to "would-counterfactuals" Boyd runs the risk of trivializing much related to the cross (by standards of libertarian freedom), as an increasing number of determined elements are put in place to ensure the cross, thus removing, it would seem, the moral responsibility Scripture ascribes to those rejecting and crucifying Christ.

In the end, my own view is that consistent open theism will follow the line of thought expressed earlier in Sanders, not Boyd, on this point. Having said this, I remain open to hearing more from Boyd and from other supporters and critics alike, to see if open theism can account for the pivotal event in all of history, the certainty of the crucifixion of Christ to pay for the sin of fallen human beings. It seems clear that with either route one takes (that of Sanders or that of Boyd), the certainty of the cross is jeopardized, and hence the gospel of grace, in its historical unfolding, is compromised.

2. Open theism's denial of God's exhaustive definite foreknowledge renders uncertain, by extension of the uncertainty of Christ's crucifixion, the resurrection of Jesus by which alone do believers in Christ have hope (1 Cor. 15:17).

Are the predictions of Jesus' future resurrection in Psalm 16 and by Jesus himself (e.g., Matt. 16:21) probabilistic, or conditional in nature? Does Peter understand these predictions this way in Acts 2:24-32 as he quotes

Psalm 16? Surely not. In Acts 2:31, Peter states, "[David] foresaw and spoke about the resurrection of the Christ, that he was not abandoned to Hades, nor did his flesh see corruption." But if the resurrection was not in question, then neither was the crucifixion merely probabilistic or conditional. Rather, both were set, fixed, certain, sure, and absolutely foreknown by God.

Again, one must ask whether Scripture itself encourages the kind of thinking espoused in open theism. Is there any hint in Scripture that the resurrection of Christ, when as yet a future reality, was uncertain? Are we led to think that God's ultimate victory over sin and death is really a risky venture in which God might possibly fail? And yet how many (!) free moral choices and actions are connected to the events leading up to the crucifixion and resurrection of Christ? But God pronounced with certainty and full authority hundreds of years in advance that his Son would not suffer decay. A certain resurrection requires a certain crucifixion, which requires God's foreknowledge of all those human choices and actions affecting these central events. The open view simply cannot account for what Scripture demands: the absolute and fixed plan and prediction of God regarding his Son's future and certain death and resurrection.

3. Open theism's denial of God's exhaustive definite foreknowledge jeopardizes the substitutionary nature of Christ's death for our sin.

Because God cannot know in advance just who will be living at any and every point of human history, therefore, when Christ died on the cross, he simply could not, in any real sense, have substituted for "you" or for "me" in his death and payment for sin. While his death could have been quite literally in the place of, or as a substitute for, those living up to the point of his death, this could not be the case with those to be conceived and born yet future. While advocates of limited and unlimited atonement differ over those for whom Christ died, all agree that when he died, he died in the place of sinners, i.e., actual sinful people whose deaths and payments for sin he took upon himself. Hence, the substitutionary nature of the atonement can obtain only if God knows not only those prior to Christ's death but also those yet future for whom Christ died.

In Boyd's response to this objection, he observes that in the open view,

God could offer his Son to pay for "every *possible* sin"[35] that might be committed. But in answering this way, he simply affirms the point that I have made. No *actual* substitution can be made, for God cannot know, when Christ hangs on the cross, any *actual* person who will yet be conceived. His death must be seen as a substitution in general, not a specific substitution for sinners who deserved the judgment he received on their behalf.

4. Parallel point: Open theism's denial of God's exhaustive definite foreknowledge jeopardizes Christ's actually bearing "our sins in his body on the tree" (1 Pet. 2:24).

At the point in human history when Christ was crucified, not only would it be impossible for God to know whether and who would come to exist in the future (so he could not actually substitute for them in his death), in addition, God would also be clueless regarding what sin(s) would be committed in the future. Therefore, there could be no actual imputation of our sin to Christ (e.g., Isa. 53:6, " . . . the Lord has laid on him the *iniquity of us all";* 1 Cor. 15:3, "Christ died for *our sins";* 2 Cor. 5:21, God made Christ *"to be sin* who knew no sin . . ."; 1 Pet. 2:24, "He himself *bore our sins in his body* on the tree . . ."). Since no future sin yet existed, on openness grounds, God could not know any of that future sin for which Christ's atonement was meant to pay. The effect of this and the previous point is to see the crucifixion, as it relates to people conceived after Christ's death, as an impersonal and abstract sort of substitution and payment. He cannot really have died personally in *their* place nor for *their* very own sin. In fact, Christ would have had reason to wonder, as he hung on that cross, whether for any, or for how many, and for what sins, he was now giving his life. The sin paid for could only be sin in principle, and not sin by imputation, and the people died for was a blurry, impersonal, faceless, nameless, and numberless potential grouping.

IV. The Gospel's Consummation Assuring the Certainty of the Fulfillment of God's Good and Wise Saving Purposes

Finally, the Christian church has ever rejoiced in the hope of the certain victory of God over all that stands against him. And this hope has been

---

[35] Boyd, "Christian Love and Academic Dialogue," 242.

understood not only to include God one day bringing an end to the world as we know it, but centrally that when he does consummate history, *he will have accomplished what he purposed and designed for this world.* But of this, we simply cannot be sure, if the open view is accepted. After all, to the extent that one holds that God took a significant risk in his creation of the world, one must admit that it may turn out that God gets less than he wanted. How much less? The fact is, we simply cannot know. The gospel—that announces to those in Christ the surety of our lives in God's hands and the confidence of knowing that God's purposes will succeed—becomes less than good news if the open view is accepted. Consider implications for life now and beyond when one denies of God his exhaustive knowledge of the future.

1. Open theism's denial of God's exhaustive definite foreknowledge undermines the Christian's hope that affliction, suffering, and trials in life are permitted by God for what he knows will turn out to be ultimately good purposes (e.g., Rom. 8:28; c.f. Rom. 5:1-5; James 1:2-4).

Any assurance we might have had that the hardships and trials of life are part of a bigger wise and good plan is now taken away. God's plans change, and frankly many, many things happen that he wishes did not. God simply cannot give assurances that things will work out for good because he doesn't know how the future will unfold. Face it: we may encounter gratuitous evil at any turn, unexpected and unwanted by God, and utterly pointless[36] in its purpose for us. Don't expect God to know what you and I cannot know, viz., that there are good purposes ultimately for this suffering. Accept it: this is the nature of life lived with a God lacking such knowledge of the future.

One of the most sobering aspects of the open view is what it does to Christian confidence in God. We are commended throughout Scripture to put our hope and trust in God alone. No one else can be trusted fully, but he can be, we are told in many ways in text after text. But what shall we now say of this openness proposal in which "God"

---

[36] Recall Sanders's quote: "When a two-month-old child contracts a painful, incurable bone cancer that means suffering and death, it is pointless evil. The Holocaust is pointless evil. The rape and dismemberment of a young girl is pointless evil. The accident that caused the death of my brother was a tragedy. God does not have a specific purpose in mind for these occurrences" (*The God Who Risks*, 262).

learns that the advice he gave us turns out not to have been best? What shall we say of a "God" who looks back, and in retrospect regrets his own previous decision or action? How shall we trust a "God" when walking into a foggy and misty future, when that same God, with the best of motives, gave admittedly poor direction at crucial junctures in the past?

Without the confidence that God works *all things* together for good, to those who love God, to those who are called according to his purpose, we will despair. How strengthening it is, when facing tragedy, to know God's wise and loving hand is guiding precisely what occurs. But open theism takes from the church this confidence, and so open theism presents to the church a false understanding of God.

2. *Open theism's denial of God's exhaustive definite foreknowledge calls into question the church's ultimate eschatological hope that God will surely accomplish all his plans and purposes, exactly as he has told us in Scripture that he will; and openness assurances that he will succeed ring hollow, in that not even God knows (i.e., can know) what unexpected turns lay ahead and how severely these may thwart his purposes or cause him to change his plans.*

Openness advocates want it both ways. They want high risk, and they also want high assurance of God's success. They cannot have it both ways. Clearly, what wins in the open view is risk; what loses is assurance of God's success. If even God cannot now know the outcome of his purposes with free creatures, we certainly cannot be sure whether those plans and purposes will prevail. At best, we can hope that God will somehow get most of what he wants. But we simply cannot be sure that he will—nor can he be sure! In the end, the gospel's very consummation is affected by the open view's denial of God's exhaustive definite foreknowledge. In the end, and only then, will God and we know just how successful his plan has been. Until then, we hope for the best, but we also fear the worst. Once again, we see the contrast with the true gospel of certain hope and the end of fear, based on the confidence that God knows the end from the beginning, and that the consummation will be just as he has planned. What glory, what joy, and what blessing—in the true gospel of our gracious and glorious all-knowing God.

CONCLUSION

Four areas central to the certainty and reality of the gospel are deeply compromised by the open view. The surety and specificity of God's plan, in eternity past, to save sinners; the saving acts of justification and sacrificial atonement for sin in the life of Old Testament Israel; the certainty and nature of the very substitutionary death and resurrection of Christ our Savior; and our confident and expectant hope for life now and for eternity—all require massive reformulation, given open theism's central commitments. In the end, when seen through the lens of the open view, this reformulated gospel is no longer the same gospel cherished by the church and taught by the Scriptures. As such, it ought not to be commended by Christians or accepted as a viable evangelical understanding. When a theological proposal has compromised the very gospel itself, it has moved beyond the bounds. May God grant courage, clarity, charity, and fidelity to chart the way forward in exploring and expounding the true wonder of the glorious gospel of Jesus Christ, to the honor of the triune God who alone secures it—and us—to the end.[37]

---

[37] I would like to express special thanks to Justin Taylor, Paul Kjoss Helseth, and Ashton G. Wilkins, all of whom read various versions of this chapter and offered valuable critical reflections. I did not always (perhaps foolishly) follow their counsel, but in many respects this chapter is stronger for their input.

PART FIVE

Drawing Boundaries and Conclusions

10

Why, When, and for What Should We Draw New Boundaries?

Wayne Grudem

Introduction

Christian groups usually have doctrinal statements that define the "boundaries" of their organizations. How can they know whether to add new topics to their doctrinal statements from time to time? This is the question of drawing new boundaries.

I will consider four questions in this essay:

A. Why should Christian organizations draw boundaries *at all?*
B. Why should Christian organizations draw *new* boundaries?
C. *When* should Christian organizations draw new boundaries?
D. For *what doctrinal and ethical matters* should Christian organizations draw new boundaries?

A. Why Should Christian Organizations Draw Boundaries *at All?*

When I say "Christian organizations" I mean all kinds of organizations, certainly including both local churches and denominations, and also mission organizations, specialized ministries like Campus Crusade for Christ or Focus on the Family, educational institutions (including

Christian schools, colleges, and seminaries), other kinds of organizations like Christian book publishers, Christian radio stations, professional groups like the Evangelical Theological Society (ETS), and so forth. The four questions I am asking here are relevant, I believe, for all Christian organizations.

By the term "boundaries" I am referring primarily to doctrinal statements that are enforced by an organization. Usually "enforcement" occurs when people are required to agree with a doctrinal statement either for membership or for certain kinds of leadership in that organization.[1]

For example, churches and denominations hold ordination councils, and churches interview prospective pastors. These activities serve as means of enforcing their doctrinal statements. Theological seminaries and Christian colleges likewise interview prospective faculty members at length, asking if they agree with the institution's statement of faith. Mission boards also interview prospective missionaries regarding their doctrinal soundness and allegiance to the doctrinal distinctives of the mission board. The Evangelical Theological Society (a professional society for evangelical scholars) simply requires that members annually sign an affirmation of the ETS doctrinal statement, and so there is a mild sort of enforcement by the "honor system," and, to some extent, by peer pressure. Such doctrinal enforcement mechanisms, when they function correctly, tend to keep people who differ with the beliefs of the organization from gaining influence and making the organization into something different.

If someone is admitted to a position of influence and then changes his mind about what he believes (for example, if a pastor decides he no longer believes in the deity of Christ), then another kind of "enforcement" comes into effect. In such cases, Christian organizations usually have procedures to follow whereby a person who no longer holds to the organization's beliefs can be removed from a position of influence.

But *why* should Christian organizations have such boundaries, such enforced doctrinal statements? There are several reasons.

---

[1] In addition to formal doctrinal statements, Christian organizations usually have some other policies and traditions that also serve as "boundaries" to protect the organization's character and distinctives. Some of these other boundaries are written, some are oral, and some may merely be practiced by habit. What I say in this essay will also have some application to these less formal boundaries, but they are not the focus of my attention.

1. False Teaching Harms the Church

To say "false teaching harms the church" is perhaps just to state the obvious, but in a day marked by much pluralism and subjectivism it bears repeating. The very *existence* of the epistles in the New Testament testifies to the importance that the apostles placed on sound doctrine! In the epistles, sound doctrine is taught again and again, and error is implicitly or explicitly corrected. This is the case in every New Testament epistle.

I am not at this point defining *what kinds of false teaching* do such harm to the church, for that is a task that comes at the end of this essay. At this point it is enough to note that *some* false teaching harms the church (as it did in the first century), and the New Testament epistles give several examples of such harmful teaching.

Sometimes false doctrine in the early churches threatened the gospel itself. Paul was concerned that false teachers would come to the churches of Galatia, even preaching a "different gospel" (Gal. 1:6), in which case Paul says they should be "accursed" (vv. 8, 9).[2] And he told the Galatians that if they gave in to those who wanted to require circumcision, Christ would be of "no advantage" to them (Gal. 5:2). The implication is that salvation itself was at stake because people could not be saved through a false gospel.

False teaching was a continual threat in other churches as well. For example, Paul warned the elders at Ephesus that "fierce wolves" would come in, "not sparing the flock," and that even from among the elders themselves, there would arise "men speaking twisted things, to draw away the disciples after them" (Acts 20:29-30).

When writing to Timothy about the church at Ephesus, Paul said that those who teach a "different doctrine" (1 Tim. 6:3), far from promoting the peace and unity of the church, and far from giving the church greater insight through conversations about their novel ideas, actually harmed the church by their "unhealthy craving for controversy and for quarrels about words, which produce envy, dissension, slander, evil suspicions, and constant friction among people who are depraved in mind and deprived of the truth" (vv. 4-5). Paul also warned Timothy to

---

[2] Unless otherwise noted, Scripture quotations in this chapter are from the English Standard Version of the Bible.

"avoid" the "irreverent babble and contradictions" of certain false teachers, for by professing what they called "knowledge," Paul says that some of them had *"swerved from the faith"* (vv. 20-21). In his subsequent letter to Timothy, Paul again warned Timothy to "avoid" such "irreverent babble," for, he said, *"it will lead people into more and more ungodliness"* (2 Tim. 2:16). In fact, Paul knew that this was already happening, for Hymenaeus and Philetus were "upsetting the faith of some" (vv. 17-18). He also warned that in latter times some would *"depart from the faith* by devoting themselves to deceitful spirits and teachings of demons" (1 Tim. 4:1).

With respect to the churches in Crete, Paul wrote to Titus that elders had to be able both "to give instruction in sound doctrine and also to rebuke those who contradict it" (Titus 1:9). He knew that false teachers there were "upsetting whole families by teaching for shameful gain what they ought not to teach" (Titus 1:11).

Peter, in writing to probably hundreds of churches in "Pontus, Galatia, Cappadocia, Asia, and Bithynia" (1 Pet. 1:1; cf. 2 Pet. 3:1), warned that false teachers would arise among the people, and that they would "secretly bring in *destructive heresies"* (2 Pet. 2:1), that *"many will follow* their sensuality," and that "because of them the way of truth will be blasphemed" (v. 2).

Jude, in a similar way, urged his readers to "contend for the faith that was once for all delivered to the saints" (Jude 3) because certain false teachers had "crept in unnoticed" and, far from being harmless, they were people who "pervert the grace of our God into sensuality and deny our only Master and Lord, Jesus Christ" (Jude 4).

After reading such verses, we might wonder if any of us have the same kind of heart for purity of doctrine in our Christian organizations, and the same sort of sober apprehension of the destructiveness of false doctrine, that the New Testament apostles had in their hearts.

If we ever begin to doubt that false teaching is harmful to the church, or if we begin to become complacent about false doctrine, thinking that it is fascinating to ponder, stimulating to our thoughts, and worthwhile for discussion, then we should remind ourselves that in several cases the New Testament specifies that the ultimate source of many false teachings is Satan and his demons:

Now the Spirit expressly says that in latter times some will depart from the faith by devoting themselves to *deceitful spirits and teachings of demons.* (1 Tim. 4:1)

And the Lord's servant must not be quarrelsome but kind to everyone, able to teach, patiently enduring evil, correcting his opponents with gentleness. God may perhaps grant them repentance leading to a knowledge of the truth, and they may escape from *the snare of the devil,* after being captured by him to do his will. (2 Tim. 2:24-26)

For many deceivers have gone out into the world, those who do not confess the coming of Jesus Christ in the flesh. Such a one is the deceiver and the antichrist. (2 John 7)

2. If False Teaching Is Not Stopped, It Spreads and Does More and More Damage

Speaking personally, I think that my profession as a scholar contributes easily to a tendency to overlook the increasing damage that is done by false teaching when it is not corrected but is allowed to continue in a church or in a Christian organization. In fact, professional academics whose minds are trained by constant practice to see the errors in false teaching can easily slip into thinking that all believers will have those same analytical skills and that all believers will quickly recognize false teaching for what it is and pay no heed to it. But if we think this we deceive ourselves into a wrongful complacency. Again and again the New Testament writers warn that false teaching is deceptive, and that false teachers *do* draw people away after them. Consider the following passages:

Your boasting is not good. Do you not know that a little leaven leavens the whole lump? (1 Cor. 5:6, regarding a man living in incest and the Corinthian church tolerating his presence in the church)

A little leaven leavens the whole lump. (Gal. 5:9, in this case with those who preached the necessity of circumcision)

[And] their talk will spread like gangrene. Among them are Hymenaeus and Philetus, who have swerved from the truth, saying that the resurrection has already happened. (2 Tim. 2:17-18)

Here Paul pictures false teachers quietly working their influence among unsuspecting church members, spreading silently and invisibly like "gangrene" or "leaven." In practical terms, once a church or a Christian organization allows some vocal advocates of a false teaching (or even one) to have a position of influence, then those people become precedents by which others can be allowed in. For example, if Professor X has been teaching at a certain seminary for fifteen years, and then he suddenly decides that he no longer believes in the inerrancy of the Bible, and if the seminary allows him to continue teaching there, they have a serious problem. This is because he or others can argue, "We have no right to refuse to hire Professor Y or Professor Z, who also deny inerrancy, since we did not exclude Professor X. You don't think we should fire our friend Professor X, do you?" And so the anti-inerrancy teaching gains more and more influence.

Paul warned the elders at Ephesus:

> I know that after my departure fierce wolves will come in among you, not sparing the flock; and from among your own selves will arise men speaking twisted things, to draw away the disciples after them. (Acts 20:29-30)

This passage pictures great damage. It portrays wolves among a flock of sheep. The longer they remain the more damage they will do. Paul does not say, "Oh, the sheep will see the problem and they'll reason with the wolf and they'll all come to a new, deeper understanding of life."

Sometimes the problems will come from without ("fierce wolves will come in among you"), but sometimes the problems will come from within, for Paul tells these elders, whom he loved and trusted, "*from among your own selves* will arise men speaking twisted things . . ." We must recognize that most false teaching in the history of the church has come from people with a sincere profession of faith in Christ, and many of them were devout, genuine Christians who had a love for Christ and strong faith—but they were deceived by some wrong idea. Even the apostle Peter was deceived at one point, and Paul had to correct him publicly:

> But when Cephas came to Antioch, I opposed him to his face, because he stood condemned. For before certain men came from James, he was eating with the Gentiles; but when they came he drew back and sepa-

rated himself, fearing the circumcision party. And the rest of the Jews acted hypocritically along with him, so that even Barnabas was led astray by their hypocrisy. But when I saw that their conduct was not in step with the truth of the gospel, I said to Cephas before them all, "If you, though a Jew, live like a Gentile and not like a Jew, how can you force the Gentiles to live like Jews?" (Gal. 2:11-14)

Therefore the argument that a person is a strong Christian and has had a fruitful ministry in the lives of many does not prove that his teaching is correct, or that it is harmless.

3. If False Teaching Is Not Stopped, We Will Waste Time and Energy in Endless Controversies Rather Than Doing Valuable Kingdom Work

Several times Paul urged his readers to "avoid controversies." I do not think that he meant they should avoid profitable doctrinal discussions or even useful debate, for Paul himself often argued with his opponents' positions in his epistles, and he would spend many hours reasoning with people. For example, at Corinth, "he reasoned in the synagogue every Sabbath, and tried to persuade Jews and Greeks" (Acts 18:4). In the apostolic council in Acts 15, there was "much debate" (v. 7). And when Apollos came to Achaia, "he greatly helped those who through grace had believed, for he powerfully refuted the Jews in public, showing by the Scriptures that the Christ was Jesus" (Acts 18:27-28). Similarly, Jude appeals to his readers "to contend for the faith that was once for all delivered to the saints" (Jude 3), and Paul wanted church leaders to be able to do this as well, because he said that elders had to be "able to give instruction in sound doctrine and also to rebuke those who contradict it" (Titus 1:9).

Therefore when Paul urged readers to "avoid controversies," he did not mean all controversies, but rather the fruitless, endless controversies that disrupt the peace of the church, that hinder us from doing more productive ministry, and that show no indication of moving toward resolution. Here are some of his warnings:

But avoid irreverent babble, for it will lead people into more and more ungodliness. (2 Tim. 2:16)

> Have nothing to do with foolish, ignorant controversies; you know that they breed quarrels. (2 Tim. 2:23)

> But avoid foolish controversies, genealogies, dissensions, and quarrels about the law, for they are unprofitable and worthless. (Titus 3:9)

> If anyone teaches a different doctrine and does not agree with the sound words of our Lord Jesus Christ and the teaching that accords with godliness, he is puffed up with conceit and understands nothing. He has an unhealthy craving for controversy and for quarrels about words, which produce envy, dissension, slander, evil suspicions, and constant friction among people who are depraved in mind and deprived of the truth, imagining that godliness is a means of gain. (1 Tim. 6:3-5)

When Paul tells Titus and Timothy to "avoid" such controversies and to "have nothing to do" with them, it shows us that there comes a point when it is no longer wise for a church to continue arguing over certain controversies. The church or organization should come to a decision, and then it should go on to other things.

4. Jesus and the New Testament Authors Hold Church Leaders Responsible for Silencing False Teaching Within the Church

Sometimes Christian leaders can become complacent—thinking that a few people who teach false doctrine aren't doing that much harm in the church or the Christian organization, and not many people are believing them—and therefore no harm will come by allowing them to continue to have a platform to promote their views from time to time.

But that is not the view of Jesus or the New Testament authors. They see the destructive influence that false teaching has in a church, and they expect that those in authority will remove the platform that these false teachers have. Consider these verses:

> For there are many who are insubordinate, empty talkers and deceivers, especially those of the circumcision party. *They must be silenced,* since they are upsetting whole families by teaching for shameful gain what they ought not to teach. (Titus 1:10-11)

But *false prophets* also arose among the people, just as there will be *false teachers* among you, who will secretly bring in destructive heresies, even denying the master who bought them, bringing upon themselves swift destruction. And many will follow their sensuality, and because of them the way of truth will be blasphemed. And *in their greed they will exploit you with false words.* Their condemnation from long ago is not idle, and their destruction is not asleep. (2 Pet. 2:1-3)

But if these false teachers are similar in many ways to the "false prophets" in the Old Testament, what should be done with them? In the Old Covenant, a false prophet who said, "Let us go after other gods . . . and let us serve them" (Deut. 13:2) was to be punished with death: ". . . that prophet or that dreamer of dreams shall be put to death, because he has taught rebellion against the LORD your God" (v. 5). In the New Testament, the corresponding penalty to putting a false prophet to death would be putting the person outside of the church, and this is similar to what John says should happen to those who do not confess that Jesus Christ has come in the flesh:

If anyone comes to you and does not bring this teaching, do not receive him into your house or give him any greeting. (2 John 10)

Most sobering are the rebukes of the risen Lord Jesus himself against churches that tolerated the presence of false teachers. Jesus rebuked the church at Pergamum *merely for having among them* people who held to certain false teachings:

But I have a few things against you: you have some there who hold the teaching of Balaam, who taught Balak to put a stumbling block before the sons of Israel, so that they might eat food sacrificed to idols and practice sexual immorality. (Rev. 2:14)

He also rebuked them because they had some there who held "the teaching of the Nicolaitans" (Rev. 2:15).

Similarly, Jesus rebuked the church at Thyatira:

But I have this against you, that you tolerate that woman Jezebel, who calls herself a prophetess and is teaching and seducing my servants to practice sexual immorality and to eat food sacrificed to idols. (Rev. 2:20)

What was wrong? They merely *tolerated* in their midst a false teacher, and Christ rebuked them.

These false teachers were so harmful to the church that these churches' failure to exclude them brought Christ's displeasure and rebuke. Such passages combine to indicate that the Lord Jesus holds churches responsible, and holds Christian leaders responsible, for silencing false teaching within the church and within Christian organizations.

5. Objection: Doctrinal Boundaries Don't Do Any Good, Because They Cannot Be Enforced

Sometimes people will object to the claim that we should exclude false teachers from the church or a Christian organization by using doctrinal boundaries. They will claim (1) that people will be dishonest and say that they agree with our doctrinal statements when they don't, and (2) that leaders simply won't have the courage to enforce these boundaries, especially when close friends are involved with teaching the false doctrine.

In response, we can agree that doctrinal boundaries will not solve every problem in a Christian organization. But they still do much good, first, because when they are made known they prevent most people who hold other viewpoints from joining a church or organization. Second, while some who hold false teachings may be dishonest about them, as soon as they begin to teach them, their views will be known. And not all of them will be dishonest, but some will frankly admit that they have different views, hoping to persuade others. Third, the existence of doctrinal boundaries gives leaders in an organization a clear standard to use in choosing new leaders and in exercising discipline for those who begin to adopt a different viewpoint. If there is no such written doctrinal boundary, then exercising discipline against leaders is exceptionally difficult.

B. WHY SHOULD CHRISTIAN ORGANIZATIONS DRAW NEW BOUNDARIES?

When I speak of "new boundaries," I do not mean boundaries that would make an organization fundamentally different from what it was from its beginning. For example, the Evangelical Theological Society has included, since its beginning in 1949, both Calvinists and Arminians, both Pentecostals and cessationists, both advocates of infant baptism and advocates of believer's baptism, and also members who hold differing views on the millennium, on church government, and on a number of other issues. I do not believe that the ETS should ever try to exclude Arminians (for example) and become the "Reformed Theological Society" because that would make it a fundamentally different and fundamentally narrower organization from what it was at its beginning.[3]

Rather, when I speak of "new boundaries," I mean boundaries that for the first time state explicitly what was already believed and assumed to be true by the vast majority of the members of an organization for many years. There are times when certain things that everyone believed in the past come to be challenged by people within an organization. Then the members of the organization see a threat that the organization might become significantly different than what it was in the first place. In such a case, "new boundaries" are put into place *to keep the organization from becoming something significantly different* from what it has been.

This process may be summarized in the following principle.

1. False Teaching Changes, So Old Boundaries Do Not Protect Against New Problems

We can notice remarkable changes in the kinds of false teaching that need to be excluded if we compare the New Testament with the creeds of the early church, and then with the creeds of the Reformation, and then with our modern age.

The New Testament writers opposed several different kinds of false teaching, such as telling believers, "Unless you are circumcised according to the custom of Moses, you cannot be saved" (Acts 15:1; cf. Gal. 5:1-6), or teaching that "there is no resurrection of the dead" (1 Cor. 15:12), or insisting on "worship of angels" (Col. 2:18), or saying that "the resurrection has already happened" (2 Tim. 2:18). The New Testament authors also warned against other teachings that would come in the future, some of which may have already been present, such as scoffing at the promise that Jesus would return (2 Pet. 3:3-4), or forbidding marriage (1 Tim. 4:3), or saying that Christians could not eat

---

[3] However, there may be times when a Christian organization or a denomination should become more restrictive than it was from the beginning, because the church is always to be reforming itself in the light of further understanding of Scripture.

certain kinds of foods (1 Tim. 4:3; Col. 2:16), or denying that Jesus is the Messiah (1 John 2:22), or denying that Jesus Christ actually came "in the flesh" (2 John 7).[4]

But by the time of the Nicene Creed (A.D. 325 and 381) the church was dealing with entirely different problems, problems concerning the doctrine of the Trinity. The Nicene Creed affirmed the full deity of the Son and of the Holy Spirit in distinction from those who were denying these things. Then in the next century, in the Chalcedonian Creed of 451, there was a need for a new boundary, a need to affirm the unity of the divine and human natures of Christ in one person, with "the property of each nature being preserved."

But when we come to the Reformation in the beginning of the sixteenth century, the church is facing entirely different problems, and the great Reformation creeds address problems that did not face churches at the time of the New Testament, and that did not face churches at the time of Nicea or Chalcedon. The leaders of the Reformation found it necessary to draw boundaries that excluded the doctrines of purgatory and indulgences (which were sold to shorten people's supposed time in purgatory). They found it necessary to establish doctrinal boundaries that insisted on justification by grace alone through faith alone, and they insisted that "Scripture alone" (*sola Scriptura*) was the ultimate authority for doctrine (in contrast to the Roman Catholic view that Scripture and the authoritative teaching of the church are both sources of doctrinal truth). The Reformers also affirmed the priesthood of all believers (as opposed to the Roman Catholic emphasis on the need to approach God through the priesthood). Except for the doctrine of justification by faith alone (addressed especially in Romans and Galatians), *none of these problems had been necessary to address explicitly in the ancient creeds or in the New Testament writings*, because the false teachings that

---

[4] For a detailed survey of the kinds of false teaching opposed by New Testament authors, see Craig L. Blomberg, "The New Testament Definition of Heresy (or When Do Jesus and the Apostles Really Get Mad?)," *Journal of the Evangelical Theological Society (JETS)* 45 (2002): 59-72. Though Blomberg lists numerous areas of doctrinal concern found in the New Testament, the point of his article is to argue that Jesus and the apostles are deeply concerned about only a very short list of doctrinal matters: "the full deity and the full humanity of Christ," "salvation by grace through faith" (including a life of submitting to the resurrected Jesus and exhibiting the fruit befitting repentance), "Christ's still future, visible return," "keeping security and perseverance in balance," avoiding "defeatism," "triumphalism," and "perfectionism," and obeying a few standards of Christian conduct (70). Beyond this short list, Blomberg is reluctant to endorse the addition of any doctrinal boundaries (70-71).

required such new boundaries had not been present in the church in earlier ages in any significant way.[5]

In the twentieth century, the church faced new problems. For example, the denial of the inerrancy of Scripture troubled many denominations, and statements about inerrancy were placed in some doctrinal statements (for instance, in the statement of the Evangelical Theological Society at its founding in 1949, or in the statement of the Evangelical Free Church at its founding), but such statements had not been needed in the Nicene Creed or the Chalcedonian Creed because in those earlier centuries everyone just assumed biblical inerrancy to be true.

In recent years within the evangelical world, other problems have arisen, such as the affirmation of annihilationism (the view that unbelievers will be "annihilated" and simply cease to exist, rather than undergoing eternal conscious punishment, after they die), and inclusivism (the idea that people who have never heard of Christ or trusted in him will be saved by his atoning work anyway). And some within the evangelical world have now argued against the idea of the atonement as penal substitution.[6] With regard to a contemporary ethical matter, I

---

[5] This is one reason why Blomberg's article, "The New Testament Definition of Heresy" (see previous footnote), while it contains a very helpful survey of the types of false teaching opposed by the New Testament authors, should not be used as a sort of "maximal" list of the kinds of teachings churches and Christian organizations should exclude today. Blomberg suggests that Christians who have insisted on boundaries in addition to those specified in his survey have been too restrictive, for he says, "By way of contrast [to the New Testament authors], the last century of American evangelicalism has majored on creating extensive doctrinal statements to separate itself from outsiders, usually adding numerous *adiaphora* to more central matters" (71). But Blomberg fails to take into account at least three additional factors: (1) New heresies have arisen in every generation, heresies that contradicted the teaching of the Bible but were not explicitly opposed by New Testament authors because nobody was advocating them in the first-century church. (2) Paul's gentle correction of some errors (such as the idea that Christ had already returned, in 2 Thess. 2:1-12) may not indicate that he thought the error unimportant, but might be due to several other factors, such as his expectation that the specific church (for example, the Thessalonians) would respond readily to his gentle correction, or perhaps that he thought the error was merely the result of misunderstanding or lack of sufficient teaching (so he did not need, in Blomberg's words, to "really get mad"). (3) The expression *adiaphora* (literally, "things that do not differ") has generally been applied to matters of personal conduct on which Scripture does not require one particular kind of conduct for all Christians (such as moderate use of alcohol, or abstaining from meat [Rom. 14:2], or observing certain days as special [Rom. 14:5]). While Christians have differed over what activities belong in the category of *adiaphora*, they have agreed that the category refers to matters about which Christians have personal freedom to make individual decisions. But Blomberg uses the term *adiaphora* in a different way, to refer to all matters of Christian doctrine except his brief list of doctrines about which the New Testament writers "really get mad," thus implying that in other areas it is inappropriate to draw boundaries. As the history of development of the creeds shows, many things beyond Blomberg's short list were not at all considered *adiaphora*, but were found to be essential for preserving the life and health of the church.

[6] See Joel B. Green and Mark D. Baker, *Recovering the Scandal of the Cross* (Downers Grove, Ill.: InterVarsity Press, 2000).

expect that evangelical churches and organizations will soon find themselves having to articulate a doctrinal standard regarding homosexuality, because of the immense pressure in our culture and because of the pattern in more liberal denominations of already giving various degrees of approval to homosexual conduct.

Therefore, *because we now face several new problems with false doctrine* (and I have listed here several views which in my judgment do constitute significantly harmful false doctrine), *old doctrinal formulations that do not address these questions are inadequate.* They do not sufficiently protect the church and protect Christian organizations from the influence of these viewpoints.

I believe that the Evangelical Theological Society is a good example of an organization that will soon need to add new written boundaries to its doctrinal statement. The original doctrinal statement of the ETS in 1949 was very simple: "The Bible alone, and the Bible in its entirety, is the Word of God written, and therefore inerrant in the autographs." Then at a later point, because of a growing influence from some non-Trinitarian people who had joined the ETS, an additional sentence was added: "God is a Trinity, Father, Son, and Holy Spirit, each an uncreated Person, one in essence, equal in power and glory."

Fifty years ago an affirmation of belief in inerrancy worked quite well to separate genuine evangelicals from those who were not. However, it seems to me that today these two sentences in the ETS statement are not enough to exclude some serious theological errors that are affirmed by some members of the ETS, in particular the belief in "open theism," but also some of the other issues mentioned above. It seems appropriate and even necessary, then, that the ETS should adopt a revised, longer doctrinal statement that would put more effective boundaries in place. Such a statement (to reaffirm what I said earlier) should not try to make the ETS different from what it always has been, but should aim to keep the ETS from becoming different from what it always has been.

I am also convinced that other Christian organizations and denominations will soon need to add new boundaries to protect against these new forms of false teaching, and if they don't, as explained in the first section above, these new false teachings will harm the church, will spread and do more and more damage, will consume huge amounts of time and energy in unproductive and endless controversies, and will soon bring the Lord's displeasure upon these organizations for tolerating such harmful false teachings.

2. Why Does God in His Sovereignty Allow These Various False Teachings to Come into the Church in Different Ages?

If we believe that God is sovereign over history, and sovereign over his church in particular, then we might look at the history of the church and ask why God chose to allow this diverse array of false teachings to trouble his people throughout the history of the church.

a. THE PURIFICATION OF THE CHURCH

I can suggest three reasons why God would allow such false doctrine to have influence within the church (though there may be more reasons as well). The first is for the purification of the church. Paul tells us,

> . . . Christ loved the church and gave himself up for her, that he might sanctify her, having cleansed her by the washing of water with the word, so that he might present the church to himself in splendor, without spot or wrinkle or any such thing, that she might be holy and without blemish. (Eph. 5:25b-27)

Now we might ask, will this sanctification or purification process be carried out gradually throughout the church age, or will none of it happen until the very moment when Christ returns? The parallel Paul draws with the husband's love and care for his wife suggests that he has in mind an ongoing process of purification of the church throughout the church age. In fact, the pattern of God's work among his people throughout Scripture is to work in them *gradually* to fulfill his purposes, whether it be calling Abraham to himself and then over centuries making the people of Israel into a great nation, or bringing the promised Messiah to earth through the people of Israel, or spreading the gospel to the Jews and then to the Gentiles, or proclaiming the gospel to all nations on earth, or causing the influence of the kingdom of God to spread gradually throughout the earth as yeast works its way through a lump of dough or as a mustard seed grows into a large tree (see Matt. 13:31-33). Similarly, in our own individual lives, the process of sanctification is a gradual one that continues throughout life. In fact, the entire story of God's work found in Scripture is a story in which God gradually reveals more and more of his glory over time and throughout the stages of his work of redemption.

Therefore Ephesians 5 has in mind a gradual and increasing process of purifying the church over time, until the time when Christ will be able to "present the church to himself in splendor, without spot or wrinkle or any such thing . . . holy and without blemish" (Eph. 5:27).

In fact, we can look back on history and see a process of gradual purification of the church. As I mentioned in another context,

> Sometimes that process of purification has been marked by specific historical events; for example, in 325 and 381, the Nicene Creed; in 451, the Chalcedonian Creed; in 1517, Martin Luther's 95 theses; even in 1978, the International Council on Biblical Inerrancy's "Chicago Statement on Biblical Inerrancy." At other times, there has been no one defining moment, but a gradual rejection of misunderstanding and a growing consensus endorsing biblical truth in some area. For example: the rejection of the militarism of the Crusades and their attempt to use the sword to advance the Church; or the realization that the Bible does not teach that the sun goes around the earth; or, in the 16th and 17th centuries, the marvelous advances in doctrinal syntheses that found expression in the great confessions of faith following the Reformation; or, in the 17th and 18th centuries, the realization that the civil government could and should allow religious freedom; or, in the 19th century, the growing consensus that slavery is wrong and must be abolished; or, in the 20th century, the growing consensus that abortion is contrary to Scripture. Other examples could be given, but the pattern should be clear: Jesus Christ has not given up his task of purifying his Church. The long-term pattern has not been 19 centuries of decline in the purity and doctrinal and ethical understanding of the Church, but rather a pattern of gradual and sometimes explosive increase in understanding and purity.[7]

But all of those advances have come through controversy. As the church has struggled to define its own beliefs clearly in distinction from

---

[7] Wayne Grudem, "Do We Act As If We Really Believe That 'The Bible Alone, and the Bible in Its Entirety, Is the Word of God Written'?" (1999 ETS Presidential Address) *JETS* 43 (2000): 13. In this statement, I am not talking about the doctrinal confusion among denominations dominated by liberal theology, where many have abandoned the truthfulness of Scripture and belief in the God of the Bible, but rather I am talking about the vast central body of Christians who have fully believed the Bible throughout history.

false doctrine, it has grown in its understanding of the teachings of Scripture. So God has used controversy to purify his church. In the process of controversy, old errors have been corrected, and the church has refined its understanding of many things it had believed implicitly but not in a detailed or deeply understood way. Thus, the doctrine of the Trinity came to be understood much more fully and clearly through the doctrinal controversies of the fourth century. Similarly, the doctrine of biblical inerrancy came to be understood much more fully through the inerrancy controversies of the last part of the twentieth century. In our present time, controversies over the nature of spiritual gifts and over appropriate roles for men and women in the home and in the church are also resulting in much deeper understanding of the teachings of God's Word on those subjects. Through controversy, God purifies the church.

b. TESTING THE FAITHFULNESS OF GOD'S PEOPLE

But I think there is another reason why God allows false teachings to have influence in the church. Through these false teachings, God tests the faithfulness of his people. Will we be faithful to him in the face of some influential false teaching advocated by winsome people, many of whom we consider our friends?

In the Old Testament, God told his people he would allow false prophets among them to test their hearts:

> If a prophet or a dreamer of dreams arises among you and gives you a sign or a wonder, and the sign or wonder that he tells you comes to pass, and if he says, "Let us go after other gods," which you have not known, "and let us serve them," you shall not listen to the words of that prophet or that dreamer of dreams. *For the* LORD *your God is testing you, to know whether you love the* LORD *your God with all your heart and with all your soul.* (Deut. 13:1-3)

Now I am not saying that everyone who teaches false doctrine in a church or Christian organization today is like a false prophet in the Old Testament who said, "Let us go after other gods . . . and let us serve them." I believe that throughout the history of the church many who advocated a certain false teaching were genuine believers who were making a serious mistake in teaching something that was wrong. And even today many who deny biblical inerrancy or who advocate open theism are genuine believers. But there is still a parallel here, because we can see a similar purpose of God for allowing such false teaching to have influence in the church. God is watching our response to it, and watching our hearts, to see if we will be faithful to him and to his Word.

Believing the Bible is not always the easiest or most popular thing to defend. There are many things that God asks us to believe that are not really logical contradictions but are mysteries or paradoxes, matters that we cannot fully explain. For example, the doctrine of the Trinity, or the hypostatic union of Christ (the union of Christ's human and divine natures in one person), or God's sovereignty and our responsibility, are doctrines that fall in this category. Why can we not explain fully what the Trinity is like? It is because there is nothing in all creation that is exactly like the Trinity! There is no other being that consists of three distinct persons, with each person possessing the whole of that being in himself, and yet the three together are only one being, not three. How can this be? It is not a contradiction, but it is a mystery beyond our comprehension.

And then there are other doctrines in which God does not ask us to approve something that is evil or wrong, but asks us to believe things that are emotionally hard for us to receive, at least in this age. Such doctrines include the doctrine of hell (with the eternal conscious punishment of the wicked), and the doctrine of God's sovereignty in relationship to evil, for example.

In these matters that are not easy to defend, and in many more, the question is, will we believe them, not because we can explain them fully, and not because we enjoy them and take delight in them in our present state of understanding, but simply because God's Word teaches them and we submit to his Word?

Throughout our lives as Christians, from time to time God will test our hearts to see whether we will be faithful in believing all that he teaches in his Word. If we are faithful, and if we pass the test, then God will often entrust us with more stewardship in the work of his kingdom.

c. TESTING OUR ATTITUDE TOWARD FALSE TEACHERS

I think there is also a third reason why God allows various false teachings to have influence in the church. God is also testing our attitude of heart toward the false teachers. Will we act in love and gentleness toward those with whom we disagree?

When he looked back on the splits that occurred in the Presbyterian church in the 1920s and 30s, Francis Schaeffer (who had been part of the conservative group that left the Presbyterian church) said,

> At the same time, however, we must show forth the love of God to those with whom we differ. Thirty-five years ago in the Presbyterian crisis in the United States, we forgot that. We did not speak with love about those with whom we differed, and we have been paying a high price for it ever since . . . we did not talk of the need to show love as we stood against liberalism, and, as the Presbyterian Church was lost, that lack has cost us dearly.[8]

Paul reminds Timothy,

> And the Lord's servant *must not be quarrelsome* but *kind to everyone,* able to teach, patiently enduring evil, *correcting his opponents with gentleness.* God may perhaps grant them repentance leading to a knowledge of the truth, and they may escape from the snare of the devil, after being captured by him to do his will. (2 Tim. 2:24-26)

As we confront others who teach what we consider to be false doctrine today, God is testing not only our faithfulness regarding what we believe and what we write into our doctrinal statements but also how we act toward those with whom we disagree. Will we continue to act toward them with love and kindness, even when we come to the point when we feel we must exclude their teaching from what is allowed in our organizations or our churches?[9] God is testing our hearts toward these people with whom we disagree.

---

[8] Francis Schaeffer, *The Church Before the Watching World* (Downers Grove, Ill.: InterVarsity Press, 1971), 69-70.

[9] Paul's own insistence on excluding people who persist in teaching false doctrine demonstrates that it is not impossible to act in love toward others even when (in sorrow) excluding them from a church or organization. Many pastors who have faithfully carried out church discipline to the point of excluding someone from fellowship know that this is possible, for they know that they have acted with love and deep sorrow at the same time. Greg Boyd seems to pit love against any kind of disciplinary action, however, in his objection to any process by which the Evangelical Theological Society might move to exclude open theists: see Gregory A. Boyd, "Christian Love and Academic Dialogue: A Reply to Bruce Ware," *JETS* 45 (2002): 243.

C. WHEN SHOULD CHRISTIAN ORGANIZATIONS DRAW NEW BOUNDARIES?

1. After a False Teaching Has Become a Significant Problem

It is impractical and impossible to rule out all future doctrinal errors before they appear. We do not even know what they will be! Probably twenty years ago no one would have expected that we would be dealing with a controversy over whether God knows our future choices. In fact, in 1952 C. S. Lewis could write, without fear of contradiction, "Everyone who believes in God at all believes that He knows what you and I are going to do tomorrow."[10] Therefore it would have been impossible to deal with this matter before it arose as a problem in the church. In other words, problems must be dealt with after they arise, and after they begin to gain some following and thus become a significant problem for the church.

2. Before the False Teaching Does Great Harm, and Before It Has a Large Following Entrenched in the Organization

Here is a matter that requires much wisdom from God. While we cannot draw new boundaries to exclude false teaching before it appears, and while we do not want to make our doctrinal statements hundreds of pages long by excluding strange teachings that hardly anyone has heard of and that have gained no following at all, we still cannot wait too long. If we wait too long to exclude a false teaching, it will gain more and more influence and may soon become entrenched in the church or organization. For example, several more liberal denominations—such as the Presbyterian Church (U.S.A.), the United Methodist Church, and the Episcopal Church—now have so many vocal advocates of the legitimacy of homosexuality that it is practically impossible to exclude them from the denomination. Bible-believing members who have remained in those denominations are heavy-hearted about the situation. The denominations waited too long, and the false teaching became entrenched.

Regarding the Presbyterian Church, again Francis Schaeffer commented:

> Let us again go back to the Presbyterian struggles of the 30s when true
> Christians did not remember to keep this balance [of showing both the

---

[10] C. S. Lewis, *Mere Christianity* (New York: Collier, 1952), 145.

holiness of God and the love of God simultaneously]. On the one hand, they waited far too long to exert discipline, and so they lost the denomination, as did the Christians in almost every other denomination. On the other hand, some of them treated the liberals as less than human, and therefore they learned such bad habits that, later, when those who formed new groups developed minor differences among themselves, they continued to treat each other badly. Beware of the habits you learn in controversy. Both must appear together: the holiness of God and the love of God exhibited simultaneously by the grace of God. It will not come automatically. It takes prayer.[11]

On the other hand, I think a good example of acting at the right time is found in the recent actions of the Southern Baptist Convention, when it added several statements to its official statement of faith, the "Baptist Faith and Message."

On June 9, 1998, the Southern Baptist Convention added an entire article (Article XVIII) on the family, which affirmed that "the husband and wife are of equal worth before God, since both are created in God's image," but also that "a wife is to submit herself graciously to the servant leadership of her husband." It also excluded the validity of homosexual "marriage" by saying, "marriage is the uniting of one man and one woman in covenant commitment for a lifetime."

Then on June 14, 2000, the Southern Baptist Convention adopted changes to the "Baptist Faith and Message" that affirmed inerrancy ("all Scripture is totally true and trustworthy," Article I); that denied open theism ("God is all powerful and all knowing; and His perfect knowledge extends to all things, past, present, and future, including the future decisions of His free creatures," Article II); that rejected the idea that baptism in the Holy Spirit is subsequent to conversion (regarding the Holy Spirit, the statement affirmed, "At the moment of regeneration He baptizes every believer into the Body of Christ," Article II. C); that denied racism ("every person of every race possesses full dignity and is worthy of respect and Christian love," Article III); that denied inclusivism ("There is no salvation apart from personal faith in Jesus Christ as Lord," Section IV); that restricted the role of pastor to men ("While both men and women are gifted for service in the church, the office of pastor is limited to men

---

[11] Schaeffer, *The Church Before the Watching World*, 71-72.

as qualified by Scripture," Article VI); and that defined clear positions on contemporary ethical issues ("In the spirit of Christ, Christians should oppose racism, every form of greed, selfishness, and vice, and all forms of sexual immorality, including adultery, homosexuality, and pornography. We should work to provide for the orphaned, the needy, the abused, the aged, the helpless, and the sick. We should speak on behalf of the unborn and contend for the sanctity of all human life from conception to natural death," Article XV). Interestingly, the Convention broadened its boundary in one area, with regard to appropriate activity on Sunday. The previous "Baptist Faith and Message" had said that "the Lord's Day" should include "refraining from worldly amusements, and resting from secular employments, works of necessity and mercy only being excepted," but now in the new statement, it says, "Activities on the Lord's Day should be commensurate with the Christian's conscience under the Lordship of Jesus Christ," Article VIII).[12]

It seems appropriate to me that the Southern Baptist Convention added these explicit doctrinal boundaries when it did. These matters had become issues of concern in the current culture and among many Christians, and the overwhelming vote to approve these changes (approximately 90 percent, according to news reports at the time) showed that there was strong support among the messengers to the annual meeting to make these changes. Many of these issues had become controversial since the last major revision of the "Baptist Faith and Message" in 1963.

Other denominations and organizations will probably come up with lists that differ from the Southern Baptist list in various ways, depending on their organization's purpose, composition, and history, but the important thing is that organizations have a process by which they consider the need for such changes from time to time, and that they make such additions in a timely manner, before the wrong teachings do much harm and become entrenched in the organization.

3. But Who Has the Authority to Make These Changes?

Among evangelical churches and organizations, we do not have a pope to decree doctrine for us. Nor have we ordinarily had church councils

---

[12] The text of the statement is available at www.sbc.net/bfm.

such as that at Chalcedon in 451. Instead, in the evangelical world, decisions are made by tens of thousands of organizations in a gradual process, as their governing bodies, or the organizations as a whole in some kind of formal meeting, come to a decision on doctrinal matters. Almost always such decisions are preceded by vigorous debate and discussion, and by much study on the part of the people involved. Over the course of time, the direction of the church is determined by tens of thousands, or even hundreds of thousands, of churches and denominations and organizations deciding these things one at a time. They do that based on the best information available to them, and working within the governing processes that each one has set up.

Is this a good system? Personally I think it is a very workable system, and one that in the long run results in the Lord's purposes being accomplished. The alternative to such a system would be some kind of worldwide church government, but that (to my mind) would concentrate too much power in the hands of too few people, and would likely lead to far worse decisions in the end.

For those of us who are scholars, we have a significant responsibility in this process, for we often write the materials that are read by study groups and church leaders as they make decisions on these questions. It is our responsibility to be truthful and accurate in what we publish, to represent the arguments fairly, and above all to be faithful to Scripture as God by his grace enables us to do so.

D. For *What Doctrinal and Ethical Matters* Should Christian Organizations Draw New Boundaries?

There is no simple answer to the question of what matters should be included when we draw new boundaries. This question requires mature wisdom, thoughtful judgment, extended prayer, and widespread discussion on the part of leaders and members in churches and organizations.

In order to help in this decision making process, I list here some questions that should be asked. It is important to remember that these questions should be weighed and not just counted, for some of them will be more relevant than others, depending on the individual situation.

As I ask these questions, I realize that I am differing with some who would say, "If we begin to draw new doctrinal boundaries, we won't know where to stop." There are many things in life that we would never do if we followed the warning, "Once we begin we won't know where to stop." Eating is one example. Sleeping is another. Preaching a sermon is a third! I hope the questions that follow will give us guidance in knowing where to stop drawing new boundaries as well as where to add them.

Here then are the questions that I suggest each church or organization should ask when considering whether to draw a new boundary (usually in the form of adding to a doctrinal statement) in order to exclude a particular wrong teaching.

1. Certainty: How sure are we that the teaching is wrong?

Have the advocates of this teaching been given a fair hearing? Has there been enough time to reflect on the matter carefully?

And is there a growing consensus among God's people generally that this new teaching *cannot be right?* I believe this question is important because I think that among God's people who are reading his Word and praying daily, honestly seeking to be obedient to him, God gives a generally reliable sense or "spiritual instinct" about when a particular teaching simply cannot be consistent with Scripture.[13] For example, I think that there was a growing consensus among Bible-believing Christians in the 1960s and 70s that, except to save the life of the mother, abortion simply *cannot* be right. Prior to the 1960s there was uncertainty and discussion and debate, and various viewpoints were expressed, but through that process a growing consensus emerged, and a settled certainty of conviction took hold among God's people.

I think it is the same today with the doctrine of "open theism." There is a growing consensus among God's people, when they learn about it and are given enough information, that this teaching simply cannot be consistent with the teachings of the Bible.

---

[13] I would make one qualification here: this spiritual instinct among God's people is reliable only if they have had access to enough true information to make a correct decision. But if they have been allowed to read and hear information on only one side of a controversy (as in a church or denomination where a study packet of material is all on one side), they generally do not have an adequate basis for making an informed judgment.

2. Effect on other doctrines: Will this teaching likely lead to significant erosion in other doctrines?

Some doctrines are absolutely important to maintain because of their effect on other doctrines. Examples would include doctrines such as the Trinity, or the deity and humanity of Christ in one person, or the inerrancy of Scripture, or justification by faith alone. If we abandon one of those doctrines, many other doctrines will be lost as well.

In the early part of the twentieth century, Protestant liberals began to emphasize the love of God so much (and who could object to that?) that they came to deny the wrath of God. They denied that God exercised personal wrath toward his sinful creatures.

At that point someone might have said, "So what? This is just one attribute of God, and I can't see that it's that important." But the result was highly destructive, because once they denied the wrath of God, then they had to deny that Jesus bore God's wrath against our sins when he was on the cross. They had to deny the substitutionary atonement of Christ. And once that happens, then the whole Christian gospel is lost.

I think that this example has significant parallels to the current debate about open theism. The advocates of open theism are denying "just" one attribute of God (his exhaustive foreknowledge with respect to future human, angelic, and demonic choices), and so someone might ask why that is so important. But, as several authors in this volume have shown, once God's attribute of exhaustive foreknowledge is denied, many other things begin to change as well, and the God who results from this process is no longer the God of the Bible.

3. Effect on personal and church life: Will this false teaching bring significant harm to people's Christian lives, or to the work of the church?

As with question two, this question asks about the effect of a false teaching, but this time with respect to living the Christian life and with respect to the work of the church.

For example, the advocacy of homosexuality as a legitimate practice brings significant destructive consequences to people's lives. Or, to take another example, inclusivism (the idea that people can be saved without hearing about Christ) tends quickly to destroy the motivation for evangelism and tends to destroy missionary activity.

4. Historical precedent: Is this teaching contrary to what the vast majority of the Bible-believing church has held throughout history?

This was an important consideration with respect to the inerrancy of Scripture. The vast majority of God's people throughout history assumed without question that God's Word was completely truthful, no matter what their differences were on other doctrines. This fact did not absolutely prove that inerrancy was true (for our only absolutely authoritative source for doctrine is Scripture alone, not Scripture plus tradition), but it is an important consideration nonetheless. It meant that those who denied inerrancy were in the difficult position of saying that the vast majority of God's people throughout the entire history of the church were wrong.

With respect to open theism, this argument is, if anything, even stronger. Probably 99.9 percent of Christian believers throughout history have believed that God knows all future events. The very few exceptions (such as the Socinians—who advocated false teaching in other matters as well) are a tiny minority. Therefore open theism has a huge burden, because it must demonstrate that 99.9 percent of God's people throughout history have been wrong on this issue.[14]

5. Perception of importance among God's people: Is there increasing consensus among the leaders and members that this matter is important enough that the false teaching should be explicitly denied in a doctrinal statement?

This is a very important consideration because it takes into account the deep spiritual instincts of God's people, not just regarding the rightness or wrongness of a doctrine, but regarding its importance. In the open theism debate, an increasing number of God's people are

---

[14] Someone might object, wasn't the doctrine of justification by faith alone discovered by Martin Luther in the early sixteenth century, and wasn't the doctrine of believer's baptism discovered by the Anabaptists in the sixteenth century? Not exactly. Evidence for both of these positions can be found in the writings of the early church fathers, though their viewpoints were later obscured, and they were not as fully developed as they would be when opposition and controversy arose.

thinking and saying, "Something fundamental is at stake here. A God who does not know the future is simply not the God of the Bible. This is not the God I have known and trusted for my whole life." The continued propagation of open theism within the church then becomes very troubling to them.

In this case, as well as in a number of other cases, my own personal evaluation is that the spiritual instinct of God's people who are thinking this way is correct.

6. Purposes of the organization: Is the teaching a significant threat to the nature and purposes of the organization?

In asking this question I am attempting to take into account the fact that God raises up different organizations for different purposes. For example, the Evangelical Theological Society provides an excellent opportunity for dialogue among Calvinists and Arminians, Baptists and paedobaptists, premillennialists and amillennialists and postmillennialists, and so forth. To exclude any one of those viewpoints would make the ETS something different from what it is and always has been. It is a very broad organization, while still being evangelical. To try to rule out some of those views would be a significant threat to its nature and purpose. On the other hand, allowing the ETS to include theological liberals who deny inerrancy and deny that the Bible is our unique and absolute authority would also be a significant threat to its nature and purposes, and would soon make the ETS a far different kind of organization.

The situation is somewhat different with denominational groups and denominational or theologically distinct seminaries. For example, the Presbyterian Church in America is Reformed in its doctrinal convictions. If it were to begin to admit Arminians into leadership, it would be a significant threat to the nature and purposes of the denomination, and I do not think that it would be appropriate for them to do so. It would fundamentally change who they are. Or, to take another example, I do not believe that historic Pentecostal groups such as the Assemblies of God should allow into their leadership people who deny that spiritual gifts like speaking in tongues and healing and prophecy continue today. To do so would be a significant threat to the nature and purposes of that denomination.

So each evangelical organization must ask itself, what things are fundamental to preserving our purpose and identity?

With respect to open theism, this is again an important question. Personally, my own view is that open theism is so serious an error, and so far over the line of what is doctrinally acceptable, that I do not think its advocates should be allowed to continue as members of the Evangelical Theological Society.

7. Motivations of advocates: Does it seem that the advocates of this teaching hold it because of a fundamental refusal to be subject to the authority of God's Word, rather than because of sincerely held differences of interpretation based on accepted hermeneutical standards?

I realize that people often quote the Bible verse, "You shall not judge people's motives." But that verse is not in the Bible; it is just an evangelical saying that people repeat over and over. I agree that there is some wisdom in it, because we cannot be sure of what is in other people's hearts, and so we can easily make mistakes, particularly when we assume that we know what is in their hearts without hearing it directly from them. So we need to be cautious in this area.

But there is another side to this matter. For example, after a half hour of serious dialogue with someone who holds another view, we often can get a good sense of that person's fundamental commitments. That is what we mean when we say (positively), for example, "I differ with John Doe on predestination, but I so appreciate what is in his heart." Or we might say (negatively), "I know John Doe says he's not preaching this doctrine because of the money he earns from it, but it just doesn't ring true to me." God has made us in such a way that we instinctively evaluate people's motivations and heart attitudes all the time, whether or not we say anything about it; but we must do so with caution.

In fact, if we look through Paul's epistles, from time to time he did speak about the motives of his opponents:

> Yet because of false brothers secretly brought in—*who slipped in to spy out our freedom* that we have in Christ Jesus, *so that they might bring us into slavery*—to them we did not yield in submission even for

a moment, so that the truth of the gospel might be preserved for you. (Gal. 2:4-5)

It is those who want to make a good showing in the flesh who would force you to be circumcised, and only *in order that they may not be persecuted* for the cross of Christ. (Gal. 6:12)

Their end is destruction, their god is their belly, and they glory in their shame, with minds set on earthly things. (Phil. 3:19)

For such men are false apostles, *deceitful workmen*, disguising themselves as apostles of Christ. (2 Cor. 11:13)

For people will be lovers of self, lovers of money, proud, arrogant, abusive, disobedient to their parents, ungrateful, unholy, heartless, unappeasable, slanderous, without self-control, brutal, not loving good, treacherous, reckless, swollen with conceit, lovers of pleasure rather than lovers of God, having the appearance of godliness, but denying its power. Avoid such people. (2 Tim. 3:2-5)

(It would be impossible for Timothy to obey that command without "judging people's motives"!)

. . . there will be false teachers among you, who will secretly bring in destructive heresies. . . . And in their greed they will exploit you with false words. (2 Pet. 2:1-3)

They have eyes full of adultery, insatiable for sin. . . . They have hearts trained in greed. (2 Pet. 2:14)

Many other examples could be found, especially if we look at Jesus' interaction with his hostile critics such as the Pharisees, but the point should be clear: the Bible simply does not command us not to judge people's motives.

With regard to some specific type of false teaching, after some interaction with one of its responsible advocates (not just with a fringe follower of the teaching who may be ill-informed or unsanctified, or even an unbeliever, but with a responsible advocate) we might ask ourselves, for example, "Deep down inside, is he (or she) just embarrassed by the offense of the cross?" Or we might ask, "Deep down inside, is he embarrassed by the exclusive claims of Christ to be the only way to God?" "Is he driven by a desire to be accepted or approved by liberal scholars?" "Is he craving for attention, for praise, and for being called 'creative' and 'innovative'?" "Is his case built again and again on hermeneutical novelties, special pleading, and methods of interpretation that we could not adopt elsewhere?"

On the other hand, to take an example where I think the motivations are good on both sides, we could think about differences among evangelicals over the length of the days of creation in Genesis 1. Some Christians believe these are six twenty-four-hour days. Other sincere believers think these days were millions of years long. As I have talked to and read things written by advocates of both positions, it does not seem to me that there is a wrong motivation on either side. I do not think that people on either side of the question have any deep refusal in their hearts to be subject to Scripture. Rather, I think this is a case of sincerely held differences based on accepted hermeneutical standards, and people are just weighing various factors more or less heavily and coming to different conclusions on a complex question.

8. Methods of advocates: Do the advocates of this teaching frequently manifest arrogance, deception, unrighteous anger, slander, and falsehood rather than humility, openness to correction and reason, kindness, and absolute truthfulness?

In 1923, J. Gresham Machen, in his classic book *Christianity and Liberalism,* wrote about liberal Presbyterian professors and pastors who believed one thing but said another just to keep their jobs and their influence. They signed the doctrinal statement even though they disagreed with it, and there was a fundamental dishonesty in what they were doing.[15]

If the advocates of a particular doctrine, especially the most responsible advocates, frequently manifest deception, falsehood, unrighteous anger, and arrogance, then we have a further indication that what they teach is not the "wisdom from above" that James speaks about:

---

[15] See J. Gresham Machen, *Christianity and Liberalism* (Grand Rapids, Mich.: Eerdmans, 1923), 162-170.

But the wisdom from above is first pure, then peaceable, gentle, open to reason, full of mercy and good fruits, impartial and sincere. And a harvest of righteousness is sown in peace by those who make peace. (James 3:17-18)

9. Some wrong questions to ask

It is important to add that there are some questions that should not be part of our consideration in deciding which doctrinal matters to exclude with new boundaries. These are questions such as the following:

- Are the advocates my friends?
- Are they nice people?
- Will we lose money or members if we exclude them?
- Will the academic community criticize us as being too narrow-minded?
- Will someone take us to court over this?

Such questions are all grounded in a wrongful fear of man, not in a fear of God and trust in God.

E. CONCLUSION

This chapter was not only about open theism but about the general problem of when to add new doctrinal and ethical boundaries. But it is appropriate here to make specific application to that particular question, because in today's evangelical world, the widespread and forceful public advocacy of open theism now requires us to evaluate this belief and to ask whether our churches and organizations should draw new boundaries to exclude it. As I indicated with regard to several of the criteria listed in the previous section, I believe that on several grounds open theism is a serious enough doctrinal error that it should now be excluded by new boundaries. In addition, other chapters in this book have argued persuasively that open theism leads naturally to an abandonment of biblical inerrancy, a loss of belief in the trustworthiness of God, and a loss of the gospel itself. The price of allowing it to remain and flourish in our midst is too great.

But I do not want to end with an appeal concerning open theism alone. It is only one of many doctrinal permutations now threatening the evangelical community. For each one of these issues, we should be satisfied neither with pleas for snap dismissal from fellowship nor with pleas for blanket avoidance of the question of new boundaries. The only right solution is careful consideration of each new matter with prayer and searching of Scripture, and then, as God gives us wisdom, humility, love, and courage, we must bring each matter to a resolution, knowing that for each decision, whether to include or to exclude, we will one day give account to our Creator. Will we have the resolve to make such decisions?

We look back with admiration and thanksgiving on the heroes of the faith from previous generations. They defended the substitutionary atonement, the virgin birth, the deity of Christ, the Trinity, the inerrancy of Scripture, justification by faith alone, and other important doctrines. During and after the Reformation, some paid with their lives.

But we look back with disappointment and shame on those who failed to take a clear stand, for example, against racism and slavery in our country.

Now God has entrusted us with a stewardship in this generation. Many of us have positions of leadership and influence in our churches and in the evangelical world. Now the choice of whether to do something or nothing about false doctrine is up to us.

Isaiah 56:10 talks about a tragic situation. Israel is about to be destroyed and her watchdogs cannot bark:

> His watchmen are blind; they are all without knowledge; they are all silent dogs; they cannot bark, dreaming, lying down, loving to slumber. (Isa. 56:10)

Will we be like this? Will we be blind, silent watchdogs?

Or will we earnestly "contend for the faith that was once for all delivered to the saints" (Jude 3)? Will we do so with gentleness, with wisdom, and with sorrow if we need to part with friends? Will we also do so with courage to do what is right and what is necessary in order to remain faithful to God and to his Word?

11

GROUNDS FOR DISMAY:
THE ERROR AND INJURY OF
OPEN THEISM

John Piper

As I have wrestled with open theism in my own denomination, I have tried to articulate for the churches the reasons this defection from historic Christian teaching is so serious. As a pastor I see open theism as theologically ruinous, dishonoring to God, belittling to Christ, and pastorally hurtful. That, of course, is not the intention of open theists. But intentions of the heart are not my concern here. I can't see them. Only God can. And he is merciful. In what follows I will try to sum up the reasons for my concern.

1. Assuming that open theism remains a marginal novelty, not a central unifying force, when a church or denomination or school gives legitimacy to open theism's denial of historic Christian views of God's foreknowledge, this erodes their common vision of the God they worship together.

Legitimizing the "open view" of God undermines the biblical foundation of historic Christian unity and leads us to unite around an increasingly ambiguous view of God. For example, to say that we all worship an omniscient God would be evacuated of common meaning, because openness teaching and historic Christian teaching have radically different views of what is meant by "all-knowing."

If a historic, unifying affirmation of faith can be made porous enough to absorb this false teaching, it will cease to define unity and will become an ambiguous cloak for serious disunity. It is not the opponents of open theism who threaten the unifying power of historic affirmations of faith; that unifying power is threatened by the effort to force into them a false doctrine that they were never intended to affirm.

2. Embracing the legitimacy of the openness view of God would put any institution seriously out of step with the entire unified history of the Christian church.

It would move toward the margins of orthodoxy. Every orthodox Christian communion for two thousand years has affirmed the exhaustive, definite foreknowledge of God. Departures from this view have been rejected as unorthodox by every major branch of the Christian church. It is also ironic that embracing open theism would be done in the name of unity, when, actually, it would be putting any contemporary church or denomination or school at odds with the vision of God's foreknowledge that has served the unity of the church for twenty centuries.

3. Protests to the contrary, the openness view of God really does imply that God makes mistakes, because of his uncertainty about the future.

For example, in Jeremiah 3:19b-20, God says, "I said, 'You shall call Me, My Father, and not turn away from following Me. Surely, as a woman treacherously departs from her lover, so you have dealt treacherously with Me, O house of Israel,' declares the LORD" (NASB).[1] Boyd says that God predicted one thing and that another came about: God "thought something would occur that did not occur."[2] ". . . God can infallibly think that a particular possibility has the greatest chance of occurring, even if it turns out that a less likely possibility actually

---

[1] Unless otherwise noted, Scripture quotations in this chapter are from the English Standard Version of the Bible.

[2] Gregory A. Boyd, *God of the Possible: A Biblical Introduction to the Open View of God* (Grand Rapids, Mich.: Baker, 2000), 61.

occurs."[3] Boyd does not call this a "mistake," because he does not believe it is a mistake when you mis-predict on the basis of the best knowledge available. But most people do call this a mistake—including fellow open theist John Sanders, who writes: "God himself says that he was *mistaken* about what was going to happen."[4]

4. The open view of God imputes to him a massive ignorance and a continual process of learning and adapting, which is unworthy of the biblical vision of God.

Since *"God can't foreknow the good or bad decisions of the people He creates until He creates these people and they, in turn, create their decisions,"*[5] therefore God is learning billions of new certainties every hour, and is adjusting his plans continually to deal with these new certainties. This is a very serious departure from the glorious, biblical vision of God who knows infallibly all that shall come to pass.

5. God's foreknowledge of all that shall come to pass is viewed by Isaiah as evidence of God's unique deity among all the gods.

It is one of the "evidences of . . . [God's] peculiar glory, greatly distinguishing him from all other beings."[6] For example, Isaiah quotes God

---

[3] Ibid. Boyd quotes the text as follows, "I thought you would call me, 'My Father' and would not turn from following me [literally, with the NASB, "I said, 'You shall call Me, My Father, and not turn away from following Me'" (wā'ōmar 'ābîy tiqr⁽ᵉ⁾'ū lîy ûmē'aḥăray lō' tāšûbū)]. Instead, as a faithless wife . . . you have been faithless to me" (Jer. 3:19-20). His conclusion is stated in a rhetorical question: "If God tells us he thought something was going to occur while being eternally certain it would not occur, is he not lying to us?" What Boyd does not say is that with a literal translation the same problem lands on his view. If God "says" something is surely going to happen which he does not know is surely going to happen, is he not lying to us? The answer to that is, No, not if there is the implicit qualification, "given the ordinary expectations under these conditions." That is what I think God meant here and in Jeremiah 3:7. The difference between Boyd and me at this point is that I believe God knew what the people would really do, when he implied that ordinary human probabilities would seem to lead to repentance. But Boyd believes that God did not know what they would do. The openness handling of this text shows how vulnerable God would be if the open view is right. God would do his very best in predicting on the basis of infinite knowledge of the present, and would miscalculate, because of human self-determination. The implications of this are huge. It means that all talk of God's managing the world on the basis of known human influences is not very encouraging, because it is the essence of human self-determination that the most utterly unexpected choices can arise from the human will and surprise God.

[4] John Sanders, *The God Who Risks: A Theology of Providence* (Downers Grove, Ill.: InterVarsity Press, 1998), 74, emphasis added.

[5] Gregory Boyd, in Gregory A. Boyd and Edward K. Boyd, *Letters from a Skeptic: A Son Wrestles with His Father's Questions About Christianity* (Wheaton, Ill.: Victor, 1994), 30, emphasis added.

[6] Jonathan Edwards, *The Freedom of the Will*, ed. Paul Ramsey, vol. 1 of *The Works of Jonathan Edwards* (New Haven, Conn.: Yale University Press, 1957), 22.

as saying, "remember the former things of old; for I am God, and there
is no other; I am God, and there is no one like me, *declaring the end from
the beginning and from ancient times things not yet done,* saying, 'My
counsel shall stand, and I will accomplish all my purpose'" (Isa. 46:9-
10). From this and other important texts in Isaiah, we can see that the
denial of God's foreknowledge is an unwitting assault on the glory and
deity of God.

*6. Jesus teaches that his ability to predict the free acts of responsible
people is an essential part of his divine glory, so that the denial of this
foreknowledge is an unwitting undermining of the deity of Christ.*

For example, in John 6:64 Jesus says, "'there are some of you who do
not believe.' (For Jesus knew from the beginning who those were who
did not believe, and *who it was who would betray him.)*" Then in John
13:19, Jesus says at the Last Supper, "From now on I am telling you
before it comes to pass, so that when it does occur, you may believe that
I am" (author's translation).

What does "I am" mean? It is the name of God in Exodus 3:14, and
it is the designation Jesus uses in John 8:58 to describe his preexistent
deity: "Jesus said to them, 'Truly, truly, I say to you, before Abraham
was, I am.'" These are the words that God uses of himself in texts like
Isaiah 43:10 ("'You are my witnesses,' declares the LORD, 'and my servant whom I have chosen, that you may know and believe me and
understand that *I am*'" [author's translation]). Therefore, the warrant
Jesus gives for believing that he is divine is that he can predict the human
evil acts which he infallibly foreknows are going to befall him in the next
hours, including the betrayal of Judas (see John 13:21-27 and Matt.
26:2), and the denials of Peter (Luke 22:31-34). Therefore, denying that
Christ knew all that would befall him tends to undermine our confidence
in the deity of Christ.

*7. The denial that God foreknew the sinful volitions of responsible crea-
tures tends to undermine our confidence in the plan of redemption.*

The Bible teaches that God made provision for salvation from the
effects of the fall before the foundation of the world. Thus, he foreknew

that there would be a fall and that there would be effects of it that needed a plan of redemption. For example, in 2 Timothy 1:9 Paul says that from all eternity God has planned to give us grace in Christ Jesus as our Savior. "[God] has saved us and called us with a holy calling, not according to our works, but according to His own purpose and grace which was granted us in Christ Jesus from all eternity" (NASB). In other words, God not only foreknew in eternity the sinful choice that Adam (and Lucifer before him) would make, but he also planned to give us grace through Jesus Christ in response to the misery and destruction and condemnation resulting from the fall that he foreknew. Therefore to say that *"God can't foreknow the good or bad decisions of the people He creates until He creates these people and they, in turn, create their decisions,"*[7] is to imply that God could not infallibly see the fall coming and plan for it the way Paul said God did. In this way, our confidence in the accomplishment of redemption would be weakened because our view of God would nullify the eternal plan of redemption spelled out in Scripture.

8. The attempt of open theism to make an exegetical defense of the denial that God foreknows all that shall come to pass is not successful.

None of the passages of Scripture that is brought forth against the exhaustive definite foreknowledge of God teaches that God does not have such foreknowledge. Rather this denial is *inferred* from circumstances that *seem* to require it. For example, reference is sometimes made to texts where God changes his mind from what he said he would do (Isa. 38:1, 5; Jonah 3:4, 10), is sorry for what he has done (Gen. 6:5-6; 1 Sam. 15:11), seems surprised (Jer. 26:1-3), says "perhaps" (Jer. 3:6-7), and puts people to the test (Gen. 22:9-12). In all these texts, the denial of God's exhaustive foreknowledge is an *inference* that *seems* necessary to some interpreters. However, in the history of the church right up to our own day, plausible explanations have been given to each of these texts which cohere with the wider, more explicit teaching of Scripture that God foreknows all that shall come to pass.

---

[7] Boyd, *Letters from a Skeptic*, 30, emphasis added.

9. The denial that God foreknows all that shall come to pass is practically and pastorally harmful.

Bad theology hurts people. Sooner or later wrong thinking about God leads to wrong believing. And wrong believing leads to the weakening of moral and spiritual life, and finally to condemnation. Most Christians see intuitively that denying God's foreknowledge of free actions will tend to undermine the confidence of the church that God can guide persons and nations, that he can answer prayer concerning the hearts of the erring and lost, that he can predict the future, that he can be assured of final triumph, and that all things will work together for the good of those who love God and are called according to his purpose. Some generation will pay the price of this wrong thinking about God. And the closer the wrong thinking gets to the center of God and his personal perfections and his saving ways, the sooner and the more painful will be the payment. Eternal things are at stake in the denial of the exhaustive, definite foreknowledge of God.

10. The alleged practical and pastoral gain from openness theology does not materialize.

The hope of open theism to lessen the crisis of faith in times of calamity is not realized. Even if God did not foreknow from eternity an evil human plan to cause a calamity (as openness theology would say), nevertheless he does see the plan as it develops and certainly foresees that evil is about to happen several hours or minutes or seconds before it does. Moreover, in both openness theology and historic Christian theology, God has the right and power to intervene in those last hours or minutes or seconds to stop hurricanes, heal diseases, hold back floods, discharge devils, strike terrorists blind, or otherwise hinder someone on his way to murder. Why he does not intervene in any particular calamity is not answered adequately by openness theology. In all these cases, even though (on openness assumptions) God did not foreknow the calamity from eternity, he still saw the calamity around the corner and did not intervene. A heartbroken mother may still ask, "Why did God not intervene to save my child?" She will not be helped by the answer that God did not foresee the calamity. In most cases he did foresee it at least in time to do something if he thought it wise. There is better counsel. The

testimony of the suffering saints for centuries has been: believing that
from all eternity God sees our pain coming, strengthens us for it, joins
us in it, and designs good by it is comforting—and biblical.

*11. The importance that we put on the foreknowledge of God is not
marginal or eccentric.*

It has broad historic precedent and many sober-minded contemporary
representatives. The errors of openness theology have been challenged
throughout the history of the church. For an extensive list of those who
represent the historic view of God's exhaustive, definite foreknowledge,
see Steve Roy's dissertation, "How Much Does God Foreknow? An
Evangelical Assessment of the Doctrine of the Extent of the
Foreknowledge of God in Light of the Teaching of Open Theism,"[8]
chapter 2, "A Survey of the History of the Doctrine of Divine
Foreknowledge." A list of contemporary defenders of the historic view
can be found in the bibliography of this volume (*Beyond the Bounds*).

*12. Evangelical denominations and educational institutions move away
from orthodox Christian faith not in obvious giant steps, but for lack
of vigilance over incremental defections from biblical truth.*

Each progressive deviation seems too small to justify a confrontation.
It doesn't seem worth the controversy and tension. It seems like a dis-
traction from the main message of the gospel and the mission of the
church. Nevertheless, it is the very message and mission that are being
undermined. This is why the apostle Paul gave himself not only to
proclamation but to "the defense and confirmation of the gospel"
(Phil. 1:7). Denominations and schools would do well to heed the
words of Keith and Gladys Hunt, in their history of InterVarsity. Their
warning to InterVarsity applies to us:

> Many organizations go off-track by the time they reach their fiftieth
> anniversary. Doctrinal statements are not enough; they need to be con-
> stantly checked and their finer points taught and emphasized. It is easy
> to "get on with the mission" and belatedly discover that the faith that

---

[8] Ph.D. diss., Trinity International University, 2000.

began the movement has eroded away. If history tells us anything, it's that theological drift occurs almost imperceptibly over long periods of time. One little change here, another there.[9]

Similarly, from the British perspective Pete Lowman describes the demise of the World Student Christian Federation:

> In short, WSCF had virtually all the ingredients of an evangelical student movement of lasting effectiveness. What it lacked was a doctrinal concern that would have ensured that its voting members—and above all, its leaders—stayed loyal to a faith based unambiguously on the Word of God; and commitment like the apostle Paul's, that would have seen the maintenance of the divinely-revealed gospel as more crucial than unity with all those who seemed religious. Only one weakness; but through that weakness the WSCF made shipwreck. IFES-linked groups have no cause to be complacent. There, too, but for the grace of God, we might be drifting.[10]

13. False teaching can come from a godly person whom God is using for other good purposes.

Harmful teaching does not generally originate in people who are unqualified to teach and lead people to Christ. In Acts 20:30 Paul reminds the elders of the church at Ephesus that, "Even *from your own number* men will arise and distort the truth in order to draw away disciples after them" (NIV). Even someone as great and godly as the apostle Peter needed to be rebuked by Paul in Galatians 2:14: "I said to Peter in front of them all, 'You are a Jew, yet you live like a Gentile and not like a Jew. How is it, then, that you force Gentiles to follow Jewish customs?'" (NIV). Serious and damaging error generally starts in the teaching of an otherwise sound and helpful leader.

The story of churches and schools that have left their founding biblical vision points up the shortsightedness of putting personality above truth. The history of such defection is a strong historical warning not to

---

[9] Keith and Gladys Hunt, *For Christ and the University: The Story of InterVarsity Christian Fellowship of the U.S.A. 1940–1990* (Downers Grove, Ill.: InterVarsity Press, 1991), 379.

[10] Pete Lowman, *The Day of His Power: A History of the International Fellowship of Evangelical Students* (Leicester, U.K.: Inter-Varsity Press, 1983), 44. On the reality of "drift," see Arnold L. Cook, *Historical Drift: Must My Church Die?* (Camp Hill, Pa.: Christian Publications, 2000).

put piety and effectiveness above simple conformity to Scripture when a particular truth is in question. It is a remarkable and wonderful thing for all of us that God will use us in all our imperfections and mistakes. We would be hopeless without this grace. Thankfully J. I. Packer is right when he points out that truth is crucial and God will bless a small amount of it:

> It is certain that God blesses believers precisely and invariably by bless-
> ing to them something of his truth and that misbelief as such is in its
> own nature spiritually barren and destructive. Yet anyone who deals
> with souls will again and again be amazed at the gracious generosity
> with which God blesses to needy ones what looks to us like a very tiny
> needle of truth hidden amid whole haystacks of mental error.[11]

But God's willingness to bless millions of Christians whose doctrine is defective is no sign that God endorses false teaching or reckons it harmless. That God will bless a sick person is no reason not to fight disease.

Our plea in this book has been that Christians keep focused on the issue and not be distracted into matters of personality or politics or procedures. Do not be overwhelmed or confused by the subtle distinctions behind the issue of God's foreknowledge. There are many views in the church as to *how* God can know all that shall come to pass. But we may be thankful that, as with all other major doctrines, we have the distilled biblical wisdom of the church in the simple and straightforward conclusion *that* God foreknows infallibly all that shall come to pass. May God give us the grace and wisdom and courage to keep the issue clear: It is a biblical truth that *God foreknows infallibly all that shall come to pass.* And this truth is important enough to be a part of affirmations of faith that define Christian orthodoxy.

14. Open theism's denial of God's good purposes in evil events is unbiblical and undermines the hope it aims to preserve.

Open theists deny that one may say "a good divine purpose lies behind all particular events."[12] Pastorally, the way this plays out is as follows:

---

[11] J. I. Packer, *Keep in Step with the Spirit* (Old Tappan, N.J.: Fleming H. Revell, 1984), 20.
[12] Gregory A. Boyd, *God at War: The Bible and Spiritual Conflict* (Downers Grove, Ill.: InterVarsity Press, 1997), 41, see also, 20, 38, 40, 49, 53, 166.

> Within the limits set by God, an individual may purpose to do things which are utterly at odds with God's ultimate purpose. Thus, when an individual inflicts pain on another individual, I do not think we can go looking for "the purpose of God" in the event. . . . I know Christians frequently speak about "the purpose of God" in the midst of a tragedy caused by someone else. There was a young girl this year at Bethel who was killed by a drunk driver, and a lot of students were wondering what purpose God had in "taking her home." But this I regard to simply be a piously confused way of thinking. The drunk driver alone is to blame for the girl's untimely death. The only purpose of God in the whole thing is His design to allow morally responsible people the right to decide whether to drink responsibly or irresponsibly.[13]

John Sanders puts it this way:

> God does not have a specific divine purpose for each and every occurrence of evil. . . . When a two-month-old child contracts a painful, incurable bone cancer that means suffering and death, it is pointless evil. The Holocaust is pointless evil. The rape and dismemberment of a young girl is pointless evil. The accident that caused the death of my brother was a tragedy. God does not have a specific purpose in mind for these occurrences.[14]

This view of reality contradicts many teachings in Scripture and robs the wounded and grieving of biblical hope in the sovereign goodness of God, of whom Joseph said, "As for you, you meant evil against me, but God meant it for good" (Gen. 50:20).

How God governs all events in the universe without sinning, and without removing responsibility from man, and with compassionate outcomes is mysterious! But it's what the Bible teaches. God "works *all things* according to the counsel of his will" (Eph. 1:11).

"All things" includes rolling dice (Prov. 16:33), falling sparrows (Matt. 10:29), failing sight (Ex. 4:11), financial loss (1 Sam. 2:7), the decisions of kings (Prov. 21:1), the sickness of children (2 Sam. 12:15), the suffering and slaughter of saints (1 Pet. 4:19; Ps. 44:11), the completion of travel (James 4:15), repentance (2 Tim. 2:25), faith (Phil.

---

[13] Boyd, *Letters from a Skeptic*, 46-47.
[14] Sanders, *The God Who Risks*, 262.

1:29), holiness (Phil. 3:12-13), spiritual growth (Heb. 6:3), life and death (1 Sam. 2:6), and the crucifixion of Christ (Acts 4:27-28).

From the smallest thing to the greatest, good and evil, happy and sad, pagan and Christian, pain and pleasure—God governs all for his wise, just, and good purposes (Isa. 46:10). Lest we miss the point, the Bible speaks most clearly to this in the most painful situations. Amos asks, "Does disaster come to a city, unless the LORD has done it?" (Amos 3:6). After losing his ten children, Job says, "The LORD gave, and the LORD has taken away; blessed be the name of the LORD" (Job 1:21). Covered with boils, he says, "Shall we receive good from God, and shall we not receive evil?" (Job 2:10).

True, Satan is real and active and involved in this world of woe! In fact, Job 2:7 says, "Satan went out from the presence of the LORD and struck Job with loathsome sores from the sole of his foot to the crown of his head." Satan struck him. But Job did not get comfort by looking at secondary causes. He got comfort by looking at the ultimate cause. "Shall we not accept adversity from God?" And the author of the book agrees when he says that Job's brothers and sisters "showed him sympathy and comforted him for all the evil that *the* LORD had brought upon him" (Job 42:11). James underlines God's purposeful goodness in Job's misery: "You have heard of the steadfastness of Job, and have seen the purpose of the Lord, how the Lord is compassionate and merciful" (James 5:11). Job himself concludes in prayer: "I know that you can do all things, and that no purpose of yours can be thwarted" (Job 42:2). Yes, Satan is real, and he is terrible—and he is on a leash.

Therefore denying that "a good divine purpose lies behind all particular events" is false. More than that, it undercuts the very hope it wants to create. If we deny that God could have used a million prior events to save a college student, what hope then do we have that God will use all the hard things of life to bless the surviving loved ones (spiritually or physically) in the hour of trial? The Bible teaches that God could have restrained the evil that killed the college student (Gen. 20:6). "The LORD brings the counsel of the nations to nothing; he frustrates the plans of the peoples" (Ps. 33:10). So he could nullify the impulse to swerve a car. But it was not in his plan to do it. Let us beware. If we spare God the burden of his sovereignty, we lose our only hope.

All of us are sinners. We deserve to perish. Every breath is an undeserved gift. We have one great hope: Jesus Christ died to obtain pardon and righteousness for us (Eph. 1:7; 2 Cor. 5:21), and God will employ his all-conquering, sovereign grace to preserve us for our inheritance through life and death (Jer. 32:40). We surrender this hope if we sacrifice this sovereignty.

I can hardly overstate the pastoral dismay I feel over Boyd's sentence, "Thus, when an individual inflicts pain on another individual, I do not think we can go looking for 'the purpose of God' in the event"; or Sanders's insistence that there is "pointless evil." As far as I can see it flies in the face of God's hard and merciful comfort in Hebrews 12:3-11. The teaching of this passage is that the persecution that Christians are receiving, as they follow the example of Jesus' own endurance, is the discipline of a loving Father with the purpose of producing in us and those around us more holiness. So it seems that individuals are inflicting pain on others (to use Boyd's sentence), and that this is interpreted by the writer of Hebrews as the discipline of God who has a clear purpose in it. Therefore, the writer *does* look for "the purpose of God" in the pain inflicted by others on Christians:

> In your struggle against sin you have not yet resisted to the point of shedding your blood. And have you forgotten the exhortation that addresses you as sons?
>
> > "My son, do not regard lightly the discipline of the Lord,
> >   nor be weary when reproved by him.
> > For the Lord disciplines the one he loves,
> >   and chastises every son whom he receives."
>
> It is for discipline that you have to endure. God is treating you as sons. (Heb. 12:4-7)

What follows in the text is a description of the purpose that God has in our being treated so painfully by others. Verses 10b-11: "[God] disciplines us for our good, that we may share his holiness. For the moment all discipline seems painful rather than pleasant, but later it yields the peaceful fruit of righteousness to those who have been trained by it."

So here are two kinds of biblical situations that contradict Boyd's claim that "when an individual inflicts pain on another individual [we should not] . . . go looking for 'the purpose of God' in the event": The sufferings inflicted on Jesus by others (Heb. 12:3; Acts 4:27-28) and the sufferings inflicted on Christians by others (Heb. 12:4-11). In both cases the teaching of Scripture is that God did indeed have a purpose in the very acts of inflicting pain: the salvation of his people in the one case (through Jesus' suffering), and the sanctifying of them in the other (through our suffering).

15. The suffering saints bear witness to the preciousness of God's all-knowing, sovereign care.

I realize that this is not proof of truth. But since open theists use stories to intensify their claims, it may be good to balance the accounts. I offer only one from twenty-two years of pastoral experience with suffering saints.

This is from a letter I received during one of the debates about open theism in our denomination. Reference had been made by an open theist to a tragic situation in which a young woman's husband had abandoned her and shattered her dreams of going with him to the mission field. She asked why God would permit her to marry a man who would abandon her. She was counseled by the open theist that God did not know the man would do this. This was meant to help her keep trusting God.

A young woman in our church heard that, and wrote to me astonished at such counsel. Her situation was worse. I will not share the details but only say that she too, and her children, were forsaken. She said,

> If God does not know everything the future holds, how is he any different from any other friend on whose shoulder I might cry? He may be good, and loving and righteous, but if he is not in control of what happens to me tomorrow, how can I have any confidence that he can work all things together for good?
>
> The confidence that God knows what he is doing has gotten me through the last five years. I believe that God knew from the beginning what _____ would do—that he cannot be surprised by any-

thing. And because I believe that, I can believe that God intends this whole thing for my good. It's not just that everything will turn out all right in the end; it's that right now he is working his purpose out in my life, to move me to the next degree of glory. If that working includes suffering, how much better it is to know that it is purposed by a loving, all-powerful God, who "gives unto each day what he deems best"!

In conclusion, I say again, as a pastor who longs to be biblical and God-centered and Christ-exalting and eternally helpful to my people, I see open theism as theologically ruinous, dishonoring to God, belittling to Christ, and pastorally hurtful. My prayer is that Christian leaders will come to see it this way, and thus love the church by counting open theism beyond the bounds of orthodox Christian teaching.

A BIBLIOGRAPHY ON OPEN THEISM

Justin Taylor

WORKS CRITIQUING OPEN THEISM

Ascol, Thomas K. "Pastoral Implications of Open Theism." In *Bound Only Once: The Failure of Open Theism*, edited by Douglas Wilson, 173-190. Moscow, Ida.: Canon, 2001.

Barrick, William D. "The Openness of God: Does Prayer Change God?" *The Masters Seminary Journal* 12 (2001): 149-166.

Bavinck, Herman. *The Doctrine of God*, translated by William Hendrickson. Grand Rapids, Mich.: Eerdmans, 1951; Edinburgh: Banner of Truth, 1977.

Beckman, John C. "Quantum Mechanics, Chaos Physics and the Open View of God." *Philosophia Christi* 4 (2002): 203-214.

Brand, Chad. "Genetic Defects or Accidental Similarities? Orthodoxy and Open Theism and Their Connections to Western Philosophical Traditions." In *Beyond the Bounds: Open Theism and the Undermining of Biblical Christianity*, edited by John Piper, Justin Taylor, and Paul Kjoss Helseth, 43-73. Wheaton, Ill.: Crossway, 2003.

Bray, Gerald L. "Has the Christian Doctrine of God Been Corrupted by Greek Philosophy?" In *God Under Fire: Modern Scholarship Reinvents God*, edited by Eric L. Johnson and Douglas S. Huffman, 105-117. Grand Rapids, Mich.: Zondervan, 2002.

———. *The Personal God: Is the Classical Understanding of God Tenable?* Carlisle, U.K.: Paternoster, 1998.

Caneday, A. B. "God in the Image and Likeness of Adam—Clark Pinnock's Use of Scripture in His Argument 'God Limits His Knowledge.'" *Journal of Biblical Apologetics* 1 (2001): 20-27.

————. "Putting God at Risk: A Critique of John Sanders's View of Providence." *Trinity Journal* 20 NS (1999): 131-163.

————. "Veiled Glory: God's Self-Revelation in Human Likeness—A Biblical Theology of God's Anthropomorphic Self-Disclosure." In *Beyond the Bounds: Open Theism and the Undermining of Biblical Christianity*, edited by John Piper, Justin Taylor, and Paul Kjoss Helseth, 149-199. Wheaton, Ill.: Crossway, 2003.

Carson, D. A. "How Can We Reconcile the Love and the Transcendent Sovereignty of God?" In *God Under Fire: Modern Scholarship Reinvents God*, edited by Eric L. Johnson and Douglas S. Huffman, 279-299. Grand Rapids, Mich.: Zondervan, 2002.

————. "The Open God Theology." Audio MP3 of sessions held at the EFCA Mid-Winter Ministerial Conference, Leawood, Kans., January, 2001. Available from www.lifeaudio.com/christwaymedia.

Charnock, Stephen. *The Existence and Attributes of God*. Grand Rapids, Mich.: Baker, 1996; orig. 1682.

Craig, William Lane. "Hasker on Divine Knowledge." *Philosophical Studies* 62 (1992): 57-78.

————. *The Only Wise God: The Compatibility of Divine Foreknowledge and Human Freedom*. Eugene, Ore.: Wipf & Stock, 2000.

————. "What Does God Know?" In *God Under Fire: Modern Scholarship Reinvents God*, edited by Eric L. Johnson and Douglas S. Huffman, 137-156. Grand Rapids, Mich.: Zondervan, 2002.

Craigen, Trevor. "Isaiah 40–48: A Sermonic Challenge to Open Theism." *The Masters Seminary Journal* 12 (2001): 167-187.

Davis, William C. "Does God Know the Future? A Closer Look at the Contemporary Evangelical Debate." *Modern Reformation* 8, no. 5 (September/October 1999): 20-25.

————. "Does God Know the Future via 'Middle Knowledge'?" *Modern Reformation* 8, no. 5 (September/October 1999): 24-25.

————. "Why Open Theism Is Flourishing Now." In *Beyond the Bounds: Open Theism and the Undermining of Biblical Christianity*, edited by John Piper, Justin Taylor, and Paul Kjoss Helseth, 111-145. Wheaton, Ill.: Crossway, 2003.

Edwards, Jonathan. *The Freedom of the Will*, edited by Paul Ramsey. In *The*

Works of Jonathan Edwards, vol. 1. New Haven, Conn.: Yale University Press, 1957.

Erickson, Millard J. *God the Father Almighty: A Contemporary Exploration of the Divine Attributes.* Grand Rapids, Mich.: Baker, 1998.

Feinberg, John S. *No One Like Him: The Doctrine of God.* Foundations of Evangelical Theology. Wheaton, Ill.: Crossway, 2001.

Frame, John M. *The Doctrine of God.* A Theology of Lordship. Phillipsburg, N.J.: Presbyterian & Reformed, 2002.

————. *No Other God: A Response to Open Theism.* Phillipsburg, N.J.: Presbyterian & Reformed, 2001.

————. "Open Theism and Divine Foreknowledge." In *Bound Only Once: The Failure of Open Theism,* edited by Douglas Wilson, 83-94. Moscow, Ida.: Canon, 2001.

Freddoso, Alfred J. "The 'Openness of God': A Reply to William Hasker." *Christian Scholar's Review* 28 (1998): 124-133.

Fuller, Russell. "The Rabbis and the Claims of Openness Advocates." In *Beyond the Bounds: Open Theism and the Undermining of Biblical Christianity,* edited by John Piper, Justin Taylor, and Paul Kjoss Helseth, 23-41. Wheaton, Ill.: Crossway, 2003.

Geisler, Norman L. *Creating God in the Image of Man? The New Open View of God—Neotheism's Dangerous Drift.* Minneapolis: Bethany, 1997.

Geisler, Norman L. and H. Wayne House. *The Battle for God: Responding to the Challenge of Neotheism.* Grand Rapids, Mich.: Kregel, 2001.

Geivett, R. Douglas. "How Do We Reconcile the Existence of God and Suffering?" In *God Under Fire: Modern Scholarship Reinvents God,* edited by Eric L. Johnson and Douglas S. Huffman, 157-186. Grand Rapids, Mich.: Zondervan, 2002.

George, Timothy. "A Theology to Die For." *Christianity Today* 42, no. 2 (9 February 1998): 49.

————. "A Transcendence-Starved Deity." *Christianity Today* 39, no. 1 (9 January 1995): 33-34.

Grudem, Wayne. "When, Why, and for What Should We Draw New Boundaries?" In *Beyond the Bounds: Open Theism and the Undermining of Biblical Christianity,* edited by John Piper, Justin Taylor, and Paul Kjoss Helseth, 339-370. Wheaton, Ill.: Crossway, 2003.

Gutenson, Chuck E. "Does God Change?" In *God Under Fire: Modern Scholarship Reinvents God,* edited by Eric L. Johnson and Douglas S. Huffman, 231-252. Grand Rapids, Mich.: Zondervan, 2002.

Helm, Paul. "Is God Bound by Time?" In *God Under Fire: Modern Scholarship Reinvents God,* edited by Eric L. Johnson and Douglas S. Huffman, 119-135. Grand Rapids, Mich.: Zondervan, 2002.

———. "The Philosophical Issue of Divine Foreknowledge." In *The Grace of God, the Bondage of the Will,* vol. 2, edited by Thomas R. Schreiner and Bruce A. Ware, 485-497. Grand Rapids, Mich.: Baker, 1995.

———. *The Providence of God.* Contours of Christian Theology. Downers Grove, Ill.: InterVarsity Press, 1994.

Helseth, Paul Kjoss. "On Divine Ambivalence: Open Theism and the Problem of Particular Evils." *Journal of the Evangelical Theological Society* 44 (2001): 493-511.

———. "What Is at Stake in the Openness Debate? The Trustworthiness of God and the Foundation of Hope." In *Beyond the Bounds: Open Theism and the Undermining of Biblical Christianity,* edited by John Piper, Justin Taylor, and Paul Kjoss Helseth, 275-307. Wheaton, Ill.: Crossway, 2003.

Highfield, Ron. "The Function of Divine Self-Limitation in Open Theism: An Evaluation." *Journal of the Evangelical Theological Society* 45 (2002): 257-277.

Horton, Michael S. "Hellenistic or Hebrew? Open Theism and Reformed Theological Method." *Journal of the Evangelical Theological Society* 45 (2002): 317-341 (revised in *Beyond the Bounds,* chapter 6).

———. "A Vulnerable God Apart from Christ? Open Theism's Challenge to the Classical Doctrine of God." *Modern Reformation* 10, no. 3 (May/June 2001): 30-38.

Howe, John. *The Reconcilableness of God's Prescience of the Sins of Men, with the Wisdom and Sincerity of His Counsels, Exhortations, and Whatsoever Means He Uses to Prevent Them.* Vol. 2 of *The Works of the Rev. John Howe.* Ligonier, Pa.: Soli Deo Gloria, 1990; orig. 1724.

Huffman, Douglas S. and Eric L. Johnson. *God Under Fire: Modern Scholarship Reinvents God.* Grand Rapids, Mich.: Zondervan, 2002.

Johnson, Eric L. and Douglas S. Huffman. "Should the God of Historic Christianity Be Replaced?" In *God Under Fire: Modern Scholarship*

Reinvents God, edited by Eric L. Johnson and Douglas S. Huffman, 11-41. Grand Rapids, Mich.: Zondervan, 2002.

Johnson, Phillip R. "God Without Mood Swings." In *Bound Only Once: The Failure of Open Theism,* edited by Douglas Wilson, 109-121. Moscow, Ida.: Canon, 2001.

Jones, Douglas M. "Metaphor in Exile." In *Bound Only Once: The Failure of Open Theism,* edited by Douglas Wilson, 31-51. Moscow, Ida.: Canon, 2001.

Kelly, Douglas F. "Afraid of Infinitude." *Christianity Today* 39, no. 1 (9 January 1995): 32-33.

Lee, Patrick. "Does God Have Emotions?" In *God Under Fire: Modern Scholarship Reinvents God,* edited by Eric L. Johnson and Douglas S. Huffman, 211-230. Grand Rapids, Mich.: Zondervan, 2002.

Leithart, Peter J. "Trinity, Time, and Open Theism: A Glance at Patristic Theology." In *Bound Only Once: The Failure of Open Theism,* edited by Douglas Wilson, 123-134. Moscow, Ida.: Canon, 2001.

MacArthur, John Jr., "Open Theism's Attack on the Atonement." In *Bound Only Once: The Failure of Open Theism,* edited by Douglas Wilson, 95-108. Moscow, Ida.: Canon, 2001.

Maier, Walter A. III, "Does God 'Repent' or Change His Mind? A Study of Genesis 6:6 and Exodus 32:14." Paper presented at the annual meeting of the Evangelical Theological Society, Colorado Springs, 14 November 2001.

Merkle, Ben R. "Liberals in Drag." In *Bound Only Once: The Failure of Open Theism,* edited by Douglas Wilson, 67-81. Moscow, Ida.: Canon, 2001.

Nash, Ronald H. *The Concept of God: An Exploration of Contemporary Difficulties with the Attributes of God.* Grand Rapids, Mich.: Zondervan, 1983.

Nicole, Roger. "'Open Theism' Is Incompatible with Inerrancy." Paper presented at the annual meeting of the Evangelical Theological Society, Toronto, 20 November 2002.

Nixon, Joost F. "Open Idolatry." In *Bound Only Once: The Failure of Open Theism,* edited by Douglas Wilson, 205-217. Moscow, Ida.: Canon, 2001.

Owen, John. *Vindicae Evangelicae; or The Mystery of the Gospel Vindicated.* In *The Works of John Owen,* edited by William H. Gould, vol. 1 (London: Johnstone & Hunter, 1852; reprint, Edinburgh and Carlisle, Pa.: Banner of Truth, 1959.

Pettegrew, Larry D. "'Is There Knowledge of the Most High?' (Psalm 73:11)." *The Masters Seminary Journal* 12 (2001): 133-148.

Picirilli, Robert E. "An Arminian Response to John Sanders's *The God Who Risks: A Theology of Providence.*" *Journal of the Evangelical Theological Society* 44 (2001): 467-491.

———. "Foreknowledge, Freedom, and the Future." *Journal of the Evangelical Theological Society* 43 (2000): 259-271.

Piper, John. "Grounds for Dismay: The Error and Injury of Open Theism." In *Beyond the Bounds: Open Theism and the Undermining of Biblical Christianity*, edited by John Piper, Justin Taylor, and Paul Kjoss Helseth, 371-383. Wheaton, Ill.: Crossway, 2003.

———. "Why the Glory of God Is at Stake in the 'Foreknowledge' Debate." *Modern Reformation* 8, no. 5 (September/October 1999): 39-43.

Roy, Steven C. "God as Omnicompetent Responder? Questions About the Grounds of Eschatological Confidence in Open Theism." In *Looking into the Future: Evangelical Studies in Eschatology*, ETS Studies, edited by David Baker, 263-280. Grand Rapids, Mich.: Baker, 2000.

———. "How Much Does God Foreknow? An Evangelical Assessment of the Doctrine of the Extent of the Foreknowledge of God in Light of the Teaching of Open Theism." Ph.D. diss., Trinity International University, 2000.

———. "Your Father Knows Before You Ask: The Implications of Matthew 6 for the Open View of Petitionary Prayer." Paper presented at the annual meeting of the Evangelical Theological Society, Colorado Springs, 16 November 2001.

Schlissel, Steve M. "Moses' Bush or Procrustes' Bed." In *Bound Only Once: The Failure of Open Theism*, edited by Douglas Wilson, 191-203. Moscow, Ida.: Canon, 2001.

Schreiner, Thomas R. and Bruce A. Ware, eds. *Still Sovereign: Contemporary Perspectives on Election, Foreknowledge, and Grace*. Grand Rapids, Mich.: Baker, 2000.

Spiegel, James S. "Does God Take Risks?" In *God Under Fire: Modern Scholarship Reinvents God*, edited by Eric L. Johnson and Douglas S. Huffman, 187-210. Grand Rapids, Mich.: Zondervan, 2002.

Sproul, R. C., Jr., "Atlas Shrugged: Worshipping in the Beauty of Holiness." In

Bound Only Once: The Failure of Open Theism, edited by Douglas Wilson, 53-63. Moscow, Ida.: Canon, 2001.

Storms, C. Samuel. "Open Theism and Intercessory Prayer: Enemies or Allies?" Paper presented at the annual meeting of the Evangelical Theological Society, Toronto, 21 November 2002.

————. "Open Theists in the Hands of an Angry Puritan: Edwards on Divine Foreknowledge." In *The Legacy of Jonathan Edwards: American Religion and the Evangelical Tradition,* edited by D. G. Hart, Sean Michael Lucas, and Stephen J. Nichols. Grand Rapids, Mich.: Baker, forthcoming.

Strimple, Robert B. "What Does God Know?" In *The Coming Evangelical Crisis: Current Challenges to the Authority of Scripture and the Gospel,* edited by John H. Armstrong, 139-153. Chicago: Moody, 1996.

Talbot, Mark R. "Does God Reveal Who He Actually Is?" In *God Under Fire: Modern Scholarship Reinvents God,* edited by Eric L. Johnson and Douglas S. Huffman, 43-70. Grand Rapids, Mich.: Zondervan, 2002.

————. *How Salvation Takes Place: A Biblical and Philosophical Response to Open Theism.* Wheaton, Ill.: Crossway, forthcoming.

————. "True Freedom: The Liberty That Scripture Portrays as Worth Having." In *Beyond the Bounds: Open Theism and the Undermining of Biblical Christianity,* edited by John Piper, Justin Taylor, and Paul Kjoss Helseth, 77-109. Wheaton, Ill.: Crossway, 2003.

Thomas, Robert L. "The Hermeneutics of Open Theism." *The Masters Seminary Journal* 12 (2001): 179-202.

Tiessen, Terrance. *Providence and Prayer: How Does God Work in the World?* Downers Grove, Ill.: InterVarsity Press, 2000.

Tracy, Steven R. "Theodicy, Eschatology, and the Open View of God." In *Looking into the Future: Evangelical Studies in Eschatology,* ETS Studies, edited by David Baker, 295-312. Grand Rapids, Mich.: Baker, 2000.

Ware, Bruce A. "Defining Evangelicalism's Boundaries Theologically: Is Open Theism Evangelical?" *Journal of the Evangelical Theological Society* 45 (2002): 193-212.

————. "An Evangelical Reformulation of the Doctrine of the Immutability of God." *Journal of the Evangelical Theological Society* 29 (1986): 431-446.

————. *God's Lesser Glory: The Diminished God of Open Theism.* Wheaton, Ill.: Crossway, 2001.

———. "Rejoinder to Replies by Clark H. Pinnock, John Sanders, and Gregory A. Boyd." *Journal of the Evangelical Theological Society* 45 (2002): 245-256.

———. "What Is at Stake in the Openness Debate? The Gospel of Christ." In *Beyond the Bounds: Open Theism and the Undermining of Biblical Christianity*, edited by John Piper, Justin Taylor, and Paul Kjoss Helseth, 309-336. Wheaton, Ill.: Crossway, 2003.

Wells, David. "The Rejection of the Classical Doctrine of God and What It Says About the State of the Evangelical Movement." Foreword to *Whatever Happened to the Reformation?* edited by Gary L. W. Johnson and R. Fowler White. Phillipsburg, N.J.: Presbyterian & Reformed, 2001.

Wellum, Stephen J. *Open Theism: An Evaluation and Critique*. Ross-shire, U.K.: Christian Focus, forthcoming.

———. "The Openness of God: A Critical Assessment." *Reformation and Revival* 10, no. 3 (2001): 137-160.

———. "What Is at Stake in the Openness Debate? The Inerrancy of Scripture." In *Beyond the Bounds: Open Theism and the Undermining of Biblical Christianity*, edited by John Piper, Justin Taylor, and Paul Kjoss Helseth, 237-274. Wheaton, Ill.: Crossway, 2003.

Wilson, Douglas J., ed. *Bound Only Once: The Failure of Open Theism*. Moscow, Ida.: Canon, 2001.

———. "Foundations of Exhaustive Knowledge." In *Bound Only Once: The Failure of Open Theism*, edited by Douglas Wilson, 135-170. Moscow, Ida.: Canon, 2001.

———. *Knowledge, Foreknowledge, and the Gospel*. Moscow, Ida.: Canon, 1997.

———. "The Loveliness of Orthodoxy." In *Bound Only Once: The Failure of Open Theism*, edited by Douglas Wilson, 17-29. Moscow, Ida.: Canon, 2001.

Wright, R. K. McGregor. *No Place for Sovereignty: What's Wrong with Freewill Theism*. Downers Grove, Ill: InterVarsity Press, 1996.

WORKS AFFIRMING OPEN THEISM

Basinger, David. "Can an Evangelical Christian Justifiably Deny God's Exhaustive Foreknowledge of the Future?" *Christian Scholar's Review* 25 (1995): 133-134.

————. *The Case for Freewill Theism: A Philosophical Assessment.* Downers Grove, Ill.: InterVarsity Press, 1996.

————. "Divine Control and Human Freedom: Is Middle Knowledge the Answer?" *Journal of the Evangelical Theological Society* 36 (1993): 55-64.

————. "Human Freedom and Divine Providence: Some New Thoughts on an Old Problem." *Religious Studies* 15 (1979): 491-510.

————. "Middle Knowledge and Classical Christian Thought." *Religious Studies* 22 (1986): 407-422.

————. "Middle Knowledge and Divine Control: Some Clarifications." *International Journal for the Philosophy of Religion* 20 (1986): 169-172.

————. "Practical Implications." In *The Openness of God: A Biblical Challenge to the Traditional Understanding of God,* by Clark Pinnock, et al., 155-176. Downers Grove, Ill.: InterVarsity Press, 1986.

Basinger, Randall. "Evangelicals and Process Theism: Seeking a Middle Ground." *Christian Scholar's Review* 15 (1986): 157-167.

Boyd, Gregory A. "Christian Love and Academic Dialogue: A Reply to Bruce Ware." *Journal of the Evangelical Theological Society* 45 (2002): 233-243.

————. "Can an Omniscient God Learn?" Paper presented at the annual meeting of the Evangelical Theological Society, Toronto, 21 November 2002.

————. *God at War: The Bible and Spiritual Conflict.* Downers Grove, Ill.: InterVarsity Press, 1997.

————. *God of the Possible: A Biblical Introduction to the Open View of God.* Grand Rapids, Mich.: Baker, 2000.

————. "Is God Dependent on Us? Interview with Gregory Boyd." *Modern Reformation* 8, no. 6 (November/December 1999): 44-45.

————. "Middle Knowledge and the Open View of the Future." Paper presented at the annual meeting of the Evangelical Theological Society, Colorado Springs, 15 November 2001.

————. *The Myth of the Blueprint.* Downers Grove, Ill.: InterVarsity Press, forthcoming.

————. "The Open-Theism View." In *Divine Foreknowledge: Four Views,* edited by James K. Beilby and Paul R. Eddy, 13-47. Downers Grove, Ill.: InterVarsity Press, 2001.

————. *Satan and the Problem of Evil: Constructing a Trinitarian Warfare Theodicy.* Downers Grove, Ill.: InterVarsity Press, 2001.

————. *Trinity and Process: A Critical Evaluation and Reconstruction of Hartshorne's Di-Polar Theism Towards a Trinitarian Metaphysics.* New York: Peter Lang, 1992.

Boyd, Gregory A. and Edward K. Boyd, *Letters from a Skeptic: A Son Wrestles with His Father's Questions About Christianity.* Wheaton, Ill.: Victor, 1994.

Clarke, W. Norris. *God, Knowable and Unknowable.* New York: Fordham University Press, 1973.

Cobb, John B., Jr., and Clark H. Pinnock, eds. *Searching for an Adequate God: A Dialogue Between Process and Free Will Theists.* Grand Rapids, Mich.: Eerdmans, 2000.

Elseth, Roy. *Did God Know? A Study of the Nature of God.* St. Paul: Calvary United Church, 1977.

Fretheim, Terence E. "Divine Dependence on the Human: An Old Testament Perspective." *Ex Auditu* 13 (1997): 1-13.

————. "Divine Foreknowledge, Divine Constancy and the Rejection of Saul's Kingship." *Catholic Biblical Quarterly* 47 (1985): 595-602.

————. "The Repentance of God: A Key to Evaluating Old Testament God-Talk." *Horizons in Biblical Theology* 10 (1988): 47-70.

————. "The Repentance of God: A Study of Jeremiah 18:7-10." *Hebrew Annual Review* 11 (1987): 81-92.

Geach, Peter. *Providence and Evil.* Cambridge: Cambridge University Press, 1977.

Hasker, William. "Foreknowledge and Necessity." *Faith and Philosophy* 2 (April 1985): 121-157.

————. *God, Time and Knowledge.* Cornell Studies in the Philosophy of Religion. Ithaca, N.Y.: Cornell University Press, 1989.

————. "The Openness of God." *Christian Scholar's Review* 28 (1998): 111-139.

————. "A Philosophical Perspective." In *The Openness of God: A Biblical Challenge to the Traditional Understanding of God,* by Clark Pinnock, et al., 126-154. Downers Grove, Ill.: InterVarsity Press, 1994.

————. "Tradition, Divine Transcendence, and the Waiting Father." *Christian Scholar's Review* 28 (1998): 134-139.

Lucas, J. Randolph. *The Freedom of the Will*. Oxford: Oxford University Press, 1970.

———. *The Future: An Essay on God, Temporality, and Truth*. London: Blackwell, 1989.

McCabe, Lorenzo D. *Divine Nescience of Future Contingencies a Necessity*. New York: Phillips and Hunt, 1882. Available online at http://members.nbci.com/CPRINC/Articles/DNtitle.html.

———. *The Foreknowledge of God and Cognate Themes in Theology and Philosophy*. Cincinnati: Walden & Stowe, 1882. Available online at http://www.revivaltheology.com/mccabe.htm.

Pinnock, Clark H. "Between Classical and Process Theism." In *Process Theology*, edited by Ronald Nash, 313-337. Grand Rapids, Mich.: Baker, 1987.

———. "From Augustine to Arminius: A Pilgrimage in Theology." In *The Grace of God and the Will of Man: A Case for Arminianism*, edited by Clark H. Pinnock, 15-30. Grand Rapids, Mich.: Zondervan: 1989; Minneapolis: Bethany, 1995.

———. "God Limits His Knowledge." In *Predestination and Free Will: Four Views of Divine Sovereignty and Human Freedom*, edited by David Basinger and Randall Basinger, 141-162. Downers Grove, Ill.: InterVarsity Press, 1986.

———. *Most Moved Mover: A Theology of God's Openness*. Grand Rapids, Mich.: Baker; Carlisle, U.K.: Paternoster, 2001.

———. "Systematic Theology." In *The Openness of God: A Biblical Challenge to the Traditional Understanding of God*, by Clark Pinnock, et al., 101-125. Downers Grove, Ill.: InterVarsity Press, 1994.

———. "There Is Room for Us: A Reply to Bruce Ware." *Journal of the Evangelical Theological Society* 45 (2002): 245-256.

Pinnock, Clark H., Richard Rice, John Sanders, William Hasker, and David Basinger. *The Openness of God: A Biblical Challenge to the Traditional Understanding of God*. Downers Grove, Ill.: InterVarsity, 1994.

Rice, Richard. "Biblical Support." In *The Openness of God: A Biblical Challenge to the Traditional Understanding of God*, by Clark Pinnock, et al., 11-58. Downers Grove, Ill.: InterVarsity Press, 1994.

———. "Divine Foreknowledge and Free-will Theism." In *The Grace of God and the Will of Man: A Case for Arminianism*, edited by Clark H. Pinnock,

121-139. Grand Rapids, Mich.: Zondervan: 1989; Minneapolis: Bethany, 1995.

―――. *God's Foreknowledge and Man's Free Will*. Minneapolis: Bethany, 1985. Previously published as *The Openness of God: The Relationship of Divine Foreknowledge and Human Free Will*. Nashville: Review & Herald, 1979.

Sanders, John. "Be Wary of Ware: A Reply to Bruce Ware." *Journal of the Evangelical Theological Society* 45 (2002): 221-231.

―――. "Defining Evangelicalism's Boundaries Theologically: Is Open Theism Evangelical?" Plenary address at the annual meeting of the Evangelical Theological Society, Colorado Springs, 15 November 2002.

―――. "God as Personal." In *The Grace of God and the Will of Man: A Case for Arminianism*, edited by Clark H. Pinnock, 165-180. Grand Rapids, Mich.: Zondervan, 1989; Minneapolis: Bethany, 1995.

―――. *The God Who Risks: A Theology of Providence*. Downers Grove, Ill.: InterVarsity Press, 1998.

―――. "Historical Considerations." In *The Openness of God: A Biblical Challenge to the Traditional Understanding of God*, by Clark Pinnock, et al., 59-100. Downers Grove, Ill.: InterVarsity Press, 1995.

―――. "Open Theism and Scripture: Reducing God to Human Proportions?" Paper delivered at the annual meeting of the Evangelical Theological Society, Toronto, 21 November 2002.

―――. "The Openness of God and the Assurance of Things to Come." In *Looking into the Future: Evangelical Studies in Eschatology*, ETS Studies, edited by David Baker, 281-294. Grand Rapids, Mich.: Baker, 2000.

―――. "Theological Lawbreaker? A Response to Stephen Williams." *Books and Culture* 6, no. 1 (November/December 1999): 10.

―――. "Why Simple Foreknowledge Offers No More Providential Control Than the Openness of God." *Faith and Philosophy* 14 (1997): 26-40.

Sontag, Frederick. "Does Omnipotence Necessarily Entail Omniscience?" *Journal of the Evangelical Theological Society* 34 (1991): 505-508.

Swinburne, Richard. *The Coherence of Theism*, rev. ed. New York: Oxford University Press, 1993.

BOOK REVIEWS

Beckwith, Francis J. Review of *God of the Possible*, by Gregory A. Boyd. *Christian Research Journal* 22 (2000): 54-55.

Caneday, A. B. "Critical Comments on an Open Theism Manifesto." *Trinity Journal* 23 NS (2002): 103-107.

———. "The Implausible God of Open Theism: A Response to Gregory A. Boyd's *God of the Possible*." *Journal of Biblical Apologetics* 1 (Fall 2000): 66-87.

Carson, D. A. "God, the Bible and Spiritual Warfare: A Review Article." *Journal of the Evangelical Theological Society* 42 (1999): 251-269.

Freddoso, Alfred J. Review of *God, Time, and Knowledge*, by William Hasker. *Faith and Philosophy* 10 (1993); 105-106.

Helm, Paul. Review of *The God Who Risks: A Theology of Providence*, by John Sanders. *Modern Reformation* 8, no. 6 (November/December 1999): 46-50.

Klein, William W. "Most Moving Issue Facing Evangelicals." Review of *Most Moved Mover: A Theology of God's Openness*, by Clark H. Pinnock. *Denver Journal* 5 (2002). Available online at www.denverseminary.edu/ dj/articles02/0300/0301.php.

Luter, A. Boyd and Emily Hunter. Review of *God's Lesser Glory: The Diminished God of Open Theism*, by Bruce A. Ware. *Journal of the Evangelical Theological Society* 44 (2001): 757-758.

Mayhue, Richard. "The Impossibility of *God of the Possible*." *The Masters Seminary Journal* 12 (Fall 2001): 203-220.

Nicholls, Jason A. Review of *God of the Possible*, by Gregory A. Boyd. *Trinity Journal* 22 NS (2001): 123-127.

Nicole, Roger. "A Review Article: God of the Possible?" *Reformation and Revival Journal* 10 (2001): 167-194.

———. Review of *The Openness of God: A Biblical Challenge to the Traditional Understanding of God*, by Clark Pinnock, et al. *Founders Journal* 22 (Fall 1995): 26-29.

Porter, Timothy G. and A. B. Caneday. "Prosecuting War Crimes Committed in the Construction of a Trinitarian Warfare Theodicy: Assessing *Satan and the Problem of Evil: Constructing a Trinitarian Warfare Theodicy* by

Gregory A. Boyd." Paper presented at the annual meeting of the Midwest Regional Evangelical Theological Society, Wheaton, Ill., 22 March 2002.

Ware, Bruce A. Review of *The Case for Free Will Theism: A Philosophical Assessment*, by David Basinger. *Journal of the Evangelical Theological Society* 43 (2000): 165-168.

———. Review of *The God Who Risks: A Theology of Providence*, by John Sanders. *Journal of the Evangelical Theological Society* 43 (2000): 339-342.

Wieranga, Edward. Review of *The Openness of God*, by Clark Pinnock, et al. *Faith and Philosophy* 14 (1997): 248-252.

Williams, Stephen N. "What God Doesn't Know: Were the Biblical Prophecies Mere Probabilities?" Review of *The God Who Risks: A Theology of Providence*, by John Sanders. *Books and Culture* 5, no. 6 (November/December 1999): 16.

Wittmer, Michael. Review of *Most Moved Mover: A Theology of God's Openness*, by Clark H. Pinnock. *Calvin Theological Journal* 37 (2002): 152-154.

ARTICLES RELATED TO THE CONTROVERSY AND ITS THEOLOGICAL PRESUPPOSITIONS, OR MULTIPLE-AUTHOR VOLUMES

Bock, Darrell L. *Purpose-Directed Theology: Getting Our Priorities Right in Evangelical Controversies*. Downers Grove, Ill.: InterVarsity Press, 2002.

Boyd, Gregory A., David Hunt, William Lane Craig, and Paul Helm. *Divine Foreknowledge: Four Views*, ed. James K. Beilby and Paul R. Eddy. Downers Grove, Ill.: InterVarsity Press, 2001.

Brow, Robert. "Evangelical Megashift." *Christianity Today* 34, no. 3 (19 February 1990): 12-14.

"The Buzz: ETS Votes to Reject Open Theology." *World* 16, no. 46 (1 December 2001): 10.

Coffman, Elesha. "Did Open Debate Help the Openness Debate?" *Christianity Today* 45, no. 3 (19 February 2001): 42.

Erickson, Millard J. *The Evangelical Left: Encountering Postconservative Evangelical Theology*. Grand Rapids, Mich.: Baker, 1997.

"God vs. God" (editorial). *Christianity Today* 44, no. 2 (7 February 2000): 34-35.

Hall, Christopher A. and John Sanders. *Does God Have a Future? A Debate on Divine Providence*. Grand Rapids, Mich.: Baker, 2003.

———. "Does God Know Your Next Move?" *Christianity Today* 45, no. 7 (21 May 2001): 39-45.

———. "Does God Know Your Next Move? Part II." *Christianity Today* 45, no. 8 (11 June 2001): 50-56.

Helseth, Paul Kjoss. "Re-Imagining the Princeton Mind: Postconservative Evangelicalism, Old Princeton, and the Rise of Neo-Fundamentalism." *Journal of the Evangelical Theological Society* 45 (2002): 427-450.

Horton, Michael S. "Is the New News Good News? Shifting Views Concerning God in Our Day." *Modern Reformation* 8, no. 5 (September/October 1999): 11-12.

House, H. Wayne. *Charts on Openness Theology*. Grand Rapids, Mich.: Kregel, forthcoming.

Koop, Doug. "Evangelical Theological Society Moves Against Open Theists: Membership of Pinnock and Sanders Challenged by Due Process," 22 November 2002 internet posting at www.christianitytoday.com/ct/2002/145/54.0.html.

Mohler, R. Albert. "Does God Give Bad Advice?" *World* 15, no. 24 (1 June 2000): 23.

———. "A New Low? 'The Word Made Fresh': Revisionist Theologians Offer Instead More Stale Liberalism." *World* 17, no. 13 (6 April 2002): 26.

Moore, Russell D. "Open Theism Closed." *SBC Life* (May 2002): 17.

Morey, Robert A. *Battle of the Gods: The Gathering Storm in Modern Evangelicalism*. Southbridge, Mass.: Crown, 1989.

Morgan, Timothy C. "Theologians Decry 'Narrow' Boundaries." *Christianity Today* 46, no. 7 (10 June 2002): 18.

Neff, David. "Foreknowledge Debate Clouded by 'Political Agenda': Evangelical Theologians Differ over Excluding Open Theists," 19 November 2001. Available online at www.christianitytoday.com/ct/2001/147/13.0.html.

———. "Scholars Vote: God Knows Future. But Supporters of Open Theism Say They'll Stay in the Evangelical Theological Society Despite Resolution." *Christianity Today* 46, no. 1 (7 January 2002): 21.

Oden, Thomas C. "The Real Reformers Are Traditionalists." *Christianity Today* 42, no. 2 (9 February 1998): 45.

Olson, Roger E. "The Future of Evangelical Theology." *Christianity Today* 42, no. 2 (9 February 1998): 40.

————. "Postconservative Evangelicals Greet the Postmodern Age." *Christian Century* 112 (3 May 1995): 480-483.

Pinnock, Clark H. "A Pilgrim on the Way." *Christianity Today* 42, no. 2 (9 February 1998): 43.

Piper, John. "We Took a Good Stand and Made a Bad Mistake: Reflections on the Baptist General Conference Annual Meeting, St. Paul, June 25-28, 2000." Available online at www.desiringgod.org/library/fresh_words/2000/070500.html.

Piper, John with Justin Taylor (appendix by Millard Erickson). *Resolution on the Foreknowledge of God: Reasons and Rationale.* Minneapolis: Bethlehem Baptist Church, 2000.

Plowman, Edward E. "Open and Shut: A Baptist Group Rejects 'Open Theology,' but Not Its Chief Advocate, While Presbyterians Debate Beliefs." *World* 15, no. 28 (22 July 2000): 26.

————. "What Does God Know? And When Does He Know It? Baptist Denomination Debates, but Arrives on the Other Side of Sovereignty." *World* 14, no. 27 (17 July 1999): 23.

Sanders, John, Clark Pinnock, Greg Boyd, William Hasker, Richard Rice, and David Basinger. "Truth at Risk: Six Leading Openness Theologians Say That Many Assumptions Made About Their Views Are Simply Wrong." *Christianity Today* 45, no. 6 (23 April 2001): 103.

Yong, Amos. "Divine Omniscience and Future Contingents: Weighing the Presuppositional Issues in the Contemporary Debate." *Evangelical Review of Theology* 26 (2002): 240-264.

Scripture Index

PERSON INDEX

SUBJECT INDEX